# CASE STUDIES
# IN ORGANIZATIONAL COMMUNICATION 2

Advertising Budget $12,000 ??
Travel Budget ?? $19,000 ??

Base • 90-110 ... 90 being min
commission • 1% of all bookings
@ 2.5 million = 25,000

2 year gaurenty of 120·130 ... 120 MM
company car • Ford 500 } mm
                chl 300
                Buick La Cross)

→ Education?

I need to know more about
the 401k plan ... is there
a contribution, if so, what?

They have an IRA
3% contribution

Blue cross Blue shield

• Health
   - medical
   - prescription
   - Dental
   - Flex spending
• Long term / short term disability

• Rep agreement

# THE GUILFORD COMMUNICATION SERIES

*Editors*

Theodore L. Glasser, *Stanford University*
Howard E. Sypher, *University of Kansas*

*Advisory Board*

Charles Berger      Peter Monge        Michael Schudson
James W. Carey      Barbara O'Keefe    Linda Steiner

*Recent Volumes*

CASE STUDIES IN ORGANIZATIONAL COMMUNICATION 2:
PERSPECTIVES ON CONTEMPORARY WORK LIFE
Beverly Davenport Sypher, *Editor*

REGULATING MEDIA: THE LICENSING AND SUPERVISION OF
BROADCASTING IN SIX COUNTRIES
Wolfgang Hoffman-Riem

COMMUNICATION THEORY: EPISTEMOLOGICAL FOUNDATIONS
James A. Anderson

TELEVISION AND THE REMOTE CONTROL: GRAZING ON A
VAST WASTELAND
Robert V. Bellamy, Jr., and James R. Walker

RELATING: DIALOGUES AND DIALECTICS
Leslie A. Baxter and Barbara M. Montgomery

DOING PUBLIC JOURNALISM
Arthur Charity

SOCIAL APPROACHES TO COMMUNCIATION
Wendy Leeds-Hurwitz, *Editor*

PUBLIC OPINION AND THE COMMUNICATION OF CONSENT
Theodore L. Glasser and Charles T. Salmon, *Editors*

COMMUNICATION RESEARCH METHODS: A SOURCEBOOK
Rebecca B. Rubin, Philip Palmgreen, and Howard E. Sypher, *Editors*

PERSUASIVE COMMUNICATION
James B. Stiff

REFORMING LIBEL LAW
John Soloski and Randall P. Bezanson, *Editors*

MESSAGE EFFECTS RESEARCH: PRINCIPLES OF DESIGN AND ANALYSIS
Sally Jackson

CRITICAL PERSPECTIVES ON MEDIA AND SOCIETY
Robert K. Avery and David Eason, *Editors*

# Case Studies in Organizational Communication 2

## Perspectives on Contemporary Work Life

Edited by
**Beverly Davenport Sypher**

**THE GUILFORD PRESS**
New York    London

© 1997 The Guilford Press
A Division of Guilford Publications, Inc.
72 Spring Street, New York, NY 10012

Printed in the United States of America

This book is printed on acid-free paper.

Last digit is print number:  9  8  7  6  5  4  3

**Library of Congress Cataloging-in-Publication Data**

Case studies in organizational communication 2: Perspectives on
  contemporary work life / edited by Beverly Davenport Sypher.
      p.    cm. — (The Guilford communication series)
    Includes bibliographical references and index.
    ISBN 1-57230-207-0 (hc). — ISBN 1-57230-208-9 (pbk.)
    1. Communication in organizations—Case studies.
  I. Sypher, Beverly Davenport.    II. Series.
  HD30.3.C372   1997
  658.4'5—dc21                                        96-48478
                                                          CIP

# ACKNOWLEDGMENTS

Michelle Givertz and Michelle Violanti have been invaluable assistants on this project. Both are "storytellers as counselors" in their own right. Their attention to detail and persistence made completion of this book possible. I am also grateful for the support from the College of Liberal Arts and Sciences and the Department of Communication Studies at the University of Kansas. My students and my colleagues, and especially Howard Sypher, continue to provide a sounding board and a springboard for my ideas and aspirations. My greatest accomplishments, Ford and Sloan, give me hope that home and work can be intertwined in mutually beneficial ways.

BEVERLY DAVENPORT SYPHER

# CONTENTS

# Introduction

## BEVERLY DAVENPORT SYPHER

The case studies presented in this volume are in effect co-constructed narratives about work life. The employees talk, we listen. We talk, they listen. They know more than they can say, and likewise, we know more than we can say. They have allowed us into their conversations, and we them. They have helped us make sense of their sensemaking (Weick, 1995). These cases are our attempts to weave their stories into ours, a necessarily creative process. As Bateson (1994, p. 57) points out, "The webs of perception and meaning that human beings construct tend toward integration. What does not fit is likely to remain invisible, unnamed, unattended to." So as Weick (1995) reminds us, sensemaking is more about invention than discovery. This holds true when we are trying to make sense out of employees' sensemaking as well as when they are making sense of their organizational world.

Each case study is a view—a view of what we see, a view of how we choose to report what we see, a view of others' views. Multiple sources of evidence are brought to bear: symbols, argument styles, products, processes, buildings, texts, technology, and narratives. We have reports of the taken-for-granted; reports of the not-so-obvious, reports of the underside, other side, dark side, and "inside."

What this volume presents are reports of contemporary work life where teams can manage themselves; where values, conflicts, and emotions get negotiated and renegotiated; and where companies can make it and employees can too. We have winning ways and strange ways, wrong ways and other ways. We see that beneficial constraints are just as likely as oppressive ones, and even though the difference between the two is often a judgment call, it is one that we must keep making and debating. In this volume, not much attention is devoted to Conquergood's (1991) "borderlands," but a good bit is written about the heartland of work where all the jobs are—the high-tech, the manufacturing, and the social services.

As the next few pages suggest, case studies have a variety of functions. With some claims to what the case is, the following section describes what case studies can do for us theoretically and pedagogically. They are a way of knowing; they are rhetorical; they are narratives, and as such they are often more memorable and believable than other forms of evidence. Among other things, they can enhance critical thinking, decision making, perspective taking, and oral and written persuasive communication abilities.

## THE VARIOUS FUNCTIONS OF CASE STUDIES

Case studies have been used in a variety of ways and for a number of years, but, curiously, their use in the communication field seems to reflect new interest. Perhaps this interest stems from a heightened appreciation of communication "as a practical discipline" (Craig, 1990), or perhaps we have become more aware of the reflexivity of theory and practice, and case studies provide a context for documenting practice and explaining theory. At the same time, case studies serve an epistemic function by providing an alternative way of knowing about communication generally and organizational communication specifically. In effect, the texts created to document practices are also admissible as evidence in our search for epistemic convergence. At the same time, case studies enliven our classroom and enrich our textbooks, which is probably why they are most often used pedagogically.

The widespread use of case studies in our field has been heavily influenced by business school practices, especially those at Harvard and Stanford, where the focus is on problematic management situations (Bonoma & Kosnik, 1990). Consequently, the problem–solution format has dominated our thinking about case study writing and analysis. Although this type of approach helps develop critical-thinking skills, there are other approaches that can do the same; moreover, developing critical-thinking skills, albeit very important, is but one of the possible functions of case studies. This chapter reviews a variety of ways in which case studies can be used by first focusing on their epistemic significance and then highlighting their rhetorical and narrative functions as well as their skill-enhancement possibilities.

### The Epistemic Function of Case Studies

Case studies, by their very nature, are ways of knowing. They are "a chunk of reality . . . the anchor on academic flights of speculation" (Lawrence, 1953, p. 215). They provide a way to apprehend, to make known, and to make sense of what is known. They allow us to "experience the experience" of organizational life in ways that are often better than the experience itself. "A well-designed case, like a good short story or even a 2-hour movie, can put us in touch with a world that would take years to experience fully on our own. The characterization of events, like the facial caricature, enables ways of seeing phenomena that only the best trained or most experienced eye could see in actual situations in actual time frames" (Deetz, 1990, p. ix). For example, in this volume, Miller (Chapter 5) brings to life what is happening in the delivery of human services, and Ray (Chapter 10) captures the personal and political exigencies in a rape crisis center. Bingham's (Chapter 21) narrative of a sexually harassed waitress gives the reader an experience that he or she would certainly not want to experience firsthand. We can come to know these situations by being put in touch with a world we may never have nor ever will experience.

Case studies also illustrate that social knowledge is "reproduced" or "invented" rather than discovered or produced (Weick, 1995; Condit, 1990), constructed and reconstructed through "story[ing] and restory[ing] our lives" (Clandinin, 1992). We pass on our "genetic structure" of knowing through the choices we make about what we look at, experience, and report; what gets passed on is knowledge "born" of human interactions and experiences. Thus, the people who reproduce knowledge through case studies are contributing offspring or other ways of knowing. In this way, "understandings either pass on their genetic structure to new generations or [they] pass on" (Condit, 1990, p. 323).

The O'Keefe, Lambert, and Lambert (Chapter 2) case in this volume is one example. O'Keefe's (1988) research suggests that individuals can have systematically different ways of understanding and responding to the communicative demands of a situation. That is, underlying message design logics compel people to produce messages with different motives and necessarily different content. The O'Keefe et al. case study of scientists in the research and development unit of a pharmaceutical company demonstrates how differences in message production resulted in interpersonal conflicts. The understanding of this situation was conceived from a "gene pool" of knowledge about message design logics and was born out of the authors' and participants' interactions that reproduced an understanding in a new context. Thus the case study helps forward the theory and vice versa. As Deetz (1990, p. ix) suggests, "Theory that does not help answer a real problem is forgotten [or "passes on," as Condit says], and experience alone rarely teaches." So in the case presented by O'Keefe, Lambert, and Lambert, experience suggested the question, and theory shaped the answer and our understanding of it.

However, the reader's understanding, as generated through the reported case, is not necessarily or altogether prior; it is contingent—contingent on the way the case is developed, argued, or presented. In this sense, case studies are epistemic; as a rhetorical form, they are a way of knowing. As Pierre Thevenaz points out, "Man [*sic*] acts and speaks before he knows. Or better, it is by acting and in action that he is enabled to know" (quoted in Scott, 1967, pp. 259–260). Case studies provide opportunities for students and authors to act, to speak, and thus to know. The more we empower students to ask the questions and act out or speak out about their views, the more they will know and thus the more case studies will fulfill an epistemic function.

## The Rhetorical Function of Case Studies

The epistemic nature of case studies is based, in part, on the assumption that they are arguments. In this vein, they provide us with opportunities to teach some rhetorical principles about evidence and argument structure. "The exemplary case study is one that judiciously and effectively presents the most compelling evidence, so the reader can reach an independent judgment" (Yin, 1984, p. 143). One way of using case studies, then, is to have students identify, evaluate, and even argue about what constitutes evidence. And what in case studies is presumed to count as evidence?

The Sypher, Shuler, and Whitten (Chapter 1) case about GEAR for Sports' winning ways is one example of an argument. What are the "winning ways"? Who is winning? These might be questions to pose when analyzing this case study as an argument. Cheney's (Chapter 4) description of the Mondragón worker-cooperative is another case that could be examined as an argument. We might ask students to negotiate their own values and provide arguments regarding Mondragón's potential for success. The same format could be used to analyze Mazloff's (Chapter 7) case of the employee assistance program at the Harding Company. What solutions are likely to work and why? What might count as evidence in the arguments for certain solutions? These are the same kinds of questions we might ask when following a problem–solution format, but too often solutions are chosen without good justifications, and too often students forget to focus on the evidence for the argument they are making. Equally as often, they forget that the choice of a certain solution is an argument to be made.

The actors' views captured in their discourse rather than the writer's interpretations of it are certainly a defensible starting point for generating evidence for a particular course of action. In reviewing *Case Studies in Organizational Communication* (Sypher, 1990), Charles Redding (personal communication, October 1989) wrote, "Don't let the case writer tell me the employee was introspective or worried and angry. Show me through their behavior and words and let me draw the conclusions." Just as a good movie does not and cannot tell viewers everything there is to know about a character and his or her thoughts, a good script, like a good case study, leaves room for interpretation and creativity on the part of the reader and includes dialogue that enhances interpretation.

As Yin (1984) contends, compelling evidence is often derived from the convergence of findings from multiple methods of research, which yield multiple viewpoints and perspectives. Thus students should have to identify and evaluate multiple forms of evidence and use it to construct an argument for the disposition of a case. This kind of exercise can be done orally or in writing by starting with directed questions *prior* to the students' reading and analysis of the case (Douglas, 1990). These questions should focus attention on the subtle and direct communicative behaviors that lend credence to arguments and perspectives. Thus one can determine whether the case has made a good argument and such analysis has the potential to increase students' persuasive abilities.

## The Skill-Enhancement Function of Case Studies

Without question, the use of case studies in the classroom has the potential to enhance communication and communication-related abilities. The assumption is that when we see communication at work, we learn from it; however, we rarely learn from experience alone. Opportunities to act, observe others in certain situations and analyze the actions have even greater potential to enhance learning. Through role playing and guidance in argument construction, students have the chance to act, to take part in constructing and reconstructing the situation to which they are exposed and to analyze potential consequences. These actions require message-reception abilities (listening and interpreting) as well as message-construction abilities. In role playing, students must practice speaking and thinking as persons in a given situation. In class discussions, they have to make oral arguments for interpretations or solutions. Outside of the basic public-speaking course, this skill is too seldom practiced, even though it is often used as an outcome measure of students' overall college performance. Recent research has suggested that significant improvements in persuasive ability can be made in the course of one semester with guided instruction in audience- or person-centered thinking (Sypher, Russo, & Curtis, 1994). Case studies were a central feature of the course in the Sypher et al. study.

Case study analysis has the potential to increase students' persuasive ability because it has the potential to increase perspective-taking skills. Through role-playing exercises or by arguing for certain solutions to problems, students get repeated opportunities to think in terms of the other. With guidance and feedback, they are able to expand their understanding of the psychological characteristics and subjective experiences of others.

The Kleinberg (Chapter 9) case provides just such an opportunity for students to assume the role of parties representing both sides in the negotiation of a Japanese buyout of a U.S. company. Students can work on taking the perspective of the participants in the negotiations and can make arguments for options that could be attempted by each side. By proposing options and taking the perspective of the actors in the negotiation, students can potentially develop both persuasive and perspective-taking abilities. These exercises increase students' strategic repertoire by giving them more experience in constructing other-oriented arguments. At the very least, such exercises have the potential to increase the quantity if not the quality of one's strategic or persuasive repertoire. Such were the benefits observed in the Sypher et al. (1994) study. With the use of case studies, students evidenced significant improvement in persuasive abilities, abilities that have been shown to predict individual and organizational success (Sypher & Zorn, 1986).

In addition to enhancing persuasive and perspective-taking abilities, case study analysis also helps students develop decision-making skills, which are among the most valuable communication-related abilities that organization members can possess (DiSalvo, 1980). Many organizational decisions are made under time constraints and without complete information. These decisions require people to be able to assimilate large amounts of information (Hartman, 1992). By asking students to read and analyze a case in the time frame of a class period, we are simulating the environment in which many work-related decisions will be made.

The development of oral and written communication skills as well as decision-making skills is linked to an enhanced capacity to think clearly and critically, one of Bok's (1986) central goals of higher learning. Perhaps by viewing solutions as arguments and focusing on evidence and other-oriented strategies, we can enhance communication and communication-related abilities as well as critical thinking. It is our challenge to find creative ways to make this happen and not depend solely upon the customary problem–solution format. That format clearly has its place, but it is only one approach.

## The Narrative Function of Case Studies

Most often case studies are thought of as narratives. Even though a case has elements of narration, exposition, *and* argumentation (Towl, 1969), the narration aspect seems to get the most attention. Critics usually encourage others to make a better narrative rather than a better argument when writing cases. While evidence is often taken for granted and only addressed when it is seemingly missing or poor, the criterion employed most often in judging a case study is whether the case has narrative structure, that is, a plot, some characters, and a sequence of events that unfold with drama and suspense. According to Yin (1984), the reader should be enticed into reading more; thus, like a good book, the case should be engaging. As narratives, case studies should have a beginning and an end; however, case studies are more often like critical events (Pettigrew, 1979) than histories. They can never tell the complete organizational story because it is ongoing. They can never tell *the* organizational story because there are multiple stories. Goodall and Eisenberg's (Chapter 22) "dispossessed" show how case studies are obligated to frame events in meaningful chunks. The boundaries of analysis depend upon such a structure, and within these bounds narrative theory can be used to analyze and evaluate case studies.

For example, Fisher (1984) offers two dimensions, fidelity and probability, on which we could structure a narrative analysis. We can have students examine the fidelity of the narrative by asking how the case resonates with readers. In effect, fidelity is the logic of good reason, a focus on the facts of the case. We can ask, Does it make sense? Are the facts consistent? Are the events easy to follow? Is the time frame clear? Probability is another criterion for evaluating narratives. Evaluating by this characteristic instructs us to guide our case study discussion with questions about the believability of the case; that is, Does it ring true? Does it seem likely? Is it consistent with what we know? Is there a logical and coherent development of characters and events? This last criterion of narrative analysis suggests a focus on the "goodness" rather than the "truthfulness" of the narrative. Both criteria might prove useful in analyzing Deetz's (Chapter 11) study of discursive power in knowledge-intensive work or Contractor and O'Keefe's (Chapter 12) study of the politics of information systems.

Clearly, the cases with identifiable characters and a sequence of events (e.g., Bingham, Chapter 21; Whitten, Chapter 18; Allen & Tompkins, Chapter 3; Wilhelm & Fairhurst, Chapter 14; and Zorn, Chapter 19) might be even more usefully analyzed according to Fisher's probability and fidelity criteria. But even without the development of characters like that in the Deetz (Chapter 11) case and the Contractor and O'Keefe (Chapter 12) case, a good case study, like a good story, calls forth both questions.

Fisher also offers an alternative way of viewing cases as narratives. Narratives provide *solutions* to problems, which is contrary to the idea that cases must be thought of as problems to be solved. Case studies can illuminate how theoretical concepts can be applied in successful communicative situations (Kreps & Lederman, 1985). Cases such as Rogers and Allbritton's (Chapter 15) Public Electronic Network in Santa Monica, DeSanctis, Jackson, Poole, and Dickson's (Chapter 17) electronic communication at Texaco, Barker's (Chapter 6) self-managing teams, and Sypher et al.'s (Chapter 1) GEAR for Sports all point out various reasons why communication practices have made a difference in the quality of lives or the quality of work lives of those studied. In recasting cases as narratives, then, we can potentially make the cases that celebrate a success as engaging and believable as those that focus on a problem. Too often it is the celebratory cases that are called into question: When a solution works, some seem to find the case harder to believe.

Many who responded to *Case Studies in Organizational Communication* said that the problem-oriented cases were more engaging, and worked best in the classroom, and that the success stories were too often met with suspicion. Perhaps it is our biases that lead to these conclusions. Our biases seem to be that good things don't happen often enough, that reports of good stories make it sound much too easy, and that in the success stories, there is nothing left to solve. Such biases tend to undermine the value of success stories.

Perhaps the reason the problem cases are more engaging is that we find more engaging things to do with them. This approach also suggests somewhat of a bias toward a logic that communication only exists to fix things, that it is a tool to make things right, and that we understand it best when there is something to fix, something to make right. While this is certainly one approach, an equally useful logic focuses our attention on the prescriptions embedded in the socially constructed reality. Fisher's (1984) alternative approach to narrative analysis suggests that a case study can be a solution and offers guidelines for writers and readers that have been ignored or implicitly rather than formally employed.

Most importantly, narrative theory suggests ways to engage students more in the cases in which communication functions to create empowering and successful situations. By having students focus on how problems were solved rather than speculating on how they would solve them, we all stand to see how narratives provide solutions and thus how the storyteller acts as counselor. Also, having students focus on what situational factors made the solutions successful aids them in recognizing that no one solution is going to work across all situations and that they need to consider the environmental factors that make proposed solutions possible. In this way, the relationship between theory and practice may be made clearer.

To review, case studies serve a variety of functions, and the recent renewal of interest in them can only grow with an expanded repertoire of uses. If we can construe cases in multiple ways, we can develop additional, innovative teaching methods. Case studies are important because as narratives about work, they can be universal and crucial to our understanding of organizations and organizational communication. As narratives, they are also potentially more memorable and believable than other report forms (Martin & Powers, 1983), especially when no disconfirming information is available. As arguments, case studies have the rhetorical force to create understandings, generate hypotheses, and explain theories. Case studies are both descriptive and prescriptive. The problems require us to provide solutions, while the narratives, especially of the communicative successes, provide solutions for us. In short, case studies provide an engaging and intellectually rich alternative to other methods of teaching and knowing.

## REFERENCES

Bateson, M. C. (1994). *Peripheral visions.* New York: HarperCollins.

Bok, D. (1986). *Higher learning.* Cambridge, MA: Harvard, Universitiy Press.

Bonoma, T. V., & Kosnik, T. J. (1990). *Marketing management: Text and cases.* Homewood, IL: Irwin.

Clandinin, D. J. (1992). Narrative and story in teacher education. In T. Russell & H. Munby (Eds.), *Teachers and teaching: From classroom to reflection* (pp. 124–137). London: Falmer.

Condit, C. M. (1990). The birth of understanding: Chaste science and the harlot of the arts. *Communication Monographs, 57,* 323–327.

Conquergood, D. (1991). Rethinking ethnography: Towards a critical cultural politics. *Communication Monographs, 58,* 179–194.

Craig, R. T. (1990). The speech tradition. *Communication Monographs, 57,* 309–314.

Deetz, S. A. (1990). Foreword. In B. D. Sypher (Ed.), *Case studies in organizational communication* (pp. viii–x). New York: Guilford Press.

Dewey, J. (1910). *How we think.* Boston, MA: Heath.

DiSalvo, V. S. (1980). A summary of current research identifying communication skills in various organizational contexts. *Communication Education, 29,* 283–290.

Douglas, M. E. (1990). The case method: Nontraditional interpretation and closure. *Journal of Education for Business, 65,* 251–254.

Fisher, W. R. (1984). Narration as a human communication paradigm: The case of public moral argument. *Communication Monographs, 51,* 1–22.

Hartman, L. D. (1992). Business communication and the case method: Toward integration in accounting and MBA programs. *Bulletin of the Association for Business Communication, 55*(3), 41–45.

Kreps, G. L., & Lederman, L. C. (1985). Using the case method in organizational communication education: Developing students' insight, knowledge, and creativity through experience-based learning and systematic debriefing. *Communication Education, 34,* 358–364.

Lawrence, P. R. (1953). The preparation of case material. In K. Andrews (Ed.), *The case method of teaching human relations and administration* (pp. 215–244). Cambridge, MA: Harvard University Press.

Martin, J., & Powers, M. E. (1983). Truth or corporate propaganda: The value of a good war story. In L. Pondy, P. Frost, G. Morgan, & T. Dandridge (Eds.), *Organizational symbolism* (pp. 93–108). Greenwich, CT: JAI Press.

O'Keefe, B. J. (1988). The logic of message design: Individual differences in reasoning about communication. *Communication Monographs, 55,* 80–103.

Pettigrew, A. (1979). On studying organizational cultures. *Administrative Science Quarterly, 24,* 570–580.

Scott, R. L. (Ed.). (1967). On viewing rhetoric as epistemic. *Central States Speech Journal, 18,* 9–17.

Sypher, B. D. (Ed.). (1990). *Case studies in organizational communication.* New York: Guilford Press.

Sypher, B. D., Russo, T. C., & Curtis, A. (1994, July). *The development of persuasive abilities in college students.* Paper presented at the annual meeting of the International Communication Association, Sydney, Australia.

Sypher, B. D., & Zorn, T. E. (1986). Communication related abilities and upward mobility: A longitudinal investigation. *Human Communication Research, 12,* 421–431.

Towl, A. (1969). *To study administration by cases.* Cambridge, MA: Harvard University Press.

Weick, K. E. (1995). *Sensemaking in organizations.* Thousand Oaks, CA: Sage.

Yin, R. K. (1984). *Case study research: Design and methods.* Newbury Park, CA: Sage.

# CHAPTER 1

## Making Sense out of Creativity and Constraints
### Winning Ways' GEAR for Sports

BEVERLY DAVENPORT SYPHER
SHERIANNE SHULER
PAMELA A. WHITTEN

It does not take long for an outside observer to realize what an immensely successful company Winning Ways is. Inside the mahogany-trimmed front doors, one is immediately surrounded by the elegance that handsome profits can produce. On the production side of the building, friendly employees, unsolicited, brag about the quality of their product. On the office side of the company, one might overhear a 10-year employee describing Winning Ways' phenomenal growth as the "Cinderella" of sports apparel.

The Kansas City-based Winning Ways has a two-decade track record of success in manufacturing various types of sports apparel, but their most recent division, GEAR for Sports, has become the central focus of their business and market identity. The high-quality, high-priced items fill the shelves of college bookstores around the country, and high school products are on the way. Destination resorts, major corporations, and the U.S. military have contracted with Winning Ways to silk-screen or embroider their logos and names onto fine-quality garments.

Given the career history of Winning Ways' founder, Bob Wolff, the success of the company is hardly surprising. In 1974, Wolff founded Winning Ways after a 16-year career in the binocular import business. Before that he sold women's gloves and maternity clothes as a result of a retail internship while a student at Northwestern University. "When my cousin-in-law offered me a spot in his binocular business, I jumped at the chance. I learned the Orient, and I learned about business," Wolff recounted in an interview. "Realizing that net worth was more important than net income" and that family businesses are always going to promote family members rather than in-laws, Wolff left that business and laid the groundwork for what has become a multimillion-dollar, privately owned venture into the sports apparel business.

At 39 years old, Wolff saw the tennis boom coming and decided, sensibly, that tennis players needed tennis clothes. In 1974, when he founded Winning Ways, hardly anyone was designing, importing, and selling warm-up suits. In that first year of business, Wolff's Winning Ways made $2.5 million dollars filling the niche he had foreseen.

From this beginning, Wolff guided the company into licensing the Wilson Sporting Goods name and moving sports apparel into the mass market. Whether producing private labels for Sears and Roebuck or specialized garments for Wilson Sporting Goods, Wolff seemed to keep seeing the future. The first year Winning Ways produced Wilson products, they generated almost $10 million, and in 1985, barely more than a decade after setting up shop with a metal desk and partition dividers, Bob Wolff moved into the college bookstore business with his GEAR for Sports division. In 4 years, the sales from GEAR division alone exceeded $30 million, and by 1991, the sales of the various divisions of Winning Ways exceeded $100 million. In fact, Winning Ways has become the largest supplier of imprinted sportswear to college bookstores in the United States.

So many things Wolff touched had turned to gold that a friend gave him a crystal ball that still adorns his desk. When asked how he did it, the founder replied, "I was blessed with vision." That vision may have developed with the binocular business, but it was certainly clarified through his Winning Ways.

This case study demonstrates how impassioned leadership, sustained vision, good communication, and continual learning make organizations successful.[1] In large part, it reveals the multiple dimensions of the Winning Ways personality by focusing on high achievement, the driving energy and passion, the concern for employees, and the willingness to change. It also demonstrates that organizational sensemaking is much more about invention than discovery (Weick, 1995). Winning Ways' management and employees have invented and reinvented themselves and the way they work both individually and collectively, and their sense of who they are is revealed in their words and actions. In short, the successes of Winning Ways have been made possible because of the excitement, the products, the innovativeness, and the ability to change.

However, the flip side of this corporate personality reveals that with creativity and change come tension. Some employees we talked to thought they had lost a sense of who they were, and as Weick (1995, p. 14) reiterated, "Whenever sense is lost, the loss is deeply troubling." This case also points out the troubles this organization confronts in sustaining success.

The frenetic energy at times appeared unfocused and misunderstood, and the continual learning has created fear and frustration. The rapid growth called for the recruitment and training of the kind of employees that have been hard to find, and all of this must be accomplished in a social milieu in which gender, race, and management decisions intersect in complex and conflictual ways. The observations and descriptions in the next section illuminate the ways in which creativity is enacted at Winning Ways. Pride in the product and building, passionate leadership, employee recognition, and performance opportunities are all distinctive. A closer look, however, revealed the inherent tensions produced from the success. These constraints are detailed as the case unfolds.

## ENACTING CREATIVITY

Bob Wolff articulated a vision, modeled the frenetic behavior that still characterizes the everyday work practices of many managers, and symbolized his values through language choices, company rituals, and various concrete artifacts. In many respects, the product and the building are the heroes at Winning Ways. The employees take pride in the product, the physical structure in which it is produced, and the historic legacy of its founder. These values, along with "innovativeness" and "conscientiousness," are what Winning Ways calls "watchwords." In many ways, these linguistic choices represent the employees' "frames of mind" (Weick, 1995, p. xii). These words matter as much to them as to us. They suggest their "sensemaking," that is, their interpretations of who they are and their explanations for why they act the way they do, and their expectations for future actions. One need only walk through the front door to see this sensemaking symbolized.

The lobby is a multisensory experience. It is an elegant, two-story rotunda with high-end sports apparel displayed in mahogany showcases. The leather-sleeved varsity jackets and embroidered sweatshirts are quick eye-grabbers. The entire scene, from the beautifully appointed reception area to the double staircase and soothing walled fountain, creates a picture of a successful organization that values quality and knows the importance of visual cues in fostering pride. Every month this setting serves as the scene for the "casual" gathering of company employees to honor the "Employee of the Month."

The symbolic logic of the building is evident; the impression management was strategic. Architects painstakingly met with every member of management when designing the new facility. "We wanted it to be a place that expressed to them [employees] their importance to our success. The building sets a standard for the performance of the people within it. It is a statement about our company personality," Wolff wrote in a Winning Ways publication. The building, though, is not the only evidence of creativity at Winning Ways. The financial success of the company is one thing, but the talk of the employees is convincing. A central theme in the discourse is passionate leadership.

### "When People Are Fired Up, They Are Hard to Extinguish"

This statement appears in a company brochure and on a framed wall hanging in Bob Wolff's office. Winning Ways' leaders indeed appeared "fired up." They spoke quickly, interrupted often, and espoused lots of platitudes. There seemed to be constant motion and constant change underlying the Winning Ways vision. They talked about "riding the waves" and "sailing faster" and "a willingness to reach long and hard." Organizational tacking and turning were hardly obstacles; they were part of the process. This language also suggests that "rich vocabularies matter in a world of action where images of actions rather than actions themselves are passed from person to person" (Weick, 1995, p. 183). It is not surprising that this philosophy was being enacted by a group of young, passionate leaders who often worried out loud about "surviving," "exploding," or "just simply making it." "We're whipping ourselves knowing we could be better," said Dave Geenans, the 33-year-old director of manufacturing. "It's healthy, but you have to be careful."

Dave is a good example of passionate leadership at Winning Ways. He left a lucrative job with one of the country's largest jeans makers to become Winning Ways' comptroller. With little production management experience, Dave was soon promoted to director of manufacturing. "I had some ideas," he said, "about how to make things work better." Just watching him work demonstrates that he has a whole slew of ideas. He always appeared in motion, seldom in his office and never at a loss to explain a new idea about how things are going to be better. In the middle of a conversation, a production employee walked in to ask Dave where the article was that Dave had recommended he read. The article turned out to be a chapter from Hayes, Wheelwright, and Clark's (1988) *Dynamic Manufacturing: Creating the Learning Organization*. Dave had photocopied the first chapter, "People Make It Happen," and had underlined the following sentences: "Creating a coherent, integrated approach to managing people is a long-term proposition. . . . It can only be *created* and *nurtured* into a lasting advantage, through consistent and painstaking effort. On the other hand, it can be quickly undermined by a few inconsistent, thoughtless actions." One might argue that texts (ones organizations produce as well as ones they tout) are an incomplete view of organizational reality because they are not "living." Weick (1995), however, argues that texts are an artifact of organizational sensemaking that gives insight into the organization's state of mind and likely behavior (Weick, 1995). For example, when asked what he had read lately, Geenans excitedly mentioned *Love and Profit* (Autry, 1991) and *Reengineering the Organization* (Lowenthal, 1994) and even offered a copy of something else he had dog-eared for himself and others.

Dave always seemed to be learning and sometimes seemed frustrated about the difficulty of putting into practice what he knew. He once commented, "Everybody sees eye to eye on the values but we don't always know how to get there." According to Dave, "Supervisors should have nothing to do with the function of the job but [everything to do with] creating the environment. We constantly have to work on that." And when asked how to create this environment, he said, "You create trust. You say things and you do it." Dave appeared to be driven and once wondered aloud if he could keep the momentum to see his ideas through. In fact, Bob Wolff worried about "keeping him [Dave] under control": "Sometimes he needs someone to put on the brakes, someone with the pedals on their side like those driver's ed people."

Employees were quick to brag about their wonder boss. A production employee claimed that "because Dave Geenans gives people respect, they respect him back. We have a lot of black-and-white rules we're supposed to follow, but Dave understands that not every situation is black and white. Dave is very direct and you always know where you stand with him, but his real strength is that he is driven by ideas." A line worker on the production side said, "He knows how to get people to perform. He does this by walking around and sharing his thoughts with you and asking what you think and how you feel about issues as well." As Dave once said, "We don't call our people associates but we don't call them employees either. . . . I generally call them by their name."

Once, when implementing a new team project throughout the production department, Dave brought in a pair of live guinea pigs. The guinea pigs served the dual purposes of symbolizing that the employees were not acting as guinea pigs in some team experiment and of exemplifying how important cooperation within and between teams is by making all teams responsible for the daily care of the guinea pigs.

Dave also seemed to recognize that leaders cannot be effective without giving an important role to followers. He believes that the employee's "foot is on the accelerator and the manager's foot is on the brake. . . . you [the manager] can only go so far before you take the foot off the brake and let them take it . . . and provide a leader in there that can help steer." One couldn't help but wonder if this "accelerator and brake" talk had become ritualized. Several employees used the same analogies, the same metaphors, and the same examples. They had invented who they were and how they were acting.

Dave talked about the importance of feelings and self-esteem and self-worth for all employees. He once stated, "I don't believe a happy worker is productive; I believe a productive worker is happy." Geenans wanted employees to be productive, but he also wanted them to like their work life, and he seemed to behave as though he agreed with Max DePree (1989), the Howard Miller Company CEO, who said that making employees like the manager is a moral obligation and one of the best ways to make great things happen in corporations.

Dave also talked with pride of the leadership potential he saw in others. Employees chuckled when they talked about John's shaky start as production manager. A production employee claimed that she had seen John grow as a manager: "He's better than when he started and he's learning by experience." A screen printer told the story about how she initially thought that John was "out to take care of number 1." One day she arrived on her shift all excited because she and her husband had finally purchased their very first new car. At the end of her shift, she found an anonymous $200 company check in her employee box with a note saying that it was for gas money. When she asked John about it, he simply smiled and told her not to look a gift horse in the mouth.

During a bimonthly production management meeting, Dave pushed back from the table where John was sitting and watched him run the meeting. He talked later about watching John develop and feeling rewarded when John did well. At one group meeting John encouraged the shift managers "to share your experiences with one another and learn from each other." John also encouraged the supervisors to be good to the dedicated and hardworking production employees. He said, "Be creative, give employees a little more vision. You've got to build commitment to get everyone involved. Always try to be upbeat; it's got to be fun. And remember to recognize and reward people." The repeated themes in the managers' talk suggested that impassioned leadership was infectious.

### "Change Is an Absolute"

Change is a fact of life for any organization, and Winning Ways is certainly no exception. Leaders in this organization have changed their focus, changed their products, and changed their markets. Change, they argued, "is an absolute." The changes, however, were not and could not be solely business oriented. Dave and the managers he supervises were constantly introducing organizational changes. How work gets done and how relationships are maintained were continually discussed.

Many of the production employees talked about the creation of teams. A few years ago, production management felt that too many employees were focusing only on their individual jobs rather than on the teamwork necessary to produce Winning Ways products. Coordination and cooperative efforts were not as strong as they could and should have been, Dave said. The team concept was developed to actualize a philosophy that he felt strongly about: "The sense of community is the more important driver here. We can't survive without each other." So teams of 10 to 15 people were created to enable employees to learn from each other and to work better together. The implementation of teams "flattened out" the production process, and the team soon became the "communication mechanism" replacing the multiple levels of production assistants and managers. Each production team came up with a team name and designed a team T-shirt, which they wore every Friday. One team, the final audit group, designed their T-shirts with a shark coming out of a box saying, "Just when you thought this order was gone. . . ." Other teams were equally creative in visualizing their work woes on their T-shirts.

Early on, teams enthusiastically competed for the coveted "Team of the Month" award. A production worker explained that the teams were developed to increase efficiency and reduce mistakes. Another production employee claimed that management developed the team approach to increase company spirit. Although some employees disagreed about the impetus for the creation of a team approach, some became very emotional about its effects. One employee quite literally got choked up when talking about the difference a team approach made: "I feel like a lot of people here got a lot closer. . . . Now we talk to each other, not about each other."

Just like the energetic leaders that founder Bob Wolff hired to run Winning Ways with a vision that paralleled his own, Bob also has been the architect of many new projects. A few years ago, he launched a plan to increase upward communication from employees to him. Once a month, a representative from each department would attend one of Bob's communication meetings armed with questions from fellow employees. The representative would present the questions to Bob at the open meeting. After the meeting ended, each representative would report back to coworkers about the types of questions asked by other departments and Bob's responses to all of the questions.

A more recent example of an ambitious project was undertaken by Dave. With its emphasis on a quality product, Winning Ways rejects any and all articles that are not perfect. These rejects, however, are costly for the company. Concerned about the tension between the need to stop any questionable item from leaving the warehouse and the need to limit the number of costly rejects, Dave called all the managers together to develop a problem-solving strategy. Dave's goal was to develop a new means to solve problems the first time so they did not reoccur. Rather than just writing up a printer for a botched order, for example, Dave wanted employees to search for the underlying problem. In this case, the real problem was a faulty system being used by customer service to record orders. Dave recognized that getting at the root of problems would prevent their reoccurrence and save the company money.

At this special problem-solving meeting, Dave outlined the long-term goals rather than a step-by-step set of guidelines. He ended the meeting by urging that managers take action even if it meant taking small steps at first. He said, "Attack at least one problem a day—it can be a small one and I'll be happy." Again, a new way of thinking about work was initiated.

## A Focus on Employees

The strength of Winning Ways does not exist only in specialized events and projects. Standard, everyday practices portrayed a company that had produced a degree of openness in which employees felt they had the freedom to express their opinions. A production employee stated that people ask her opinions about things "constantly, all day long." An employee in the credit department felt that top management's doors were always open, literally and figuratively. "If I have a problem, moral or work-related, I can go talk to them." She felt so comfortable about expressing her view that she proudly boasted that "she gives her opinions even when they are not asked for." Another employee claimed that people from all different levels ask for his opinions all the time. He pointed out one recent example when "his department, which is considering going back to one shift for everybody, asked each individual how they felt about this and how it would affect their life." In addition to the solicitous and open communication patterns that are encouraged at Winning Ways, at least one department has implemented a formal employee involvement program in which suggestions are given and problems can be solved by the people who know the job best.

Another feature of Winning Ways is its recognition of the people who work there. There are a variety of means through which the company displays its appreciation for employees. The first indication can be found in the actual work environment. There are plaques with engraved names, announcements on bulletin boards, and newsletter stories of good performance. That they feel appreciated is also evident in employees' talk. One employee said she was pleased with the fact that things constantly change; she gets moved around a lot, which prevents her job from getting stale. Employees are quick to offer that this is the "best place" they have ever worked. One person told us she likes the fact that this company "does not stand over you with a stop watch" like all the other manufacturing firms she had worked for. Another even expressed amazement that Winning Ways gives her the freedom to use the bathroom any time she needs to, not just at prescribed break times! (Unfortunately, there is a good bit of evidence that suggests that women, especially, suffer more humiliation and urinary problems because of restricted bathroom privileges in some man-ufacturing plants.)

Winning Ways is also a company that often puts its money where its mouth is when showing employees how much they are valued. One would be hard pressed to find an employee who does not brag about the perks provided by Winning Ways. As one employee told us, these perks are not just the typical bonus of canned hams at Christmas. Winning Ways em-ployees enjoy a blow-out picnic that has become a company ritual. At these picnics, employees feast on barbecue (a much-appreciated delicacy in Kansas City) and play games on company time. The most anticipated event at the picnic is the presenting of a host of coveted employee awards, some of which result in employees flying off to vacation destinations. Yet it is not just the expected perks that make employees feel special. Many times Winning Ways has surprised employees with a special impromptu lunch. It is also not uncommon for management to give away Kansas City Royals baseball tickets or coveted University of Kansas basketball tickets.

It is not only in the work environment or the prizes and cash awards that one can observe how employees are appreciated. The environment fostered at Winning Ways made it feel like a good place to work. One of the buyers was pleased that people were encouraged to interact at Winning Ways: "It's a fun atmosphere—there is a lot of joking and fun." A coworker also expressed pride in the fact that Winning Ways fosters a team spirit: "I've been at some places where they don't even realize from one depart-ment to the next that it's a team effort. Here, we're all striving for the same objectives. . . . everybody works really well together and has a really good attitude." Someone in inventory control stated that the nurturing family atmosphere "is more than just lip service." This caring, family atmosphere is exhibited on a daily basis in big and small ways. A credit department employee said she tells new coworkers about a typical example: "My daughter had triplets a couple of years ago, and they announced it over the loud speaker to all 600+ employees because so many people realized it was an event going on in my life and there are just a lot of caring people here."

In addition to a pleasant work environment, nice prizes and awards, and a warm, family atmosphere, Winning Ways displays its appreciation of employees through the many opportunities it offers. An employee in the printing department has experienced these opportunities through a vari-ety of training and cross-training programs. A packer was offered the op-portunity of leadership training even though she felt there was no imme-diate promotion in sight. She said just being encouraged to participate in this training made her feel valued. Some employees appreciated the chance to try new things like switching shifts if they got bored or trying a new kind of printer. One person told us that at Winning Ways, "Promotion doesn't just mean moving up. It also means having the opportunity to move around in the company." Finding these "performance opportunities" is what Zuboff (1988) called the major management challenge of the decade. The Winning Ways employee explained that there are plenty of opportunities for traditional promotions and "employees have the ability to manage their own destinies": "To get promoted at Winning Ways, all you have to do is figure out what you want to do and then go ask your boss or coworkers what you need to do to attain that position."

One woman recently took advantage of these opportunities and literally created her own "performance opportunity." Hired as a graphic artist, she wanted to recreate a more employee-focused company newsletter after the former newsletter editor left Winning Ways. She made the suggestion to upper management, and they told her to "go for it." If she were successful, they told her that she would have a new job. Her efforts so impressed upper management that they created a full-time internal communication staff job and hired her to fill it. Success stories like this are not uncommon at Winning Ways.

With impassioned leadership, innovative changes, and a focus on employees, Winning Ways appeared to be an exemplary company that tried to do things right while trying to "do the right thing" (Bennis, 1989). Yet, like all organizations, Winning Ways exists in a world where constraints challenge creative efforts. The same growth that provided new jobs, employee rewards, company profits, nice surroundings, and performance opportunities for managers also has led to less personal contact with the founder, increased pressure to adapt to new ways of working, a greater demand for skilled labor, continuous change, and consequently different conversations to understand and cope with the world they have created.

The constraints, however, seemed to be embedded in various levels of consciousness. Some members knew things had changed, but most captured it in terms of the loss of "family," a loss that was, as Weick said, deeply troubling. The founder/father figure was not around as much nor as willing as in the past to hand out bonuses of various types. With changes came pressures, and only the more visionary were able to construe the constraints in a larger environmental frame.

## CONFRONTING CONSTRAINTS

With all the creative action at Winning Ways, it can be difficult to see the constraints that produce tension. As Dave said, "It's important to have good intentions," but even organizations that are trying to do the right things are constantly tested and challenged by both the larger environment and the social reality that has been created to get the work done. Some constraints are specific to the organization, while others are created by society and the marketplace.

In order to better understand an organization like Winning Ways, it is helpful to understand the state of manufacturing today. While the production of goods was once the main activity of organizations employing nonfarm workers, these types of organizations now make up less than 16% of the total nonfarm employment in the country (U.S. Bureau of Labor Statistics, 1996). Zuboff (1988) said almost a decade ago that our work in this country is now much more about "working with" rather than "working on" machines.

Among organizations classified as manufacturing, there is a great deal of variation; from work in the dangerous and unpleasant meat-packing industry (for a profile, see Stull, 1995) to the superclean production of computer chips by employees wearing "spacesuits" and working in highly sterile conditions. In terms of working conditions, Winning Ways can best be described as somewhere between these two extremes.

While there has been a growing movement in the United States to implement new "empowering" and participative structures (McCaffrey, Faerman, & Hart, 1995), manufacturing organizations have tended to lag behind these trends. Winning Ways appeared to be somewhat of an exception. Even though employees work with some degree of repetitiveness, specialization, and control at Winning Ways, Taylorism hardly seems to be the pervading philosophy that Suzaki (1993) says it is in many manufacturing organizations. The employees' language, their behavior, their reading material, and the organization of their work suggests otherwise. More often they evidenced participative decision making, upward and informal communication, a focus on relationships, and an understanding of individual differences. As in most organizations, there was the push and pull of autonomy, but one could hardly describe Winning Ways in classical management terms. Employees of Winning Ways said their workplace was better than other workplaces, and they expressed seemingly genuine appreciation for the positive differences. They also had come to expect the benefits previously outlined in this case, especially the fact that they would be treated well and listened to at work. Many of the tensions evidenced at Winning Ways were a result of these expectations being violated, and some of the greatest constraints were associated with success and rapid growth.

## "Growth Has Its Problems"

By all accounts, Winning Ways has experienced tremendous growth in the past few years. While the employees talked about the opportunities that have come with the recent growth, they inevitably felt the drawbacks. Perhaps the most strongly felt consequence of growth was the perceived decline in the "family" feeling.

### "Bring the Family Back"

One production worker said, "People who have been here for awhile see it [growth] as chipping away at family atmosphere. People see it as losing something that they had before." While all employees, both office and manufacturing, used to know each others' names, now that is really impossible. One employee who has been around awhile said, "It's just sad because I saw how it used to be. It used to be family-oriented as a company." In fact, Dave once said, "You just can't do some of these things once you're past about 700. Huge companies just can't and don't respond to employees." Winning Ways was approaching that number. In fact, they had doubled the workforce in less than five years.

One office employee spoke wistfully about the good old days. "They used to let us have casual day where we could wear GEAR stuff and jeans and now that's really limited. I don't understand because that's our business and they have this perception that they're a three-piece suit company. When we moved into this building they wanted us to look like the building." When they moved to the new, bigger building, employees began to talk about "the wall" that separated production from offices as almost unscalable. However, "the wall," a language choice of symbolic and concrete construction, is not unique to Winning Ways. Separation of work activities is a common feature of manufacturing organizations that has for years been shown to cause divisions between "staff" and "production" employees (Parker, 1995).

Although the office side is posh, "the wall" acts as a border for some luxuries, such as air conditioning and privacy. In the summer, production-side spirits seemed to wilt as temperatures rose too high to be combated by fans or Gatorade. Employees reported that tempers tended to be shorter and that some employees had suffered from heat exhaustion. Different kinds of work have meant different kinds of work environments.

As Winning Ways has grown, upper management, or the "higher ups," as they have become known, have become more distant, residing in a posh suite of offices known as "the Oval Office," the second floor of offices that hugs the lobby rotunda. The initially positive impression of the building was beginning to show signs of stress: it was already too small, "the wall" was more than concrete, and Bob Wolff's "oval office" was too often unoccupied. Nonetheless, Bob Wolff was still revered among the manufacturing employees. He still likes to walk around the production floor and to talk to employees, even though he is not on site nearly as often as he used to be. One second-shift employee said, "He got kind of mad at us, because, other shifts come out and talked with him and we were still working. . . . We were trying to impress him." While most people still talk about him in positive ways, the older employees talk about how he is not around as much and say that they miss having the personal contact with him that they once had. On his infrequent days in the office, Wolff was characterized by his "drive-bys," the term used to describe the way he cruises around and questions managers about what is going on. The intonation in the description suggested these were, at the very least, anxiety producing for some managers. "The family" apparently had reinvented itself just as the leaders had.

### "Someone Forgot the Candy"

Also due in part to growth, some of the perks have been discontinued. Employees looked forward to special lunches, roses on Valentine's Day, and Halloween candy. As the company has grown, some of those perks have decreased. As Wolff pointed out, "Those lunches cost $6,000 now!" Even though employees recognized the increased costs for things like dinner, many felt that "they're making more money now" and could afford the expense. From management's perspective, it was not as if someone had made a decision to eliminate these fringe benefits. "Someone just forgot to bring the Halloween candy," one manager said, "it wasn't really a decision to discontinue it." On the other hand, no one took the responsibility for continuing it. To some employees, discontinuing appreciated gestures, no matter how small, has become symbolic of too much growth.

Some also recognized these changes as potential communication problems. Although they moved to the current building just 5 years ago, they have already outgrown it. Recently, overcrowding has made it necessary for the art department to move out of the headquarters and back into the "old building." Many saw this decision as coming from the "higher ups" who do not always listen to the employees. "I understand why they are doing it, but I think it will create more communication problems," said one member of the art department.

With growth inevitably comes change. While most Winning Ways employees saw change as necessary, some employees grumbled that just when they figured out one system, a new one was introduced. Dave, however, was sold on change, believing that even change just for change's sake was healthy. So even though "change is absolute," it also has led to uncertainty and confusion.

### "We're Better on Form Than Substance"

As this quote from Dave indicates, the energy and willingness to embrace change has led to several new projects that were welcomed at first, but that were later dismissed as "one more idea somebody just read about." However, the commitment to try new forms of management and new ways of working distinguishes Winning Ways from the Tayloristic patterns on which many manufacturing organizations are still relying. Changing ingrained patterns is difficult, however, and can cause new and different problems (e.g., Hirschhorn & Gilmore, 1989). One result of the commitment to change at Winning Ways is that employees are sometimes confused or unaware that programs have been instituted. Lack of follow-through was a consistent complaint. When the team concept was first introduced, it was implemented with an apparent flourish. However, as is often the case (see Westley, 1990), the sudden changes were seen as somewhat superficial. While the new language of teamwork and cooperation affected the way people thought about each other, the actual work did not change in substantial ways. Problems quickly arose when turnover and new hires changed team membership.

"These teams—it was real hot and heavy for about three months and then it was gone. They don't finish what they start," said one production worker. Things like team dinners, special meetings, and awards are no longer happening. While people are still wearing the T-shirts, most new employees are not sure what they are for or how they came about. Although there is an understanding that the company as a whole still wants to have a team approach, one employee said, "We don't talk team so much. It's like anything else around here. When an idea is first implemented, that's all you hear about and then it fizzles out."

This confusion about teams has implications for the way work gets done on a daily basis. One woman who works in manufacturing complained that she is never sure whether it is more important to work cooperatively in a team or to get ahead by working competitively to earn individual points. "You know, one day they want you to have teamwork, next they want you to have points, then it's teamwork again, then points. So I said, 'Make up your mind!'" One manager commented that this was a problem with the "change for change sake" philosophy, indicating his frustration with the lack of follow-through on implementing a team structure.

Another new idea that died was the new emphasis on problem solving. "We talk about it a lot," Dave said, but it never seemed to take hold. This new idea may fall by the wayside, just as did Bob Wolff's upward communication meetings with employees. According to one employee, these meetings just "sort of stopped. . . . usually these [new ideas] don't last too long, they work great for awhile and then it all sort of falls by the wayside," she sighed. When asked about the meetings' discontinuation, Wolff said, "Oh yeah, I need to start those again. They have sort of just been forgotten."

Training and development is another area that has seen constant change and lack of focus. An example was the hiring and promotion of employees from production to do training. Many people thought this approach was abandoned because one member of the senior management did not like the idea, and these employees were demoted back to operations to make way for a new training approach. A new training manager was hired, but the woman who took the position left in three months. A few months later, Wolff said they would not hire another training director and that necessary services would be contracted out. While there appears to be a recognized need for employee development and leadership skills, and lip service is certainly given to the importance of people, the prevailing trend leans to hiring expertise from the outside (both consultants and supervisors) rather than developing potential internally.

Employees complained that Winning Ways used to put more emphasis on promoting people from within the company who had experience, potential, and willingness to learn. Now, however, they appear to be looking outside the organization to fill some managerial and supervisory roles. This is a source of tension, especially among older workers without a "piece of paper." One packer noted, "I used to think people got promoted pretty fair but now I think it has a lot to do with your education. That's good but there's a lot of people with good experience that aren't getting promoted. It didn't used to be that way. It used to be that if you were here a long time and knew your job, you got promoted. Now it seems like it's education more." So with growth came new needs, new priorities, and new problems, both perceived and real.

## "All the Legal Crap" and Other Constraints

In addition to the constraints resulting from internal changes, some tensions are imposed by the larger organizational environment. Sometimes the values of an organization are called into question by the realities created by the broader culture. At times, Winning Ways seemed to struggle with the difficulty of balancing human needs and organizational needs. "Even though we are aware of all the legal crap, we do the right thing," Dave says. "You can't legislate corporate culture. . . . It's hard to be fair." The tension produced from this struggle is evidenced internally by employee complaints about the glass ceiling and incidents of harassment. External factors also make for a slim labor pool and continual turnover.

### The Glass Ceiling

Winning Ways suffers from some of the same problems that face other contemporary U.S. organizations. Only a small number of senior management is female in corporate America; the numbers are even lower for manufacturing organizations. So it is not surprising that Winning Ways has few women managers. There is only one woman on the Winning Ways senior management team and very few women in managerial and supervisory roles throughout the company. Especially in production, many female employees are starting to ask why more of them are not getting promoted. The glass ceiling is felt by several women who are frustrated with the lack of upward mobility (for a discussion of the glass ceiling phenomenon, see Buzzanell, 1995). One woman asserted, "Any woman in any skill, it seems like you can't get past that computer. You'll never be a manager or a supervisor, you'll be behind the computer or be a laborer. They won't even give you the chance—in four years I haven't seen one woman get promoted to a job where they could support themselves on their own. I feel like they give them to the men because they're the head of the household."

Upper management, however, was not unaware of these feelings. Dave noted that the most often checked-out book in the "training library" was *The Promotable Woman*. The recent addition of the one woman vice president was used as an example by Bob Wolff, who said, "We don't have a problem with discrimination; we just don't have that many women drawn to manufacturing." One female production worker blamed the lack of women managers on an incident in the past in which a woman who was in a supervisory position "blew it and ruined it for the rest of us." Most managers, however, see the problem as too few women to promote. Perceptual differences, it appears, are just as problematic as real differences.

### Harassment

In addition to talk about the glass ceiling, another "hot button" topic of conversation was harassment. Like all companies, Winning Ways is not immune to these types of problems; they have recently dealt with both sexual and racial harassment. The pervasive nature of conflict related to race and gender in society make dealing with these issues almost inevitable in any organization. These issues have been discussed frequently among the employees, who found it difficult not to take sides. In the harassment situations, multiple perspectives were evidenced. The victim, the perpetrator, the managers, and the other employees all had considerations of their own regarding the conflict. We were asked, "When an organization values all employees and wants to see them succeed, what should be done when a long-time employee is accused of harassment?" To ignore the problem would be unfair to the victim and to other employees and would also open up the possibility for legal action. To simply fire the perpetrator was considered by some to be a loss to the organization.

In the recent incident of sexual harassment, Winning Ways tried to balance these constraints by moving the accused to a different job. The incident of racial harassment was handled in a similar fashion. Outplacing the accused perpetrator to a subsidiary business in an outlying community seemed an appropriate compromise to management but was a frustration to some employees. While these solutions avoided certain conflicts, they also caused some employees to wonder what behavior was being rewarded. The decision provided a new and challenging work situation for the alleged perpetrator and also allowed the organization to continue to benefit from his many years of experience. The benefit for the victim was to remove the harasser from the work situation. This is one more example of how an organization benefits by outsourcing to subsidiary businesses started up in nearby rural areas with high unemployment. It is also an example of how sexual harassment has implications for those involved as well as coworkers and the organization as a whole. No solution was seen as easy, and none was thought fair by all.

## Market and Economic Conditions

A final constraint that many organizations face is tied to market and economic conditions. Winning Ways is located in Johnson County, Kansas, an upper-middle-class community with a shortage of people who are willing to work at hourly manufacturing jobs. Many of the production workers do not live nearby, and some commute an hour or more to work each day. Although they do like the "perks," production employees complained about the low pay and infrequent raises at Winning Ways. One packer who is supporting himself through college remarked, "there for a while, the people at McDonald's were making better money." Not surprisingly, turnover in production is 42%, which Dave reported was higher than the industry average. Even with a recent dollar-an-hour raise, the labor pool appeared scant. The combination of continued growth, an inadequate labor pool, and high turnover has caused Winning Ways to reconsider some of its policies and think about more changes. In order to meet customer demands, Winning Ways is finding that they must outsource about 50% of their embroidery orders instead of completing them internally. These market pressures are exciting in one sense because they signify the success of the product, but they cause a great deal of stress on the part of both managers and employees. These pressures, when added to the other constraints, challenge creativity and redirect efforts. Indeed, "change is absolute."

## CONCLUSION

As Eisenberg and Goodall (1993) argue, organizations must constantly strive for a balance between creativity and constraints. Perhaps it is more of a juggle than a balance. Sometimes there is more creativity; sometimes there are more constraints. The interdependence of organized activities suggests constant trade-offs. Winning Ways is a maverick, change-oriented, creative organization with impassioned leadership, excitement, and a hero of a product, and considering all things, it is "a great place to work" according to most employees. However, they also face constraints stemming from growth, constant change coupled with a perceived lack of follow-up, a shaky commitment to formal training and development, an inadequate labor pool, and social pressures and problems. But as Dave says, "The constraints are where the choices are."

The leaders have come to expect that dealing with constraints is part of their winning ways; problems are merely interruptions in the process. They seem to be aware of Weick's (1995, p. 182) challenge that "talking the walk" (i.e., "walking is the means to find things worth talking about") is more opportunistic and adaptive than "walking the talk" (which can appear hypocritical and can become inert and reduce risk and innovation). In responding to the talk, they need to continue to be the kind of authors of language and histories that make opportunities seem possible, not lost. The way they have constructed their past success suggests a great deal of trial and error. Learning from the errors is the part of their accounts that makes continued winning ways seem likely.

## NOTE

1. This case is based on observations and interviews with key informants over a 2-year time frame. Additional in-depth interviews were conducted with a stratified random sample of employees during a 3-month period in the summer of 1994.

## KEY TERMS

EMPLOYEE INVOLVEMENT: employee participation in decision making, problem solving, or other organizational activities beyond just doing the tasks required by a particular job.

EMPLOYEE RECOGNITION: a way to show appreciation for the efforts of employees through either informal means or formal rituals.

IMPASSIONED LEADERSHIP: committed and dynamic leadership that inspires others to follow one's example.

ORGANIZATIONAL ENVIRONMENT: the surroundings of an organization (its offices, building, etc.) that help shape organizational activities and reflect values; also refers to the sociocultural, economic, and political milieu in which the organization is embedded.

ORGANIZATIONAL HERO: usually a person but sometimes a product that represents the idealized view of the company or organization.

ORGANIZATIONAL IMPRESSION MANAGEMENT: the strategic action taken by organizations to create a positive image to internal and external publics.

ORGANIZATIONAL SYMBOLISM: reflections of organizational culture, including language choices of members as well as meaningful objects, representations, or both of how people think and act.

ORGANIZATIONAL VALUES: the bedrock, or foundation, of organizational culture that is assumed to drive action, guide behavior and produce cultural artifacts

ORGANIZATIONAL SENSEMAKING: the process at work of retrospectively constructing meanings for events and subsequently acting in relation to those interpretations.

PERFORMANCE OPPORTUNITY: jobs or tasks that make the employee feel like he or she is making a contribution.

TEAM MANAGEMENT: organizing the job so that employees work together cooperatively and rely on horizontal communication rather than just following the formal "chain of command."

THE GLASS CEILING: subtle inequality in organizations that prevents women from advancing past a certain point up the organizational hierarchy.

"THE WALL": a common way to refer to separation between office and production units in manufacturing organizations.

VISION: the idealized organizational mission advanced by leaders who attempt to inspire others to share in its realization.

## DISCUSSION QUESTIONS

1. If Winning Ways is typical of the contemporary U.S. workplace, what challenges should you expect as an employee and as a manager?
2. Give some examples of organizational symbolism at Winning Ways.
3. Give some examples of organizational impression management at Winning Ways.
4. Give some examples of organizational sensemaking at Winning Ways.
5. How is leadership enacted at Winning Ways? Give some examples of how their impassioned leaders communicate.
6. How does the language of employees both create and reflect the reality of life at Winning Ways?
7. Analyze the various causes and suggest possible solutions for each of the constraints evidenced at Winning Ways.

## REFERENCES

Autry, J. A. (1991). *Love and profit: The art of caring leadership.* New York: Avon Books.
Bennis, W. (1989). *On becoming a leader.* Reading, MA: Addison-Wesley.
Buzzanell, P. M. (1995). Reframing the glass ceiling as a socially constructed process: Implications for understanding and change. *Communication Monographs, 62,* 327–354.
DePree, M. (1989). *Leadership is an art.* New York: Dell.
Eisenberg, E. M., & Goodall, H. L. (1993). *Organizational communication: Balancing creativity and constraint.* New York: St. Martin's Press.
Hayes, R. H., Wheelwright, S. C., & Clark, K. B. (1988). *Dynamic manufacturing: Creating the learning organization.* New York: Free Press.
Hirschhorn, L., & Gilmore, T. N. (1989). The psychodynamics of a cultural change: Learnings from a factory. *Human Resources Management, 28,* 211–233.
Lowenthal, J. N. (1994). *Reengineering the organization: A step-by-step to corporate revitalization.* Homewood, IL: Irwin.
McCaffrey, D. P., Faerman, S. R., & Hart, D. W. (1995). The appeal and difficulties of participative systems. *Organization Science, 6,* 603–627.
Parker, M. (1995). Working together, working apart: Management culture in a manufacturing firm. *Sociological Review, 43,* 518–547.
Stull, D. D. (1995). *Any way you cut it: Meat processing and small-town America.* Lawrence: University of Kansas Press.
Suzaki, K. (1993). *The new shop floor management.* New York: Free Press.
U.S. Bureau of Labor Statistics. (1996). *Current employment statistics.* Available WWW: http://stats.bls.gov:80/blshome.html.
Weick, K. E. (1995). *Sensemaking in organizations.* Thousand Oaks, CA: Sage.
Westley, F. R. (1990). The eye of the needle: Cultural and personal transformation in a traditional organization. *Human Relations, 43,* 273–293.
Zuboff, S. (1988). *In the age of the smart machine: The future of work and power.* New York: Basic Books.

# CHAPTER 2

# Conflict and Communication in a Research and Development Unit

BARBARA J. O'KEEFE
BRUCE L. LAMBERT
CAROL A. LAMBERT

In the fall of 1990, we were contacted by Dr. Frank Ridley, head of the research and development (R&D) unit of a company we will refer to as Northwestern Pharmaceuticals.[1] Northwestern is a large, midwestern drug manufacturer that is a subsidiary of a still-larger midwestern chemicals company. Ridley was concerned about a situation that had been developing in his department over the preceding two years. Three scientists who needed to work together to develop the key component of a new product had developed serious interpersonal conflicts—significant enough to disrupt their ability to function effectively as a team. The case reported in this chapter is based on our analysis of the conflict in the R&D unit at Northwestern Pharmaceuticals and the intervention we undertook to help the team resolve its conflicts and resume making progress on its research problem.

The details of the narrative presented in this case study are drawn from a variety of sources. The background of the case was derived from discussions with Ridley, his supervisor, and one of his peers, as well as from our own prior experience with the company (Carol Lambert has a long-standing business relationship with Northwestern). Information about the perspectives and behavior of the individuals involved in the case were drawn from tape-recorded interviews and meetings with Ridley and the research team as well as notes from discussions with relevant supervisors and coworkers. For all of these interviews and meetings, all three coauthors were present, and our contemporaneous field notes also provided data for this case study. The primary corpus of material collected in this study consists of (1) field notes on background discussions; (2) tape recordings and field notes from individual interviews (1–2 hours each) with Ridley and the research team conducted at the beginning of the intervention, which covered each participant's perspective on the history and details of the conflicts they were experiencing; (3) a tape recording of a meeting held about a month later in which Ridley and the research team met with us to discuss their goals for change; (4) a video- and audiotapes of a training session in which the research team participated in a series of role-played conflict scenarios; and (5) field notes of exit interviews (1–2 hours each) with Ridley and each member of the research team.

## DEVELOPMENT OF THE CONFLICT:
## BACKGROUND AND PERSPECTIVES

Interviews with Ridley and his supervisor provided a detailed picture of the historical development of the conflict in R&D. Ridley reported that he had been trying to build a team of researchers to develop a delivery system for a new drug product. Northwestern had managed to beat its competitors in the race to develop the new drug, but it had run into problems finding an appropriate delivery system for the treatment. A delivery system is a method of administering a drug, for example, as a pill or an injection. In this case, the drug needed to be administered in a timed-release form, and none of the usual methods for timed-release administration was appropriate. Northwestern needed to develop a new approach to the drug delivery problem. To do so, Ridley began assembling a research team to tackle the problem. He looked for individuals who would bring complementary strengths and capabilities to the team.

Interviews with all four principals showed a great deal of consensus about the origins and development of the conflict. All four emphasized their belief that many of their problems arose from the fact that crucial differences among the team members had become sources of conflict rather than of strength within the team.

Ridley began assembling the team with the selection of a senior scientist, Dr. Hugh Robinson, who was already in the company. Then he hired a more junior scientist, Dr. Lowell Edwards, who he thought would complement Robinson's strengths. As he assembled this team, Ridley had the additional goal of providing Robinson with an opportunity to develop his managerial skills. He wanted to give Robinson the opportunity to lead a team and to mentor junior colleagues. So he hired a less-experienced scientist and told Robinson that he would be responsible for leading the drug delivery team.

As it happened, Edwards and Robinson represented somewhat different scientific specialties, and Edwards's area was a newer, and in some eyes more methodologically sophisticated, approach to pharmaceutical science. When Edwards was recruited, he was given the impression that he would be chief of his own lab. While both Edwards and Robinson did in fact have their own independent labs and lab staffs, Robinson asserted his position as leader of the drug delivery team by trying to supervise Edwards's work. Edwards felt that Robinson should treat him as an equal and resented Robinson's attempts to supervise him. Soon after his arrival, Edwards began complaining to Ridley about Robinson's supervision, and Ridley came to believe that Robinson and Edwards were not very compatible colleagues.

Partly in response to his conflict with Edwards, Robinson had formed another working relationship with a researcher from another department. The creation of cross-departmental teams was promoted at Northwestern through its use of "matrix management" methods. With matrix management, an organization has multiple, coexisting organizational structures. There is the classic structure of the organization, with its formal departments and lines of authority. But overlaid on this classic structure is an organization by project, in which employees from different departments are assigned to work on a particular project under a project manager. Each employee then reports both to his or her line supervisor as well as to the project manager; the project managers themselves work as a team to coordinate the activities of the employees. The matrix management system was an early effort to help organizations find more "agile" structures able to respond flexibly to changing business conditions and opportunities.

A previous project had helped Robinson form a working relationship with Bill Scully, a scientist from the animal science group. He found Scully easy and comfortable to work with, and Scully was willing to continue a partnership with Robinson. So, rather than partnering with Edwards to run the clinical trials needed to test the new drug delivery system, Robinson asked Scully to help him work on the new delivery system. This effectively cut Edwards out of the loop. This was not a situation that Ridley found acceptable. He wanted the drug delivery team to use the new ideas and methodologies that Edwards could contribute to the project. He had been looking for a third member to add to the team, and he decided that he would try to find someone who would work easily with both Edwards and Robinson and serve as "glue" to bind the team together. The person he found was Dr. Morris Carter.

Carter was also a less-experienced scientist, and his theoretical and methodological preferences were closer to Edwards's than Robinson's. He and Edwards immediately formed a natural alliance, but neither felt particularly comfortable with Robinson. Edwards, of course, had developed a degree of hostility toward Robinson as a result of the failed attempts at supervision; this was aggravated by a growing disrespect for the older scientist.

Carter also began to feel resentment toward Robinson. Robinson seemed to have little regard for lines of command. Each of the three scientists had his own lab with a staff of technicians. The technicians reported to their lab chief. However, Robinson acted as though all three labs working on the drug delivery project were part of the same team. If Carter was not available, he would go ahead and ask Carter's technicians to perform tests for him. Carter felt that Robinson should never give orders to his lab staff. He thought Robinson should ask him to have his staff do the work—that would respect Carter's line of authority. Carter was quite upset by this behavior and by similar incidents in which Robinson directed Carter's staff to do things.

This history of alienation and resentment set the scene for a major conflict within the R&D division. Northwestern was under considerable pressure to get their new product to market. The company had already built a plant to manufacture the drug, on the assumption that R&D would quickly develop a delivery system. However, for a number of technical reasons, it was taking a long time to figure out how to deliver the drug. The drug delivery team became a central focus of attention within the company as the development time on the new product lengthened.

Finally Robinson found what he thought would be a breakthrough solution to the problem. But rather than involving Carter and Edwards in testing the new delivery system, he asked his friend Scully to help him test it. Robinson and Scully got very good results in their tests, and they presented their findings at a departmental seminar. Based on their results, Ridley committed the R&D division to development of Robinson's drug delivery system.

Carter and Edwards were very upset that they had not been given the task of testing the new delivery system, and they immediately began to complain privately to a number of different R&D employees about Robinson's findings. They argued that Robinson's methods were old-fashioned and that since Robinson had a stake in finding that the system worked, he (and his friend Scully) should not have been involved in testing the new delivery system.

Robinson heard about these complaints and became very angry. He felt that Carter and Edwards had made the decision themselves not to be part of the team and that they were simply jealous of his success. He felt that the two younger scientists were a dangerous and divisive force in the R&D unit and that they were likely to slow product development even further.

In this context, all joint work between Robinson and Carter and Edwards stopped. As the conflict escalated, they refused to share data or resources willingly. This created problems because some of their work required that they do so. They stopped talking with each other directly and communicated only via e-mail or independent meetings with Ridley. Progress on the new product stalled, and Ridley began to get pressure from his supervisor to get things moving. As Ridley tried to figure out what was going wrong, he became more involved in the conflict himself, spending the greater part of each working day listening to each side and trying to find ways to help them work more effectively together. Nothing he did seemed to help; in fact, his best efforts only appeared to make the situation worse.

As the development time on the new product lengthened, Ridley began to feel pressure from his supervisor to move the project along. The conflict within the drug delivery team was becoming common knowledge throughout the organization, and Ridley was urged to figure out how to make the team work more effectively.

## THEORETICAL ANALYSIS: EFFECTS OF DIFFERENCES IN MESSAGE DESIGN LOGIC

To understand the dynamics of this situation, we turned to O'Keefe's theory of message design logic. This section outlines her theory, discusses the role of threats to one's face ("face threats") in amplifying design logic differences, and applies this extended model to the analysis of interpersonal conflict situations.

### Message Design Logic: An Outline of O'Keefe's Model

O'Keefe (1988) argued that communication is grounded in implicit (unconscious) assumptions about meaning. Most contemporary theories of communication agree that messages are understood in relationship to a context. Consider the example of one person who asks another, "Is it just me or is it warm in here?" Depending on the situation, this could be intended and taken as a sincere question or as a request to turn on the air-conditioning; if uttered by a friend, it might be taken as a request, but by a boss, as an order. Similarly, when a speaker compliments a hearer on a "nice" point or a "nice" dress, what "nice" means depends on what it is being used to praise. Features of the situation help to determine what words mean and what the upshot of a message is. Hearers rely on information about the features of a situation to understand messages, and speakers take this into account in designing messages.

To figure out what an utterance means, a communicator must make assumptions about the context and about what features of the context are relevant to the message. These assumptions influence both the process of selecting things to say and of constructing the meaning of messages that are heard. The theory of message design logic begins with an analysis of how speakers select things to say and how hearers construct what messages mean.

This analysis of message selection and construction processes begins with a model of how message design works in general (for a technical discussion, see O'Keefe & Lambert, 1995). The basic model is shown in Figure 2.1.

Prior to communicating, a message producer is in a state of activation—many thoughts are available for expression. Of these thoughts, some subset is selected for expression. These form the content of the message. This process reflects the *pars par toto* principle: the part stands for the whole. The message recipient hears the message and makes additional inferences about its meaning; this reflects the *totum ex parte* principle: the whole from the part.

An individual's message design logic supplies both the selection principles and the construction principles used to decide what thoughts can appropriately stand for the whole context and what whole context is associated with a particular set of expressed thoughts. That is, a design logic is a way of using information about the context to reason about the meaning of the message.

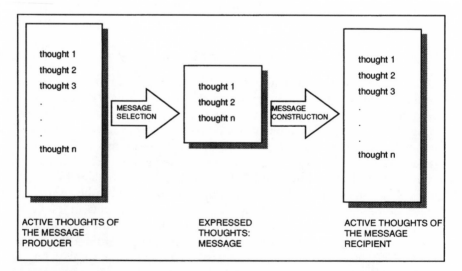

**FIGURE 2.1.** Communication as the reciprocal activation of thoughts based on the *pars par toto* and *totum ex parte* principles.

As it turns out, different individuals can have systematically different ways of looking at situations and deciding what thoughts are relevant for message selection and construction. O'Keefe (1988) hypothesized that there are at least three distinct ways that individuals reason about the meaning of messages, three different message design logics; the expressive, the conventional, and the rhetorical. Each design logic provides its own distinctive selection and construction mechanisms.

An expressive design logic provides very weak mechanisms for selection and construction. With an expressive design logic, most selection is based on activation strength: More highly activated thoughts will be expressed before less activated thoughts. Principled selection is based primarily on editing and suppressing obviously dangerous thoughts. Similarly, message construction is limited, and relatively few inferences are made about the meaning of the message. Where inferences are drawn, they are primarily based on idiosyncratic associations.

As a result, an expressive message design logic focuses on the expressed content of messages. Those using an expressive design logic appear to believe that communication is a process of expressing and receiving encoded thoughts and feelings. Characteristically, those using an expressive logic fail to distinguish between thought and expression; in producing messages, they "dump" their current mental state, and they assume that others produce messages the same way. Expressive communicators do not generally alter expression systematically in the service of achieving effects, nor do they ordinarily find anything other than "literal and direct" meaning in incoming messages. Their messages have a distinctively "reactive" quality, in the sense that they react to contingencies rather than anticipating them.

A conventional design logic provides a much stronger set of mechanisms for selection and construction. In terms of selection, assumptions about the social system provide the basis for fairly subtle calculations about the social value of expressed thoughts. Consequently, thoughts are selected not just on the basis of how strongly they are activated but also on the basis of their relevance to the social situation. Similarly, message construction is based on assigning each thought a value within this social calculus.

In general, then, a conventional message design logic provides ways of managing the force or point of messages. It appears to reflect a view of communication as a game played cooperatively, according to social conventions and procedures. Within conventional logic, thought and expression are related in a less direct way, since expression is subordinated to the achievement of other instrumental goals. Language is still treated as a means of expressing thoughts, but the expressed propositions are specified by the social effect one wants to achieve. (Utterance content is specified in the sense that uttering a given set of propositions under certain conditions counts as performing an action that is associated in sociocultural practice with the effect the message producer wants to achieve; for example, uttering a certain kind of proposition under the right conditions counts as performing a request, and performing a request is a way to get certain wants satisfied simply by exploiting conventional obligations among persons.) Conventional communicators treat communicative contexts (the roles, rights, and relations that situations contain) as having fixed parameters (that is, they take social structure—roles and norms—to be both manifest to all and relatively inflexible), and they design messages by performing what they take to be the contextually appropriate actions.

Finally, a rhetorical design logic provides a very complex set of mechanisms for selection and construction. Thoughts are selected for expression based on a model of their likely effects on the recipient, and messages may contain elements that present the situation as contrary to what it really is. Similarly, in interpreting messages, recipients using rhetorical message design logics evaluate message elements in terms of their effects and use this information to understand the goals of the message producer.

As a result, a rhetorical message design logic can be used to manipulate both messages and their contexts. A rhetorical message design logic seems to reflect a view of communication as the creation and negotiation of social selves and situations. The rhetorical view subsumes knowledge of conventional ways to achieve goals within the view that social structure is flexible and created through communication. For the rhetorical communicator, social reality is created by what and how something is said or written, and so messages are designed to portray a scene that is consistent with one's wants; the discourse of others is closely interpreted to determine the nature of the drama and the perspective they are enacting. Individuals using a rhetorical logic anticipate interactional problems and evade them by offering explicit redescriptions of the situation.

## Face Threats and Differences in Design Logics

One feature of social situations is especially critical to the way message design logics interact: the relationship between instrumental goals (accomplishing whatever task needs to be done) and identity goals (establishing and maintaining appropriate identities for participants). The interplay between instrumental goals and identity goals has been modeled by Brown and Levinson (1987) in their work on politeness. Their work is based on Goffman's (1967) analysis of "face." Face is the moral dimension of identity, "the positive social value a person claims for himself" (p. 5). Face is created and sustained in and through communication with others; it is an aspect of the "front" an individual puts forward. In short, face is the person as publicly defined and represented, the self that is "on the record." The inner self remains implicit and is "off the record," not part of one's public identity.

Brown and Levinson (1987) suggested a modified analysis of face. They suggested that face actually consists of two wants: the want to have one's wants be valued by others (positive face); and the want not to be impeded by others (negative face). Many actions are intrinsically threatening to the face wants of actors or their interactional partners—for example, requests are intrinsically threatening to the negative face wants of the target of the request since a request necessarily involves some degree of imposition.

Brown and Levinson (1978, 1987) argued that the various forms of politeness within a language could be understood as rational resolutions of goal conflicts that arise when a speaker undertakes a face-threatening action: To achieve his or her goal, the speaker needs to be clear, but being clear will mean being more face-threatening; and conversely, to save face, the speaker must sacrifice getting the point across. However, speakers can also remedy face threats through the use of redress.

Most theorists agree that indirectness essentially consists of communicating by implication. A speaker says one thing that, under the circumstances, warrants the inference that the speaker means to communicate a second intention or idea as well. The fact that "face" is part of one's "front" makes indirection a useful way to convey face-threatening intentions. By keeping face-threatening intentions unspoken, "off record," indirect messages can convey potentially face-threatening messages without affecting the hearer's face; if the face-threatening message were spoken "on-record," the hearer's face would necessarily be diminished.

But communication by implication depends on the hearer making the correct inference about the speaker's intentions, and so it is less certain to make the point of the message clear to the hearer. Hence both direct and indirect communication have payoffs and tradeoffs: Being direct makes it more likely that one will get one's point across but creates increased possibilities for face threat; being indirect reduces face threat, but may fail to get the point across or to secure the hearer's acknowledgment of the point.

Message producers have a second linguistic device to use in managing conflicts between their intentions and the hearer's face wants: face-relevant elaborations, which Brown and Levinson call "forms of redress." Since face is a symbolic entity that is created through communication, it can be manipulated symbolically. A person can give "face" by offering verbal descriptions, accounts, or reassurances to another. Although it is more efficient to simply perform a face-threatening act baldly, with no redress, adding in redress mitigates the face threat by giving face in return. Consequently, as a speaker gives higher priority to saving face, he or she should be more likely to employ forms of redress; the lower the priority given to saving face, the less likely a speaker should be to use redress.

Whereas Brown and Levinson assumed that every person deals with face threats using the same adaptive strategies (indirectness and redress), O'Keefe (1988) argued that different design logics provide different tools for dealing with face issues. An expressive design logic relies on simple editing to modify messages to protect face—the issue is simply whether or not to say whatever is face-threatening, not how to say it. A conventional design logic relies on indirectness and redress, on conventional politeness strategies as well as editing. And a rhetorical design logic makes yet another type of strategy available for managing face wants: context redefinition.

One significant consequence of these differences in strategies for managing face issues is that differences in message design logic are likely to be most significant and apparent in precisely those situations in which communication about identities is most perilous: those involving intrinsic conflicts between instrumental aims and face wants. In these situations, the explicit communication is generally related to the instrumental goal. The identity communication involves how politeness strategies are used to send implicit messages. But when different individuals use different strategies to encode and decode politeness, they are likely to misunderstand the identity messages of their partners.

The situation we studied at Northwestern Pharmaceuticals—one in which individuals needed to resolve substantive differences about the best way to solve a research problem—comprised an array of instrumental conflicts, each of which implied its own threats to face. As the individuals involved in the situation tried to deal with their instrumental conflicts, they often failed to deal successfully with the identity and relationship issues connected with the instrumental conflict. In large part this was due to an inability to recognize or appreciate the implicit messages generated by different design logics.

## Understanding and Misunderstanding: An Analysis in Terms of Message Design Logics

In conflict situations, the primary consequence of differences in design logic is a great potential for miscommunication between individuals who use different logics. A communicator using an expressive design logic lives in his or her own little world: Unless information is provided explicitly and directly, an expressive communicator tends to ignore it. An expressive communicator is less able to perceive social structures that are not marked by explicit organizational labels. For an expressive communicator, a supervisory relationship must be encoded explicitly in a job title or a clear hierarchy. A situation in which different individuals head different independent labs creates considerable ambiguity about what the hierarchy might be; it invites an expressive communicator to ignore real status differences among lab chiefs.

At the same time, we would expect those using conventional and rhetorical design logics to perceive status differences even when they are not explicitly encoded. An organizational structure like the one in the R&D division at Northwestern promotes misunderstanding between expressive communicators and those using other design logics, since rhetorical and conventional communicators will organize their behavior and make interpretations in ways that assume status differences that expressives may not see.

An individual who uses an expressive design logic will be understood by conventional and rhetorical communicators as speaking systematically and according to a plan when in fact they are just saying whatever comes to mind. Similarly, an expressive communicator will often be oblivious to the many things that conventional and rhetorical communicators convey by implication rather than through direct communication.

These misunderstandings should be particularly troublesome when expressive and rhetorical communicators interact, since both tend to elaborate their messages more than do conventional communicators but based on radically different principles. Expressive communicators say what they think, while rhetorical communicators say what they think needs to be said to influence the hearer in a particular way. This leads expressive communicators to attribute beliefs to rhetorical communicators that they may not have, and it leads rhetorical communicators to assume that expressive communicators mean to do things when they may have no such intentions. Sometimes expressive and rhetorical communicators become aware of the differences in the way they design messages, which leads expressives to think that rhetorical communicators are dishonest ("They say things they don't really believe") and rhetoricals to think that expressive communicators are callous ("They say what they want, regardless of what effects their words might have").

There is also potential for miscommunication between conventional and rhetorical communicators. Conventional communicators treat situations as fixed: If they talk in a particular way, it is because they think the situation requires that way of talking. But rhetorical communicators treat situations as fluid: To talk a particular way is to invoke a particular kind of situation. For a rhetorical communicator, a way of talking or acting may be used as a way of changing the situation rather than of conveying what they think the situation is. Hence when a rhetorical deals with a conventional communicator, he or she often has the impression that the conventional is rigid, unwilling to view the situation in different ways. Similarly, a conventional communicator can see the rhetorical communicator's efforts to redefine a situation as inappropriate or mistaken. A summary of expected types of miscommunication is provided in Table 2.1. As a comparison of the diagonal with the off-diagonal cells suggests, when individuals use similar design logics, relatively simple communication problems arise from disagreements about key features of the situation; but when design logics differ, communication problems are created both by differences of opinion and by differences in selection and construction processes.

Even more important, it is difficult for communicators using different design logics to understand their communication problems. One of the most important predictions made by this theory is that communication problems attributable to design logic differences are often not perceived as communication problems per se (O'Keefe, 1988). For example, this model hypothesizes that expressive communicators perceive the kind of context redefining expressions used by rhetorical communicators as fundamentally dishonest or wrong: an expressive communicator would never knowingly say anything counterfactual unless he or she were lying, so when a rhetorical communicator implicitly redefines the situation by

**TABLE 2.1.** Type of Miscommunication as a Function of Message Design Logic

| Message producer | Message recipient | | |
|---|---|---|---|
| | Expressive recipient | Conventional recipient | Rhetorical recipient |
| Expressive producer | Inability to connect due to differences of opinion and value | Lack of communication seen not as editing but as assent; unfocused remarks overinterpreted as having a particular point | Overattribution of systematicity and planfulness; perception of inconsiderateness and uncooperativeness |
| Conventional producer | Failure to hear off-record messages; ritual messages heard literally | Misattribution of intent based on incompatible assumptions about social structure | Conformity to rules and routines viewed as expressing commitment to existing contextual structures |
| Rhetorical producer | Messages viewed both as unnecessarily elaborate (i.e., "loquacious") and as insufficiently direct | Context definition viewed not as offer but as assertion (true or false); failure to see coherence based on complex plans | Misattribution of intent based on incompatible assumptions about goals |

describing it in a new way, the expressive communicator can only interpret this as some kind of dishonesty or mistake. Instead of being interpreted as reflecting different views of language, the difference will be seen as reflecting bad traits (dishonesty) or bad beliefs (being wrong about the situation).

Hence we expect that individuals are more likely to believe that their problems are communication problems when communicating with a person who uses a similar message design logic. When design logics are similar, messages are mutually intelligible but unsuccessful, leading to a clear perception that communication is not working. But when design logics differ, the very structure of behavior seems unintelligible or malformed, leading to attributions of bad intentions, mistaken beliefs, or undesirable personality characteristics. Rather than seeing communication as the problem, interactants form negative impressions of each other. This is clearly displayed in Table 2.1: The diagonal entries (involving matching design logics) hypothesize simple communication problems deriving from conflict, whereas the off-diagonal entries (involving different design logics) hypothesize complex problems in which a message producer's rational communication choice leads to a message recipient's perception of bad intentions or qualities.

## ANALYZING AND AMELIORATING THE CONFLICT AT NORTHWESTERN

Our application of O'Keefe's (1988) theory to the situation at Northwestern Pharmaceuticals involved two stages. In the first stage we gathered information about the message design logics used by the individuals involved in the case and used this to understand their conflicts. In the second stage we implemented an intervention designed to ameliorate their conflicts.

### Message Design Logics in the R&D Unit

To determine what message design logic was employed by each individual involved in this case, the entire R&D division was surveyed. Employees completed a questionnaire in which they responded to two hypothetical scenarios involving communication and conflict at work by writing what they would say to handle the situation. These role-played messages were classified by two coders as reflecting an expressive, conventional, or rhetorical message design logic. At the time they evaluated the questionnaires, the coders were unaware of the identities of any Northwestern employees (for details of the method and coding, see O'Keefe, Lambert, & Lambert, 1993).

The scenarios used, sample messages, and explanations of how we evaluated the messages are given in the appendix of O'Keefe et al. (1993).

Based on this assessment we inferred that Frank Ridley and Hugh Robinson used a rhetorical design logic, Morris Carter used a conventional design logic, and Lowell Edwards used an expressive design logic (the first letter of each employee's surname reflects his design logic). Our model of how people use different design logics formed the basis for a multistage intervention designed to restore effective communication within the drug delivery group.

## Analysis and Intervention

We first applied our model to understand Ridley's performance as a supervisor. As described by himself and his subordinates, Ridley was open and collaborative in his approach to supervision. He seldom gave orders; rather, he discussed the many sides of an issue. He rarely made decisions without discussing an issue with everyone involved, and he expected decision making to reflect a consensus arrived at through discussion. Faced with a conflict in his group, his natural response was to consult with everyone involved and to use discussion to resolve the problem.

As we would expect from their use of a common design logic, Ridley and Robinson understood each other well. Although they were not particularly friendly, each reported that he could follow the other's reasoning and found the other scientist's behavior quite understandable. On the other hand, both Edwards and Carter described Ridley's use of discussion rather than authority to resolve conflict as weak and confusing. Edwards in particular found Ridley hard to understand, even though he and Ridley were quite friendly and spent time together outside of working hours. Edwards reported that he never felt that Ridley had given him adequate supervision; after a conversation with Ridley, Edwards never knew what it was that Ridley wanted him to do because for all his talk, Ridley never seemed to say explicitly what he wanted from Edwards.

One of the first recommendations we made to Ridley was to be much more direct in communicating with subordinates, and particularly with Edwards. We advised him to tell employees what he wanted them to do if he had a particular task he needed to assign or a requirement he wanted them to satisfy, or what he advised them to do if he had a preference or recommendation. Ridley was surprised; he felt that giving directives explicitly failed to show respect for the message recipient. But he made a concerted effort to adapt his style for Edwards and Carter. In an interview several months after our intervention, Edwards commented spontaneously on how much better he felt about his communication with Ridley, who now was being much clearer about his goals and requirements.

Our second focus was on the composition of the drug delivery team. In retrospect, it was not surprising to find that Robinson had not been an effective supervisor for Edwards. First, Robinson's authority to supervise Edwards was derived solely from Ridley's saying that he should head the drug delivery team. Unlike Ridley, he had no special institutional status to underwrite his authority. Second, Edwards felt that his own qualifications were in some ways superior to those of Robinson, and so he resented Robinson's supervision. Finally, Robinson's supervision style confused Edwards. As Edwards explained, he found Robinson contradictory. On the one hand, Robinson was insufficiently authoritative. Robinson would discuss alternatives with Edwards without ever indicating explicitly which alternative he thought Edwards should pursue. Edwards liked a previous supervisor, a German who made it clear who was the boss and who acted "like a father" (as Edwards put it) to Edwards. In Edwards's view, Robinson did not mentor him but, rather, treated him as just another person on the team. On the other hand, Edwards felt that Robinson sometimes demeaned him; for example, Robinson would ask him to leave a meeting to get needed data as though he were a flunky or ask to see his work before he was ready to present it.

Nor were we surprised at the manner in which the question of authority was resolved. Edwards went directly to the individual he saw as having legitimate authority—Ridley—and complained to him about Robinson's supervisory style. Ridley, typically, responded to these complaints with empathy and talked to all parties to reach some kind of consensus. The consensus was that Robinson did not care for Edwards either, and it would be best if Edwards would report directly to Ridley. However, Robinson was left feeling that Ridley had not backed him up.

Since Ridley had interpreted the conflict between Robinson and Edwards as a matter of incompatible personalities, he tried to deal with the situation by creating a more compatible mix of individuals in the team. Both we and Ridley were struck by his intuition that Carter fell between Edwards and Robinson on a dimension that Ridley could not identify explicitly. The three message design logics are ordered in terms of how well an individual's understanding of communication integrates contextual variation in meaning, with a conventional design logic falling between expressive and rhetorical logics.

Even though Ridley was successful in finding a third scientist whose communication style should have enabled him to be successful in communicating with both Edwards and Robinson, Ridley failed to consider a number of other factors that exacerbated rather than alleviated factionalism within the R&D unit. Edwards and Carter were younger; Robinson was older. Edwards and Carter were hired from academic positions; Robinson had been in industry for many years. Edwards and Carter both used the newer theoretical and methodological approach to pharmaceutical science; Robinson used classical theories and methods. Edwards and Carter were new and knew very few people at Northwestern; Robinson had been there for some time and had an extensive network.

Because of their many similarities in knowledge, interests, and values, an alliance between Edwards and Carter was almost foreordained. Unfortunately, they became both more isolated and more certain that their view of events was correct as they supported each other. They felt that they represented the best new methods and theories in pharmaceutical science and consequently that they had something unique to offer. But they felt that the older scientists at Northwestern were unwilling to work with them.

At the same time, both reported having conflicts with various coworkers over knowledge ownership issues. For example, early in his work at Northwestern, Edwards had had a falling out with another employee when he felt he was not given appropriate credit for an idea. Carter had reported having unpleasant interactions with Robinson after Robinson asked him to explain a new methodological technique; Carter told Robinson he could explain it, but he thought Robinson should just turn over data analysis to him since it was not his job to teach Robinson. Shortly after Edwards and Carter were hired, other scientists at Northwestern began trying to use the new methods. But the way they did this was to try them out themselves, consulting Edwards or Carter for feedback and advice. Instead of seeing this as evidence of their growing influence and acceptance, Edwards and Carter saw this as evidence that they were being excluded. They felt that they should be asked to do the analysis, to be a central part of any team using the new methods.

In short, both Edwards and Carter were somewhat inept in the way they set about building a place for themselves at Northwestern: They were quick to claim credit for group work, quick to conclude that others did not appreciate their contributions, prone to confront others aggressively rather than to seek accommodation and understanding, and frequently tactless. This ineptitude was not helped by their alliance, since each alone might have been less assertive and demanding. All things considered, Carter appears to have been a poor choice from the standpoint of creating a functional team, since his alliance with Edwards tended to distance them both from the rest of the organization rather than to help them to accept organizational values and practices and meld seamlessly into a team with Robinson.

Of course, it may be that any candidate who represented the new approach would have allied with Edwards. Robinson had made it clear that he did not need colleagues but could work with other individuals in his network. Once he and Edwards had fallen out, it was unlikely that they would work together well. Under these circumstances, little could be done to avoid factionalism, although things might have gone more smoothly if Ridley had hired someone who used a rhetorical design logic, who would be more likely to be tactful in negotiating a place for the new approach in the existing culture.

To deal with this nexus of problems, we recommended that Ridley stop tolerating the factionalism: He should tell the drug delivery team that he would no longer accept communication problems as an excuse or account for a lack of progress. Moreover, members of the team were to resume all the normal communication activities (day-to-day coordination through conversation, reports sharing data and ideas, direct negotiation and resolution of conflicts, etc.) associated with an ongoing research project. Robinson should be instructed to work with Edwards and Carter and to discontinue his informal collaboration with Scully.

Communication within the drug delivery team had deteriorated to the point that Robinson was interacting with Edwards and Carter only through e-mail, not face-to-face. This had the additional bad consequence of giving all three scientists a cache of old messages that were available for endless interpretation and reinterpretation. Since none of the three interpreted messages in a manner similar to the others, this promoted a flood of unproductive communication within the team and with Ridley. We additionally recommended that Ridley prohibit the use of e-mail to deal with anything but routine requests and information exchange. Any conflict-related communication had to be done face-to-face.

Finally, we recommended to Ridley that he require the drug delivery team to resume the normal sharing of information and resources. They were to complete and circulate reports as required by the organization's protocol and they were to conduct regular meetings. They were to resolve conflicts among themselves rather than constantly asking Ridley to intervene. We also advised Ridley to take steps to end the collaboration between Robinson and Scully by talking to Scully's supervisor. These steps reestablished Ridley's control over the drug development process and put the team back on a footing in which they had to work together.

Our third focus was on restoring trust and communication within the drug delivery team. Here we took two steps. First, we held a meeting with Ridley and the three scientists in which their difficulties working together were discussed and Ridley's expectations were made clear. All three coauthors were present at this meeting, which was focused on the question of what goals the four principals would like to set for the intervention. However, the actual discussion was broad and intensive in its coverage of the principals' perceptions of their team and its problems. This discussion provided the principals with an opportunity to evaluate and discard a number of beliefs that were promoting conflict within the team and to build a consensual view of the situation. The discussion was tape-recorded for later analysis and served as a key resource in designing materials for a training program (described next).

Second, we provided a workshop in which the three scientists were helped to understand their different ways of looking at messages. For this workshop, we prepared a number of hypothetical scenarios for discussion; each scenario was based on a real incident described to us by one or more team members. For the scenarios shown in Figure 2.2, the workshop par-

### COLLABORATION SCENARIO

Suppose that you have a coworker, Bill Jones, working with you in your unit. Bill is a scientist whose position is at a level comparable to yours in the organization. You have worked with Bill for four years; you like him very much and feel that you work well with him. You value his friendship and support a great deal.

Last week you and Bill had an interesting conversation in which you identified some common complaints about the way reports are produced and circulated by your units. The conversation with Bill led you to think about what should be done to solve these problems. You have come up with some ideas you think should be implemented, and you have drafted a proposal to give to your boss, George Hill, in which you outline the problems and some solutions for them.

Earlier today you sent a draft of the proposal to Bill. In the cover memo you asked him for any feedback he might be able to give and said that you would like to send it to George by the end of the week.

Bill comes to your office, carrying the proposal. He looks irritated and says, "I thought we were working together to solve these problems. Why did you go ahead and write a proposal on your own?"

What would you say to Bill?

### AUTHORITY SCENARIO

Suppose that a technician, Joe Walsh, has been assigned to work under you on a project. Joe has proved himself to be a very capable and responsible worker and you are pleased to have him on your team.

Last week you left town to attend an important conference. You left Joe in charge of completing an important project. He was given very clear instructions about what he was to do and just what you expected him to accomplish before your return.

At 8:00 A.M. sharp on the day you returned Joe showed up in your office. He explained that he was unable to complete the project and apologized profusely. When you pressed him for an explanation, you learned that another senior scientist, Marie Petrowski, had insisted that he help her with a very time-consuming procedure while you were gone. Joe said that although he told Marie that he had other work to do and did not have time to help her, she insisted that he make time for her project. She threatened to have Joe fired if he didn't "act like a team player."

You immediately walk down to Marie's office and ask why she insisted that Joe work on her project. Marie says, "Well, I had a deadline to meet and Joe is the only one around here who really knows how to do that procedure. I had to have his help, and since you weren't here I couldn't consult you."

What would you say to Marie?

**FIGURE 2.2.** Scenarios presented in communication workshop at Northwestern Pharmaceuticals.

ticipants were asked to indicate, in writing, how they would handle each situation. These written responses were compared and discussed. Each participant had an opportunity to explain what he would do to handle the situation and why he would handle it in that particular way. This helped the participants see, in a concrete way, that there are different, logically consistent ways to reason about communication and to see that their colleagues were different but nonetheless reasonable and well intentioned. For selected scenarios, workshop participants were assigned roles different from those they had played in the original incident, and the scene was reenacted, videotaped, and analyzed. This helped participants conceptualize key incidents from the perspective of the others involved.

Ridley and the three members of the drug delivery team reported that the meeting and workshop were important to reestablishing more normal, that is, more businesslike and less affectively charged, communication within the drug delivery group. Although the three scientists never became a well-integrated and highly functional team, they were able to begin communicating directly and effectively about the work they did together. They became less suspicious of each other and more willing to be generous in interpreting the behavior of the others. All in all, Ridley felt that the intervention had been a success.

## CONCLUSION

One point that should be considered as we conclude this case is the general implications of the theory of message design logic for interventions in ongoing relationships. O'Keefe (1988) argued that differences in message design logic are differences in competence: Those who use an expressive design logic are less capable communicators than those who use conventional design logic, who in turn are less capable than those who use a rhetorical design logic. These differences in competence were clearly exemplified in the case of the drug delivery team at Northwestern, where many of the interpersonal difficulties were caused by Edwards's and Carter's inability to deal tactfully with Robinson, especially combined with Robinson's sensitivity to the implicit meanings of behavior.

Because of this, one natural assumption is that the theory of message design logic promotes the view that one design logic—the rhetorical design logic—is superior and that we should intervene by training everyone to use the best available logic. But in fact we think that the Northwestern case points to a fact that has been emphasized by O'Keefe: Every design logic provides a logically consistent and potentially satisfactory way for an individual to use language. Edwards and Carter were, if anything, happier and more successful than Robinson. So it is not at all clear that we should recommend that they be trained to use a more sophisticated design logic, even if we were already in a position to provide such training.

In fact, in our intervention, we focused on training all the team members in more general strategies designed to help them recognize and accommodate to diversity in message design logic. It is possible to help anyone—regardless of the design logic they employ—to better appreciate the different ways that language can be used, if only by demonstrating that people do differ in their evaluations of different ends–means associations and that when they differ, they have reasons for believing what they believe. To create a stronger and more tolerant community, we need to encourage communication that is flexible and able to accommodate not just differences in design logic but other important human differences as well.

## NOTE

1. To protect the privacy of the participants in this project, both the company name and the names of individuals used in this case study are fictitious. All events described are factual and occurred as reported.

## KEY TERMS

CONVENTIONAL MESSAGE DESIGN LOGIC: a method of message design in which message content is selected based on its relevance to accepted norms and roles in a social situation and in which message construction involves associating expressed messages with conventionally defined roles and actions—messages are taken to represent meanings associated with social positions.

EXPRESSIVE MESSAGE DESIGN LOGIC: a method of message design in which message content is selected primarily based on its salience or strength of activation and in which message construction involves relatively few inferences about what meaning might lie behind the expressed message: messages are taken as straightforwardly representing the thoughts of the message producer.

FACE: the positive social value claimed by an individual in a social situation.

FACE-THREATENING ACT (FTA): any action that in its essence involves a threat to face.

FACE WANTS: wants associated with face; positive face wants are wants to be positively valued by others and negative face wants are wants to be free of imposition by others.

INDIRECTNESS: communication by implying meaning rather than by saying what is meant.

INSTRUMENTAL GOAL: the outcome sought by engaging in a particular activity; task goal.

MATRIX MANAGEMENT METHODS: a method of managing organizations in which the formal organizational structure is overlaid with a second structure of project-oriented, cross-departmental teams.

MESSAGE DESIGN LOGIC: the specific principles and strategies of inference used by a communicator to accomplish *pars par toto* (message selection) and *totum ex parte* (message construction) operations. A message design logic is used to determine which of a set of thoughts can appropriately stand for the whole context and what whole context to associate with a particular configuration of expressed thoughts.

PARS PAR TOTO PRINCIPLE: the part stands for the whole—message selection.

REDRESS: giving face by saying or implying that someone is valued or that one does not intend to impose.

RHETORICAL MESSAGE DESIGN LOGIC: a method of message design in which message content is selected based on its relevance to a model of the listener's beliefs and motivations and in which message construction involves associating expressed messages with psychological states and processes: messages are taken to represent meanings associated with specific identities.

TOTUM EX PARTE PRINCIPLE: the whole is constructed from the part—message construction.

## DISCUSSION QUESTIONS

1. Read the authority scenario in Figure 2.2 carefully. Based on the information in this chapter, write what you think individuals using each of the three (expressive, conventional, or rhetorical) design logics would say. Be specific: Write exactly what you think someone would say; don't just describe the general action you think they would perform. It will help to use the model shown in Figure 2.1. What kinds of thoughts will individuals have about this situation? How will different selection mechanisms lead to different sets of expressed thoughts?
2. Now explain what inferences you think each type of communicator (expressive, conventional, or rhetorical) would make when he or she interprets the three messages you wrote in answer to Question 1. Where would the key misunderstandings arise? It will help to use the model shown in Figure 2.1. What are the expressed thoughts in the message being interpreted? How will different construction mechanisms lead to different inferences about the speaker's intentions, beliefs, and characteristics?
3. Now predict what would happen as diverse communicators interacted in the collaboration scenario shown in Figure 2.2. How would each type of communicator respond to the situation? How would each type of message be interpreted by others?
4. Some additional data collected at Northwestern (for a report, see O'Keefe et al., 1993) show that employees and their supervisors perceived each other as most effective when they used a rhetorical design logic and least effective when they

used an expressive design logic. What additional evidence would we need to conclude that it is more functional to use a rhetorical message design logic than the other two logics? If we have that evidence, should we develop training programs to try to change the logic an individual uses? What might we do to try to help individuals develop more sophisticated views of communication?

## REFERENCES

Brown, P., & Levinson, S. (1987). *Politeness: Some universals in language usage.* Cambridge, England: Cambridge University Press.

Goffman, E. (1967). *Interaction ritual: Essays on face-to-face behavior.* Garden City, NY: Anchor/Doubleday.

O'Keefe, B. J. (1988). The logic of message design: Individual differences in reasoning about communication. *Communication Monographs, 55,* 80–103.

O'Keefe, B. J., & Lambert, B. L. (1995). Managing the flow of ideas: A local management approach to message design. In B. Burleson (Ed.), *Communication Yearbook 18* (pp. 54–82). Newbury Park, CA: Sage.

O'Keefe, B. J., Lambert, B. L., & Lambert, C. A. (1993, November). *Effects of message design logic on perceived communication effectiveness in supervisory relationships.* Paper presented at the annual meeting of the International Communication Association, Washington, DC.

# CHAPTER 3

# Vocabularies of Motives in a Crisis of Academic Leadership

"Hell Hath No Fury..."

BRENDA J. ALLEN
PHILLIP K. TOMPKINS

Families and formal organizations, though similar in many respects, are treated as distinct by social scientists. Marriage and the family is a topic of study for sociologists and for interpersonal specialists in communication; organizations are studied by separate disciplines in many different fields. Rarely, if ever, are models from one domain applied in the other. In this case study, we employ a model from sociology about families (specifically, divorcing couples) to analyze a series of organizational events.

## NARRATIVE

### The Showdown

The encounter became known as the "Black Friday Ambush." On January 15, 1994, Judith Albino, president of the University of Colorado (CU), was scheduled to meet privately with a group of deans and a vice chancellor who intended to ask her for her resignation. Albino had invited the group to continue a discussion begun earlier that week at CU-Boulder, the flagship of the four-campus system. The deans had aired their complaints about Albino's leadership and had forewarned her that they had signed a letter asking her to resign. On that fateful Friday, the unsuspecting delegation entered a room filled with news reporters, photographers, university staff members, and Albino, who was flanked at her conference table by six members (out of nine) of the university's elected Board of Regents. Under the glare of television lights, Albino greeted the group and declared, "I would like for you to know that I do not intend to resign as president of this university." She then asked for the letter. The vice chancellor for academic affairs (second-in-command at the Boulder campus) handed Albino the letter, which read:

> Over the past two years, the University of Colorado has been confronted with some very difficult problems, including new kinds of budgetary constraints, a deteriorating public image, and challenges from the State Legislature. We believe that you have tried your utmost to deal with these problems. You have worked hard and have maintained your courage in an environment that has generally been discouraging and unfavorable.
>
> Despite your efforts, many of the University's problems remained unmitigated. Relations with the Legislature stand at one of the lowest points in the recent history of the University. The external image of the University, as portrayed through the President's office, has weakened to the point that the University may be losing the allegiance of its alumni, of the business community, and of a traditionally supportive segment of the general public. Faculty and administrators struggle with the disruptive consequences of your failure to lead effectively, and to convey accurately the mission and strengths of the University.
>
> Given the grave circumstances of the University, we believe that it is essential for you to resign immediately your position as President of the University of Colorado. Reversal of the present downward momentum seems impossible without a fresh start, and this can only be achieved through new leadership. We make this request after much thought and discussion, and without personal antipathy toward you.

Seventy-eight persons (including department chairs, all nine academic deans from the Boulder campus, and representatives from other campuses) had signed the letter.

After barely glancing at the document, Albino read from a prepared statement that advised the insurgents to search within themselves for a commitment to work with her: "You have told me that you do not believe that I understand the mission of the Boulder campus, and you fault me for not promoting goals that were set in the 1970s and 1980s," she said. "You're right," she continued. "I don't support those goals. They are not enough to get us into the 21st century." After deflecting blame about poor leadership back to the deans, she asserted, "This University will go forward. It's time for you to decide if you will go with it." Upon concluding her remarks, she opened the floor to the six regents, each of whom expressed personal support for her. Some of them chastised the deans and denounced them for insubordination. The deans were not permitted to speak, and Albino ended the meeting because she had to attend ceremonies for the Martin Luther King, Jr. holiday.

Afterward, the stunned detractors conducted a press conference in another room. Appalled that the university's chief executive officer had aired their dirty linen in public, one dean characterized the meeting as an "ambush." Group members explained that the letter and petition had been circulated for several weeks among distinguished professors in the College of Arts and Sciences at CU-Boulder and at other units, including those from the other three campuses. Thus the deans maintained that they had not initiated the rebellion. Rather, they maintained, they had responded to widespread faculty discontent that had been brewing since Albino assumed the presidency.

Later that afternoon, one of the signatories said, "We're definitely not going to back down. We believe the president's treatment of this conference was a very open demonstration of the problems that confront us. The president has been almost consistently very defensive. She has given blame to problems to almost everyone around her."

## Before the Ambush

The showdown had been 3 years in the making. In 1990, CU's president, Gordon Gee, hired Albino as vice president of academic affairs and Dean of the system-wide graduate school. Albino came to CU from the State University of New York, in whose system she had worked for 17 years as a faculty member and in various administrative posts (e.g., associate provost and dean of the graduate school).

Gee left CU later that year to assume the presidency of Ohio State University. By March 1991, a costly job search had culminated with a list of five candidates, but the regents found none of them suitable. In a controversial and impromptu move, without soliciting faculty input, the regents appointed Albino to the presidency. She had not applied for the position, and she had been on campus only 11 months. Thus Albino became the first female president of the institution, earning the highest salary of CU presidents ever.

From the outset, varying degrees of conflict plagued the new president. She had assumed the role during daunting times: Across the nation, public confidence in higher education was ebbing, and state funding for public universities was decreasing. Moreover, recent legislation in Colorado had engendered tighter budgetary constraints, even as demands for higher education within the state stood to increase by 30%.

As she attempted to manage these and other inherited problems, Albino was handicapped by contrasts between her personality and her predecessor's. Gee had been an affable and ardent leader; Albino was reserved and low-key. Observers often described her as aloof and arrogant, and critics contended that she had poor public relations skills.

Albino faced other criticisms that seemed excessive, if not unfair. She was falsely accused of living in a million-dollar mansion that was paid for by tax dollars. In fact, Gee had built the presidential residence without dissent. Although Gee's wife had been on CU's payroll in two different positions with no complaints, when Albino's husband attempted to assume the job of heading maintenance and university functions at the presidential mansion, numerous objections arose. The couple withdrew the plan. Albino's husband took the job anyway, without pay and without the staff that Gee's wife had employed.

After a local newspaper reported that sabbaticals cost $4 million annually, with little accountability in the system, Albino was harshly criticized for her attempts to defend the 100-year tradition. A regent said that her public comments were "not convincing." Other complaints surfaced regarding her ability to serve as a liaison between the university and the public, state legislators, the regents, and the Colorado Commission on Higher Education. When newspaper accounts revealed that Gee had authorized bonuses to high-ranking school officials (including Albino) totaling hundreds of thousands of dollars, Albino had to deflect criticisms about how the university was run.

Behind the scenes, deans, faculty, and advisory committees tried to apprise Albino of their concerns. They reported that she would not listen and that she often seemed to interpret constructive suggestions as personal attacks. Some critics said that Albino did not understand the rationale behind university policies and practices. They assailed her leadership and managerial abilities, and they claimed that she was ineffective in her role as liaison between faculty and administrators and regents.

In September 1993, despite a simmering sense of unrest, the regents voted unanimously to extend Albino's contract until 1996. Two months later, however, three regents met secretly to call for the president's resignation. "We've got to stop the bleeding," said one of them. Meanwhile, the Council of Chairs and other faculty members at the Boulder campus steadfastly were enlisting support to oust Albino.

## After the Ambush

The day after the ambush, a local newspaper printed a letter to the university community written by the president and a letter written by some members of the faculty:

> *Letter to the University Community from President Albino*
>
> As I reflect on the events of the last few days and weeks, my overriding concern is for the continued stability and progress of the University of

Colorado. Division and turmoil serve none of us in the community and distract us from our true purposes of providing excellence in research, service to the state, and a first-class quality education for our students.

It is undeniable that the Boulder campus deans and I have serious differences about the proper course for this institution to follow in meeting its mission. Last Wednesday they candidly expressed their concerns to me; on Friday I did the same. We have each now felt the sting of the other's lash. No useful purpose can be achieved by continuing along this course, which can only result in greater division and disharmony.

Much has been said about personalities and individual motives, but individuals are not the issue. In the overall scheme of things, it is not whether I am president for the next ten days or the next ten years. What is important is the University. What is important is that we agree to come together, resolve our differences and carry on the vital work of serving our students and the citizens of Colorado. We must do no less.

. . . There is no question that there has been a serious breakdown in our capacity to work together. I urge those who share my desire for resolution to let me know of their willingness and help me shape this effort. . . .

### Letter to the University Community from Four Faculty Members

A number of us who signed the letter to CU President Judith Albino requesting her resignation did so only after considerable soul searching. The faculty is institutionally a conservative body, even as it tries to remain intellectually adventurous. Most faculty spend their careers in one or two universities. Unlike presidents, who come and go every few years, faculty are there for the long haul. They do not, therefore, like to rock the boat. They know how hard it is to run a university, because they more than anyone keep it running. They are by disposition more interested in teaching and research than institutional politics. For these reasons, along with our desire to spare Judith Albino personal and public embarrassment, and to allow her to reflect privately on the implications of our request, we faculty involved in the resignation request decided to work confidentially. The motivation for our request was and remains the quality of higher education at the University of Colorado.

. . . The Office of the President faces a hard task as it explains the work of the University to a public and a legislature wondering, quite reasonably, what we do and why we do it. Many of the signers of the letter believe that the current president has not been able to do that job, notwithstanding our desire to see her succeed and our appreciation of her efforts. We are saddened by this latest example of political and personal misjudgment. . . .

On the Monday following Black Friday, Albino met with nine distinguished professors and department chairs to discuss restructuring campus governance. They rebuffed her. Later that day, the deans voted to request time to speak with the Board of Regents during their regular monthly meeting, held the following Thursday. During the next few days, concerned parties met to try to de-escalate the confrontation. One group tried and failed to negotiate a compromise that would have allowed a graceful exit for the embattled administrator.

On Thursday, the Board of Regents met for 14 hours to discuss a faculty resolution that called for Albino's resignation. Over 100 people crowded the main meeting room, while nearly twice as many more viewed the proceedings on a television monitor in an adjacent room. Several members of the dissenting faculty contingency sat cross-legged on the floor.

Representing a mix of supporters, detractors, and concerned alumni, more than 30 speakers expressed their opinions during the 4-hour public hearing, which sometimes became explosive. Regents, faculty, and Albino frequently disrupted one another's stories. One professor read from a 6-page document that outlined administrative faults, leadership failures, and problems of personal integrity and honesty, including failure to accept personal responsibility for instances of poor judgment.

Included among Albino's supporters were African-American alumni and community members who applauded Albino's efforts to address the concerns of ethnic minority groups. A leader of the student union said that although she believed in Albino, she would not take sides. "That," she said, "would be like being asked to choose between Mom and Dad."

Acknowledging her own pain, Albino expressed regrets for any pain that she had caused. "I have responded overly harshly," she confessed.

At 11 P.M., the regents concluded the lengthy meeting by voting 5 to 4 to reject the resolution asking for Albino's resignation. When an Albino supporter presented a resolution to study "communication" among the president's office and the four campuses, Board members voted 7 to 2 to complete that review by the end of August. Albino vowed, "I'll try to do the best job I can."

## The Struggle Continues

Bolstered by the narrow victory, Albino expressed her intent to draft a plan to "move the university forward." She initiated a structural study to pinpoint problems and to identify exact lines of command within the campus system. A task force of regents and a core of higher education consultants conducted a campus-wide study in which they solicited input from faculty, staff, administrators, students, and alumni.

During the ensuing months, embers of controversy smoldered and periodically sparked. Many faculty members remained firm in their intent to force Albino's ouster. In February, the Boulder Faculty Assembly

(BFA—the faculty governance body for the CU-Boulder campus) and its counterpart at the Denver campus voted no confidence in the president.

Legislators accused the regents of postponing the problem. The governor said that Albino had lost her ability to lead the state's flagship school, and he suggested that she set a specific date for her departure. After meeting with Albino, he announced that they agreed on "a number of issues, attitudes, ideas, and approaches." He stopped short, however, of supporting her decision to remain.

Among those who wanted her to leave, the prevailing sentiment was that it was just a matter of time before Albino would resign. On the other hand, her supporters continued to root for the president. They maintained that the dissidents had not leveled specific charges. They also cited figures showing that the University's financial condition had thrived during Albino's tenure. Additionally, sponsored research was up 6%; enrollment applications had risen 10%; and minority applications had increased 22%. Finally, Albino had formed a gender-equity plan for CU athletics, cut the student athletic fee, and cut the tax subsidy for athletes.

In July, Albino appointed one of the outside consultants from the structural task force as 2-year interim chancellor at Boulder. Although the new chancellor believed that Albino had outlived her effectiveness, she gave him a free hand in restoring morale. The regents supported her decision, and the chair of the system-wide faculty council commended Albino for the appointment. Nonetheless, the chair of the BFA announced that its February vote of no confidence remained in effect.

In August, the regents granted Albino a reprieve by voting 6 to 3 to begin a comprehensive 6-month evaluation process of her presidency the following March. The decision was made after an hour of acrimonious discussion among the regents.

Late in October, Albino reflected on her stormy years as president: "In the absence of specific charges against me, I concluded that I wasn't the problem. The university would not be better served, at this time, without me. I've tried during the past 9 months to stay focused on the business of the University, and on moving the university forward."

"I've learned a few things," she observed. "I spend more time with constituents, always trying to address the real question, which is not whether we get rid of Albino or not, but how do we position the university to succeed in a future that holds all sorts of uncertainties."

## INTERPRETATION

We hold that experience commonly takes the form of familiar narratives or dramas, and observers often organize their interpretations of experi-

ence accordingly. Events that occur in organizations—an increasingly important part of human experience—often become narratives. The preceding narrative is our synthesis of the discourse embedded in and surrounding recent events at the University of Colorado.[1]

We also hold, with Geertz (1973), that our narratives should be interpreted theoretically if we are to rise above a mere undifferentiated
ethnography, a story that could be told from the perspective of any or no
social science. To interpret a narrative at a deeper level, one must consider the motives of the actors. Thus our main interpretation of our narrative draws on the symbolic theory of motives developed by Burke
(1935/1954), who suggests that we pay particular attention to the discourse of agents or actors in a drama. Indeed, Burke has argued that motives reside in discourse: "To summarize: Insofar as schemes of motivation change, one may expect a change in the very motives which people
assign to their actions. A motive is not some fixed thing, like a table,
which one can go and look at. It is a term of interpretation, and being
such it will naturally take its place within the framework of our *Weltan-
schauung* as a whole" (p. 25).

To repeat, a motive is not a thing that we can see and observe. It is a
term, a term of interpretation, and one's interpretations of motives must
therefore be determined by one's vocabulary. Vocabularies, in turn, are influenced by one's era, education, culture, the company one keeps and the
texts one engages. To understand others and put them in their places, we
assign motives to them by the application of terms of interpretation. The
assigning of motives to our own actions "is a matter of *appeal*" (Burke,
1935/1954, p. 25, emphasis in original). We can thus speak of the vocabulary of motives we use to explain and justify behavior as rhetorical constructs. In reference to our narrative, we concentrate on the "motive talk"
of the principals.

Hopper (1993a, 1993b) applied Burke's theory of motives to two
studies of the discourse of divorce. In the data gathered primarily
through interviews with divorcing and divorced individuals, Hopper
found patterns in what previously had appeared to be a disorderly
process:

> In examining the vocabularies of motive that divorcing people offer,
> my purpose is not to motive-monger or seek the "real" causes of di-
> vorces, whether psychological or social. Nor is my purpose to argue,
> along with ethnomethodologists, that we should abandon the search
> for motives and focus only on the structures of accounting and motive
> imputation. Rather, my purpose is to offer empirical evidence that vo-
> cabularies of motive are indeed rhetorical constructs, and that they
> function to impose order upon sets of behaviors, circumstances, and
> events that would otherwise seem chaotic. (1993a, p. 802)

Hopper was, in other words, trying to find support for Burke's notion that the orderliness of life is accomplished in part by vocabularies of motives that serve as rhetorical constructs. Hopper's ethnographic research showed that before a divorce, the relations between the two parties could be characterized by indeterminacy and ambivalence. Both parties described themselves as having been keenly aware of problems for some time, both often considering the possibility of divorce; and yet nothing about their respective complaints and ambivalences seemed to predict which partner, if either, would initiate the divorce.

Despite indeterminacy before the divorce, divorcing people knew immediately after the fact who had initiated the action, often referring to that party as the "dumper." Once the initiator's identity had been established by the decision, "a discernible vocabulary of motives emerged that helped make the initiator's decision seem reasonable and 'motivated.' This vocabulary cut through the complexity of what was happening before and made sense out of the initiator's transition from ambivalence" (Hopper, 1993a, p. 807).

Initiators emphasized negative aspects of their marriages, and they wove that emphasis into a common vocabulary of motives that helped them to interpret their status as initiator. They stressed the importance of individual needs over commitment. Describing marriage as a functional arrangement, they explained the need for divorce in terms of unfulfilled emotional and practical needs. And they asserted that fulfillment could be achieved only by ending the relationship.

Noninitiators invoked a vocabulary of motives that helped them make sense of being left and to explain their opposition to the divorce. They emphasized commitment to the union, the relationship, and, when appropriate, to the larger family. Citing the positive aspects of the marriage and acknowledging the dumper's complaints, they often asked for another chance to make the marriage work. Despite their previous doubts and ambivalences about the marriage, noninitiators developed a forceful and bitter rhetoric of opposition. Sometimes the partner harassed the initiator. A few became violent; "some would relate sensational and lurid stories about violence, sabotage, and vandalism" (Hopper, 1993a, p. 809). In most cases, such behaviors by the "dumped" party helped to transform the relationship into one of deep antagonism.

There are similarities between families and organizations that are often obscured by subdisciplinary boundaries between the studies of interpersonal and organizational communication. Langellier and Peterson (1993, p. 54) noted that there are "ways in which the family mirrors other social institutions." While not in disagreement with that observation, we would stress the converse as well. Organizations mirror the family, no doubt because family experience occurs logically and temporally *prior* to participation in formal organizations. Formal organizations acknowledge this imitation with discourse proclaiming that the firm is "one big happy family."

We also see similarities between the discourse about divorce that Hopper describes and the discourse surrounding (potential) breakups experienced by individuals and formal organizations. Organizations often play the role of "dumper," and of course the individual at times acts as the initiator. We believe that empirical studies of the explanations given for such acts would yield distinct vocabularies of motives. Like Hopper, we do not attempt to understand actors' intentions, while we acknowledge that sometimes individuals unwittingly may adopt particular vocabularies of motives without realizing their implications.

At universities, for example, the disjunctions are typically managed in the following ways. The president who has a job offer in hand publicly announces the decision to leave as motivated by the desire to face new challenges and opportunities elsewhere. The institution usually expresses its opposition privately, while publicly expressing only regrets and best wishes. The president who is to be dumped is usually warned privately in advance, allowing the dumped party an opportunity to announce publicly a newly realized desire to "return to teaching."

What is unusual and dramatic about our narrative is Albino's decision to receive the initiating message under bright stage lights with the critics and reviewers in the audience rather than in a more private space. After silencing the administrators, and while flanked by a cast constituting a majority of regents, Albino delivered a monologue in her vocabulary of motives. Motivated by the highest ends, she said she would stay on for the good of the institution. Although presenting her case in a public forum stiffened the support from most members of the "family" sympathetic to her oppositional stance, it also served to make the resolve to dump her stronger and more widespread. It guaranteed that she would be forced to leave her position as the dumped partner, no matter what public remarks she made at her departure. "Revenge," they say, "is a dish best eaten cold."

Once the divorce was initiated privately and its opposition was announced publicly, the initiators' discourse became dogmatic and categorical. The dumpers could see no good in Albino or the relationship. Albino, the dumped party, on the other hand, necessarily began to speak of the motives of reconciliation, coming close to an apology for the ambush and blaming her problems on the "structure" of the university she had inherited from her predecessor. Her detractors sneered at the structural explanation and repeated their charge of incompetent leadership.

Thus, constrained by the rigidified roles, the parties now perceived even the organization-as-communication system in radically different ways. The transition from ambivalence to the dialectical roles and rhetorical constructs would not allow the possibility that both explanations were reasonable; each developed a deafness to the explanations of the other. And yet it is our considered opinion that both sides were correct: There are serious structural problems at the University of Colorado, but there are also serious problems with Albino's leadership and management style. When the "structural study" was released on November 1, 1994, it failed, of course, to satisfy the initiators.

We see other similarities between the crisis of authority at CU and patterns of divorce developed by Hopper. It is not a perfect analogy, and yet it does suggest places to look for motives as rhetorical constructs in the individual–organizational relationship. For example, the "marriage" between Albino and the university was troubled from the start because of the unorthodox way in which she had been appointed. Faculty felt as if they were being asked to enter into an "arranged" or forced wedding. Albino must have experienced ambivalence as well.

Our narrative documents that the relationship was never free of doubts and uncertainties. Although it was not possible to predict which party, if either, would initiate the rupture, the attempted divorce did come. And in a manner similar to Hopper's divorcing parties, the initiating party did develop a vocabulary of motives to explain its actions, as revealed in published documents and quotes. Citing a plethora of negative aspects of Albino's presidency, the initiators alleged that the fulfillment of institutional dreams and ambitions was being deferred. Albino would have to go in order for the other party, the university, to achieve its fulfillment.

Albino, as the noninitiating party, predictably developed a rhetoric of opposition. On many occasions after the ambush, she said she would not leave because of her commitment to the institution ("The kids need me"). The university would not be better off if she abandoned it, she said, thus negating any selfish motive in fighting to keep her role. Both parties would be better off, she repeated, if they worked to strengthen the relationship.

Nonetheless, the opposition did produce the "lurid stories" and a kind of "sabotage" described by Hopper (e.g., the Black Friday Ambush). Additionally, rumors swept the campus that Albino had attempted to get the chancellor to fire some of the "ringleaders." The staged rejection of the invitation to quit produced a hardened or calcified vocabulary of motives. Nothing good could now be said about Albino by most members of the Boulder campus.

As Albino and her supporters necessarily expressed the desire for reconciliation, other observers began to suggest the analogy of divorce, while often using words that depicted a "war" metaphor (e.g., "ambush," "coup"). Professional conflict mediators were called in to try to heal the 5 to 4 rift in the Board of Regents. A former dean at the Boulder campus described them as "marriage counselors," an intuitive indication of the validity of the analogy being considered here. The student's story about being unable to choose between "Mom and Dad" also reflects the applicability of the analogy. Another example is the new chancellor's remark to the BFA that Albino's appointment had not been "certified by the joint-governance system," a suggestion that the relationship was illegitimate. And, in opposing the "divorce," Albino often asserted that the initiators had not provided sufficient "grounds" for their request.

One could advance other factors in a well-rounded analysis of motives of this case. That Albino became president without the legitimizing effect of having been recommended by a faculty search committee was an egregious error. The error was fully the responsibility of an elected Board of Regents, which made the appointment; rarely, if ever, has the Board enjoyed the confidence of the faculty in recent years. The zeitgeist is partly to blame: There is a widespread cynical disrespect for institutions in general and universities in particular. The scramble for scarce resources has pitted faculties against each other and against their administrations. Albino would have had difficulties under the best of circumstances. Something short of the best of circumstances produced the conditions that finally stimulated the attempt to dump her.

Thus Hopper's model of the rhetoric of motives of divorce seems to apply in this case as an attempt to dissolve a "relationship" in an organizational setting. Our analysis indicates that the model may be applicable (1) to breakups in general, and (2) in organizational as well as interpersonal situations.

## Gender

We now move to fill in the missing part of our chapter's subtitle: "Hell hath no fury like a president scorned (or dumped)." We did realize that most readers would strain toward completing it with a gender-relevant noun. This was our subtle way of promising to consider some of the feminist dimensions of the case.

Would our narrative be the same if Albino had been a man? We think not. It is our considered opinion that gender-related issues pervade our tale, beginning with Albino's ill-advised appointment. One professor at the university contended that gender had had more to do with Albino getting the job than with her being asked to resign. A former adjunct professor who conducted research on gender and power said that "the entire evaluation process had been subjected to gender bias." And the only female dean on the Boulder campus observed that Albino "never had one day's honeymoon or one day's opportunity to outline and implement her vision without having negative stories in the press. The treatment has been very biased." She added, however, that "sexism is not the issue anymore. If anything, some of the negative feelings [toward Albino] would have been public sooner if she had not been a woman because of this feeling that people wanted her to succeed and wanted to try to be helpful." Finally, a prominent faculty member said in the discussion leading up to the vote of no confidence by the BFA, "*Speaking as a woman,* I have to vote no confidence" (emphasis added).

Albino pointedly avoided questions regarding gender discrimination. "I don't tend to view the world from that perspective," she claimed. This attitude may have been to her detriment. To extend our marriage/divorce metaphor, Albino unwittingly may have enacted the role of an independent woman of the '90s in a relationship where her partners assumed she would behave in more traditional ways. Albino rarely exhibited stereotypical "female" communication behaviors (e.g., support, cooperation, deference; see, for example, Gilligan, 1982). And her reserved, autonomous demeanor was almost the opposite of her predecessor's. Consequently, she may have alienated faculty and administrators because her behaviors did not coincide with either their perceptions regarding the president's role or their socialized expectations about how a woman should behave. A female regent aptly expressed this notion: "I've always thought her particular management style—plus being a woman—is behind the problems she's had." And "women are still most effective around men when they adopt at least some of the traditional female patterns of behavior" (Duerst-Lahti, 1990, p. 202). These factors may have contributed to the sense of distrust and unease among those individuals who eventually were compelled to seek the termination of the relationship.

## CONCLUSION

In conclusion, we believe that Burke's symbolic notion of motives has worked in explaining (1) discursive patterns of divorce and (2) discursive patterns in an organizational crisis. We are particularly pleased that the principles transcend the iron curtain between interpersonal and organizational communication. Or does it? Perhaps marriage and divorce are proper areas of research for specialists in organizational communication, for, as observed almost 60 years ago, "'Love' is shorthand for membership in 'the smallest corporation,' a partnership of two" (Burke, 1937/1959, p. 266).

## ACKNOWLEDGMENTS

The authors thank George Cheney, Joseph Hopper, an anonymous observer, and an anonymous principal for their comments on earlier versions of this chapter.

## NOTE

1. Both authors were participant-observers of the events as they unfolded; they were ethnographically immersed in the crisis. Newspaper accounts in the following newspapers supplemented our memories and notes: *Rocky Mountain News, Boulder Daily Camera, Silver and Gold Record,* and the *Colorado Daily.* Other internal documents were used as sources. Tompkins met with Albino on several occasions before and after the crisis. He was also a member of the BFA. Allen attended two breakfasts that Albino held with faculty to discuss concerns about CU, and she accompanied Albino on a trip to Denver to meet with African-American community leaders. Allen was a member of the Faculty of Color Organization at CU-Boulder.

   As coauthors, we feel the need to elaborate our individual attitudes toward Albino and the events that we described. We have slightly different "interests" in the narrative and the interpretation, despite our agreement on what we have written above.

   Allen, an African-American female assistant professor, remained a cautious Albino supporter. Although she felt that the president often displayed a lack of political and social savvy, she also thought that Albino's critics often were unduly harsh and sometimes seemed petty. In addition, she believed that Albino had matured during her tempestuous tenure, exhibiting strong potential for becoming a more effective leader. Most of the other faculty of color at CU-Boulder also supported Albino, primarily because they believed that she was diligently addressing their concerns. Many of them also admired Albino's tenacity and her determination to fight the old boy network.

   Tompkins, a white male full professor, was sympathetic to Albino's position because long before "structure" had become an issue, he had analyzed the problems of the university in class lectures. In fact, Tompkins and Albino had agreed that he would conduct a study of the four-campus system in the summer of 1993. Medical problems forced a delay of the study until other events made it impossible. Nonetheless, Tompkins remained sympathetic until the Black Friday Ambush, and he voted—with reluctance—for the BFA's motion of no confidence.

## KEY TERMS

ANALOGY: similarity in some aspects between things that are otherwise dissimilar.

DISCOURSE: communication of ideas, information, and so on orally or in writing.

ETHNOGRAPHY: a research method that entails in-depth, extended observation of the "culture" or phenomenon being studied.

METAPHOR: a figure of speech containing an implied comparison in which a word or phrase typically used for one thing is applied to another (e.g., "All the world's a stage").

MOTIVE: inner drive or intention that causes a person to behave in a particular way.

RHETORICAL CONSTRUCT: verbal attribution of why people do what they do.

WELTENSCHAUUNG: personal view of the world.

ZEITGEIST: the spirit of the times.

## DISCUSSION QUESTIONS

1. Do you accept the authors' argument that elements of the "breakup" between Albino and her detractors are analogous to those of divorcing couples? Explain your position.
2. What might Albino have done differently than her Black Friday meeting to avoid escalating the conflict?
3. Through explicit and implicit examples, identify metaphors other than divorce that are threaded through the narrative.
4. How, if at all, do you think that the narrative is influenced by the authors' roles as members of the organization that they analyzed?
5. In what ways (other than those cited in the case) does organizational communication resemble family communication?
6. In your opinion, did the fact that Albino is a woman make a difference in her behavior as well as those of her supporters and detractors?

## REFERENCES

Burke, K. (1935/1954). *Permanence and change: An anatomy of purpose* (3rd ed.). Berkeley: University of California Press.

Burke, K. (1937/1959). *Attitudes toward history* (3rd ed.). Berkeley: University of California Press.

Duerst-Lahti, G. (1990). But women play the game too: Communication, control and influence in administrative decision making. *Administration and Society, 22,* 182–205.

Geertz, C. (1973). *The interpretation of cultures.* New York: Basic Books.

Gilligan, C. (1982). *In a different voice: Psychological theory and women's development.* Cambridge, MA: Harvard University Press.

Hopper, J. (1993a). The rhetoric of motives in divorce. *Journal of Marriage and the Family, 55,* 801–813.

Hopper, J. (1993b). Oppositional identities and rhetoric in divorce. *Qualitative Sociology, 16,* 133–156.

Langellier, K., & Peterson, E. (1993). Family storytelling as a strategy of social control. In D. Mumby (Ed.), *Narrative and social control: Critical perspectives* (pp. 49–76). Newbury Park, CA: Sage.

# CHAPTER 4

# The Many Meanings of "Solidarity"

## The Negotiation of Values in the Mondragón Worker-Cooperative Complex under Pressure

### GEORGE CHENEY

> Contrary to popular assumption, solidarity is not in contradiction with efficiency. In fact, the most advanced form of capitalism uses as a basis for progress attention to the person as a member of the organization, developing his/her initiative and freedom of activity, especially within the context of teams.
> —José María Sarasua, "Our External Mission," *Work and Union* (corporate house organ of the Mondragón cooperatives) (January 1994, p. 12)

## THEORETICAL ORIENTATION

This passage, quoted from the corporate magazine of the Mondragón Co-operative Corporation in the Basque Country of Spain, captures well one of the defining tensions of modern organizational life: that between the individual and the organization. As typically discussed, this tension—especially as manifested in for-profit firms—pits individual needs against organizational efficiency. Too often the organization and the individual are largely seen as exclusive of one another and as being in unending conflict. Their interrelationship is not recognized, nor are the various ways in which these organizational and individual values are understood in practice. Still, the synthesis of the two is not easy.

Weber (1978), of course, was keenly aware of the importance of values in the development of any organization and in the rise of the modern organization as an institution. Writing at the beginning of the 20th century, Weber identified three basic "logics" of authority in social organization. Charismatic authority (focusing on the compelling and exceptional qualities of a leader), traditional authority (emphasizing a preeminent lineage or a custom), and rational–legal authority (involving a systematic attempt to regularize behavior) correspond to and are expressed in the prototypic forms of religious sects, monarchies, and bureaucracies.

Of these types, Weber was centrally and acutely concerned with bureaucracy as the emergent and soon-to-be-dominant form of organization in modernity. Differing from Marx, Weber saw the logic of social relations in the organization as ultimately more important than the nature of ownership and control over the means of production in shaping an organization's functioning and the day-to-day life within it. (Still, as one sociologist has insightfully observed, both Weber and Marx focused their attentions of forms of "severance" in modern life, specifically, how persons were becoming separated from control over some of their most defining activities; see Sayer, 1991.) Weber was simultaneously a cheerleader and a doomsayer for what he called the "iron cage" of bureaucracy. He pointed out clear advantages to this rational and systematic order. First, it was considered nonarbitrary (with respect to personnel). From this standpoint, roles would become more important than the individual persons filling them. Such a system advances the value of equality of opportunity in terms of merit. Second, bureaucracy has as its basis clear and easily applied standards. And third, it offers a blueprint for organizing giant and far-flung enterprises. At the same time, Weber feared the overconcentration of power at the apex of the hierarchical pyramid, the depersonalization of relations between and among members (i.e., "We are all cogs in a machine"), and the supplanting of a concern for basic values (e.g., "What are we here for?") with narrow calculations of technical matters (e.g., "How many widgets have we made today?").

Weber's (1978) ponderings over values and the collective never expressed themselves in a full-blown model of organization alongside his other ideal types. However, at least two sociologists have argued that such a model is in fact implicit in Weber's writings (see Rothschild-Whitt, 1979; Satow, 1975). In the view of these researchers, we ought to extrapolate from Weber's writings a type of organization that features grounding in and regular collective reflection on basic values. It is important to consider such a possibility not so much because we should feel the need to round out Weber's works but because of the imperative for exploring alternative forms of organization at a time when public confidence in all of the major institutions of our society is waning. I call this an imperative because both individual alienation and organizational ineffectiveness abound in the public and private institutions in which we participate today. We are not happy with the way most of our organizations are working or with our work within them.

The question underlying this case study[1] of a cooperative corporation is this: Can an explicitly value-based organization maintain its "integrity" over time? A reconsideration of Weber's theory for the late-20th-century world leads us to explore what is possible for an organization that attempts to be true to its overarching mission. How do the internal dynamics of the organization affect organizational integrity? Is internal deterioration, such as bureaucratic stultification, inevitable? Is goal displacement, as witnessed in so many service-oriented organizations, really unavoidable? Are external market pressures, such as the need to be bigger and more competitive (especially in the case of for-profit firms) necessarily going to demand that the organization become just like the mainstream, in the sense of being reshaped into an uncreative and unreflective standard hierarchical organization?

The case illustration that follows features just such questions. But it does so from the perspective of communication, that is, special attention is given to the ways values are understood, expressed, and transformed in the ongoing interactions that constitute much of what the organization is. After all, if we take democracy and social values seriously for an organization, then their very meanings must be subject to reflection and critique (see Cheney, 1997). Terms for values, such as "democracy" or "efficiency" become part of the ongoing process of (re)organizing. In her insightful treatment of the relation between words and values, for example, Rosenthal (1984) shows how a great deal can be "going on" under the umbrella of a common term like "growth"—a term used to refer to such diverse situations as expansion of an organization and the maturation of an individual (and in both cases with an almost unquestioned positive tone). And in an interesting study with even greater relevance to the present one, Stohl (1993) reveals how a term such as "employee participation" is understood in very different ways by managers from the various European Union nations. Also, Berggren (1992) reveals how a buzzword such as "teamwork" in organizations can function in some ways that may have little to do with small-group cooperation. Specifically, the present case analysis concerns the polysemous but inspiring value of social solidarity and the ways it is expressed, maintained, and yet transformed over time.

## BACKGROUND ON THE CASE

The Mondragón cooperatives, located in the heart of the Basque region of Spain, represent one of the world's largest and longest-lived organizations characterized by real worker ownership and governance. Founded on values of democracy, solidarity, and equality/equity, the co-ops are a conscious attempt to combine systems of individual incentive and group cooperation and welfare. The ten official principles of the Mondragón system are:

1. Open membership
2. Democratic structure
3. The sovereignty of labor
4. The instrumental and subordinate nature of capital
5. Participation in the management of the firms
6. Remunerative solidarity
7. Intercooperation (between and among co-ops)
8. Social transformation
9. Universal character
10. Education

Of these value-based principles, numbers 6 through 9 deal especially with issues that co-op members would classify under the heading of "solidarity." Indeed, the term "solidarity" is important for the co-ops on interpersonal, intergroup, and societal levels, as we will see in considering the ways in which solidarity is being (re)negotiated today.

The Mondragón cooperatives were founded through the efforts of a quiet but persistent Basque priest, José María Arizmendiarrieta, and five engineers. Years of bloodshed and strife in Spain through the Civil War (1936–1939) and World War II (1939–1945) led Don José María and his group to reflect upon new methods of social organization. After reviewing the histories of a variety of organizations, especially the experiences of utopian communities in Great Britain in the 19th century, the founders settled on a "third way" between the poles of unbridled corporate capitalism and centralized state socialism. The creation of a technical school in 1943 was followed by the development of the first manufacturing co-op in 1956 and a cooperative bank in 1959. These and all other parts of the system are cooperative in two senses: economically, in that all worker–members are also owners (there still is no outside stock held); and socially, in that each co-op is governed by a complex system of direct and representative democracy (along with governance by a congress of all co-ops).

Today the co-ops number more than 150, collectively forming the 15th largest private firm in Spain, the Mondragón Cooperative Corporation. The system currently employs more than 23,000 persons. The co-ops are centered in manufacturing (including, for example, Spain's largest maker of refrigerators), but they also include a large bank, a social security system, and a complete educational system. Many of these are "second-order" co-ops, in that they count among their membership both individuals and other co-ops. The single largest co-op today is Eroski (which roughly means "group buying" in Euskera, the Basque language), a chain of grocery stores with nearly 9,000 employee–owner–members. In addition, there are more than 250,000 consumer–members of Eroski, most of whom are citizens of the Basque Country.

Each *socio–trabajador* (worker–owner–associate–member) is an economic owner of a co-op through a complex system of investment and return. Up to 70% of the profits go to owner–members in the form of individual capital accounts and direct benefits; approximately 20% of the profits are reinvested in the co-ops themselves; and about 10% are contributed to community projects (notably, to Basque-language schools but also to drug education and AIDS-related programs).

The cooperative system is governed at the broadest level by a Cooperative Congress, which meets once a year and has proportional representation from all of the individual co-ops. At the same time, there is a corporate superstructure for the management of the daily affairs of the co-ops and representation of the co-ops in the marketplace. A president of the corporation, the closest person to being like a corporate chief executive officer, is elected by the Cooperative Congress. Each individual co-op has its own general assembly, meeting once a year to consider major policy issues. Each assembly operates on a one-person, one-vote principle, so each "*socio*" (or member) has a direct voice in its deliberations. Members of the assembly elect a governing or guiding council, which is typically the most powerful group in the day-to-day affairs of the co-op. There is also an elected social council, which deals with issues of personnel and human resources; it is designed as a check on the power of the governing council, although its charge is largely advisory. In larger co-ops, there is also a management council, whose membership is determined in part through election and in part through appointment. The manager of the co-op heads the management council. (See Whyte & Whyte, 1991, for much more on the history and structure of the Mondragón cooperatives.)

## CURRENT CHALLENGES

The Mondragón co-ops face significant social and economic challenges today. (These are detailed elsewhere; see Cheney, 1995, 1997.) This case study is based on two general categories of changes: what we might call sociocultural transformation in the larger society and the real and perceived external economic pressure. These changes provide a context for considering the complexities surrounding the term and the value of "solidarity."

The sociocultural transformation is manifested in several ways. Basque society is strongly communal yet applauds self-reliance. Basque culture still privileges orality; however, the requirements of modern institutions have made written (and electronic) communication more and more common. Basques are, generally speaking, intensely proud of their ethnic and cultural distinctiveness, especially of their ancient and complex language, Euskera (a tongue that is not a member of the Indo-European family of languages and whose exact origin remains a mystery). Of all the 17 provinces of the contemporary Spanish state, the Basque Country enjoys the greatest autonomy in its own governance; nevertheless, its linkages with Madrid remain controversial and challenged from a variety of quarters.

Today Basque society is undergoing rapid change, as are the other societies of Spain in the post-Franco era. Secularization, the advancement of women in the workforce, increased consumerism, the careerist aspirations of many young people, and the general acceleration in the pace of life are profoundly affecting the everyday lives of Basques and non-Basques living in the three provinces constituting the Spanish part of the Basque region.

These trends, especially the faster pace of life and the independent-minded orientations of young professionals, are seen as threats to social solidarity, a value central not only to the official "constitution" of the co-ops but also to Basque culture more generally. As many citizens complained to me on the street while I was there for 5 months in 1994, "Everything is changing. And people don't have the time for each other that they used to have. We're becoming more like you, the Americans, and the Germans and the Japanese, but we don't necessarily like it." Among the hundreds of people I talked with either formally or informally in 1994, I encountered virtually no dissent from this view of what is happening to the society. They justified the changes on the grounds that "we must do this to compete in the global economy."

Related to this set of concerns is the pressure for the co-ops to grow and to be more economically competitive (see, e.g., Moye, 1993). Growth, from the very beginning of Mondragón, has been seen as important to give the co-ops a broad capital base as a buffer against the economic fluctuations of the larger market and to enable the co-ops to be a visible force in that same market. And the actual pressures to compete have become more obvious and more intense since the dropping in 1992 of most barriers to trade within the European Union (which Spain joined in 1986). Originally, the Mondragón co-ops conceived of themselves as competing in a Basque market; later they saw themselves in a Spanish market, and now they see themselves in European and global markets. As one worker–member said to me during my first visit to Mondragón in March 1992, "We must grow or die."

The typical framing of the matter of market pressure is interesting from a communication standpoint. Many co-op members spoke to me in interviews[2] about the need to be more competitive and more efficient in economic terms, describing "the market" as if it were something totally out of human hands—a wholly external force (e.g., "The market requires that we expand" or "We have to respond to the market by cutting costs"). Adopting a somewhat playful investigative attitude toward such comments, I often replied, "So, *who* or *what is* the market?" Looking somewhat puzzled at first, my interviewees would usually respond by acknowledging that they, as members of the co-ops and as consumers, were also part of the very thing that they were linguistically placing "out there." The "externalizing" language used to discuss the market, not at all uncommon in the Basque Country as elsewhere, seemed to promote a sense of limited possibilities for action. That is, people seem to forget their own roles and possibilities for shaping the very market that they see themselves merely as responding to in a very reactive way. Of course, this comment raises the question of the reality versus the *perception* of market pressure in terms of the way an organization and its members "see" the environment, the way they contribute to it in various ways (see, e.g., Weick's [1979] provocative discussion of this matter), and the way they construct and reconstruct it.

Competitiveness has been a salient concern of the Mondragón co-ops, particularly in the 1990s. The cover of the April 1994 issue of the corporate house organ, *Work and Union*, depicts a young professional man running hurdles with the earth below him. In one article linked to the cover, written by one of the founders of the co-ops, this definition of competitiveness is offered as preferable to several others: "Competitiveness, in the macroeconomic context, is a characteristic of firms through which they assure their presence in the market and increase their participation in the same, in rivalry with other firms." Like many definitions, of course, this one has a somewhat circular or tautological quality about it. In a sense the definition says, "To be competitive, a firm must be competitive." (And it remind's me of Kohn's [1986] insightful observation that in our society we treat competition simultaneously as something that is *natural* and as something that needs to be *nurtured* or promoted.) At the same time, however, the definition acknowledges that an organization becomes *part* of the market through its competitive posture. Much of the argumentation along these lines within the co-ops treats social solidarity (in various forms) as subordinate to economic competitiveness, understandably insisting that the very survival of the co-ops is more important than their strict adherence to certain values. (See also Cheney & Christensen, in press.)

The issue of competitiveness is indeed questioned within the co-ops. A number of interviewees argued that the external pressures were being exaggerated and used as excuses for greater centralization and bureaucratization: for example, in a top-down move away from regional sectors to functional ones (see Kasmir, 1996). The larger point here, though, is that the need for competitiveness currently shapes and challenges a number of ideas about social solidarity.

## NEGOTIATING AND RENEGOTIATING SOLIDARITY

In the life and history of the Mondragón co-ops, "solidarity" has had several distinct and well-established meanings. As already explained, the term has a background of significance for Basque society. In this regard, the word is important for denoting camaraderie and interdependence. Within the co-ops themselves, solidarity is institutionalized in several ways. First, as captured in principle 6 (above), there is remunerative or wage solidarity. That is, the wage differential ratio from highest to lowest was statutorily set by the co-ops in 1956 at 3:1. Second, there is a strong emphasis on job security, with frequent use of lateral transfers and only rare recourse to layoffs or early retirements. Third, "intercooperation," or intercooperative solidarity, means that both benefits (or profits) and losses are socialized, that is, shared within a group of co-ops that form a single industrial sector (for example, automotive parts). Accordingly, poor financial performance by one of the co-ops in a group is directly compensated for by contributions from the profits of other co-ops in the same group. Finally, solidarity within the environment means both preservation of jobs in a locale and assistance to the wider community and to the world.

Thus before even considering the impacts of recent trends on "solidarity" within the Mondragón co-ops, we find a number of different meanings for the term, varying in context and in level of specificity. The remainder of the case describes three recent events that bring into focus tensions over solidarity and that spotlight ways in which it is being (re)negotiated. "Solidarity is hard," as one *socio* lamented to me.

First is the matter of wage solidarity today. Market pressures and the need to recruit highly paid professionals led over the years to a gradual widening of the wage differential index from 3:1 to 4.5:1 and then to 6:1, although it should be mentioned that when taxes are taken into account the third ratio actually looks more like 4:1. (As a point of contrast, the index in most large U.S. firms currently is between 200:1 and 300:1, and it shows no signs of narrowing.) Over the years, the arguments advanced in favor of these changes in the wage differential have essentially been appeals to the outside market, suggesting that wage solidarity can be "modified" in practice based upon what is going on in the larger economy.

Still, until a crucial December 1991 meeting of the Cooperative Congress, wages and salaries had never been *tied* to the market. At that assembly, the majority of representatives of individual co-ops voted to allow approximately 25 of the top officials' salaries to rise to 70% of the current market figure. Thus a direct symbolic and financial link was established between the cooperatives' pay scale and the market.

As one worker–member of FAGOR, the appliance manufacturer, told me, "The change in policy over wages represents a break from the tradition of solidarity in the co-ops. Where's the solidarity in this? Our trust in one another is broken." The same employee–member, an activist in a budding informal union called "Cooperative Groups" (formal unions are prohibited by the charter of the co-ops on the grounds that they make no sense structurally or ideologically within the context of full employee ownership), maintained that the change in policy was a problem *even if* the select salaries did not rise to meet the 70% maximum level.

In fact, as the then-President of the Mondragón Cooperative Corporation, himself an elected official, explained to me, the 25 salaries were at only about 50% of the then-current market rate. He expressed frustration about the mystery and suspicion surrounding the salaries of those 25 persons in the "*cúpula*" (what many worker–members call the managerial superstructure), but he also believed that there was no effective way to ameliorate these concerns. In his view, the basic "foundation" of solidarity had been shaken not because of the 1991 policy change but because some worker–members were conceiving of solidarity too narrowly, too technically.

In this instance of a market-oriented policy change, the symbolic power of the change in the minds of some organizational members seemed to overshadow the question of actual salaries. From their standpoint, the corporation had compromised an internal value, wage solidarity, in bowing to external market standards and had thereby undermined a distinctive characteristic of the co-ops. On the other hand, defenders of the change (such as the president) insist that some compromises are necessary for the sheer survival of the system (and by implication, its constitutive values). This instance is a reminder of how sometimes a single communication event (or "message") can deeply affect the climate and course of an organization.

A second change, important to the discussion of solidarity in Mondragón, concerns the internal structure of the organization. As the cooperatives grew in the 1960s and '70s, they were clustered in separate valleys of the mountainous Basque country. During the 1990s, however, the Mondragón Cooperative Corporation has been moving away from its traditional, regional sectors toward reorganization on the basis of industrial sectors. This development is rationalized principally on the basis of economic efficiency: specifically, in terms of grouping co-ops with similar product or service markets. Gradually, the 15 regional sectors are being supplanted by nine functional ones, including clusters concerned with machine tools, home appliances, auto parts, finance, education, and so on. This restructuring, which is developing unevenly across the co-ops because of the degree of autonomy maintained by "the base" (i.e., by individual cooperatives), has produced a strong negative reaction in at least two forms.

One is that a group of co-ops in a valley neighboring that of Mondragón seceded from the larger corporation in 1992. As the then-president and highest elected official of the breakaway group told me, "We did not want our group to be divided, with one co-op being linked to a sector based somewhere else. We derive our strength from one another [i.e., referring to each individual co-op], and we share a commitment to the local community." In this way, both intercooperative and external solidarity were defined in very concrete ways, in terms of specific connections between and among co-ops and between the co-ops and the land and the people around them.

Another negative response to reorganization was oriented more toward interpersonal relations among worker–members. One of the chief points of contention for the informal labor group mentioned earlier is what they see as the "violation" of the traditionally important regional groups of co-ops. Importantly, some of the most active members of this group are also employees of some of the oldest co-ops. They have a strong identification with the Mondragón Valley and with their local community. They are not, however, well connected to or appreciated by the upper management of the corporation, and the group has not been well integrated into the corporation's planning for the future. The "Cooperative Groups" have taken an antagonistic stance toward the corporation. The same group sees local connection as central to the definition and functioning of the co-ops. They see solidarity especially in terms of worker–members' commitments to one another, bonds that are much stronger when co-op members are citizens of the same community. At the same time, this group emphasizes the co-op's linkage to its host community. Thus any move toward reorganization along sectoral or functional lines is seen as a direct threat to solidarity. In one statement made at a general assembly meeting of one of the largest and the oldest co-ops in 1993, the group warned, "In the interest of being more modern and more efficient, the cooperatives, under the name of the Mondragón Cooperative Corporation, are trying to dismantle the basic rights of the *socios* and undermining its most advanced social dimensions." The Cooperative Groups have thus taken the position that they, much more than the leadership of the corporation, embody the defining values of the Mondragón.

For their part, many leaders within the co-ops define the reorganization as necessary "in order that we may compete." They also argue that those opposed to the changes should take a broader view of the welfare of the entire system, of the whole Corporation, its survival and growth. As explained in an issue of *Work and Union* devoted primarily to an analysis of the financial group of cooperatives: "The primary challenge is to know how structurally to unify the businesses to make them all profitable and to respond [to the market] appropriately with a single vision." This captures well the frequently articulated interest in reorganizing the co-ops according to their specific economic concerns and then allowing the corporation to speak with one voice to its relevant markets. Internal and external solidarity, as explained to me by one of the founders, are thus assigned wider roles and are not necessarily conceived of in the old, specific ways.

A final issue with respect to solidarity bears mention here. While I was at Mondragón, I had extensive conversations with a Madrid-based consultant who was conducting retraining for machine-maintenance employees in one of the largest co-ops. He was frustrated by what he saw as the use of the term "solidarity" to cover up laziness or incompetence. In particular, he heard appeals to the value of solidarity as means of deflecting criticism of members who were perhaps not performing up to expectations. As he related to me, "'Solidarity,' in this sense, has become stale and almost meaningless. It becomes for some cooperative members nothing but an excuse."

This poignant and disturbing example of a rather surprising usage of "solidarity" raises the issue of the transformations of terms: of what new uses are made of them and of how they can become detached from their former moorings. Terms for values are perhaps especially vulnerable to this kind of "evolution" because of their abstract nature, their widespread use, and their emotional significance (see Bakhtin, 1981). In organizational as well as in political life, a potent term such as "democracy" or "freedom" can command intense emotional allegiance and yet over time be divorced from traditional substantive content (see Cheney, 1997). Here, a process-oriented perspective on organizations (an particularly on democratic ones) requires attention to how the organization changes over time, in terms of the meanings it "holds" and "manages."

## EPILOGUE

While no definitive answer can be (or should be) provided here for the question of how a value-driven organization can maintain its substantive integrity, a few closing observations are helpful. First, *all* organizations need to be vigilant about the pursuit of their goals and of the possibility for goal displacement. This imperative, which was implicit in Weber's (1978) writings, is now underscored by a century of solid experience with bureaucracy in all sectors. This need is even more important in a value-based organization, such as are many firms that are owned and governed by the workers.

Second, both scholars and lay persons must be attuned to the ways value terms function in everyday talk as well as in formal discourse. Terms such as "equality" or "efficiency" or "service" can be used to bring together different ideas and different people, allowing them to coexist under the same banner, as in the mission statement of an organization (see, e.g., Cheney, 1991). Diverse perspectives and programs (e.g., about "employee participation") can be called the same thing (see, e.g., Stohl, 1993). Terms such as "teamwork" may mean substantially different things in different cultural contexts and in different organizations (Berggren, 1992). However, such ambiguities can also be used to conceal conflicting and even contradictory meanings or (intentionally or unintentionally) to manipulate situations and people (see, e.g., Eisenberg, 1984). For example, new models of grassroots democracy can be imposed on employees, benevolently done in the name of fortifying "social solidarity" (see, e.g., Stohl & Cheney, 1997). And at the same time, key terms or symbols can become empty slogans—almost devoid of specific or concrete meaning—even while maintaining emotional power (see, e.g., White, 1984). As an example, consider what has happened to the term "empowerment" in the scholarly and popular literatures on organizations and work.

Third, in this age of the globalization of markets, we must ask ourselves what is reasonable and unreasonable about drives toward more intense competition, heightened efficiency, market-determined responses, and increased speed of production and consumption. For example, some observers argue that the presumably democratic drive toward the globalization of free trade actually works in rather undemocratic ways, especially in that both its implementation and its results are being little debated (Mander & Goldsmith, 1996). Do these pursuits promote the values we care about most deeply; are they giving us what we really want? (See, e.g., Schmookler, 1993.) Is the system to which we often defer, often by saying, "That's the way it is?," truly rational in the sense of helping us as a people to maximize progress toward our most cherished goals and values? It's time to reflect carefully on what our organizations are doing for us and to us.

## NOTES

1. This case study is part of a much larger project and it draws upon a 10-day intensive tour of and 5 months of fieldwork at the Mondragón worker cooperatives in 1992 and 1994, respectively. The author gratefully acknowledges the assistance and counsel of numerous persons in and around Mondragón and elsewhere. I would like to mention specifically Pilar Abad of Cincinnati, Ohio,

and Mac Johnson of Covington, Kentucky, who each offered me a great deal of information and help, particularly through a tour of the co-ops in 1992. I would also like to mention three people at the Otalora Training Center of the Mondragón Cooperative Corporation—José María Larrañaga, Mikel Lezamiz, and Itziar Bazanbide—who become both friends and collaborators. I would like to offer the same expression of thanks to José Manuel Biaín, Fernando Recalde, and José Antonio Ugarte, of ULMA, a group of cooperatives in neighboring Oñati. Without the encouragement and efforts of all these people, my work would not have been possible. I am grateful to these observers of Mondragón for helpful conversations: Sue Eicher, Fred Freundlich, Sandra Harding, Sally Klingel, Mike Long, Terry Martin, Mike Miller, Sheila Turpin, and William Foote Whyte.

2. Interviews of two types were conducted. First, approximately 25 general-information or background interviews were done with a variety of persons throughout the co-ops. Second, about 75 interviews were conducted with stratified random samples of the memberships of three diverse co-ops: One was a recent conversion from a traditional capitalist firm; the second was a well-integrated and economically profitable part of the system; and the third had recently voted to leave the Mondragón Cooperative Corporation. Interviews lasted between 15 minutes and 2 hours; all were conducted in Spanish.

## KEY TERMS

AMBIGUITY (IN LANGUAGE): in the sense used here, a necessary, important, yet baffling aspect of all language, but especially of abstract, value-laden terms. Burke (1950/1969), the literary and rhetorical critic, urges us to consider "the strategic points at which ambiguities necessarily arise" in trying to understand human relations.

BUREAUCRACY: a systematic, nonarbitrary, rational, and generalizable model of organizational activity. As Weber predicted, bureaucracy has significant advantages and disadvantages with respect to other organizational forms. For example, while bureaucracy helps us to organize giant and far-flung enterprises, it also tends to depersonalize relations in that it treats people as replaceable parts of a system.

CENTRALIZATION (IN DECISION MAKING): an organization's effort to consolidate decision-making control in one office or part of the organization, usually at the top of a hierarchy.

COMPETITION: in the sense used here, a presumed or actual zero-sum relationship between and among organizations in the same arena or industry, where advancement or profit by one necessarily means the decline or loss by another organization. Competition has other meanings, however.

DEMOCRACY (IN THE WORKPLACE): in the context of this study, attempts to give "voice" to individuals' interests, beliefs, attitudes, and knowledge within their employing organizations. Put another way, workplace democracy means the "codetermination" by all members of an organization's basic goals and pursuits.

EMPLOYEE PARTICIPATION: used to denote specific work programs for increasing or enhancing employees' decision-making power, usually with an interest in increasing overall organization productivity. Participative decision making (or PDM), total quality management (or TQM), and quality circles are just three examples of movements in the area of employee participation.

GOAL DISPLACEMENT: as articulated by a variety of organizational theorists, an organization's tendency—especially over time—to substitute goals such as power, growth, and expediency for the stated original goals of the organization (such as making a quality product or providing valuable public service).

MONDRAGÓN COOPERATIVE CORPORATION: a system of over 150 employee-owned-and-governed cooperatives, located in the Basque Country in Spain. It is the subject of this case study.

RATIONAL–LEGAL AUTHORITY: Max Weber's term for an organizational or social relationship that relies on common adherence to a prescribed system of rules, regulations, and means of assessment (as opposed to the personal qualities of a leader or the transmission of tradition). Bureaucracy is the organizational form that best exemplifies rational–legal authority, according to Weber.

SOCIAL CHANGE: in general, the ways in which social structures are altered and sometimes completely transformed over time. Understanding how changes do occur, even in seemingly stable social arrangements, is one of the fundamental problems of social theory.

SOLIDARITY: one of the key terms of this study, not only because it is an important culturally held value for the organization in the case study but also because it has so many different but equally significant meanings (e.g., interpersonal solidarity, solidarity between and among organizations, solidarity with the community).

VALUES (IN ORGANIZATIONS): in the context of this study, relatively abstract points of reference that individuals and organizations use in guiding and in explaining their decisions. Examples of important organizational values here are democracy, solidarity, growth, equality, efficiency, and productivity.

WORKER COOPERATIVES: an organization that is completely or largely employee owned, in that there is little or no outside stock or ownership of equity. Such an organization may also be completely or largely employee governed, in that each member may have a real voice in decision making. As with other categories of organizations, there is tremendous variety between and among organizations that are called "worker cooperatives" (and the related organizational types of "collectives," "employee stock-ownership programs," etc.).

## DISCUSSION QUESTIONS

1. Do you see cooperatives such as Mondragón as being viable in other societies? Why or why not?

2. What safeguards can a democratic organization employ to preserve its governance processes?
3. When a value-driven organization drifts away from its founding principles, what should be done by its members? When should the mission of the organization be revised? When should the practices of the organization be brought back in line with its stated values? When should the organization be dissolved?
4. What values do you see as most important for an employing organization? To what extent do these values (and terms) have multiple and perhaps even conflicting meanings?
5. How can an organizational mission statement be used to bring together diverse interests represented by the different members? How can an organization's employees participate effectively in the formulation of a mission?
6. How can a for-profit firm be humane for employees yet competitive in the market?
7. What do democracy and efficiency mean to you? Be specific. In your view, can an organization be both efficient and democratic? Why or why not?

## REFERENCES

Bakhtin, M. (1981). *The dialogic imagination: Four essays* (M. Holquist, Ed.). Austin: University of Texas Press.

Berggren, C. (1992). *Alternatives to lean production: Work organization in the Swedish auto industry.* Ithaca, NY: Cornell University Press.

Burke, K. (1969). *A rhetoric of motives.* Berkeley: University of California Press. (Original work published 1950)

Cheney, G. (1991). *Rhetoric in an organizational society: Managing multiple identities.* Columbia: University of South Carolina Press.

Cheney, G. (1995). Democracy in the workplace: Theory and practice from the perspective of communication. *Journal of Applied Communication Research, 23,* 167–200.

Cheney, G. (1997). *Organizations as if people mattered: Values, democracy, and communication in a changing worker-cooperative complex called Mondragón.* Manuscript in progress.

Cheney, G., & Christensen, L. T. (in press). Identity at issue: Linkages between "internal" and "external" organizational communication. In F. M. Jablin & L. L. Putnam (Eds.), *The new handbook of organizational communication.* Thousand Oaks, CA: Sage.

Deetz, S. (1992). *Democracy in an age of corporate colonization.* Albany: State University of New York Press.

Eisenberg, E. (1984). Ambiguity as strategy in organizational communication. *Communication Monographs, 51,* 227–242.

Kasmir, S. (1996). *The myth of Mondragón: Cooperatives, politics and working-class life in a Basque town.* Albany: SUNY Press.

Kohn, A. (1986). *No contest: The case against competition.* Boston: Houghton-Mifflin.

Mander, J., & Goldsmith, E. (1996). *The case against the global economy.* San Francisco: Sierra Club.

Moye, A. M. (1993). Mondragón: Adapting co-operative structures to meet the demands of a changing environment. *Economic and industrial democracy, 14,* 251–276.

Rosenthal, P. (1984). *Words and values: Some leading words and where they lead us.* New York: Oxford University Press.

Rothschild-Whitt, J. (1979). The collectivist organization: An alternative to rational-bureaucratic models. *American Sociological Review, 44,* 509–527.

Satow, R. L. (1975). Value-rational authority and professional organizations: Weber's missing type. *Administrative Science Quarterly, 20,* 526–531.

Sayer, D. (1991). *Capitalism and modernity: An excursus on Marx and Weber.* London: Routledge.

Schmookler, A. B. (1993). *The illusion of choice: How the market economy shapes our destiny.* Albany: State University of New York Press.

Stohl, C. (1993). European managers' interpretations of participation. *Human Communication Research, 20,* 108–131.

Stohl, C., & Cheney, G. (1997). *Paradoxes and contradictions of workplace democracy and employee participation.* Unpublished manuscript in progress.

Weber, M. (1978). *Economy and society* (2 vols.). Berkeley: University of California Press.

Weick, K. (1979). *The social psychology of organizing* (2nd ed.). Reading, MA: Addison-Wesley.

White, J. B. (1984). *When words lose their meaning: Constitutions and reconstitutions of language, character, and community.* Chicago: University of Chicago Press.

Whyte, W. F., & Whyte, K. K. (1991). *Making Mondragón: The growth and dynamics of the worker cooperative complex* (2nd ed., rev.). Ithaca, NY: ILR Press.

# CHAPTER 5

## There's No Smile on Your Face, Brother John

### The Trials and Tribulations of Human Service Work

KATHERINE MILLER

Brother John stared at the pile of paper, files, books, and forms arrayed before him. "There's a desk under there somewhere, and I'm going to find it," he muttered. As the director of Pathways, a shelter for homeless men in the downtown area of a southwestern city, Brother John often found himself buried under an avalanche of paperwork. Pathways was founded in 1986 by the Catholic church as a community outreach program. Now entering its 10th year of service, the shelter provided beds to sleep in and evening meals for men who were "down on their luck." After a 1-week stay at Pathways, however, the men had to be moved along into transitional housing or into a different emergency shelter. Otherwise, they would end up back on the street. In addition to the basics of food and a bed, Pathways tried to help the men out in other ways, such as providing mail service, showers, phones, health referrals, job-training options, and drug and alcohol programs. Brother John had worked with Pathways since its founding—indeed, he had been the driving force behind the establishment of the shelter. For him, providing a stopping point for men in need was the most important kind of ministry that could be provided.

Brother John sighed, gulped down his coffee, and attacked the chaos on his desk. At the top of the pile was a memo from his overseeing Board of Directors. Apparently there were funding changes on the horizon. Though Pathways had always avoided funding sources outside the church and private donations, it looked like the board now wanted him to look into other avenues as well. Below this memo was a notice from the local homelessness alliance regarding an upcoming breakfast meeting. Brother

John checked his calendar. That day was full, but he penciled in the breakfast anyway. He believes it is critical to work with other agencies serving the homeless, and these breakfasts were great opportunities for networking. Brother John felt the tendrils of a headache starting behind his eyes as he glanced at the next letter in the pile. "Big Al" (of "Big Al's Used Car" fame) was once again complaining about "vagrants" from the shelter hanging out around his car lot. Big Al claimed that men loitered around the cars while waiting for dinner to be served at the shelter. Brother John shook his head. As far as he knew, his clients at the shelter were staying clear of local businesses, but he understood how explosive the situation could be. He'd just have to swallow his pride and pay Big Al a conciliatory visit. The next piece of paper was also depressing. A phone message from an administrator at the local hospital suggested a meeting to discuss "procedures" for handling homeless patients. "Just what homeless people need," thought Brother John. "More 'procedures' to make them feel like so many cattle going through the system."

This line of thought was interrupted by a quick knock at his office door. Before Brother John could say anything, Andrea Jensen, Pathway's assistant director, strode into the room. Not surprisingly, the always-organized Andrea had a list of items to discuss. "First," said Andrea, "we're having problems with the parish leaders at St. Gregory's. They signed up for Thursday night dinners for the next three months, but apparently they're having trouble getting enough volunteers. Gina's looking into getting another parish to help out or finding another set of volunteers to shore that night up. Second, we found drugs by the cot John Anderson slept in last night. I'm not particularly surprised about the drugs, but we need to do something about our check-in and inspection procedures. Perhaps you could talk to Chuck and Howard about it. Third, there's a family outside— with five kids, no less —that needs a place to stay tonight. I called over to the downtown shelter, and they're already full. Any ideas?"

"How about checking with the Methodist Ministries?" Brother John replied.

"Good thought," Andrea said, as she jotted a quick note to herself. "Let's see, fourth is we've got problems getting transportation to the urban work program some of the guys have been involved in. The bus routes have changed, so we need to work out some alternative. Oh, and last but not least, Rosa quit. We need to find a new receptionist."

Brother John put his head in his hands. "Not again! That's the third receptionist in as many months! Did she say why?"

Andrea finally sat down, after moving a pile of files from the only unoccupied chair in the room. "The usual litany of complaints. Clients are rude, the hours are long, the pay is lousy, the benefits are nonexistent. It isn't exactly a dream job, you know."

"I know, but this isn't exactly a dream world we live in, either. These men don't want to be on the street, you know, despite what some members of Congress think. All we can do is try to help them in whatever way we can. I feel like we're just a Band-Aid, and that's depressing, but sometimes people need Band-Aids until they can find more permanent solutions." As Brother John warmed to his topic, he began to stride around his small office. "This is frustrating work, but it's important work, too. If only we could find better ways to provide the service, better ways to coordinate our efforts, better ways to show that we care, better ways to. . . ."

Andrea started to laugh. "Slow down, John! You're preaching to the converted!" Brother John sheepishly returned to his chair. "Seriously, I agree with you. But I can understand how Rosa feels. Maybe I've been in this business too long, but I can't help but wonder if we're doing any good at all. The more men we help, the more that show up needing our help. And I'm not alone. Everyone around here is starting to feel that frustration. They might not all be quitting like Rosa, but we're all starting to fray around the edges."

"Then we need to get back on track," said Brother John with conviction. "Tell you what. We'll have a staff retreat. We'll talk through these issues and rejuvenate ourselves. Maybe next Saturday. Check with everyone on their schedules, talk to the church office about a good place, and . . . and . . . just get it organized, okay?"

As Andrea left the office, she was already making a new list. "Next Saturday it is, chief."


## THE RETREAT

Brother John looked around the room. The meeting room at St. Timothy's wasn't the poshest setting in the world, but it was comfortable enough and all that Andrea could scare up at the last minute. The Pathways staff was beginning to gather in the chairs set up around the room. There were 10 staff members, including Brother John and Andrea. Gina Houghton, the volunteer coordinator, sat next to Andrea. Gina had been working at the shelter for 4 years—almost as long as Andrea—and they were very close, both professionally and personally. Their heads were close together as they caught up on recent gossip. Andrea and Gina looked up as Chuck Morton sat down in an adjacent chair. Chuck was the shelter supervisor during daytime hours. He'd only been with Pathways for 6 months and was still trying to get to know the people and procedures. Gina and Andrea tried to include him in their conversation, but the easy flow of their interaction ceased.

Next to arrive were Hannah Melendez, Joe Ortiz, and Natalie Simpson. Hannah, Joe, and Natalie were Pathway's three caseworkers. They all had degrees in social work from the local university and had been at Pathways for less than 2 years. Though they weren't particularly close on a personal level, their shared experiences made them stick together at work. Finally, Howard Lefkowitz, Ann Trenton, and Jackie O'Donnell straggled in. Howard was the night supervisor at the shelter and had been with Pathways for 6 years. Ann had supervised the kitchen for the preceding 18 months. And Jackie had just joined Pathways as a bookkeeper. Howard, Ann, and Jackie all found seats apart from the others and sat quietly, waiting for the retreat to start.

Brother John stood up and cleared his throat. The others looked up at him expectantly. "I suppose you've all wondered why I've called you here today," he began, and the staff members chuckled a bit. The ice somewhat broken, John went on. "As you all know, we do terribly important work at Pathways. Homelessness is a national problem of momentous proportions. Some people say there are as many as 3 million homeless people in America today. But the problem of homelessness can only be addressed at the local level—one person at a time. As we all know, helping people in need isn't always easy. There aren't simple solutions, and the homeless don't always want the kind of help we can give. But that doesn't mean we can't work to improve the quality of service we provide at Pathways. And that's why we're all here today. We're going to try to get back the edge some of us have lost, and we're going to talk about ways to improve the way our shelter runs in order to help men get off the street for good." John paused, and picked up a file folder from the table beside him. "To that end, I've prepared a little agenda of issues we should talk about today. Why don't you all take a moment to look this over, and then we can get started."

John passed the papers around to everyone in the room. He gave his staff a few minutes to review the agenda, then cleared his throat. "Okay, as you can see from the agenda, I thought it would first be helpful to review some of the national trends and statistics with regard to the homeless. It's only by understanding the clientele we're dealing with and the array of services available to them that we can provide optimally for their needs." John glanced up from his papers and looked at his staff. Gina and Andrea looked at him expectantly, Chuck stared down at the agenda, and Jackie and Ann were looking vacantly across the room. However, Hannah, Joe, Natalie, and Howard stared back at him with barely concealed animosity.

John looked at his angry staff members. "Is there something wrong? Why do you all look so upset?"

There was silence for a moment, then Hannah spoke up. "This agenda is what's wrong. Item 1—the homeless in America. Item 2—services available to the homeless. Item 3—local agencies and opportunities. Item 4—coordinating for optimal service. Item 5—effective interaction with clients. Item 6—conclusions and wrap-up."

John was confused. "So what's the problem?"

"The problem," Hannah replied, "is that when Andrea told us about this meeting she said that there was concern about turnover, that there were worries about how *we* were coping with our jobs. Then we get here and all you want to talk about is the homeless. I deal with the homeless one-on-one for hours every day. I'm burned out from dealing with the homeless. I want you to deal with *me.*"

John was honestly perplexed. "But that's what we're doing. I know we're burned out, so we need to refocus our energy on what's important. On who we're working for and why we're doing this in the first place."

Hannah sat shaking her head. "You just don't get it, do you. You want to refocus your staff, but you don't seem to understand that you won't *have* a staff unless we do something more radical than learn more about homelessness." Hannah looked around the room. "Don't you guys agree with me?" The heads around her began to nod, some vigorously, some almost imperceptively. But all were nodding.

John looked around. "Okay, Hannah, you've made your point." He ceremoniously dumped his copy of the agenda in a nearby trash can. "Let's start from scratch. Let's just talk about what's bugging all of you and see where we can go from there." John handed a piece of chalk to Andrea and pointed toward the chalkboard. "Will you do the honors?"

As Andrea approached the chalkboard, an uncomfortable silence came over the room. Finally John himself broke it. "Well, folks, what's bugging me is paperwork. Reams and reams of it. There's red tape for every client we serve, for every program we institute, for every service provider we talk to. And it just gets worse."

Andrea scribbled on the board and nodded in agreement. "He's hit the nail right on the head. That's the worst part of what we do. We fill out form after form after form, and we never even get to talk to the people we're trying to help."

At that comment, Hannah, Joe, and Natalie laughed in unison. Joe spoke up, "I suppose there is a lot of paperwork, but that's not what's stressful. It's when you *do* get to talk to the guys that the stress really kicks in. Brother John, I know you started out spending a lot of time on the street with your ministry. Don't you remember? Didn't the hopelessness of it all get to you? Didn't you get frustrated with people who couldn't or wouldn't help themselves? Didn't you get exhausted at the end of a day of talking to people with such depressing lives? Sometimes it's hard to get up in the morning knowing that there's another day of misery to be faced."

Natalie and Hannah nodded as Joe spoke, then Hannah broke in again. "Joe's right. I started this job with such high hopes. I was going to save the world—or at least my little part of it. Now sometimes it's all I can do to drag myself back to the shelter. And I know I'm not treating clients very well. I just get so frustrated with them and me that I find I have to shut myself off from them and quit giving so much all the time."

Andrea wrote "BURNOUT" in large letters on the chalkboard, then turned to the group of caseworkers. "But you can't quit! You can't turn your backs on these people. You must have chosen this career because you care about people—it certainly wasn't the high pay and good benefits." Everyone in the room laughed. "So if you lose that caring, you've lost the most valuable thing you can bring to your clients."

The caseworkers looked at each other, unsure of how to respond to Andrea's words, then Gina broke in. "Andrea, you're my best friend and I love you dearly. But quite frankly, you don't understand the stress that Joe and Natalie and Hannah go through. Sure, you've got a stressful job, too. You've got a lot of responsibility, a lot of information to deal with, a thousand things to get done every day. But it's a different *kind* of stress. I'll admit, I don't have it as bad as the caseworkers, but I think I get a taste of their problems just from dealing with the volunteers all the time."

Brother John looked up at the chalkboard. On it, in large letters, were the words "BURNOUT," "PAPERWORK," "RED TAPE," "DEALING WITH CLIENTS," and "CARING" (the last with a large question mark after it). He addressed the group. "Well, I think we're getting a feeling for some of our problems. But we haven't heard from everyone. Chuck, Howard, how about you guys? You're both on the 'front lines' of shelter management. How do you view the situation?"

Chuck cleared his throat nervously. "Well, I've only been here a few months, but I can certainly see the merit in the points everyone has made here. There is a lot of paperwork and it's tough to deal with the guys sometimes."

Howard let out a derisive snort. "Come on, you guys. Almost every job has paperwork. And almost every job has difficult people to deal with. I've been at this job for years, and you can adapt to all that. What's different about *our* jobs is that we're not paid worth a damn. I've got a college degree, I've been working at this job for more than 5 years, and I still make less than $25,000. I'd find something else to do, but the job market is tight, and, well, I guess I do care about the guys. But you shouldn't wonder why it's tough to recruit people and even tougher to hold onto them."

Ann nodded. "You've got that straight, Howard. But at least you get some variety in your work and you get to talk to people. I'm back in the kitchen all afternoon supervising all those church workers. No offense, but there's only so long you can stay inspired about getting a good deal on swiss steak and vats of potato salad."

As Andrea added "UNDERPAID" and "MONOTONY" to the board, Jackie finally spoke up. "You could probably throw in 'job security' on your list, too. I know Pathways needs a bookkeeper, but even in the few weeks I've been here, there's been talk of cutting my hours back. I'm only half-time as it is, so I don't know how well all of this is going to work for me."

The chalkboard was nearly full. "Well," said Brother John, "we clearly have more problems at Pathways than I knew about. It's also clear that not everyone suffers from the same difficulties. I came in here concerned about the quality of service we were providing, and I'm starting to realize how intimately that's tied up with the quality of care we provide for ourselves. Tell you what. I promised you we'd be out of here by noon, and I know a lot of you have plans for the afternoon. During the next few weeks, I'll schedule individual meetings with each of you, and we'll see what we can do to deal with this problem. Then, 4 weeks from today, we'll reconvene here. Andrea, can you make the arrangements?"

Andrea gave him a quick salute. "You've got it, chief."

## A LONG NIGHT

Almost a month later, Brother John sat in his office late at night. The shelter was quiet. All the men had gone to sleep, and all the staff was gone except Howard. John himself was extremely tired, but he knew he had a great deal of work ahead of him for the evening. The follow-up retreat he'd called for so cavalierly was scheduled for tomorrow, and he had little idea of what he would say to the Pathways employees. One thing that was clear, after extensive discussions with all the staff members, was that the problems at Pathways were complicated. Further, any solutions—if there were solutions to be had—were sure to be complicated as well.

Brother John decided to follow his usual course of writing things down when easy solutions didn't appear to him. He'd found over the years that the act of putting problems down on paper often helped him organize the issues and made alternative ways of dealing with the problems more apparent. He started with a blank sheet of paper and wrote "STRESSORS" at the top of it. He then quickly looked through his notes from the staff interviews and jotted down all the issues that had arisen. The list was depressingly long. Brother John leaned back in his chair and studied the list and found that, indeed, there seemed to be logical ways to group the stressors.

The first group of stressors he labeled "JOB BASICS." Included under this list were items such as long hours, low pay, poor benefits, and inadequate job security. Sadly, when he looked back over the interview notes, he found that *all* of the staff members had complained about one or more of these issues. Issues of pay and benefits were "top of the list" items for

Howard and for Ann, but they were also of critical importance to the social workers and to Gina, the volunteer coordinator. John wasn't surprised. Many of these people were highly educated, and he knew they could find work in other sectors that would pay them a great deal more. Take Gina, for instance. She had a degree in communication and had even taken some graduate course work. Her work as a volunteer coordinator entailed a tremendous amount of responsibility and required a great many organizational, persuasive, and presentational skills. Yet she was paid little more than an entry-level secretary in the private sector. The situation was similarly depressing for most of the Pathways staff.

A second set of stressors was grouped under the label of "ADMINISTRATIVE" on John's paper. These stressors included paperwork, work and information overload, high levels of responsibility, limited influence, and lack of results. Again, all staffers complained about these issues to one extent or another, but the people most bothered by these issues were Andrea, Gina, and the caseworkers. As John looked over the "ADMINISTRATIVE" list, he felt both familiarity and surprise. The familiarity sprang from the fact that many of these stressors were *his* stressors. The things that bothered him most about his work at the shelter were the red tape that came with human service programs, the overwhelming sense of doing a critical job that needed to be done, and the also overwhelming sense that the critical job was not being done effectively. What surprised John was the fact that many of his staff members noted frustration over the lack of influence they had over Pathways' policies and procedures. John had always thought he was an open supervisor, listening to what his staff had to say. But even Andrea, his "right-hand gal," finally admitted that she felt that her suggestions weren't taken very seriously. Her comment was, "I know you try to listen, but when it comes down to making a decision, you let your convictions override all of our comments. Maybe that's okay—you've certainly had more experience in this arena than we have—but there doesn't seem much point in contributing when the contributions aren't taken seriously."

A third column on Brother John's page was labeled "INTERACTION." There was only one item under this heading—talking to clients—but Brother John knew that the brevity of the list was not indicative of the importance of this kind of stress to his staff. The stressful nature of client interaction was noted by everyone but Jackie, and it was clearly an overriding concern of the caseworkers and Chuck, the day supervisor. Even Toni Lawrence, the new receptionist, complained about talking to clients after only 3 weeks of work.

Brother John looked through his interview notes to try to get a better handle on this problem. The usually quiet Natalie had been quite eloquent on the subject. "It's really a balancing act for me. Of course, I really care about the guys and want to do everything I can to help them get their lives back together. And so I talk to them and talk to them to try to really understand their perspective—to feel what they're feeling. But sometimes I go too far and their problems become my problems. I feel all their pain and can't get the distance I need to be helpful to them. But if I try to protect myself from that, sometimes I start thinking of my job and the guys in very cynical ways and I lose sight of why I do this kind of work. So, like I said, it's a matter of finding the perfect balance that will give them help and keep me sane—and it isn't always easy."

So that was one piece of the puzzle. But John's notes indicated that there were other aspects of interaction that led to stress for his employees. Chuck complained about interacting with men who didn't seem to really care about getting help and often couldn't answer simple questions or perform simple tasks. And Toni highlighted the anger of many clients. "I know I'm new to the job, Brother John, but some of those people are just plain mean to me." Brother John shook his head ruefully. "What homeless person doesn't have a right to a bit of anger," he thought. But he knew that interacting with these individuals was often far from rewarding.

These three categories—"JOB BASICS," "ADMINISTRATIVE," and "INTERACTION"—essentially exhausted the list of stressors that Brother John had on his list. And as he looked over these three categories of issues, Brother John felt depression start to settle in. Instead of wallowing in that depression, though, John went back to his interview notes and pulled out a fresh sheet a paper. He wrote "COPING STRATEGIES" at the top of this second sheet and went back to work combing through the information his staff had provided to him.

Brother John found that two columns would suffice for categorizing the coping strategies his staff had revealed to him. At the top of one column he wrote "PERSONAL COPING." Under this column went a wide array of tactics his staff used to cope with stress. These included exercise, prayer, good diet, adequate sleep, and time management strategies. He also noted that several staff member had talked about "having the right attitude," and he included this under the "PERSONAL COPING" list, as well. Natalie had commented on this in her discussion of the "balancing act" of casework. "If I can just get the right attitude toward clients—the right balance—I can deal with the stress of dealing with the homeless much more effectively. I've got to keep my head caring without letting my heart get overwhelmed."

After considering the second column of coping strategies, Brother John thoughtfully headed it "SOCIAL SUPPORT." There were many disparate items under this heading, though. For instance, all three caseworkers mentioned relying on each other when the work got tough. From the interviews, Brother John could see that this reliance ran the gamut from having someone to bitch with about difficult clients to learning about new programs that might be valuable to the homeless to taking over a client interview or even an entire work shift when the stress got to be too much. Gina and Andrea also seemed to provide a great deal of support to each other, though, Brother John thought, sometimes to the exclusion of others at Pathways. Several other employees mentioned how important it was to have a supportive spouse or a group of friends who could be relied on for fun activities and heart-to-heart talks. There were downsides to these support providers, however. As Chuck noted, "I talk to my wife a lot about this place, and it helps to talk with her. But, quite frankly, she doesn't know much about what goes on in a place like this, so her sympathy doesn't always count for a whole lot." Brother John was also disturbed that the interviews with several employees—Howard and Ann, for instance—were notable for their *lack* of mention of support received from others at Pathways or at home. Brother John began to move his attention away from this column of issues, then returned to it with a start. No one had mentioned receiving social support from him. This realization struck him more profoundly than any of his musings had to that point.

Brother John sat quietly. A great many stressors, but a great many ways to cope with those stressors as well. They would certainly have a lot to talk about at the retreat tomorrow. First, he could review the stressors on the list, sharing the organizing framework he'd developed with his staff. Then, he could list the coping strategies they'd shared with him and match up appropriate coping strategies with appropriate stressors. "I could match up the time management strategies with the overload stressors and the attitude tactics with interaction problems. Then we could consider social support from various people to deal with all of the stressors." Brother John pulled out yet another sheet of paper and started jotting down all of these ideas.

After a few minutes, the pace of his writing slowed, then stopped completely. He stared out the window into the darkness. "Haven't I learned anything from these interviews?" he chastised himself. Brother John went back to the sheet of paper headed with "COPING STRATEGIES" and added a third column beside the columns titled "PERSONAL STRATEGIES" and "SOCIAL SUPPORT." This third column was titled "ORGANIZATIONAL STRATEGIES." Brother John looked thoughtfully at this column. His staff members relied consistently on each other and on themselves to cope with the stresses of work at Pathways. "It's sad," Brother John thought. "For ten years I've worried about providing care for our clients, and for ten years I've complained about the stress I have to endure in providing that care.

Yet all that time I've been surrounded by a staff that I've not given a second thought to. Hopefully, it's not too late to change all that." Then he continued to work far into the night.

## THE SECOND RETREAT

Once again, Brother John looked around the meeting room at St. Timothy's. Once again, his staff looked up at him expectantly as he stood by the chalkboard. "As you might imagine," he began, "I've thought a great deal about our problems since we last met. Talking with all of you has been a real eye-opener. I used to only see the great rewards of working with the homeless and my own frustrations in providing care to them. But I now see all of the stress you people have endured. And I now see how much you've relied on your own wits and each other in dealing with that stress. And I now see how blind I've been about things I could do to help you. So, now that my eyes are open, let me take this opportunity to shut my mouth for a change and let you tell me things that I could do to reduce the cost of caring at Pathways."

Brother John sat down. For an uncomfortably long time, there was silence. But true to his word, Brother John kept quiet. And soon the room was buzzing, and the chalkboard was filling up once again.

## KEY TERMS

APPRAISAL-FOCUSED COPING: A personal coping strategy that involves changing the way one thinks about the stressful situation.

BURNOUT: A chronic condition that results as day-to-day work stressors take their toll on an employee. Especially prevalent in human service occupations.

DETACHED CONCERN: Feeling for a client and communicating concern for them while being emotionally objective. A helpful strategy for dealing with the interaction stresses of human service work.

EMOTIONAL SUPPORT: A function of social support that involves letting another person know that they are loved and cared for by boosting their self-esteem and/or providing them with a way to vent feelings.

EMOTION-CENTERED COPING: A personal coping strategy that involves dealing with the negative affective outcomes of burnout.

INFORMATIONAL SUPPORT: A function of social support that involves the provision of facts and advice.

INSTRUMENTAL SUPPORT: A function of social support that involves the provision of physical or material assistance.

PROBLEM-FOCUSED COPING: A personal coping strategy that involves dealing directly with the causes of burnout.

STRESSORS: Aspects of the work environment that can lead to negative psychological, physiological, and organizational outcomes.

WORKLOAD: A workplace stressor that refers to having too much work, too little work, or work that is too difficult.

## DISCUSSION QUESTIONS

1. If you were a staff member at Pathways, what would you tell Brother John about things he could do to help relieve your stress? What organizational and administrative strategies could work in ways that personal coping and social support cannot?
2. In what ways is the stress of human service work different from stress in other types of work? What stressors are shared among the majority of organizational settings?
3. Brother John developed an extensive list of stressors and an extensive list of coping strategies. Hopefully, you added to the list of coping strategies in responding to Question 1, above. Now consider ways you could match up stressors with coping strategies. Are there some coping strategies that are more appropriate to particular stressors? Are there some stressors that are unlikely to be reduced by *any* coping strategy?
4. Imagine that you were asked to design a program to help new workers adapt to human service occupations. What would you teach in this workshop? How could you maintain newcomers' idealism while warning them about the organizational realities they will encounter?

## SUGGESTED READING

Ashforth, B. E., & Humphrey, R. H. (1993). Emotional labor in service roles: The influence of identity. *Academy of Management Review, 18,* 88–115.

Hochschild, A. (1984). *The managed heart.* Berkeley: University of California Press.

Kahn, W. A. (1993). Caring for the caregivers: Patterns of organizational caregiving. *Administrative Science Quarterly, 38,* 539–563.

Maslach, C. (1982). *Burnout: The cost of caring.* Englewood Cliffs, NJ: Prentice-Hall.

Miller, K. I., Birkholt, M., Scott, C., & Stage, C. (1995). Empathy and burnout in human service work: An extension of a communication model. *Communication Research, 22,* 123–147.

Miller, K. I., Ellis, B. H., Zook, E. G., & Lyles, J. S. (1990). An integrated model of communication, stress, and burnout in the workplace. *Communication Research, 17,* 300–326.

Miller, K. I., Stiff, J. B., & Ellis, B. H. (1988). Communication and empathy as precursors to burnout among human service workers. *Communication Monographs, 55,* 250–265.

Pines, A. M., Aronson, E., & Kafry, D. (1981). *Burnout: From tedium to personal growth.* New York: Free Press.

Snow, D. R., & Anderson, L. (1993). *Down on their luck: A study of homeless street people.* Berkeley: University of California Press.

# CHAPTER 6

# Disciplining a Teammate
## Control in Self-Managing Teams

### JAMES R. BARKER

Liz couldn't remember the last time that she had been this angry at one of her teammates. She fumed all the way across town as she drove to work, snapping and cursing at the other drivers along the way. Liz was headed toward her job as a worker on a self-managing team at Technicom, Inc., a computer circuit board manufacturer. She pulled into the employees' lot at Technicom, parked, and looked out toward the early morning sun. She kept turning over in her mind the problems her team had dealt with the day before, problems caused by the absence of one of her coworkers, Sharon. Liz couldn't believe Sharon had missed work yesterday and had called in late with an excuse on top of that. Sharon was a hard case on the team. She had a history of coming in late for work or of calling in at the last minute and asking for the day off to take care of personal business. Sharon was a single mother with two kids, one 3 and the other 5 years old. Getting to work at 7 A.M. each day was a big challenge for her. Liz and the other team members could appreciate Sharon's problems, but the team had a job to do. They had their own important commitments and priorities. Circuit boards had to be built and customer orders had to be filled. The team was rapidly tiring of Sharon's problems and excuses.

For Liz, the day before had been the last straw. Nothing had gone right all day long. Liz's team was already shorthanded because two team members had started their vacations on Monday. Then Sharon didn't show up for work at 7 A.M. The team had a rule that if a member had to miss work, that person would call in within 15 minutes of the start of the workday. At 7:20 Sharon called to say that one of her kids was sick (again!) and that she would have to stay home with her. Martha took the call. She hung up the phone and turned to the rest of the team, "Well, well, well, bet you can't guess who that was."

When a problem arose, such as a team member having to miss work at the last minute, the Deltas would always pull together and get the job done. They had done it before and they would do it today. But at 10:30, they ran headlong into an unexpected crisis. Ron, the plant manager, came running into the team's work area and said that he had just received an emergency order from their best customer. The team's best customer *always* had top priority. The Deltas would have to get this order manufactured and out the door that day! Liz's team quickly agreed to drop everything and shift work to that project. With Sharon missing, the rest of the team pulled together to pick up the slack. The team skipped most of their breaks during the day and only took a few minutes for lunch. Katia and Steven doubled up to package the boards as fast as they could. The two hardly said a word to each other that wasn't about doing the work, except when they grumbled about Sharon's absence.

To top it off, the team had to work 2 hours overtime to finish the order. This meant that the workers had to scramble madly both to get their work done and to take care of their after-work personal business. Martha had to cancel dinner with her neighbors. Jaime spent over half an hour on the phone trying to find someone to meet his kids after school; finally a cousin volunteered to stay with them. When Lee called her husband and told him that she would have to work late, he yelled back, "You're always working late. Why do you care so much about that lousy job?"; a bad fight ensued.

The customer's order got shipped, but at no small cost to the team. They were burned out, but everyone on the team knew that they had to be back promptly at 7:00 A.M. the next day and committed for another day of hard work. Wearily, they left the plant for their homes. Ron met them at the door to congratulate them on getting the order out, but the workers were too tired to care about praise. They had something else on their minds. Martha, Jaime, Lee, Katia, Steven, and the rest of the team were just as mad as Liz. And Sharon was the target of their anger.

Liz, angry and exhausted from the previous day's hard work, looked toward the plant entrance. "It's high time Sharon learned her lesson about working on our team." She got out, slammed her car door, and headed into the Technicom plant. It was 6:50 in the morning, Thursday, June 17. The regular morning team meeting would start in 10 minutes. The Deltas always took time at these meetings to discuss (and correct) any problems that members had with the work behavior of their teammates. Today, Liz had a problem, and she was going to see that it got fixed.

Liz, Martha, Jaime, Lee, Sharon, Katia, Steven, and five other people all worked on the Delta Team, one of five self-managing teams at Technicom. Manufacturing circuit boards for computers requires close attention to detail. Workers assemble these circuit boards by carefully placing small diodes, potentiameters, and fuses into certain positions on a piece of fiberboard about 3 inches by 5 inches. After assembly, the boards are run through a machine that solders the components onto the board. Then each board has to be tested for quality and, if necessary, repaired by hand. A small mistake, such as misaligning a diode by a fraction of an inch, could take an hour or more to repair and could cause a long delay in shipping the order, negatively affecting the team's customer service record. The work is not exactly "hard labor," but the need for constant, careful attention to the boards and the continual pressure to increase production and customer satisfaction creates its own high-stress working environment.

Technicom was a relatively small company with just over 80 workers in production. The plant sat in an industrial park on the southside of a midsized city in the western United States. The city was quite ethnically diverse and so were Technicom's manufacturing workers. Two-thirds were women.

About 2 years earlier, Technicom had restructured its production plant into teams of 10 to 12 workers and empowered them to manage themselves. Prior to this change, Technicom had been what was called a "traditional" manufacturing company. That is, the production plant consisted of several assembly lines. At the head of the line, a worker would take a blank board and put in several components, then send the board down the line to another worker who put in several more components. When the board reached the end of the assembly line, someone else took it to the soldering room. After soldering, the board went to a different part of the plant where another group of workers did quality testing and repairing. After that, the board went to a shipping area where somebody else packaged it and sent it to a customer.

In this environment, each worker had a particular task to do, such as assembling particular diodes onto the board or testing the boards for quality. Each worker did his or her job and that was that. For example, once diodes were inserted on a board, the worker who had inserted them never saw it again. Work was controlled by four levels of supervisors. Each assembly line had a line lead, who was the first-line supervisor responsible for getting the boards assembled on time and sent to the soldering room. Another first-line supervisor ran the soldering room, another the testing and repair area, and another the packaging and shipping area. These supervisors reported to a shift supervisor, who managed all the manufacturing aspects of that particular shift (the company usually worked two shifts). The shift supervisors reported to the production manager, who ran the entire manufacturing operation. The production manager reported to the vice president of operations, who was very rarely seen out on the shop floor.

But now things were different. Technicom's plant had been reengineered into five work areas for five self-managing teams. Each team was responsible for all the tasks required to assemble a board, test it, package it, and send it off to the customer. The line leads and shift supervisors had disappeared. The teams supervised their own work, and each team now reported directly to the plant manager. Technicom was a self-managing company.

## SELF-MANAGING TEAMS AT TECHNICOM

The *self-managing team* innovation has been the most popular organizational restructuring program since the late 1980s, although the concept itself has been around for a long time (Barker, 1993). Over the last few years a number of very influential business consultants, such as Peter Drucker, have touted teams as *the* way of working for the future. Also, contemporary management scholars and practitioners have argued that team-based manufacturing was much more productive and much less expensive than traditional ways of managing work. For executives at companies such as Technicom, who found themselves facing stiff competition and the need to cut costs by restructuring, self-managing teams looked to be a sure bet.

The basic premise of self-managing teams is simple: Employees can effectively control their own work if supervisors give them the chance. The team concept, as we see it today, has two roots. The first root lies in the influence of Japanese management systems on Western organizations. In the increasingly high-tech global marketplace, Western business executives find themselves needing to offer a high-quality product in order to stay competitive. They look to Japan's experience and see a direct connection between high-quality products and employee commitment to the company's success. Employees increase their commitment to the company's success when they are "empowered," that is, when senior management allows and encourages everyday workers to participate more in decision making about how work gets done. For example, in the 1980s many Western companies formed "quality circles" in which workers met to discuss ways to improve product quality. When a company adopted quality circles, they set the stage for a later conversion to self-managing teams.

The second root of self-management lies in a collection of experiences and experiments in teamwork from Western countries, such as Scandinavia and the United States, that usually appear under the headings "workplace democracy" or "semiautonomous teams." These experiences indicate that today's workers really do not need close supervision to do a good job. Many contemporary employees, when compared to workers of preceding generations, are very well educated and can readily learn not only how to direct their own work but how to work together effectively in groups as well. Besides, supervisors cost a company a lot of money in salaries, training, and benefits.

The increasingly technological demands of today's working environment also influence the need for teamwork. In today's high-tech and fast-paced world of faxes, voice mail, e-mail, teleconferences, and various forms of computer-assisted communication, workplace decisions have to be made very quickly. Workers do not have the time to send an idea up the chain of command and wait around for an executive to pass judgment and send the decision back down to them. Today's organizations need workers to act quickly and effectively. Self-managing teams can do that.

By the mid-1990s, the concept of self-management had spread far and wide across Western work organizations. Everybody was talking "teams" and "teamwork." Even academic and governmental organizations were jumping on the team bandwagon. As the consultants had predicted, teams had become *the* way to go, and Technicom had already gone.

Ron, Technicom's plant manager, was very happy with the company's conversion to teams. Before the change to teams, Technicom had really struggled. Productivity had declined, and customer orders had lagged for almost 2 years. The company president and the operation's vice president knew that Technicom had to do something dramatic if it were going to stay in business. They turned to self-management as the answer, and about 3 years earlier, they had directed Ron to implement teams in the production plant. They told Ron that the company had to change to teams, cut costs, and increase productivity to survive. Ron had to make it happen. And he did.

Ron had needed a year to plan and prepare for the change. He figured out how to reengineer the plant and designed all the training needed to prepare the workers, including training in teamwork skills. Ron had started implementing self-management 2 years earlier with five new manufacturing teams. The workers needed about 9 months to get all the kinks out of the new operation, but after that, productivity dramatically increased.

When he started the teams, Ron had completely reorganized the plant and configured five different production areas for his new teams. Each of these five teams was responsible for building different types of circuit boards. Further, each team was completely responsible for every aspect of building their boards: assembly, soldering, testing, repair, packaging, and shipping.

Since the new teams worked on their own boards from start to finish, the team members had to learn all of the jobs required in making a circuit board. Former assemblers had to learn how to do quality testing. Repairers had to learn how to package. Packagers had to learn assembly. Each team was completely interdependent. The team members had to support and work with each other for the team to meet their production demands.

At the same time, Ron also eliminated the line lead and shift supervisor positions. The chain of command now went directly from the teams to Ron. The old line leads became regular workers on the teams, while the shift supervisors took new jobs in production support. Now the teams had to make their own decisions, direct their own work, and coordinate within and among each other.

## CONTROLLING A SELF-MANAGING TEAM

Liz and the rest of the workers on her team did do well in their new role as mates on the Delta Team, but it was not a piece of cake. The team had to struggle hard as they learned how to work together. There was no line lead or shift supervisor around anymore to make decisions for them or to chew someone out for doing a bad job. They had to do those things for themselves. They had a schedule of customer orders, and they had to figure out how to get their boards assembled, tested, and shipped on time. They had to learn new ways of communicating with each other, new ways that would allow them to direct their own work.

What the teams did was create a new system of control. The old line leads and shift supervisors had been a key part of Technicom's traditional system of control before the change to teams. They provided *direction* to the workers (told them what to do and when). They *monitored* the workers' performance (ensured that they did the work that the company needed to do). And they provided the *discipline* necessary to make the system work (rewarded workers who did good work and punished workers who did not perform well so that everyone would do good work; see Tompkins, 1990).

Technicom's new self-managing teams had to create a fundamentally different system of control, a system of self-control to replace the hierarchical control provided by the old line leads and shift supervisors. The new teams had to figure out how to manage themselves. They had to learn how to direct their own work, how to monitor their own performance, and how to discipline each other.

This new system of control that arises in a self-managing team environment is called *concertive control* (Barker, 1993; Tompkins & Cheney, 1985). This term refers to the fact that the team members must work "in concert" with each other to develop a method for controlling their own work. Concertive control differs considerably from traditional forms of hierarchical control. In these systems, supervisors and managers do the monitoring, directing, and disciplining, as had been the case at Technicom before it changed to teams. In a concertive system, though, the team assumes all these responsibilities.

Self-managing teams develop a system of concertive control by agreeing on particular *values* that indicate what the team ought to do and ought not to do if it were going to be effective. That is, the team members had agreed on a set of values that they could all understand as being important factors in their ability to do good work as a team. The Delta Team had agreed on a number of values for doing good teamwork: They should give their best customer's orders top priority. They should make sacrifices to support the needs of the team. They should all speak candidly and openly at team meetings, which they called "saying your piece." They should check each other's work. They should all arrive at work on time; and there were a number of other values.

Self-managing teams further develop a concertive control system by turning these shared values into behavioral *norms*. For a team, norms are the practical side of values. They represent how the team's members can behave in accordance with their shared team values. Thinking about what one ought to do is thinking about a value. Behaving in a way one ought to behave is behaving according to a norm. The agreement that the Delta Team should always build its best customer's orders first is an example of a team value. The team choosing to build their best customer's order before a lesser customer's order is an example of a norm. The Delta Team also had a value for sharing information at meetings. They expressed this value in norms by holding regular meetings and by expecting each of the teammates to say their piece at the meeting.

Just as the Deltas, and the rest of Technicom's teams, had agreed on a number of team values, they also created a number of team norms. They had a norm that everyone should be at work promptly at 7 A.M. They had a norm that all the team members would support the final decision of the team whether they liked it or not. They had a norm that all the team workers should learn all the job tasks required in building circuit boards. A team member who had been an assembler before the change now had to learn how to test, repair, and package finished boards.

*Rules* are the final element in a concertive control system. Rules represent formalized norms and are most often written down in some manner, such as a team code of conduct. Rules are specific, clear, and constitute a binding contract for the team members. Rules are most helpful for new members who join a team after its formation. These new members cannot quickly grasp the underlying values and norms that characterize the team's way of working, but they can easily understand rules.

The Deltas had also created a number of team rules. Team members were required to work overtime when it was necessary. The team held a 20-minute meeting each morning. At this meeting they would discuss the following topics in sequence: that day's schedule, who would do what work, who would coordinate which resources, problems that team members had with each other's job performance, and, last, announcements. The team members took 15-minute breaks precisely at 9:30 A.M. and at 1:30 P.M. If a team member had to miss work for a personal emergency, that worker had to notify the team no later than 7:15 A.M. The Delta Team had made a number of rules such as these. All of them were very specific and very easy to understand.

These values, norms, and rules meant that a concertive control system was working at Technicom. The team members could use their values, norms, and rules to direct their work, to indicate for them what they ought to do and how they ought to do it. Since they were a team that worked together closely, they could easily monitor how well they each obeyed the team's norms and rules. If somebody slipped up, if they violated a norm or broke a rule, the team disciplined them. That was why the rules for team meetings set aside time to talk about any problems the team members might have with a teammate's job performance. The Deltas fixed these problems at the team meeting in front of everyone.

The Delta Team's system of concertive control had been working well for them. The team members knew what they were supposed to do to be good team members, and they made sure that everyone toed the line. Sometimes, though, a worker didn't always do the right thing in the eyes of the rest of the team. Which brings us back to Sharon.

## THE INCIDENT

The Deltas felt very strongly that a team member should arrive at work on time and make sacrifices to support the needs and goals of the team. For the team to get its work done, it needed everybody in place and ready to go at 7 A.M. With everybody on time for the team meeting, the Deltas could make good decisions about the work schedule and the coordination or problem solving that they needed to do that day. Being on time in the morning and making sacrifices for the good of the team were essential for the Deltas to direct their own work.

In the 2 years since the change to teams, the Deltas had dealt with a number of problems concerning workers coming in late. That was why they now had a number of team rules that governed tardiness.

If a team member arrived for work 5 minutes late, the team would write up a memo about this occurrence and put it in his or her file. A team member who came in 5 minutes late more than three times in a 30-day period was disciplined by being docked 3 hours' worth of wages as a penalty. To monitor the team member's punctuality, the Deltas drew up a big chart and put it on one of their area's walls. This chart showed who had and had not come to work on time each day of the current month. A team member who had to miss work because of a personal emergency was required to call in by 7:15 A.M. That way the team could deal with the situation during its morning meeting. Anyone who called in after 7:15 was disciplined by having some of his or her pay docked.

Everybody understood these rules for being on time and why they were important for the team. Almost everyone obeyed them most of the time. No one wanted to be called on the carpet at a team meeting. The team was tolerant of a lapse here and there. For example, the team would forgive being caught in traffic once in a while as long as the guilty team member accounted for the lateness to everyone during the next meeting. What the team would not tolerate, however, was someone establishing a pattern of being late. That was what Sharon had done.

Sharon arrived late for work at least once and often twice each week. The team was monitoring her behavior carefully. The week before she had told Martha, "You know, I feel like you all are watching over me all the time. I can't even go to the bathroom without you all timing how long I'm gone."

Martha had replied, "Well, we wouldn't have to do that if you would just follow our rules."

The team had tried to help Sharon as much as they felt they could. They knew she had problems getting to work on time, but she was not the only single parent on the team. Her problems weren't different from those of any other team member. They had recently given her a whole week off when one of her kids had the flu. But she kept coming in late. The team tried a few minor disciplinary actions, but that did not solve the problem.

Then came the most recent incident. Sharon's 5-year-old, Marie, had woken up too sick to go to school. Sharon had tried up until the last possible minute to arrange for someone to sit with the child, with no luck. She had noticed that her kitchen clock read 7:03 A.M. when she was on the phone pleading with a relative to watch Marie for her. The next thing Sharon knew it was 7:20 and she hadn't called in. It was too late.

## THE TEAM MEETING

All the problems caused by Sharon's absence the preceding day had finally pushed Liz and the rest of the team to the breaking point. Shortly before the meeting time, the team members began assembling, still tired and angry. Sharon made it just at the stroke of 7. No one else on the team acknowledged her presence, and she didn't look at them either. She sensed what was coming.

The team went over the day's schedule. No one mentioned the problems of the day before. They were waiting for the appropriate point in the meeting to discuss Sharon's problem. The team talked about work assignments for the day and how they would have to coordinate for the soldering room with the Beta Team. With the coordinating done, the meeting had reached the point for discussion of behavior problems. Liz stood up. Sharon drew in a breath and looked down.

Liz took a couple of steps toward Sharon and said forcefully, "Do you have any idea what kind of problems you caused for us yesterday?" Sharon continued to look down. "Well, do you?"

Martha joined in, "We had to work overtime because of you. We couldn't take lunch or anything. You know you're not the only single mother here. I can get to work on time. Why can't you?"

Katia followed, "This really hurt us bad. We almost missed a shipment for our best customer. Do you know what would have happened to us if we had missed that shipment? We might have lost their business. We have to do whatever it takes to keep our customers happy."

Steven took his turn, "You caused us a lot of trouble yesterday. We had to do a lot of extra work because of you. The rest of us pulled together. We sucked it up and got the job done. No thanks to you."

Liz walked a bit closer to Sharon, "Well, what have you got to say for yourself?"

Sharon's shoulders began to bob up and down. She was crying. "I'm sorry. I couldn't help it. It won't happen again." She didn't look up at Liz.

Liz continued, "We know it won't happen again, because you won't be working here if it does."

Steven spoke again, "We don't want to hear 'I'm sorry.' We want to hear a commitment to our team. Are you going to support us or not? Are you going to be a part of our team?"

Sharon was crying harder now. "It won't happen again. I promise. I promise."

Nobody said anything else for a while. They let her cry it out. Liz sat back down.

After a bit, Katia took out some tissues, handed them to Sharon, and said, "Look, we didn't want to hurt your feelings. We just want you to know how much we depend on you to be here. We have to be able to count on you."

"We wanted you to understand how you not being here yesterday affected the rest of us," said Liz softly. "We need you here, on time, every day." She echoed Katia, "We have to be able to count on you."

Martha said, "If we can't count on you, we'll let you go. It's as simple at that. We don't want to do that, but we will if we have to. We're a team here. We all have to work together. You have to support us. What's it going to be?"

Sharon dried her eyes. "Look, I know that I've had some problems, but I'll do better. You can count on me. I'll do better. I'll prove myself to you. I need this job. I really need this job."

Liz nodded, "We know."

Sharon continued, "I'll be on time. I won't have any more problems. I'll show you that I can be a good team member."

Steven had the last word. "All right, we'll be looking to see that."

The meeting was over. Everyone went to work. Boards were assembled, soldered, tested, repaired, packaged, and shipped to customers. Off and on during the day, several of the team members went up to Sharon and talked with her. They helped to soothe her wounds and tried to make her feel a part of the team again. By the end of the day, the team seemed to be back to normal, at least for the time being.

That evening Liz replayed the meeting as she drove home. She was sorry that the team had needed to discipline Sharon so harshly, but she did not feel guilty about it. "It had to be done. We're a team here. We have to work together. We all make sacrifices for the team," she told herself. Then her thoughts turned toward home and away from work for a little while. Seven o'clock would come soon enough.

## KEY TERMS

CONCERTIVE CONTROL: a system of organizational control that develops in team-based organizations. Concertive control refers to the team acting "in concert" with each other to develop a method for directing, monitoring, and disciplining their own work behavior. In self-management, teams develop concertive control through their shared values, norms, and rules.

DIRECTION: the first element of an organization's system of control. Direction refers to the orders or commands that managers use to tell workers how to do good work for the company. In self-management, teams provide their own direction through their shared values, norms, and rules.

DISCIPLINE: the third element of an organization's system of control. Discipline refers to the rewards or punishments that a manager uses to ensure that workers comply with the directives. In self-management, teams develop a means of disciplining themselves, usually through applying peer pressure and direct confrontation.

MONITORING: the second element of an organization's system of control. Monitoring refers to a manager's observing whether or not workers are complying with the directives. In self-management, teams develop a means of observing their own compliance with their values, norms, and rules.

NORMS: the practical side of values. Thinking about what one ought to do is thinking about a value; behaving in a way one ought to behave is behaving according to a norm. In self-management, norms represent how the team's members can behave in accordance with their shared team values.

RULES: formalized norms usually written down in some manner, such as a team code of conduct. Rules are specific, clear, and easy to understand. Rules also have a clearly defined penalty for the person that breaks them.

SELF-MANAGING TEAMS: an organizational innovation in which workers are organized into small groups and empowered to control their own work activity.

VALUES: an understanding of what ought to be done or ought not to be done in a particular situation. In self-management, teams reach a shared consensus on a set of values for doing good work on the team.


## DISCUSSION QUESTIONS

1. How does a self-managing team create concertive control?
2. What values are expressed by the team members, and how did these values become norms and rules?
3. How effective were the Delta Team's values, norms, and rules as a system of control?
4. How would a traditional first-line supervisor have disciplined Sharon? Was the team's method of disciplining Sharon more or less effective than what the former supervisor would have done?
5. Why was the team so aggressive in disciplining Sharon?
6. Was the Delta Team's treatment of Sharon fair or unfair? How so?
7. At what point should upper management intervene in a team's internal system of control?
8. What are the advantages and disadvantages of working in a concertive control environment such as self-managing teams?
9. What is your opinion of self-managing teams as *the* new way of working in today's organizations?


## REFERENCES AND SUGGESTED READING

Barker, J. R. (1993). Tightening the iron cage: Concertive control in the self-managing organization. *Administrative Science Quarterly, 38,* 408–437.

Drucker, P. F. (1994). The age of social transformation. *Atlantic Monthly, 247*(5), 53–80.

Hackman, R. J. (1986). The psychology of self-management in organizations. In M. S. Pallak & R. O. Perloff (Eds.), *Psychology and work: Productivity, change, and employment* (pp. 89–136). Washington DC: American Psychological Association.

Orsburn, J., Moran, L., Musselwhite, E., & Zenger, J. (1990). *Self-directed work teams: The new American challenge.* Homewood, IL: Irwin.

Parker, M., & Slaughter, J. (1988). *Choosing sides: Unions and the team concept.* Boston: South End Press.

Sundstrom, E., De Meuse, K., & Futrell, D. (1990). Work teams: Applications and effectiveness. *American Psychologist, 45,* 120–133.

Tompkins, P. K. (1990). On risk communication as interorganizational control: The case of the Aviation Safety Reporting System. In A. Kirby (Ed.), *Nothing to fear: Risks and hazards in American society* (pp. 203–239). Tucson: University of Arizona Press.

Tompkins, P. K., & Cheney, G. (1985). Communication and unobtrusive control in contemporary organizations. In R. D. McPhee & P. K. Tompkins (Eds.), *Organizational communication: Traditional themes and new directions* (pp. 178–210). Newbury Park, CA: Sage.

# CHAPTER 7

# The Utilization of Employee Assistance Programs at the Harding Company

DEBRA C. MAZLOFF

At least one-quarter of the United States workforce has job-related problems caused by nonworksite factors such as alcoholism, drug dependency, mental and emotional disorders, financial difficulties, family problems, or a combination of these and others (Besenhofer & Gerstein, 1991; Myers, 1984). According to the Corporation Against Drug Abuse, approximately 25% of all workers use drugs on the job and about 5% have serious addiction problems (Kittrell, 1988). Smith (1993) recently reported that a third of all employees are attempting to deal with family members' and coworkers' substance abuse. In addition to the traditionally acknowledged problem of drug dependency, organizations employ people who are being battered by spouses (Bryant, Eliach, & Green, 1990), who need to care for elderly parents (Ellis-Sankari, 1992), who feel incompetent or obsolete, and who experience serious levels of workplace burnout and stress (Walsh, 1991). Although some of these problems occur outside of the workplace, employees do not leave them at home when they go to work each day. These problems inevitably affect the quality of work and the quality of work life experienced.

These problems also cost organizations billions of dollars in lost performance due to absenteeism, accidents, grievances, turnover, and lower job satisfaction (Daly, 1993; Myers, 1984). Additionally, the healthcare crisis in the United States has forced organizations to protect against compensation claims and lawsuits (Katzman & Smith, 1989; Warner, 1987). Furthermore, the 1988 Drug-Free Workplace Act requires organizations that have federal grants or government contracts in excess of $25,000 to maintain a drug-free workplace through education, policies, and counseling (Cunningham, 1994).

In response to these problems, employee assistance programs (EAPs) have become the workplace standard. EAPs are "job-based programs operating within a work organization for purposes of identifying 'troubled workers,' motivating them to resolve their troubles, and providing access to counseling or treatment for those employees who need those services" (Sonnenstuhl & Trice, 1986, p. 1).

Today's programs offer more than alcohol or drug rehabilitation; they also offer counseling for issues such as depression, marital problems, financial difficulties, and eldercare. These enhanced programs are often referred to as "Broad-Brush Employee Assistance Programs" or "Employee Enhancement Programs" (Lubin, Shanklin, & Sailors, 1992) and share the original goals of EAPs to improve job performance, family life, and health (Shain & Groenveld, 1980).

## EMPLOYEE ASSISTANCE PROGRAMS

### Characteristics

Even though EAPs encompass much more than alcohol rehabilitation, dealing with issues such as marital problems, eldercare or child care, emotional problems, and legal and financial difficulties, they still work from the original premise: Supervisors are taught to identify troubled employees based on the employee's drop in job performance. The employees then are sent to programs that will hopefully motivate them to change the problematic behavior. Since it would be difficult to train supervisors to recognize the cause of these problems, they are often taught to focus solely on job performance (Sonnenstuhl, 1988).

To identify troubled employees and motivate them to take part in traditional EAPs, employees have been taught to use a strategy termed "constructive confrontation." Technically, supervisors, peers, or union stewards confront the troubled worker with evidence of unsatisfactory job performance, coach them on ways to improve work, encourage them to use assistance services, and remind them of the consequences of continued poor performance. This process continues either until the employee is rehabilitated or terminated. Along the way, the employee is encouraged to seek help through either in-house, community, or consortium assistance programs (Sonnenstuhl, 1988).

Along with supervisor referrals to the EAP, self-referral is often encouraged. In the late 1970s, voluntary EAPs sprang up because managers were reluctant to provide counseling training for supervisors. The assumption was that certified professionals would be better prepared to handle these problems. In this voluntary format, employees were made aware of the programs either by a supervisor or through other forms of education, and they chose to participate on their own. Today, managers are still taught to use constructive confrontation, but giving the employee the information needed to make his or her own decision is equally popular. Most organizations use a combination of self, supervisor, and peer referral (Sonnenstuhl, 1988).

Although traditional EAPs deal predominantly with existing problems, EAPs in the 1980s have also been seen as prevention programs (Miller, 1985). The idea is that EAPs should address the whole person. This approach moved the focus of EAPs from pathology to the overall wellness of the individual (Balgopal, 1989). This type is often referred to as "health promotion programs" (HPPs) or "wellness programs" (Coshan, 1991). The main purpose of these programs is to change and prevent employees' unhealthy living practices in an effort to improve the quality of work life as well as to save lives and lower healthcare costs (Conrad, 1987; Coshan, 1991). These programs provide education and training on issues such as weight control, stress, and cholesterol. HPPs work within the EAP framework by minimizing the need for constructive confrontation and highlighting the voluntary nature of these programs (Sonnenstuhl, 1988).

### Increased EAPs but Low Utilization

In 1970, there were fewer than 50 EAPs in U.S. businesses, but by 1986 more than 12,000 programs were available to more than one-third of the workforce (Blum & Roman, 1986). In the larger or more successful companies, EAPs are even more common. In 1990, 80% of Fortune 500 companies along with 20,000 other organizations used some form of EAP (Kelly, 1990). As societal pressures continue to build, there is reason to believe that EAPs will continue to grow (Sussal, 1992).

Although EAPs have become a popular choice by many U.S. organizations for meeting worker needs as well as for increasing productivity, utilization of the program by employees is often low. Employees generally are not aware of the program, of how to access services, and of whether they need to seek help (Masi & Friedland, 1988). In many cases, management implements an EAP and expects it to run itself with little support or money. In these cases, the program usually goes unnoticed and unused by employees.

Lack of awareness as a cause of low utilization rates has pushed many researchers to discuss the importance of improving communication about the EAP, although little relevant research has resulted. Instead, researchers merely speculate about its importance. An understanding of how information about an EAP is communicated seems to be an important springboard for understanding utilization better. The case study that follows attempted to answer questions of how employees at the Harding Company understood and communicated about their EAP as well as why they did not utilize the program more often.

A number of methods helped inform this case. Archival data such as posters, paycheck stuffers, and videos were collected. Observations of meetings in break room interactions and work areas produced an understanding of organizational members' work life.

Individual interviews, focus groups, and a survey also helped answer questions of what employees knew about the EAP and why they did or did not use the program. The description that follows results from a year-long study of Harding's EAP.

## THE HARDING COMPANY

The Harding Company[1] is one of the largest and most successful food distribution companies in the United States. It is consistently listed as one of *Fortune Magazine's* Top 50 Companies.

The Harding organization distributes merchandise to retailers nationally. The midwestern division distributes goods to stores in three surrounding states. The work performed varies by department, including transportation, distribution, retail services, and management. Work life varies between departments depending on the type of work done and the composition of its associates.[2]

The transportation department consists predominantly of union workers performing a number of duties. First, there are truck drivers, who either drive long distances over rural routes or drive within a metropolitan area. There are loaders, who load the merchandise onto the trucks, and hostlers, who move the cabs of the 18-wheelers to and from the different loads. Finally, utility people and mechanics service the sites and the trucks. These associates work 12-hour shifts, 3 days a week, generally starting at 4 A.M. or 3 P.M. Union employees bid for shifts, sites, and jobs based on their seniority. Each employee has performed most of the jobs in their area at one time or another and has worked at all of the different sites. Needless to say, this keeps associates in an unstable atmosphere with few connections to any specific supervisor because they are constantly changing shifts, sites, and at times, duties. The work schedules and overtime are heavily regulated by the Department of Transportation (DOT), which allows drivers to work no more than 10 hours a week overtime. Moreover, DOT regulations also require mandatory random drug testing once a month as well as mandatory alcohol awareness programs.

The distribution department also consists predominantly of union workers, who do a variety of manual warehouse jobs such as selecting orders for a load, driving forklifts, receiving orders from wholesalers, and repackaging merchandise. Unlike drivers, these associates are not regulated by the government, so they work 10-hour shifts, 5 days a week, with unlimited overtime. This results in little time off, and what time off they do receive is sporadic. For example, they may get every other day off or a half day off several days at a time. They are often expected to work 10 to 20 hours a week overtime during the busiest times of the year. The work is predominantly manual labor in warehouse conditions. These individuals are not subjected to the drug-testing policy; however, many associates think they also should be regulated since they also work with heavy equipment.

In addition to the drivers and warehouse workers, there are supervisors and superintendents who manage the individuals working on the floor and organize the delivery schedules. These associates are responsible for the coordination and supervision of approximately 100 truckloads delivered daily to different retailers throughout various midwestern states. They must also regulate trucks arriving with merchandise on an hourly basis. Although a few supervisors moved up through the ranks from driver to management, most have neither driven trucks nor worked in the warehouse. Unlike the union workers in transportation, they are not subject to DOT regulations, so they often work 12- to 14-hour days, 6 and 7 days a week. They generally take a day off when possible, but they rarely receive a full weekend off.

Most of the drivers and warehouse workers, who make up 60% of the organization, are members of the Teamsters Union. They take pride in this affiliation because they realize that the union has helped them get the benefits and pay they currently receive. Many supervisors feel that these associates think they work for the Teamsters rather than Harding. Many of the drivers concur, since they would have little trouble finding work elsewhere. A popular joke is that they could "just go down the street," since Harding's major competitor is located one block away. However, this is not the reality for the warehouse workers. They realize that they will not find work for the same pay and benefits in most places. In fact, many associates have worked for Harding for over 15 years, some even for 25 to 30 years. These individuals have job security and pensions coming from both Harding and the Teamsters. Many drivers whose jobs do not require long-distance drives that force them to leave their families for several days at a time also choose to stay with Harding for the same long tenures. Many consider this the ideal job for truck drivers.

The relationship between management and the union is tense. Both managers and union members believe that the union determines the structure of business. Although these opposing groups agree, neither is satisfied because they prefer decision making to occur mutually instead of in spite of each other. For example, management felt that the union took advantage of their influence and constrained decision-making power. One manager described the union's influence over they way work was performed as

> "just totally controlled by the union environment here, and rather than us being able to do the job the way it should be done, we have to do the job the way its going to benefit Joe Blow out there on the floor because of his seniority and the rules and what we've got ourselves into over the years with the policies established here. In contrast, union members believe that the union is responsible for better aspects of the job."

One associate said,

> "We are fortunate to have a union. We don't have no union to say that we can do this and that, it's not like that because if it wasn't for that then we would not have the jobs that we got, we wouldn't have the vacation that we get, a lot of things that we would not have."

In addition to union laborers, there are a number of professional or clerical associates who work long hours for a lot less pay than union workers receive. Clerks and professional associates are separate from the transportation and distribution departments, and in most cases they have very little interaction with laborers except when passing in the break room or at company events. These individuals work with wholesalers and retailers buying and selling goods. They have a more structured work schedule, generally working Monday through Friday from 8 A.M. to 5 P.M.

In addition to the professional and clerical associates, there is upper management, who coordinate Harding's midwestern division. Positions in this area include the division president, manager of human resources, controller, and data-processing manager. They work long hours, yet they keep schedules similar to the professional or clerical staff. Unlike their transportation counterparts, they report pride in working for Harding. Many have moved through the ranks into their current positions and have worked at other locations throughout the United States.

Harding's midwestern division has experienced a myriad of changes in its day-to-day operations as well as in its identity in recent years. One major change has been that employees no longer feel as if they are part of a family; instead, they feel as if they are a number. Management in the midwestern division was known, in the past, for taking a hands-on approach that contributed to a family atmosphere. One reason for this characterization was that the midwestern division was where Harding was founded in the early 1900s. Although today Harding does business in over 40 states, this is where one family began distributing products to customers throughout the midwestern states. The founder's son, Ned Harding, still worked at this location until his death in 1990. All employees knew Ned Harding as well as the history of the organization.

After Mr. Harding's death, corporate headquarters were moved to a new state and the original corporate offices were closed. Employees of the midwestern division were moved to a variety of locations with the goal of consolidating over 700 employees from five work sites into one. The results were a number of layoffs and even more transfers. One employee described the move as a very traumatic experience. She said,

> "It was very sad in the last weeks when we were still in Smith to know that almost every Friday someone else was leaving, that we wouldn't be seeing that person anymore. And, some of those people I had worked with for 19 years and that was really hard. It was. We had all become, like I said, we were close, [a] very close group of people and [we] worked well together and had fun together. It was sick."

With so many people located in one place, the rules were bound to change. The family atmosphere that had once been the pride of Harding associates was considered history. Associates in the cave[3] talked about the "divorce" their family was experiencing.

Another change Harding's midwestern division experienced was an organization-wide structural reengineering. The reengineering contributed to a number of changes in daily operations. Locations of offices, titles, jobs, and procedures changed. In addition to people being laid off, others were hired. The speed at which this all took place amazed most associates. One associate said,

> "When we started expanding so rapidly there was changes being made all the time and peoples' security was threatened, their security was threatened, clericals' security was threatened, jobs changed names and we needed less people here and more people there and so everybody was, you know. And what you had the whole time was turmoil."

One particular change that serves as an exemplar was management's introduction of a new punch-in system. Everyone was required to wear an ID badge with a seven-digit identification number. Many associates complained that it controlled flexible hours that supervisors used to be able to grant. For instance, one woman explained that she used to arrive an hour early to get her work finished so she could leave early. With the new numbers, she could punch in no more than 10 minutes early. Prior to reengineering, "Harding was a family, not a bunch of numbers," she said. For many associates, it seemed that the midwestern division no longer had autonomy with regards to day-to-day operations.

In response to all of the changes and turmoil, associates were asked to go far beyond a normal 9-to-5 day. A normal day could last 12 hours with very little time off. Managers felt an obligation to the organization to put in the time without time off regardless of the reason, while nonmanagement employees were often "drafted" to work overtime. One manager described his work load: "Today is my 7th day. The last time I worked 11 straight days and had 2 days off. I left here last night at 6:30, the day before they called at 8:00, called at 9:00, called at 3:00 A.M. and I was here at 4:00."

Managers described having to leave through entrances other than the loading dock if they really wanted to leave because several people tended to approach them with a problem. On the other hand, warehouse workers (the most overworked group) said they had to hide or lie to get some time off. During certain times of the year there was mandatory overtime, but still managers were asking them to put in extra shifts. When one associate was asked to work a longer shift, his response was "I got to sleep." Another individual said the thing he liked least about working for Harding was "the draft." He described it as "When you're home, you got your days off, and you're sitting at home and you answer the phone that they need you really bad, they draft you, that means you got to come to work." But he continued to explain, "You get smarter, screen your calls." Warehouse associates said they literally hid from Harding in fear that they would be pulled in for more overtime. As one driver stated, "If you didn't have laws and rules you never would get to go home. . . . Not so much in transportation, but warehouse people, hell, they work them to death." The change and turmoil constantly occurring at Harding seemed to cause management to pay less attention to associate's needs and much more attention to getting the job done.

An outsider might wonder why associates stayed with this organization for so long. Yet associates did stay. In fact, most associates had worked for Harding for over 10 years and in some cases over 20 years. Associates felt the pay and benefits were good, especially for those individuals who belonged to the union. However, many nonunion associates who worked in professional and clerical positions felt the same way.

One of the primary reasons people gave for staying with Harding was the supportive relationships associates had with one another. Although tense relationships existed on a daily basis, especially between the management and union members, most individuals said they always helped one another in emergencies. According to one associate, "Most of the people care, and they go out of their way to help you if they can." One interviewee gave an example of a woman whose house burned. Everyone contributed money and household items such as towels, clothes, and appliances. Coworkers collected money and the president donated a waterbed. In response to their help, the woman whose house burned down said,

> "They pulled 100% and helped me and that is, I am so happy for them, where I just can't express in words how they have helped me and what they did for me so far. I don't know if I could make it without their help."

In another instance, a clerk explained about a recent sick leave she took:

> "I've had an illness that's where I've been. This past year's been really hard on me and I've been off with surgery and stuff and they've been real good about that. . . . They just made me feel like my job was still going to be here, not to worry about not being able to come back to it or just that things were taken care of while I was gone, just stuff like that."

Although Harding associates felt the organization did not have the personal family-like atmosphere it once did, they still seemed to find that feeling within their departments or work groups. As one supervisor explained,

> "I work directly with people, with the drivers, I know them all very well, and I'll try to be on a more personal basis with them than just the business basis. Even though business is very important, I like to say, 'How's your family, how are you doing, how's Lonnie doing in football this year, did they win their game last night?' first and then I go to business."

Not only did supervisors try to get to know the people they worked with but employees worked with each other; a clerk explained whom she depended on:

> "The gal I work with, Jane, and I have become really good friends over the years that we've worked together and we work real well together. If one of us is having a really bad day, somebody can help out with it. Our boss is great, he really understands us. We can joke around with him."

Many employees said the personal relationships made work life at Harding easier and worth continuing, although many said work life at Harding was not easy. Associates were constantly faced with changes and turmoil. Their days were spent trying "to do more than one individual physically can." Partially the turmoil was the nature of the distribution business: Someone somewhere always needed something. In addition, Harding was trying to keep up with a changing work environment by staying competitive. Yet associates seemed to stay because they felt secure in their positions and because of good pay and benefits. Throughout most associates' extended tenure with this organization, they had made friends who, by all accounts, provided a great deal of social support.

These changes, and the nature of the work itself, were obviously stressful. Even though Harding associates reported varying degrees of support, they also reported instances of drug and alcohol problems (especially among the truck drivers), financial difficulties, management–union tensions, uncertainty, and mental and physical fatigue. These are just the kind of problems EAPs are designed to address, and Harding had a well-structured and free EAP; but ironically it had been ignored during recent years at Harding. Work life was considered hectic and tense, yet individuals still looked to one another for the help they needed. Given their problems, utilization of the EAP was especially low. This study was concerned with why.

## THE EAP AT HARDING

For all associates at Harding, an EAP is available to help them solve the problems that may arise in their lives. This program is contracted out to an EAP consortium that handles services for a number of organizations. To access the program, employees call a telephone number that will connect them with an EAP counselor. Regardless of the problematic issues, associates can go to a neutral location where they can receive counseling. This program offers services to employees and their family members for drug or alcohol addictions, marital issues, depression, financial or legal concerns, and any other stressors that may arise. Employees may use the program three times each year free of charge for each different issue. If an individual needs additional support, his or her health insurance in most cases covers the added expense. The EAP is confidential in that no one is notified, including the individual's family, unless the individual signs a waiver. The only individual at Harding who is notified is the manager of human resources. She is only told how many people use the program and for what reasons. No one's name is communicated unless the individual is in a treatment program that will keep him or her away from work. In these cases, the manager of human resources only knows the individual is using the program, but not why.

Two factors led to the decision to implement the EAP at Harding.

First and foremost, DOT and the Federal Drug-Free Workplace Act of 1988 required alcohol and drug awareness programs for associates at Harding who worked in transportation. The ability to provide awareness training was complemented well by having counseling made available to associates who needed it. In addition, like other organizations dealing with the high costs of turnover and healthcare, Harding saw the EAP as a way to keep trained associates on the job and to contribute to their well-being.

The EAP is made known to associates in a number of ways. When the program was first implemented five years ago, all associates attended small group seminars introducing the program through a talk by the president of the EAP consortium and a video. Currently, new associates are sent to an orientation meeting at which the EAP is introduced along with other benefits and, depending on time, a video is shown. A newsletter is sent out to all employees periodically as a paycheck stuffer. These newsletters address issues that may be currently affecting the organization; for example, coping with change. In addition, posters are placed throughout the work-site to emphasize the same troubling issues discussed in the newsletters. Finally, all union members are required to attend educational programs on drug and alcohol abuse due to government regulation affecting their industry. These programs also emphasize the availability of the EAP along with the drug education.

In addition to the EAP provided by the organization's management, the union has its own program called the Teamsters Assistance Program (TAP). This program works in a similar manner to occupational alcoholism programs, which were modeled after Alcoholics Anonymous's 12-step programs. In the TAP program, two teamsters, who are recovering alcoholics, provide support for the troubled union members by introducing them to rehabilitation programs as well as being "on call" for anything others may need (a place to stay, help during a relapse, someone to talk with). TAP acts more as a referral and support service than a counseling service. Like the EAP, this program offers referrals for union members troubled with alcohol and drug dependency, depression, marital disputes, and legal and financial problems. The TAP program works separately from the EAP, but it is also available to associates who are union members.

Even though there are a variety of ways the EAPs are promoted, annual associate utilization is approximately 2% of the eligible associates. This rate is low compared to the national average of 5% to 10% (Bayer & Barkin, 1990). The human resource manager said the low utilization was a function of the demographics of associates: They are predominantly middle-aged males working in labor jobs, a group of characteristically low users (Alexy, 1991; Steinhardt & Young, 1992). A number of other researchers have argued that a lack of communication contributes to a lack of utilization (e.g., Beyer & Trice, 1978; Harris & Fennell, 1988; Masi & Friedland, 1988; Olesen, 1986, Sonnenstuhl, Staudmeier, & Trice, 1988). From all reports, one might conclude that lack of communication was a major cause of low utilization at Harding.

## Communicating Harding's EAP

Although Harding attempted to make the EAP known to associates, most associates were not aware of the program. Most associates either did not know the program existed or had just heard the name but did not know the specific details of how the program worked. Most employees said they needed more information about the program in spite of the fact that Harding used videos, meetings, paycheck inserts, and mandatory training to communicate about the EAP. Why then were they so uninformed?

Those associates who had information about the EAP primarily believed that it was for substance abusers. Common responses from associates echoed one person's question, "They have that drinking program, don't they?" Another individual said, "I've always heard of somebody in for some sort of dependency area, but I've never heard of just using them that weren't in the dependency mode." More pointedly, when asked about the EAP, many associates told the story of a recovering alcoholic who wore a ponytail to represent his struggle with the disease and his successful rehabilitation.

It is not surprising, then, that associates saw the EAP as a program to combat substance dependency. Most of the communication about the EAP focused on substance abuse. For example, the video shown to employees as well as training for managers focused solely on education about substance abuse. The video's purpose was to educate associates on "how drugs and alcohol can impair workers on the worksite." It addressed alcohol, cocaine, marijuana, amphetamines, and PCP. The dangers of illicit substances were the focus of the entire video. In addition to this orientation video, drug education was the focus of supervisor training programs as well. The primary goal of these media was to fulfill DOT regulations regarding substance abuse education. Obviously creating a general understanding about their EAP and its many uses received short shrift at best.

Furthermore, other organizational factors could have brought substance abuse to the forefront of employee talk. For example, the focus on drugs and alcohol across organizational life may have caused associates to see the EAP as a crisis intervention to address these problems. In addition to the media used at Harding, random drug testing focused truck drivers' attention on this problem every month and perhaps even every day. Truck drivers and warehouse workers knew they were considered a high-risk group for having substance abuse problems. Finally, TAP, the union program, often addressed the issue of substance abuse, so a connection between the two different programs may have been made by employees. Many associates often thought I was referring to TAP when I asked them about their EAP.

Even though substance abuse was thought to be the major focus of Harding's EAP, some associates also believed that the EAP was a counseling program for couples with marital problems. Although some were aware of this feature, few believed that associates used the EAP for this reason. I was told, for example, "You never hear of people who don't have the dependency" using the EAP. "So many people have marital problems," but "I've always wondered if anyone ever used it for marital problems, you just never hear it."

Unfortunately, few associates were aware of counseling for challenges that plagued their everyday life such as stress, the birth of a new child, and financial counseling. The primary belief at Harding was that the EAP was for substance dependency and divorce, but it was almost never used for the latter and seldom for drug problems.

Although knowledge about the EAP was minimal, most associates did know that the program was free. Cost was a dominant issue discussed by members. If associates understood that Harding provided the program, they knew it was free of charge. So concerns about cost do not appear to be a part of the low-utilization puzzle.

When asked about the purpose of the EAP, most union associates reported that they did not know why Harding had an EAP. However, management and clerical associates believed it was to help troubled individuals and improve well-being, and few members believed that Harding had implemented the EAP for negative reasons. For example, one associate stated, "You put a lot of time here, sometimes you work 15- to 18-hour days. . . . It shows that the company is concerned with your well-being. And that is good to know that the company is concerned about your physical and mental state." Another individual explained, "Most managers don't want to fire anybody. They recognize somebody with a problem, they would rather help them get over that problem." Managers and clerks/professionals saw the EAP as a positive step in helping associates deal with the problems that affect their lives.

Even though the EAP was considered by many a goodwill effort, both managers and union members saw the program as a disciplinary tool. Managers were trained to use the program for discipline and were taught strategies for intervening when problems arose. Union workers usually heard about the EAP as a way to pinpoint troubled workers before they were terminated. Often union stewards were asked to serve as an intermediary to save an individual's job. One union steward explained,

"What they'll do at times if they do perceive a problem is that they'll come and tell me, this guy is coming to work drunk or he's drinking somewhere and they don't know where, he's got a problem. And then I'll go to the individual and say, 'Hey the company knows you've got a problem.'"

Both management and the union saw the EAP as an alternative to termination.

Confidentiality appeared to be another problem. Although the EAP was seen as a relatively positive force within the organization, most union and clerical associates did not believe that the program was completely confidential; management, not surprisingly, did believe it was confidential. Union and clerical associates thought that someone, either a coworker or manager, would find out they had a problem, and associates feared that someone would use the information against them at a later date. As one individual stated,

"Even though a management person or clerical whatever might seek this type of help because they felt they need it, in the back of their mind they might think, naa, some day is this going to affect the fact that I didn't get the promotion because I showed maybe I had a weakness in some area. Now granted, that should not be, but that is always a doubt in people's minds."

Even though associates did not feel that Harding specifically implemented the EAP to find out information about employees, they saw the lack of confidentiality as an inevitable consequence of seeking help. On the survey, respondents strongly indicated that they thought the EAP would not be utilized for fear of coworkers or supervisors knowing. As one recovering alcoholic said, "You come back to work and the room is full of supervisors, drivers, everyone; they know where you have been." Another individual explained her experiences:

"I needed help once and had to call around to find out about the program and it was embarrassing. We never get anything but a paycheck stuffer. . . . So you call around for information, then they know there is a problem and then you feel as if you are being watched."

The lack of confidentiality was not considered deliberate; instead, it was thought to be an inevitable consequence of seeking help.

Several reasons may account for this difference in perceptions regarding confidentiality. Management received more training about the EAP and was aware of how little information they received about people using the EAP. Already-strained relations between management and union workers also could have raised suspicions among associates. Trust is characteristically questioned by union members. Since the program was administered by management, they would obviously know more about the EAP and believe in its confidentiality. For the same reason, union members were likely to be suspicious.

The promotional materials about the EAP also presented mixed messages concerning confidentiality. The brochure stated, "Strict confidentiality is maintained in [the EAP]. In fact confidence is the most successful relationship between you and the counselor in a program like this." It also reads, "No one will be told of your participation unless you decide to do so yourself." But training programs for managers discussed how they could check on an employee's progress so the employee would know they cared. It seemed that the media these associates used most, brochures and orientation meetings, sent one message about the EAP, while supervisors' talk about the programs differed based on their training. These conflicting messages found in the different types of media appears to have contributed to the concerns regarding confidentiality.

It appeared that the lack of confidentiality employees spoke about was related to their confusion about the EAP. The purpose of the EAP was not long-term rehabilitation but short-term problem prevention. In fact, practitioners discouraged long-term counseling and stated that they did not rehabilitate employees. If a counselor met an employee with an addiction, the counselor referred the individual to the appropriate resource. Other organizational members did not need to know an individual was using the EAP if the problem was addressed at the early stages instead of in its later stages.

However, due to misunderstanding or lack of information, associates also saw the EAP as a crisis intervention. This understanding prevailed even when the messages contradicted it. Orientation meetings and brochures characterized the EAP as a prevention program instead of a crisis intervention. The brochure reads, "Although [the EAP] can help you through a crisis, it is primarily designed to help you manage the life changes we all experience such as marriage or divorce, birth of a child or raising children, relocation, a new job or promotion, death of a friend or family member, retirement." However, most employee talk dealt with problem solving, not prevention. Associates understood the program as a last resort for solving a crucial problem, perhaps because the organization did not connect the EAP to other programs addressing health promotion and quality of work life. The EAP was clearly segregated from other organizational issues that might boost employee well-being, such as charity drives, performance evaluations, and suggestion systems. Because the EAP was cut off from other services implemented by human resources, it is not surprising that employees understood the EAP as a crisis program to save their jobs.

Although promotional materials stated that this was a prevention program, the culture of the organization clearly emphasized the importance of substance abuse control. Random drug testing and addiction existed as part of Harding's culture. This ritual was a constant reminder of the stigma attached to addiction. The characterization of truck drivers as prone to addiction infiltrated the various subcultures. The alcoholic truck driver stereotype was discussed by clerical workers who had little contact with drivers. This view seemed to influence everyone's understanding of the EAP.

Based on this understanding, associates also did not use the EAP because of the way they viewed the problems that needed treatment. Since most employees believed that the EAP was a crisis intervention instead of preventive healthcare, they did not believe their everyday problems were severe enough to seek help. Employees felt they could handle their problems on their own. They believed that an individual needed to be in a serious condition before he or she would seek help. One driver explained when others might use the program. He said,

> "I guess when there is no other place to turn, I think, I don't know. But like I said, I really don't know of anyone that's used it. I'm sure there must be somebody but, in transportation I don't think we got anybody that's ever used it. Truck drivers are a breed of their own. They just go ahead and keep abusing. They think they ain't got no problems."

Apparently regardless of what they knew about the EAP, some associates were not going to use it either because they did not think their problem was serious enough or because they did not think they had a problem.

The three primary reasons employees gave for low utilization—lack of understanding, fear of a breach of confidentiality, and denial of one's problems—are related to the content and form of the messages they received. In this case, more information about how the EAP works might clarify these issues for employees, and messages more targeted to individual needs and program goals might heighten awareness and contribute to higher utilization. However, the content, form, and timing of these messages need to be carefully considered, constructed, and reconstructed.

It is clear in this case that EAP-related communication is inadequately achieving goals necessary to make the EAP a success. Associates need different information; more information may not be the answer. What is received is confusing to most associates. In addition to different information, issues of trust need to be addressed; associates still do not trust the program even if it does promise confidentiality. And in many cases, associates do not want to admit that they have problems or that their struggles can be dealt with through the EAP; but even when they do, they don't see the EAP as the source of help that it could be. The challenge to the EAP practitioners, to the human resources manager, and to the Harding supervisors and coworkers is to construct the EAP in such a way as to invite participation. Perhaps rethinking what participation means and including the associates in such conversations is the communicative beginning to changed understandings and a new kind of increased utilization.

## NOTES

1. The Harding Company is a pseudonym for the organization studied.
2. All members regardless of status are referred to as associates. Harding takes pride in stating that everyone is treated equally. No one has an assigned parking spot, and many decisions are based on seniority instead of organizational status.
3. The cave was a warehouse located literally in a cave. It was built in the ground. Working conditions were rough: There was little light, and rocks often fell from the ceilings. However, associates generally opted for this site because they said it was a smaller, more close-knit work group.

## KEY TERMS

CONFIDENTIALITY: the policy that no one, not even a supervisor or family member, will be notified of an individual's visit to the EAP. In addition, the information will not be recorded in the employee's permanent file.

CONSTRUCTIVE CONFRONTATION: a communication strategy taught to supervisors, peers, or union stewards so they can persuade employees to seek help through the EAP. The strategy involves confronting the troubled worker with evidence of unsatisfactory job performance, coaching them on ways to improve work, encouraging them to use assistance services, and reminding them of the consequences of continued poor performance. The process continues until the employee is rehabilitated or terminated.

EMPLOYEE ASSISTANCE PROGRAM (EAP): job-based programs operating within a work organization for the purposes of identifying "troubled workers," motivating them to resolve their troubles, and providing access to counseling or treatment for those employees who need those services.

HEALTH PROMOTION PROGRAM (HPP): a wellness program. These programs combine educational, organizational, and environmental activities to support behavior that is conducive to the health of employees and to change unhealthy living practices.

MULTIPLE METHODS: a combination of both quantitative and qualitative research methodologies used to create a more holistic picture of how communication creates an understanding of organizational phenomenon. By producing different types of evidence, the researcher can better balance the limitations of different methodologies.

UTILIZATION: the number of employees who visit an EAP counselor.

## DISCUSSION QUESTIONS

1. What is an EAP? What benefits can an EAP provide organizational members? What are the barriers some EAPs must overcome?
2. What contributed to the lack of utilization at Harding?
3. What media were used to promote EAPs at Harding? What other media or strategies can be used to promote the EAP?
4. How can EAP utilization be improved? What promotion strategies can be implemented in the workplace?
5. What role might organizational culture play in the success or failure of the EAP?

## REFERENCES

Alexy, B. B. (1991). Factors associated with participation or nonparticipation in a workplace wellness center. *Journal of Nursing and Health, 14,* 33–40.

Balgopal, P. R. (1989b). Occupational social work: An expanded clinical perspective. *Social Work, 34,* 437–442.

Bayer, G. A., & Barkin, A. C. (1990). Employee assistance program utilization: Comparison of referral sources and problems. *Employee Assistance Quarterly, 5*(4), 1–10.

Besenhofer, R. K., & Gerstein, L. H. (1991). Referrals to employee assistance programs (EAPs): Characteristics of hypothetical supervisors, EAPs, and substance abusing workers. *Employee Assistance Quarterly, 7*(2), 41–62.

Beyer, J. M., & Trice, H. M. (1978). *Implementing change: Alcoholism policies in work organizations.* New York: Free Press.

Blum, T., & Roman, P. (1986). Alcohol, drugs, and EAPs: New data from a national survey. *ALMACAN, 16,* 33–36.

Bryant, V., Eliach, J., & Green, S. L. (1990). Adapting the traditional EAP model to effectively serve battered women in the workplace. *Employee Assistance Quarterly, 6*(2), 1–10.

Conrad, P. (1987). Wellness in the workplace. *Millbank Quarterly, 65*(2), 255–275.

Cunningham, G. (1994). *Effective employee assistance programs: A guide for EAP counselors and managers.* Thousand Oaks, CA: Sage.

Daly, J. L. (1993). Perceptions of substance abuse program effectiveness and communication practices in Florida municipal government. *Employee Assistance Quarterly, 8*(3), 73–88.

Ellis-Sankari, J. (1992). Eldercare belongs in EAP. *Employee Assistance Quarterly,* 7(4), 1–16.

Harris, M. M., & Fennell, M. L. (1988). Perceptions of an employee assistance program and employee willingness to participate. *Journal of Applied Behavioral Science, 24*(4), 423–438.

Katzman, M. S., & Smith, K. J. (1989). Evaluation of occupational health promotion programs. *Employee Assistance Quarterly, 4*(3), 27–45.

Kelly, R. J. (1990). Hall of famers look ahead. *EAP Digest, 11.1,* 30.

Kittrell, A. (1988, February 1). Employers lack AIDS strategy. *Business Insurance, 22.5,* 3, 21–22.

Lubin, B., Shanklin, H. D., & Sailors, J. R. (1992). The EAP literature: Articles and dissertations. *Employee Assistance Quarterly, 8*(1), 47–90.

Masi, D. A., & Friedland, S. J. (1988). EAP actions and options. *Personnel Journal, 67,* 61–67.

Miller, R. (1985, December). Incorporating health education into employee assistance programs. *Health Education,* 25–28.

Myers, R. (1984). *Establishing and building employee assistance programs.* Westport, CT: Quorum Books.

Olesen, W. (1986). Videotape boosts Xerox's EAP. *EAP Digest, 18*(2), 61.

Shain, M., & Groenveld, J. (1980). *Employee-assistance programs: Philosophy, theory and practice.* Lexington, MA: Lexington Books.

Smith, J. E. (1993, June 22). Substance abuse: It's a problem for workers and the bottom line. *Kansas City Star,* p. D-13.

Sonnenstuhl, W. J. (1988). Contrasting employee assistance, health promotion, and quality of work life programs and their effects on alcohol abuse and dependence. *Journal of Applied Behavioral Science, 24*(4), 347–363.

Sonnenstuhl, W. J., Staudmeier, W. J., Jr., Trice, H. (1988). Ideology and referral categories in employee assistance research. *Journal if Applied Behavioral Science, 24.4,* 383–396.

Sonnenstuhl, W. J., & Trice, H. M. (1986). *Strategies for employee assistance programs: The crucial balance.* Ithaca, NY: ILR Press.

Steinhardt, M. A., & Young, D. R. (1992). Psychological attributes of participants and nonparticipants in a worksite health and fitness center. *Behavioral Medicine, 18,* 40–46.

Sussal, C. M. (1992). Why does the EAP really succeed? An object relations theory analysis. *Employee Assistance Quarterly, 8*(1), 35–45.

Walsh, S. M. (1991). Employee assistance and the helping professional: The more things change, the more they stay the same. *Employee Assistance Quarterly, 7.2,* 113–118.

Warner, K. E. (1987). Selling health promotion to corporate America: Uses and abuses of the economic argument. *Health Education Quarterly, 14*(1), 39–55.

# CHAPTER 8

# Reengineering at LAC
## A Case Study of Emergent Network Processes

DEAN H. KRIKORIAN
DAVID R. SEIBOLD
PATRICIA L. GOODE

A communication satellite is, practically speaking, a microwave repeater in orbit (Atkins, 1993). It is lifted by rockets or the Space Shuttle to an altitude of nearly 200 miles before being sent along a nearly circular path orbiting the earth at approximately 17,000 miles per hour forward velocity, its altitude and forward velocity being correlated so that the satellite maintains its position over the earth's surface. Such satellites are thus called "geostationary" because they are *stationary* with respect to the *earth*'s surface. These satellites beam signals to and from high-altitude microwave earth stations, and satellite-linked communication services will pervade our lives over the next century: mass-audience TV shows, Direct TV, pay-per-view, digital music, and video-on-demand, among others.

Increasing competition among satellite manufacturers, based on an area-wide recession and recent post-Cold War cuts in defense spending, has produced uncertainty and a "turbulent environment" (Emery & Trist, 1965) for the satellite industry. Furthermore, with advances in cable TV and fiber optics, once-dominant satellite manufacturers now received outside competition. These environmental threats have been neutralized to a great degree by recent advances in satellite technology, including very small aperture terminals (VSATs), lighter satellites, and on-board processing (a so-called thinking satellite).

However, companies within the satellite industry continue to compete in a global market that is reaching saturation. Due to bandwidth restrictions, satellite "parking spots" are limited in number. Along with low-cost labor, deregulation, recession, and the availability of affordable new technology, superior organizational processes determine competitive advantage in the satellite industry. These strategic processes will be defined and enhanced by combining tasks that cross functional boundaries and allow quick responses to customers. Total quality improvement efforts (e.g., total quality management [TQM] programs) and process reengineering have become everyday business practices. Process reengineering (Hammer & Champy, 1993) has received recent notoriety as a means to cope with problems like those evident in the satellite industry; it is an example of the way that "clean slate" change can produce substantial cost savings for organizations. Between 1993 and 1994, a large aerospace company (which we refer to as LAC throughout this chapter) involved in the production of communication satellites reengineered the way they communicated information by implementing a company-wide database system. Through the use of a multifunctional process change team (PCT), LAC explored and refined its business information infrastructure by streamlining organizational communication. The PCT discarded outdated rules and assumptions, and its members reached consensus on many new and improved ideas during decision-making processes.

This case study of reengineering at LAC is developed in five sections. First, the data collection methodology is reviewed. Brief reviews of the process reengineering and emergent network literatures, which provide theoretical bases for the case study, are offered in the second and third sections. Fourth, the case study is explicated by identifying the PCT's "case for action" and "vision" for the company's satellite anomaly process. The final section analyzes how elements of the PCT's emergent network combined to form a reengineered process.

## METHOD

Denzin (1978) defines *participant observation* as simultaneously combining "document analysis, interviewing of respondents and informants, direct participation and observation, and introspection" (p. 183). Each of these methods has had a rich and prominent place in ethnographic case studies of organizations (Schwartzman, 1993). In this case study, data collection was based on reviews of minutes of weekly team meetings, personal interviews, and personal recall. Rather than simply observing the actions as "outsiders looking in," the authors were integral members of the PCT who helped facilitate PCT meetings and record and distribute meeting minutes (the third author was actually the project leader). We note this vantage point as "insider recollection," and we mean to represent a more accurate depiction of case events due to the authors' involvement in the project and stake in its outcome. While realizing the potential for bias in such instances, the actual outcomes of the case provide validity checks on the authors' interpreta-tions. The authors also cross-checked facts to ensure reliability of events.

## PROCESS RENGINEERING

The prevalence of process reengineering can be seen by the 1994 *State of Reengineering Report* (cited in Champy, 1995), in which 621 companies, representing a sample of 6,000 of the largest corporations in Europe and North America, were given questionnaires on their use of reengineering projects. Seventy-five percent of the 124 European companies and 69% of the 497 North American companies used reengineering, with half of the remaining companies reporting that they were considering reengineering projects (Champy, 1995). Probably the most visible symbol of process reengineering is Hammer and Champy's 1993 book, *Reengineering the Corporation*, a 6-month *New York Times* best-selling book that has been translated into 14 languages. Hammer and Champy preach "clean slate" process change: throwing old processes away and beginning anew. Defined as "the fundamental rethinking and radical redesign of business processes to achieve dramatic improvements" (Hammer & Champy, 1993, p. 32), *process reengineering* looks to reduce non-value-added (i.e., nonproduc-tive) tasks and to streamline operations.

Hammer and Champy specify a two-step process in prescribing process reengineering. First, a *case for action*, the reason the company must reengineer, must be developed to provide a structure for the study of change in the organization. Defining the reasons for change identifies key processes on which to focus initial reengineering efforts. Second, a *vision*, reflecting an ideal goal state toward which the company should strive, must be developed. In Hammer and Champy's view, reengineering is en-acted by visionaries looking forward and facilitating organizational change processes. We will use process reengineering principles to help frame the PCT's case for action and its vision. The next section on "emer-gent networks" will provide the theoretical basis for mapping organiza-tional communication change processes. Such a theoretic base provides guidelines for identifying changes in organizational processes through analysis of emergent communication patterns.

## EMERGENT NETWORKS

While process engineering provided the impetus for change, the change is better described as *emergent networks* changing over time and building upon past experiences emphasizing connections between elements in a system. Monge and Eisenberg (1987) define the fundamental process in emergent networks as *reorganizing*, which "represents the changes that occur . . . as [people] alter their communication linkages with one another" (p. 311). This reorganizing process can be reconceptualized as semipermeable (i.e., somewhat open to influences outside the system) system boundaries (Putnam & Stohl, 1990) being altered and reconstructed by the interaction of people in social networks (Fulk, Schmitz, & Steinfield, 1990). As an example of emergent organizational networks in practice, Lewis and Seibold (1993) found that a new organizational work arrangement was modified by connections among individuals within work groups involved with the use of the innovation.

In summary, by looking for emergent communication patterns of interactions, one can better visualize process changes over time. Specifically, in analyzing the case study, we will look at ways in which change processes "feed" off each other and form an emergent network. In discussing the case study that follows, it is also important to recall the structural features of process reengineering (case for action and vision). Throughout the study one should particularly observe the conflict between existing structures and ongoing processes, as this tension is often the impetus for organizational change.

## REENGINEERING AT LAC

As mentioned at the outset, increasing industry-wide competition as well as decreasing federal support forced layoffs at LAC and caused upper management to rethink daily production processes. A recent financial assessment at LAC found that manufacturing and test problems were significant contributors to the cost of satellite production. As a result, the PCT was formed by upper management to streamline the way LAC processed satellite manufacturing and test problems (anomalies) such as defective parts, inadequate designs, and workmanship errors. By analyzing processes, the PCT would have better tools to fix problems, not just their symptoms. The membership of the PCT reflected all functional manufacturing and test areas as well as product assurance, systems engineering, database administration, and information technology—a multifunctional task team. While the PCT was commissioned and funded by top management, it was agreed at the start of the project that continued funding was contingent on progress and tangible results. In the next section we review the five major problems of the satellite anomaly process identified by the PCT: (1) re-do processes; (2) non-value-added processes; (3) splintered processes across business units; (4) lack of standardized metrics to measure processes; and (5) customers as outsiders to process.

## Case for Action

In process reengineering, the "case for action" serves to identify major organizational problems, which in turn creates the need (and basis) for reengineering. Key barriers in reducing anomalies (defined earlier as unexpected occurrences to satellite hardware or software) were identified by the PCT.

### Problem 1: Re-do Processes

The expense of the hardware re-do process had become a significant barrier in product development. Re-do consists of rework, repair, retest, and redesign ("re" is a costly prefix) in any part of the satellite production process. Re-do is normally caused by variability in design, production, and test operations (e.g., defective parts or fluctuating power readings). Estimates concerning the cost of re-do at LAC were in the multimillion-dollar range. From a human resources perspective, re-do can be personified in terms of the number of people taken off a certain design enhancement team to solve a pressing "parts alert" problem. The financial numbers can be easily calculated in terms of person-hours on the re-do effort.

### Problem 2: Non-Value-Added Processes

Many task processes added no value to the overall quality and timely delivery of the end product. Redundant and overlapping tasks led to collection of non-value-added data both for management and for those performing the hands-on work. In some areas, anomaly task processes were documented manually, which made it difficult to retrieve data and communicate problems *across* functional areas. Without clear understanding and shared agreement concerning the process in question, it was difficult to determine what additional data were needed to indicate the health of the process.

### Problem 3: Splintered Processes

The PCT found that the "splintering" of processes among business units hindered the detection of company-wide problems. This reflected a classic tension between differentiation and integration in organizations (Lawrence & Lorsch, 1967). Differentiation of the anomaly process into subparts led to an internal focus within each organizational subarea (e.g., many areas had developed their own data-tracking systems), thereby undermining the synergistic (integration) potential of the organizational units.

Common processes, materials, and parts were used to some extent across the organization, but for the most part, problems were not viewed from the perspective that other areas might be affected by the same problem. This caused *suboptimization,* or inefficiencies, especially where processes could be combined. Commonality across functional areas was seen in examples of engineering design changes, test failure processing, and hand soldering. In these areas, local processes helped identify process problems across the organization.

### Problem 4: Lack of Standardized Metrics

Anomaly output reports at LAC were found by the PCT to lack "standardized metrics" (i.e., agreed upon measures allowing for measurement of process). PCT members recognized that standardized metrics implied that one had carefully determined the right areas to standardize so that one compared similar processes. Examining different processes can lead to comparing "apples to oranges."

For example, the production processes of mechanical and electrical hardware were inherently different and should not have been compared. For this reason, the PCT determined that customized report generation for different processes was also necessary, even though this effort was time consuming and often lacked focus. Hence, the PCT determined that both standardized and customized reports would be included in the design of the database system.

### Problem 5: Customers as Outsiders

External customers were considered outsiders in the anomaly process. Customer opinion was considered only when LAC was in "firefighting" mode—that is, dealing with crises reactively rather than proactively. The PCT recognized this problem and looked for ways to work with the customer rather than respond to the customer. For example, they found that there were few or no computer linkages to customers. Moreover, customers' right to access to anomaly database information had always been questioned by apprehensive functional area personnel. Strict security concerning company-sensitive information would need to be guaranteed and proven on the system, PCT members determined. This *privacy dilemma* posed interesting questions for future implementation of database technology: How much access to company information could LAC allow customers? The privacy dilemma juxtaposed both the need to communicate with external customers and the need to protect proprietary and other company-sensitive information.

## The Vision

In looking forward, team members proposed solutions to each of the five process problems. This section identifies these solutions, provides organizational commentary, examines how solutions were communicated, and gives specific examples of implementation. As a result of this vision for a more integrated process, the PCT was able to move toward a reengineered solution to LAC's production problems.

The first solution concerned the use of anomaly data to prevent re-do's. Upon examining recent cost figures, a division manager at LAC exclaimed, "We need to significantly reduce the number of re-do's to remain competitive." PCT members determined that use of anomaly data must somehow relate to an element of the process that needs improving to prevent anomaly recurrence and reduce the number of re-do's. That is, after determining the cause of an anomaly, corrective action (i.e., feedback) was designed to reflect an improved process to prevent anomaly recurrence.

PCT members began by conducting their own research concerning re-do's through extraction of data that indicated the cost of each re-do effort and how many re-do's were occurring late in the anomaly process (where it is most expensive). PCT members mapped existing re-do processes using a technique for structuring communication and analysis called "flowcharting." Flowcharts are generally not meant to be replications of actual processes; rather, they serve as rough outlines to ensure commonality of basic underlying structures (Seibold & Krikorian, 1997). By flowcharting re-do's at different stages in the anomaly process, the PCT created a shared vision, allowing for standard reports to identify potential problems leading to early detection and correction of anomalies.

As an example, the PCT was tasked by upper management to look at the recent recurrence of anomalies in one functional area. After gathering cost data, the PCT then flowcharted the process under review, identifying how problems identified at later stages, when not corrected, led to more costly re-do's. Analyzing and communicating this information using a standardized process represented a major step toward reducing re-do's and improving cycle time, that is, time from design to launch in the case of satellites. Cycle time reduction reflects improved processes, which contribute to bottom-line cost savings for the company as a whole.

A second solution concerned the need for a centralized database. Before the PCT was formed, the typical attitude of production engineers was expressed by one: "The database I use serves my purposes, why do I need to change?" Changing to an unfamiliar and cumbersome system took time that was not readily available to engineers embroiled with problems in their own area.

By collecting anomaly data into one centralized database, employees had easy access to all relevant process anomaly data. This functioned to converge data for each phase of the entire process centrally, rather than suboptimizing with separate databases. The resultant centralized database also replaced multiple systems, simplifying the subprocesses (and their interfaces) and leading to better understanding of data needs across the company.

The PCT began training organizational members on the centralized database system (a "road show," as PCT members termed their traveling training). The team members had to create and present charts reflecting changes in the anomaly database system. In communicating this information, members quickly encountered a persistent problem: The standardized database needed increased user-friendliness. As a result, all areas were consulted about their existing systems and were asked what functions they most valued in an anomaly database system. From a communication standpoint, the existing system was reorganized to accommodate the users' information needs cross-functionally.

A third solution was concerned with scope expansion: conception to completion processes. The original goal in representing the anomaly process only stressed the factory (i.e., production and test) processes of product development. After being presented with the recent status report on the PCT's progress, a vice president asked, "Can the company's manufacturing anomaly database combine with a similar launch process database?" The PCT was then tasked to see if they could incorporate other areas, including supplier defects, mission control, and on-orbit anomalies, into the reengineered anomaly process. Several areas of process improvement were noted. For instance, parts histories could be incorporated in the database so that anyone discovering an anomaly could follow a few simple commands to learn if any similar problems occurred elsewhere in lot testing at the manufacturer or LAC. This allowed anyone in the organization to look at where and when anomalies occurred, as well as the impact that the anomalies had on the overall process. This ongoing and circular information flow permitted continuous process monitoring and improvements. This process previously was ill defined, but it was determined by the PCT to be critical to satisfying customer requests for information as well as to internal problem solving. By using technologies such as e-mail, the organization utilized existing communication channels to convey information across organizational levels.

A fourth solution was concerned with developing standard and customized reports. Upon receiving a confusing monthly anomaly report, a frustrated associate program manager remarked, "How can monthly anomaly reports help me understand *my* problems on *my* program in a straightforward manner?"

Standard reports play a pivotal role in early detection of anomalies.

They raise the flag for more detailed anomaly investigations. Standardized metrics of anomaly data across groups were necessary to allow each functional group to automatically receive monthly anomaly reports. For example, each functional division manager received charts using the same metrics, such as (1) top causes of hardware anomalies over the preceding month, (2) length of investigation time for specific anomalies, and (3) level of testing of anomaly occurrence. Even groups with low-proximity links would logically look for the same type of data to allow themselves to use already-implemented improvements. By identifying processes, one uncovers the detailed information at the level to where problems and not symptoms can be corrected. Statistical process control techniques can be further utilized to keep a process within control (i.e., to achieve reduced process variation) because the processes they are measuring have been identified and standardized across the company. Because of the functional differences of areas at LAC, the PCT also needed a way to allow users to customize reports to suit their own particular needs.

*Focus sessions,* a communication and qualitative method of guided roundtable discussion of specified topics (see Marshall & Rossman, 1995), commenced with key functional area personnel to develop new and improved metrics and also to identify and customize report options. The database system was also made more user-friendly with more updated and accurate information, increasing usage, and customizability. Now, instead of waiting to receive monthly reports, employees could create their own reports when needed. In summary, customized reports allowed users to "get what they want," and standardized reports allowed users to automate what they typically consider to be a tedious, thankless, and trivial task.

A fifth and final solution emphasized customer focus. In reaction to the access by customers' and nonarea LAC personnel (so-called internal customers) to their data, unit engineers often replied, "Why do I want *the customer* looking at *my* data?" The PCT formed a subcommittee, or *task team,* to look at security issues in anomaly database access, realizing the importance of tailoring access levels to meet individual security needs. The flexibility-of-access issues were solved most efficiently by a smaller task team of key players, including systems developers, division computer programmers, and information technology experts. Knowing when to break a larger group into smaller, more effective subgroups requires both knowledge of facilitation and communication processes (Seibold & Krikorian, 1997). For instance, members needed to address issues such as: How can we communicate better? Do all of us need to be here at this meeting when only four people seem interested? Should I request tabling this issue—it has dragged on rather long—and the next issue is why I came to the meeting, anyway?

The security task team, with input from other members of the PCT, devised a scheme providing four database access levels on a "need to know" basis and programmed these restrictions into the database access codes as (1) read-only (e.g., external customers); (2) input and read-only (e.g., data administrators); (3) limited data-change capabilities (e.g., engineers); and (4) system-change capabilities (e.g., database administrators). This solution helped solve the privacy dilemma by providing multiple levels of access to include the needs of the customer, hence increasing customer satisfaction.

By including both internal and external customers in the anomaly process, PCT members also established built-in cost savings initiatives at LAC. For example, report and status generation could be performed by the customer and anomaly notification could be automatically routed via e-mail distribution lists. This reduced the time LAC employees spent in "reactionary mode" while responding to customer requests for anomaly reports.

In summary, five solutions were proposed by the PCT to problems identified by them in the case for action part of their reengineering efforts: (1) the use of anomaly data to prevent re-do's, (2) a centralized database, (3) scope expansion, (4) developing standardized and customized reports, and (5) customer focus. All of these solutions address process problems identified in the previous section. Integral to these solutions was the communication-related techniques used in their implementation: (1) flow-charting, (2) training, (3) e-mail, (4) focus sessions, and (5) task teams. In the next section, the problem–solution process will be analyzed by comparing and contrasting process reengineering with emergent communication networks.

## ANALYSIS

Figure 8.1 depicts the problem–solution process developed by the PCT. This process reflects Hammer and Champy's (1993) prescriptions for process reengineering, which assumes there is "one best way" in solving problems as noted by the "is" and "should be" model. Their conception of "process reengineering" does not provide any other mechanisms for arriving at solutions. This neglects solution interaction and interdependence, and human interaction does account for the potential of an *emergent process*. Hence, we see the notion of *process* reengineering as a misnomer that actually downplays the role of "process." For this reason, we suggest Hammer and Champy's prescription would be better termed "structural reengineering," or even "restructuring," as reengineering often is operationalized in the real world as a method for *downsizing* (i.e., layoffs) in organizations. Gouillart and Kelly (1995) echoed these concerns, citing

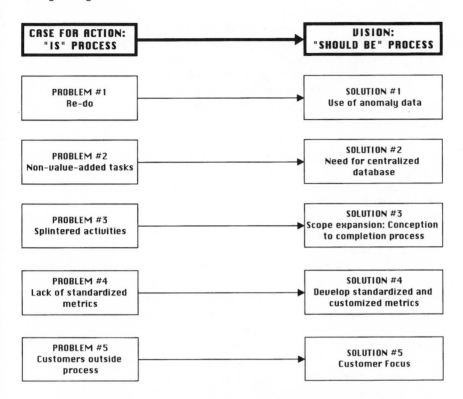

**FIGURE 8.1.** The process change team's problem–solution process.

reengineering as helpful in its reframing dimension, but they discounted its radicalism as "pedestrian" methodologically.

The LAC case study provided several examples in which solutions involving person and work groups evolved through communication regarding the anomaly process. This interactive and interdependent process of determining problems and solutions, while virtually ignored in Hammer and Champy's depiction, may best be explained as an emergent network. Figure 8.2 shows this resultant emergent network of anomaly processes at LAC and specifies the connections between system elements as the criteria for process evaluation.

We reconstruct this resultant emergent network by providing the details behind why connections exist between solutions in Figure 8.2. First, the use of anomaly data (Solution #1) was operationalized by (1) building a centralized database (Solution #2), (2) incorporating a conception to completion process (Solution #3), (3) developing measures of anomaly data (Solution #4), and (4) providing information to customers (Solution

#5). Because all functional areas are affected by the use of anomaly data to preclude future re-do efforts, this solution may be considered more central in the emergent network. Therefore, the arrows in Figure 8.2 reveal the connections from Solution #1 to all other solutions.

Second, the need for a centralized database (Solution #2) reflected informational flow of (1) anomaly data into the database (Solution #1), (2) scope expansion through increased usage by functional areas (Solution #3), and (3) the development of customized reports from the database (Solution #4). Hence, arrows are drawn from Solution #2 to each of these three solutions.

Third, scope expansion (Solution #3) (1) provided more uses of anomaly data (Solution #1), (2) used one centralized database (Solution #2), and (3) developed measures of anomaly processes (Solution #4). These effects are represented in Figure 8.2 arrows from Solution #3 to the three other solutions.

Fourth, developing standardized and customized metrics (Solution #4) (1) allowed for more use of the anomaly database (Solution #1), (2) established the need for a central information repository (Solution #2), (3) allowed for scope expansion based on shared meaning (Solution #3), and (4) provided options for customer access (Solution #5). Metric development also played a central role in the resultant emergent network; Figure 8.2 shows Solution #4 linked to all other solutions.

Finally, customer focus (Solution #5) illustrates (1) a reduced num-

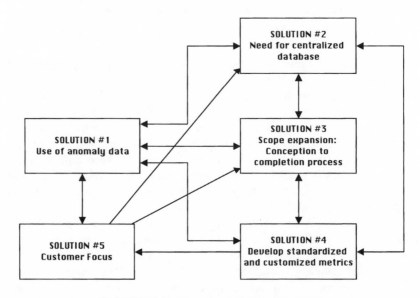

**FIGURE 8.2.** The emergent network at LAC.

ber of anomalies by identifying them at early stages in the process (Solution #1) through creation of multiple database access levels, (2) enhanced usage of the centralized database (Solution #2), and (3) incorporation of the customer in scope expansion processes (Solution #3). The arrows from Solution #5 to other solutions represent the final connections of the PCT's emergent network. It should be obvious to the reader that the solutions in the study "feed upon each other," as evidenced in Figure 8.2. In this respect, Figure 8.2 should give the reader an idea of how seemingly simple changes can result in widespread change. In observing process, one can better understand how and why change occurred. Observing points in the process where reinvention occurred or when more effective communication techniques (e.g., flowcharts, focus groups, or task teams) were used show how improvements in communication are a significant factor in reducing cost and improving process. Indeed, things seem much more complex than the simple prescriptions provided by Hammer and Champy as depicted in Figure 8.1.

As a final note, by combining the structure of reengineering with the process of emergent networks, we have illustrated the construction of a dynamic model of social systems (see Hanneman, 1988). This process was developed in the case as follows: (1) identifying the problems of the anomaly process, (2) identifying solutions to the problems (i.e., subsystem identification), (3) connecting solutions to corresponding problems (i.e., basic connectivity), and (4) connecting solutions as a means for information flow (i.e., control connections). In light of our previous analysis, we can see how Hammer and Champy (1993) stop after the second item—one problem has one solution. In analyzing the case from an emergent network perspective, we completed step 3 as reflected in Figure 8.2. Step 4 is left as an exercise for the reader and will take the form of recommendations for policy formation on topics concerning the PCT (see Question 3, of the Discussion Questions).

## CONCLUSION

The PCT gathered people from across the organization who would not normally communicate. The original scope of this project concerning anomaly reduction seemed relatively innocent: the combination of similar paper forms, a few work instruction changes, and an upgraded database. These were improvements, but nothing radical. By constructing a case for action calling on the multifaceted experiences of team members, the PCT facilitated convergence of a shared vision. By analyzing how proposed solutions "feed" on each other, a communication perspective on "emergent networks" can be used to better understand the dynamics behind "reengineered" processes in a typical large organization. Finally, the case analysis reflects the importance of grounded theory and principles to help explain change processes in organizations. A prescriptive approach such as process reengineering (Hammer & Champy, 1993) may work in describing simple, straightforward tasks, but it should not be used to describe widespread change.

## ACKNOWLEDGMENTS

The authors would like to thank Jim Potter, John Lammers, Rob Whitbred, Noshir Contractor, and Maureen Heald for comments on earlier versions of this chapter.

## KEY TERMS

CASE FOR ACTION: why a company must reengineer; provides structure for the study of change in an organization.

CONNECTEDNESS: a network analytic measure of the relative centrality of system elements. Connectedness is operationalized by the equation $L / (N-1)$, where $L$ is the number of links between elements in a system and $(N-1)$ is the total number of possible links.

DOWNSIZING: an operationalization of reengineering in the form of layoffs.

EMERGENT NETWORKS: a theoretical construct emphasizing processes that change over time and build upon past experiences emphasizing connections between elements in a system.

FLOWCHARTS: a technique for structuring communication and analysis; meant not to replicate actual processes but to serve as rough outlines to ensure commonality of basic underlying structures.

FOCUS SESSIONS: a communication and qualitative method of guided roundtable discussion on specified topics.

PARTICIPANT OBSERVATION: a method that simultaneously combines document analysis, interviewing of respondents and informants, direct participation, observation, and introspection.

PRIVACY DILEMMA: the conflict that arises from the need to communicate with external customers and the need to protect proprietary and other company-sensitive information.

PROCESS REENGINEERING: the fundamental rethinking and radical redesign of business processes to achieve dramatic improvements.

REORGANIZING: the fundamental process in emergent networks; represents the changes that occur as people alter their communication linkages with one another.

SUBOPTIMIZATION: inefficiencies, especially where processes could be combined.

TASK TEAM: a subcommittee analyzing a specific issue given to a larger group.

TRIANGULATION: a technique often used in case studies that uses different perspectives in order to generalize findings beyond the specific case.

VISION: reflects an ideal goal state toward which a company using reengineering must strive.

## DISCUSSION QUESTIONS

1. What are the causes of each of the five problems identified in the case? Do you think each cause was driven by forces internal or external to the PCT? Why?
2. What are the solutions to each the five problems identified in the case? What communication techniques were used in implementing solutions? What other communication techniques would you use in these situations?
3. Recalling Hanneman's fourth point for dynamic systems, "connecting information as a means to control flow (i.e., control connections)," and given what you know about the case study, what recommendations would you make to the vice president of LAC about forming policy on issues regarding the PCT?
4. It is important to realize that there are many ways to represent system elements in dynamic processes. As an exercise, devise your own connections between solutions based on your own analysis of case study events. Is your resultant emergent network similar to Figure 8.2? Why or why not?
5. *Triangulation* is a technique often used in case studies that uses different perspectives in order to generalize findings beyond the specific case. Specifically, Denzin (1978) lists four basic types of triangulation: (1) data triangulation—a variety of data sources are used; (2) investigator triangulation—different researchers are used; (3) theory triangulation—multiple theories are used; and (4) method triangulation—a number of methods are used. In what ways are the four types of triangulation used in the case study? Based on this answer, do you feel that the authors are able to generalize their results of the case study based on triangulation? Why or why not?
6. *Connectedness* is a network analytic measure of the relative centrality of system elements. It is operationalized as the number of links between elements in a system $(L)$ divided by the total number of possible links $(N - 1)$; thus, Connectedness $= L / (N - 1)$. (Rogers & Kincaid, 1981). For Figure 8.2, calculate (1) the connectedness *from* each solution as represented by arrows from the solution; and (2) the connectedness *to* each solution as represented by arrows to the solution.

## REFERENCES

Atkins, W. J. (1993). *Fundamentals of satellite communications: Introduction to satellite communications course material.* Unpublished manuscript.

Champy, J. (1995). *Reengineering management.* New York: HarperBusiness.

Denzin, N. K. (1978). *The research act.* New York: McGraw-Hill.

Emery, F. E., & Trist, E. L. (1965). The causal texture of organizational environments. *Human Relations, 18,* 21–32.

Fulk, J., Schmitz, J. A., & Steinfield, C. W. (1990). A social influence model of technology use. In J. Fulk & C. W. Steinfield (Eds.), *Organizations and communication technology* (pp. 117–140). Newbury Park, CA: Sage.

Gouillart, F. J., & Kelly, J. N. (1995). *Transforming the organization.* New York: McGraw-Hill.

Hammer, M., & Champy, J. (1993). *Reengineering the corporation: A manifesto for business revolution.* New York: HarperCollins.

Hanneman, R. A. (1988). *Computer-assisted theory building.* Newbury Park, CA: Sage.

Lawrence, P. R., & Lorsch, J. W. (1967). *Organization and environment: Managing differentiation and integration.* Homewood, IL: Irwin.

Lewis, L. K., & Seibold, D. R. (1993). Innovation modification during intraorganizational adoption. *Academy of Management Review, 18,* 323–354.

Marshall, C., & Rossman, G. B. (1995). *Designing qualitative research* (2nd ed.). Thousand Oaks, CA: Sage.

Monge, P. R., & Eisenberg, E. M. (1987). Emergent communication networks. In F. M. Jablin, L. L. Putnam, K. H. Roberts, & L. W. Porter (Eds.), *Handbook of organizational communication: An interdisciplinary perspective* (pp. 304–342). Newbury Park, CA: Sage.

Putnam, L. L., & Stohl, C. (1990). Bona-fide groups: A reconceptualization of groups in context. *Communication Studies, 41,* 248–265.

Rogers, E. M., & Kincaid, D. L. (1981). *Communication networks: Toward new paradigm for research.* New York: Free Press.

Schwartzman, H. B. (1993). *Ethnography in organizations* (Qualitative Research Method Series, Vol. 27). Newbury Park, CA: Sage.

Seibold, D. R., & Krikorian, D. H. (1997). Making meetings more successful. In L. R. Frey & K. Barge (Eds.), *Managing group life: Communicating in decision-making groups* (pp. 272–305). Boston: Houghton-Mifflin.

# CHAPTER 9

# Negotiating a Japanese Buyout of a U.S. Company
## Concepts of Work as Subtext

JILL KLEINBERG

The globalization of business increasingly directs our attention toward the negotiating practices of persons throughout the world, encouraging cross-national comparison (Adler, 1996). It is generally assumed that societal culture affects negotiation behavior. As Shenkar and Ronen (1987, p. 263) explain, "Conduct during negotiations is influenced by attitudes and customs, which to a great extent are embedded in a negotiating team's cultural and social traits. Different attitudes and customs can yield significant differences in psychological processes such as selective perception and interpersonal attraction." It is assumed as well that cultural differences in conduct and in psychological processes such as perception make successful completion of cross-national negotiation problematic. Cross-cultural understanding and accommodation, therefore, are essential (Adler, 1991).

Most of the research on cross-national, cross-cultural negotiation, in one way or another, focuses on the cultural "rules," explicit or tacit, for conducting negotiation. The emphasis, for example, may be on verbal and nonverbal tactics like the use of promises, threats, normative appeals, silence, facial gazing, touching, and so forth (Graham, 1985). Or it may be on what some researchers term "discourse style" or "discourse strategy," that is, the logic underlying the way a cultural group puts thoughts and words together in order to persuade (e.g., Friday, 1991; Young, 1982). Furthermore, negotiation is generally viewed as a distinct organizational activity, physically and cognitively demarcated by the conference room, the table around which negotiators sit, and the hours occupied by trying to reach resolution of particular issues.

This case study approaches cross-national, cross-cultural negotiation holistically, adopting an anthropological ethnographic framework. Negotiation outcomes are not explained solely by the negotiating behavior of participants. Rather, negotiation is seen as embedded in organizational concerns that transcend the specific matter under consideration. And, while the negotiators' culturally informed style of persuasion, their verbal and nonverbal tactics, unquestionably affect the course of negotiation, cultural influences can be conceived more broadly than nation-specific assumptions about how to conduct negotiation.

The case study reported here focuses on negotiations surrounding the buyout of a U.S. company by a Japanese-owned and managed firm operating in the United States. The two organizations maintained a close business relationship prior to the buyout and expect to continue to do so in the future. The case offers an opportunity to consider how national cultural differences influence organizational communication and how organizational communication as cultural performance both reflects and creates organizational realities.

## NEGOTIATION AS CULTURAL PERFORMANCE

Ethnography implies cultural description of a social setting—that is, the ethnographer seeks to comprehend the "native's" world from the native's point of view (Gregory, 1983). Culture can be defined as "the acquired knowledge that people use to interpret experience and generate social behavior" (Spradley, 1979, p. 5). Cultural knowledge is widely shared by a group of people; its configuration is distinctive to the group, and it is constructed, passed on, and reinforced (or modified) among group members through social interaction. Acquired cultural knowledge may be explicit, as in norms that people can consciously articulate, or it may be tacit, the unconscious assumptions that many scholars consider to be the innermost core of culture.

Negotiation is not simply an activity shaped by the cultural knowledge that participants bring to it. To paraphrase Pacanowsky and O'Donnell-Trujillo (1983, p. 131), negotiation is "cultural performance," which brings to completion a sense of reality. Through their interaction, negotiators construct the understandings by which they make sense of their social setting, they reinforce existing cultural knowledge, and they create new cultural knowledge.

Negotiation as cultural performance is consistent with Mangham and Overington's (1983, 1987) theatrical model of human action in organizations. They are concerned with "characterization," that is, with how actors choose to play their role. They are concerned even more broadly with "the conditions that allow for performance," that is, the setting, the rough script, the rehearsals, the role of the director, and so forth (1987, p. 83). The "text" of the negotiation, who says and does what, emerges out of the performance.

A cultural-performance approach to negotiation suggests we examine cultural knowledge as "subtext" that both gives form to and is reflected in the text. Mangham and Overington define subtext as the players' "'naive' theories of action and motives which enable them to formulate characters whose conduct will 'make sense'" (1987, p. 92). Subtext, in large part, derives from the constraints of the situation and the history of the participants and their organizations.

Part of the cultural knowledge that the Japanese and Americans brought to the buyout negotiation concerned what I have labeled, inclusively, "concepts of work." Such cultural knowledge encompasses largely tacit understandings widely shared in the societal culture about such things as authority, trust, and decision making. Given the context of negotiations, assumptions about work were critical. The Japanese and Americans involved in the negotiations planned to continue to work together, albeit on a different basis than formerly. Not only did each party's culturally patterned "concepts of work" help shape the agenda, they simultaneously colored mutual perceptions and influenced the negotiation "text" (Mangham & Overington, 1987) that emerged. In addition, the negotiators' cultural knowledge reflected assumptions about the way they made sense of their own specific organization.

The notions of characterization, text, and subtext can all be thought of as being to some extent culturally infused. In the case study that follows, the buyout negotiation reveals cultural rules about negotiating and subtextual cultural knowledge about concepts of work and organization-specific assumptions. Thus the text that is produced is cultural performance in the way it is accomplished, just as the accomplishment itself, the text of the performance, is cultural by virtue of the shared understandings it reflects.

Negotiation data analyzed here were gathered through participant observation and intensive ethnographic interviews. These interviews and observations were conducted on a daily basis over the course of a year. Over a 2½-month period, I observed four separate negotiating sessions and an agreement-signing meeting. In addition to the transcripts of over 20 hours of tape-recorded negotiation and interviews with key participants, the data set includes extensive field notes of observations along with related documentary materials.

The following sections describe the context of the negotiations; reproduce excerpts from negotiation transcripts to illustrate cultural influences on the interactive construction of character, text, and subtext; and provide a brief analysis of this particular cross-national, cross-cultural negotiation.

## The Context of Negotiations

This case is a study of LASCO (Los Angeles Subsidiary Company, a pseudonym), a subsidiary of a large Japanese trading company. LASCO, which employed around 120 persons, including 11 Japanese sent by the Tokyo headquarters to hold key management positions in the subsidiary, formed the hub of the trading company's multinational "computer peripherals group." The bulk of the group's sales, as well as product research and development, emanated from LASCO. The trading company itself had no manufacturing capability; it subcontracted production to various Japanese manufacturers but sold the products under the trading company brand name.

Negotiations mainly involved the owner-managers of a U.S. company, called here ROCA, which had served almost 2 years of a 5-year contract as exclusive sales representative for LASCO's video terminals product line. ROCA, in fact, had been formed expressly for the purpose of selling LASCO video terminals. Its owners, Tom and Jerry,[1] had become acquainted with each other while working for different companies in the computer electronics industry. They approached Matt (the American name adopted by Mr. Tateishi), the president of LASCO, with the idea of a sales company to handle their products, and LASCO loaned them start-up money. By the time of the negotiations, ROCA employed 15 people in Los Angeles and regularly supplied 35 distributors in the United States. A subsidiary company, ROCA Europe, was one point of negotiation.

At issue was a proposed buyout of ROCA by LASCO, thereby bringing responsibility for video terminals sales directly under LASCO management. Sales had grown tremendously since the LASCO–ROCA business relationship began, and Matt sought greater control of the burgeoning business. At the same time, Tom and Jerry, who were, respectively, president and vice president of ROCA, found themselves spending most of their time managing an expanding company instead of performing the sales activities they both enjoyed. Consequently, the purchase of ROCA seemed a good move for both parties. With the buyout, LASCO planned to create a new sales subsidiary, LASCO Terminals, to handle the video terminals business, once the responsibility of ROCA. Prior to the formal LASCO and ROCA negotiations, representatives had reached certain understandings. Nevertheless, both sides acknowledged that despite their mutual desire to reach agreement, successful negotiations hinged on acceptance of particular conditions still in question.

Prenegotiation understandings included:

- LASCO would agree to pay $500,000 in "front-end" money to Tom and Jerry on liquidation of ROCA.
- Tom and Jerry would complete the 3 years remaining on the original contract as management-level employees of the new sales subsidiary, Tom as vice president for marketing and Jerry as vice president for sales; officially, however (for tax reasons), Tom and Jerry would form a "management services" firm, ROCA Consulting, and LASCO would employ their services through that firm.
- LASCO would pay ROCA Consulting a commission of 1.5% of video terminals annual gross sales for a 3-year period.
- The new business arrangement would begin on April 1.
- ROCA Consulting, with money loaned by LASCO, would buy 10% ownership of LASCO Terminals.
- LASCO would purchase ROCA's assets, such as office furniture.
- Tom and Jerry would be members of LASCO Terminals' Board of Directors, although they would not be "officers" of the company.

Three points were left for negotiation: One concerned the date until which LASCO would pay ROCA the 10% sales commission guaranteed by the original contract. Jerry, in particular, considered this a key issue. ROCA paid its distributors a commission on orders placed by customers at the time the Japanese manufacturer shipped the order out of the factory. Tom and Jerry were concerned about the possibility of significant financial loss if a large number of video terminals ordered prior to the new agreement were delivered after the formation of LASCO Terminals.

A second point was the future business relationship between ROCA Europe and ESCO (European Subsidiary Company), LASCO's sister subsidiary in England. The critical question was whether ROCA Europe would continue to have responsibility for sales of trading company brand name terminals and, if so, on what basis.

Finally, ROCA and LASCO needed to negotiate the terms of the service agreement. At issue were Tom's and Jerry's salaries for consulting (settled early on as $350,000, $400,000, and $450,000 over 3 consecutive years) and the circumstances under which the 3-year agreement between LASCO Terminals and ROCA Consulting could be canceled.

## The Negotiation Drama

As the negotiation drama unfolded, each of the characters constructed their roles. Matt and Terry were the two central Japanese characters representing LASCO. Matt's U.S. assignment had been unusually long—nearly

*[handwritten: unlike most Japanese]*

12 years. Most of this time he had been president of LASCO, which he helped establish. At age 47, he had a reputation among trading company colleagues for being a risk taker as well as a quick and autocratic decision maker. Terry was LASCO's 41-year-old vice president of administration and Matt's longtime protégé. The key players from ROCA were Tom and Jerry, ROCA's president and vice president. At age 45 and 43, respectively, both men had an extensive background in computer electronics sales. Only Tom had had management experience prior to the formation of ROCA.

Besides these four men, the (American) lawyers for each side at various times played an important part in the negotiation drama. They were Roger, representing LASCO, and Daryl, representing ROCA.

Characterization began even before the first negotiation session formally got underway. Matt seated himself at the head of the long oval conference table, and Terry sat to Matt's left, along one side of the table. Tom and Jerry sat across the table from Terry. The lawyers for each side, Daryl and Roger, sat beside their clients.

*[handwritten margin note: Non-Verbal]*

Matt acted as both "director" and player in the negotiations. Terry was LASCO's detail person. Tom was the person from ROCA who tried to keep things moving smoothly, while his counterpart, Jerry, presented himself as a hard-hitting negotiator, a jokester, and an all-around good guy.

The negotiations began with Matt laying out the two basic goals of the negotiation: (1) to agree on the conditions of the buyout and (2) to agree on the terms of the management services contract. As soon as the negotiations got underway, Terry passed out copies of a document listing the nine items that were to be negotiated.

As the negotiation proceeded Matt frequently identified possible problems that were likely to occur with regard to the agreement. He played, in his opinion, a "hard-nosed negotiator," telling me after one session, "I'm acting [like a] very very tough guy, intentionally." Terry, on the other hand, more often offered conciliatory remarks.

*[handwritten margin note: Typical American Jump before Thinking. Japanese will be more Patient.]*

Jerry's presentation of self differed markedly from both Terry's and Matt's. He spoke spontaneously, excitedly, and much more frequently than anyone else, used repetition for emphasis, jumped into discussions with an extreme or exaggerated stance, and sometimes paid little attention to accuracy of fact. Tom maintained a calm, relaxed posture in comparison. Additionally, he typically softened Jerry's negotiating stance and corrected his factual lapses. Tom also joked, but much less often than Jerry or Matt.

Cultural assumptions about work were repeatedly revealed through dialogue. For the Americans, the assumptions revolved around trust, manageable risk, autonomous action (personal and organizational), and money. For the Japanese, the assumptions focused on trust, personal qualities deemed "managerial," the identity and future of the computer peripherals group, and interunit relations within the trading company. Even though both revealed assumptions about trust in a work setting, the meanings of trust were quite different for Japanese and American negotiators.

## Negotiating Sales Commission Issues: Trust, Money, and Manageable Risk

The Japanese and American negotiators demonstrated their differing conceptualizations of trust when trying to determine how long to pay the 10% sales commission. Matt repeated the refrain "You should believe"—that is, Tom and Jerry should believe in the good intentions of LASCO to play fairly, implying that they need not belabor the specific aspects of the agreements. Tom's and Jerry's discourse, however, suggested that details could not simply be left to trust. They enumerated the things that could go wrong. Jerry even brought up the possibility of willful manipulation by LASCO. Tom and Jerry wanted the avowed good intentions to be formally ensured in the agreement.

The text excerpted below additionally illustrates the prominence of the subject of money in Tom's and Jerry's discourse as well as their preoccupation with reducing risk to manageable proportions.

MATT: Okay, number 3. Anyway, as part of our present commission, our obligation to pay to ROCA up to March 31st is only towards, uh, invoice [of product received by customer] by that date.

TOM: Right.

MATT: And then, after April 1st, if we cannot collect the money from the customer for that particular invoice, we have the right to ask ROCA for the invoice.

JERRY: What? (*Laughter*) What is this? Wait a minute, no, what did you just say, please?

TOM: What he's saying, that you're gonna go out there and unload the barrel ship 5-million-dollars worth of product in March. If they can't collect, then they get that money back.

JERRY: Well, the only other problem is what . . . what keeps them from delivering April 1st, instead of March 30th?

MATT: It's, uh, 100% in the control of LASCO. (*Laughter*)

JERRY: That's the problem.

MATT: You should believe us.

JERRY: We had almost a million dollars not make it one month, that got slipped into the next month. Why?

MATT: Because our accounting, way of the, uh, accounting procedure in my country, every sales will close on 26th of every month. After that, we cannot, uh, enter to the computer.

JERRY: Why don't we just go one extra month [under the old commission agreement]? . . . The problem we're having, Matt, is, I mean—and honestly it's a problem—we're shipping anywhere from $300,000 to 500,000 worth of equipment between the 26th and 30th of every month . . . sometimes up to a million dollars . . . and we had $400,000 of stuff this last month that went out on the 1st, on the 2nd, because they [LASCO] couldn't get it out.

TOM: What Jerry's talking about is that we've been paying, we pay our guy's commissions based on, uh, when the product is shipped [to LASCO from the Japanese factory] . . . And even though you miss a month, you know, [and] we don't get it [ROCA's commission] until the next month, we're still payin' our guys when they [the manufacturer] make the shipment.

MATT: Uh-huh. *not giving to much information*

TOM: We just want to make sure we don't have a half-million-dollar differential that you say you're paying after the 31st, that could balance our books out . . . okay, just so . . . you know, right around that date we have a clear understanding, you know, with a little flexibility in there somewhere.

Matt adjusted LASCO's stance, indicating that Tom and Jerry would receive the 10% commission on any product paid for (by the customer) by April 15. They accepted this, but Jerry pursued a related issue: unusual slippage in delivery.

JERRY: Now, how 'bout the other half of the formula? . . . All of a sudden we see, in some significant manner—15%, 20%—some amounts falling into April. . . . I think something should be triggered then, because that means either the factory is delaying it or, you know, somebody is delaying the shipments into April and taking them out of March.

MATT: Yeah, something needs to happen then. But, uh, it is kind of out of our control. Factory delay, delivery out of [our] control.

JERRY: Well, but you just told me earlier that LASCO had total control, so, uh . . . (*Laughter*)

MATT: No, uh, if the product is at our hand here. But, unless, otherwise, it's out of control . . . if, uh, shipment boat sank, what happen then?

*Typical American* / *impossible*

*very*

The debate continued. Matt suggested that the potential problem be handled by carefully checking March purchase orders (POs) with Sam, a Japanese colleague who headed LASCO's present video terminals group.

MATT: So, the only solution is, when, uh, briefing, uh, PO, you should discuss with Sam. PO by PO basis, this is including in the March shipment or not.

*NO TRUST*

Jerry was not satisfied. He worried about the possibility of significant slippage of products into April that were supposed to be shipped in March.

JERRY: So what is the recourse is all I'm asking, you know?

TERRY: Are you worrying about the, uh, happenings beyond our control, or intentionally, you know . . .

JERRY: I would say, I would say to get April off to a nice start [for LASCO Terminals], intentionally you might ship, you know, a portion of that business from late March to early April. It doesn't hurt to come out flying you know. . . . Matt, I can't, I can't call up [the Japanese manufacturer] and say, "Well, why did you ship this on the 1st or the 3rd," [and learn that] because verbally somebody called and said, "Let's ship everything from the 1st to the 5th instead of from the 26th or the 20th. . . . Let's move half of it over, because, you know, we help you out sometimes, you help us out sometimes." Do you understand the position?

MATT: No. ← *he can not understand the lack of Trust*

JERRY: You don't understand the position?

MATT: You should believe.

JERRY: Oh, I do believe, but see, in believing I can . . . by instituting something that makes it even easier to believe, right?

TERRY: The person [at the Japanese manufacturing company] who is handling the accounting and, you know, daily inventory control of shipment, doesn't know our [LASCO–ROCA] deal.

MATT: Yeah.

TERRY: So they will do as usual.

JERRY: But Sam [the Japanese manager of LASCO's Video Terminals Group] could sit and call [manufacturer's name].

TERRY: So it depends on whether you can believe Sam or Matt or myself . . .

*Again, typically Americans want everything spelled out!*

Jerry continued to press for a clause protecting ROCA's interests, given a specified amount, that is, a "trigger point," of slippage. The debate over the issue of slippage ended inconclusively. It was briefly resumed later in the first session when the lawyers were present.

Jerry also brought up the question of what would happen if "6 or 8 months after the subsidiary is operating, someone sues for money back." Does ROCA Consulting have the obligation to pay LASCO for returned product? The general consensus was "no," but again Jerry wanted formal protection. He wanted to ensure that ROCA Consulting's risk was minimized.

The potential problems of late product delivery and the return of payment to dissatisfied customers did not actually arise in subsequent negotiation sessions. By the time a LASCO–ROCA agreement was signed, however, LASCO had extended the cutoff date for the 10% commission to April 30, 1 month beyond the originally proposed date, and agreed to a date after which Tom and Jerry would not be liable for returned product shipped while ROCA was LASCO's sales representative.

So to Tom and Jerry, trust was to be earned by specifying conditions and meeting them; conditions were repeatedly linked to money and manageable risks. To Matt and Terry, trust was to be assumed, and players were to believe problems would be worked out agreeably.

## Negotiating ROCA Europe–ESCO Relations:
## Interunit Relations, Money, and Trust

Discussion of the future relationship between ROCA Europe and ESCO provided insight into the complexity of relations between subunits of the trading company involved in the computer peripherals business. Decision making clearly occurred within a multiunit framework and Matt was well aware that proper protocol had to be followed. This part of the negotiation was critical to Tom and Jerry's financial calculations. Tom and Jerry trusted Matt to see that ROCA Europe's interests would be protected.

MATT: I think, uh, as I told you from the beginning of our negotiations, that Europe is out of my control, out of my responsibility. So, I will try to convince the president for ESCO to take the, uh, minimum 3 years, [that] ROCA Europe should be the exclusive rep for ESCO as far as this video terminal business is concerned. That I will try to let them accept, but I cannot guarantee.

TOM: When will we know?

MATT: Uh, the president of ESCO and, uh, Tsutsui [executive responsible for day-to-day operations of ESCO] will be here by the 20th of this month for transaction of this, uh, deal . . . so, I'd like to delete entire paragraph on Europe from the present agreement. But I understand your concern, so I will try the best and, uh, when UK [United Kingdom] president and, uh, Tsutsui come over here, we will arrange a meeting with you.

TOM: Okay, all right. So we make a deal directly with them?

MATT: Yes.

TOM: Okay.

MATT: But right now we are 90% no problem.

TOM: Okay.

JERRY: What's the 10%?

MATT: Ten percent is, uh, they like to actually interview your guy [i.e., Kristian, who runs ROCA Europe] over this. Because without, uh, knowing him, he [ESCO's president] cannot commit to use as exclusive rep.

TOM: Uh, Tsutsui knows Kristian.

MATT: Yes, Tsutsui knows, but, uh, new president.

Tom told Matt that Kristian would be in Los Angeles the same week as the ESCO people, so Matt planned the meeting for a time Kristian could attend.

MATT: So, that's why I would like to propose that the entire article regarding Europe be deleted from the, uh, contract.

JERRY: I understand what you'd like to do, but you understand that we can't? Okay?

MATT: (*Raises eyebrows*) So, it means that you cannot accept?

JERRY: This is a very integral part of the whole, the whole deal. It always has been. . . . Do you understand that this is, you know, close to half the [buyout] deal?

MATT: (*Raises head in questioning manner and makes a long "ummm" sound*) Because my impression was when, uh, I shared communication with you on this entire deal . . . I thought the European deal is not so significantly affect deal.

TERRY: We have seen that the, uh, European deal is, uh, out of [our control] . . . as Matt said, would try best to have the ROCA Europe to be the exclusive rep of ESCO, but as far as LASCO position is concerned, this deal, Europe deal, entirely separate. That's the basis we have been negotiating.

JERRY: We understand that it's a separate basis, but we also have been, you know, brought this far based on [the understanding that] C. K. [C. K. Tani, president of ESCO] has been, you know, informed of it; he approved of it; he liked it. And there would be two separate documents, but basically that it would happen. . . . It's a very important part of the whole arrangement, and it's close to 50% of the deal.

TOM: It's not 50%, but it's a building stone, big block.

JERRY: It changes everything else. It will change everything else if it doesn't go.

TOM: We can, you know, for purposes of right now, Matt, we can delete it from the package that we're talking about as a separate [deal] . . . but realizing that, before we sign, we'll have that other thing. We'll have the European thing signed.

MATT: But, uh, my understanding from the beginning after starting negotiation with you, the European deal, is, uh, . . . ESCO operation has, uh, choices. One is either they will use ROCA Europe as a sales rep, commission 5%, minimum 3 years, exclusively for European sales, or, ESCO can hire now the, uh, employee of ROCA Europe as the employee of ESCO. Right?

JERRY: No.

MATT: Well, anyway, the Europe deal, we feel, as I said, uh, separate the deal. So, let's, uh, put aside.

JERRY: When you say put aside, there's nothing we can do about it until you sit down with C. K. Or, it sounds like, it sounds like we can't do anything until they interview, uh, Kristian and all, all they're looking at is possibly hiring him. . . . That's not our understanding.

MATT: Well, if so, then, uh, I have to change our proposal to, uh, ESCO.

TOM: Do a sales, do a sales job on C. K.

Japanese cultural knowledge about interunit relations was evidenced again during a lull in the first negotiating session while the players waited for the lawyers. The context was an animated discussion about logos. Utterances of the Japanese players reflected their concern for the identity and future of the computer peripherals group. Tom and Jerry brought mockups of potential LASCO Terminals logos developed by ROCA's ad agency. General interest in the logos stemmed from the rapid expansion of the computer peripherals business worldwide. The need to coordinate LASCO's choices with decisions at the Tokyo headquarters complicated the issue.

The following exchange additionally provided insight into yet another of Tom and Jerry's assumptions about work, in this instance, their sense of autonomous action, which was clearly at odds with Japanese assumptions about consultative decision making.

JERRY: Let's ask the question we've heard from two different sources: either the trading company [headquarters] or LASCO is looking to produce a new logo?

MATT: Yes.

JERRY: Yes, LASCO, or, yes, Japan is looking for a new logo?

MATT: Japan. . . . All product distributed worldwide, through distributors. It means, with the trading company's model number or name only. . . . All distribution product, standardized logo should be there. That is the [headquarters'] focus, idea. We agreed, but the problem is they [already] chose a, uh, logo. We don't accept that logo.

JERRY: So, you can't use LASCO's [present] logo?

MATT: No.

JERRY: Well, okay. But can't we pick our own [logo]? LASCO Terminals?

MATT: That is . . . up in the air right now.

Tom displayed the logo mock-ups. The objective was to make LASCO a household name; they wanted the letters "LASCO" to be widely recognized in ads for any LASCO-affiliated company. He cautioned Matt that speed was essential with regard to this decision. *Speed does not typically happen in Japanese culture*

MATT: (*To Jerry*) So, you have to talk with everybody concerned.

JERRY: (*At blackboard, gesturing and pacing*) For what? . . . It's easy. We just checked almost everybody concerned. Sam says he likes that [logo]. Tom and I say we like that. So now it's up to you. You make the decision anyway. Doesn't matter what we say.

MATT: So, let me think it over a couple of days. . . . I have to talk to our marketing people and, uh, everybody concerned.

JERRY: Okay, this is our marketing people. (*Laughter*)

MATT: No, LASCO.

JERRY: Well, this is LASCO Terminals.

MATT: Yeah, but, uh, in the future, we have to have a group image, one logo.

JERRY: Well, how 'bout if we bring the, uh, printer people in [right now], to see what they think of that [proposed logo], right? They'd like to see that.

MATT: Can you, uh, leave it, uh, couple of days?

TOM: Sure.

## Negotiating the Management Services Agreement: Money, Autonomous Action, Manageable Risk, Interunit Relations, Managerial Qualities, and Trust

In negotiating the management services agreement, most of the subtextual cultural themes were again revealed. Tom and Jerry were keenly aware of the autonomy they would give up by becoming part of the LASCO Terminals organization, and they expressed their intent to preserve as much personal autonomy as possible under the new arrangement. Their preoccupation with the terms of the agreement again revealed both their monetary concerns and their desire to control risk. The Japanese subtext more subtly reflected notions about the personal qualities a manager should have and about the way interunit relations affected decision making. In addition, the issue of trust resurfaced.

Debate first centered on cancellation of the management services agreement:

MATT: So, I . . . uh, we have two problems or, I should say, two points we should discuss [about the management services agreement]. One is compensation, how much we should compensate. The other one, the number two point is: On what kind of occasion can we terminate this services agreement without any obligations within [i.e., before] 3 years. For example, if for some reason, we have to close LASCO Terminals, still have obligation to pay or not?

TERRY: I don't think so.

MATT: I don't know. We did not discuss in such a detail.

JERRY: Obviously, I think the draft we have is a no-cut deal, as they call it [i.e., the contract cannot be canceled].

TOM: No . . . we didn't, uh, we didn't address that in our deal.

Matt guided the discussion toward possible reasons for ending the services agreement prematurely. He wrote the following on the board:

Termination—automatic after 3 full years
Cancellation—without any obligation
  1. LASCO Terminals business stopped by any reason
  2. Criminal [case against Tom or Jerry]
  3. Disability [of Tom or Jerry]
  4. Death [of Tom or Jerry]

Attention focused on point 1, the reasons LASCO Terminals might stop operating. Among the points mentioned were U.S. government intervention, competition making the business unprofitable, or the Tokyo headquarters shutting down the company.

JERRY: The problem with doing any of this, and not making it, as I say, a no-cut deal on our account . . . we tend to, uh, we tend to lose our ability to control item 2 [on the agenda], and item 2 is very important to us. So if we lose control of that, we've lost control of a lot of things. . . . If you think you're going to shut the business down, that's not why we're here. . . . I don't wanna see number 1 happening. If there's a possibility of that, then we'd better start and renegotiate this whole deal.

TOM: You know we've gotta sit on, uh, we've gotta keep the services agreement going. 'Cause . . .

JERRY: Forget the services agreement. Just look at what were losing [by giving up ROCA].

TOM: I know.

JERRY: We should invoke some rule, some penalty for that. That should be another item we should have: If for some reason [the Tokyo headquarters] can't maintain the company . . . cancellation clause, right? To us. To the benefit of the poor guys who gave up a running business. Does that make sense?

TERRY: To some extent.

JERRY: To some extent?

TERRY: To some extent.

JERRY: Say that a little bit louder. (*Laughter*) Mark the date, would you? (*Laughter*)

The players later returned to the subject of cancellation after the lawyers joined the negotiation. Jerry reiterated earlier arguments, despite being told by everyone that it was unlikely LASCO Terminals would go out of business. His comments indicated his awareness that, in contrast to Tom and Jerry, the Japanese enjoyed employment security within the trading company.

JERRY: However, if they feel . . . that there might be some reason for canceling the agreement, then we're not dealing in good business practice. At least from our side, we're sitting here saying, "We're gonna be here for some time, other than death or disability," and they're saying,

"Well, maybe the government looks like it's gonna shut this thing down." If that's the case, let's cancel all deals. I mean, everything falls apart then. Our management services contract falls apart, our one-and-a-half percent for three years falls apart, and, uh, theoretically, Tom and I are left holding the bag.

MATT: Uh, we say, uh, the government—force majeure. Out of [our] control, although we desire to continue.

JERRY: Granted . . . but, you all [the Japanese] go back. Either you sit here, or you all go back to Japan, and you still have a position within the company. Where we sit [exposed], you know, for taking less money. Well, you know we're selling certain rights now, based on this [deal] going on for a certain, you know, period. Where, theoretically, we might have been able to ensure some stability in our long-term lives, you know, financial stability. . . . And, if you're saying, based on any one of these [reasons], you can change your mind, then that . . . you know, we have the most to lose, even though we're the smallest entity. Personally, we have the most to lose.

MATT: So Jerry, the bottom of your concern is, in the event this LASCO, or the trading company, decides to go out of the business, uh, you, uh, concerned how much you will be compensated? . . . We show you that figure and that is the end of this discussion?

JERRY: Right. That's correct. So, you'll put a figure in there?

ROGER: You see, by ending the discussion, you cut off the legal fees that I can charge. (*Laughter*)

Barring an event on the scale of nuclear war, Matt verbally guaranteed ROCA Consulting 3 years of monetary compensation, in the form of commissions and salary for management services. He then explored the circumstances under which LASCO Terminals could substitute other persons for Tom or Jerry, or simply forgo any actual services by ROCA.

MATT: How about, uh, difference of opinion of the management?

*LASCO* ROGER: What flexibility do you want in that case?

MATT: Two flexibilities. One is we like to have the right to ask to this management [services] company to replace . . .

JERRY: Okay. To replace Tom and I. And what is the second one?

MATT: The second one is . . . we don't terminate. We'll pay just 3 years, but, uh, I like to tell them [Tom and Jerry], no need to come over.

*ROCA* DARYL: Well, members of the management team, under the management

contract, are subject to the direction of the board of directors. . . .
They will do what you tell them to do.

ROGER: So, you know, if you want a substitute, what you really do is, you
say, "Jerry stay home," you pay Jerry, and then we go hire a substitute
over here and just pay him ourselves. . . . The only time they have a
duty to provide a substitute [at their own expense, while still being
paid according to the services contract] is when there's a criminal
[act] . . . a death . . . a disability.

DARYL: With your reasonable discretion as to who.

MATT: So, as we said, as long as we are keeping the payments for the 3
years.

ROGER: They have no right to do anything, if we tell them to do nothing.

MATT: Then, they cannot refuse.

ROGER: Correct.

In the third negotiating session, discussion got down to the actual
work role and work behavior of Tom and Jerry within LASCO Terminals.
They were officially "consultants." Would they be bound by the policies
and regulations that govern regular employees? Questions arose about vacation time, days off, work hours, overseas trips for ROCA Europe business, and so forth.

ROGER: Okay, shall we talk about this?

TERRY: I think so.

JERRY: Talk about what?

TERRY: Okay. Mostly, you guys are not employee[s], although you have to
follow the, uh, company policies and regulations, . . . right?

JERRY: Uh-huh.

TERRY: For example, according to, uh, employee policy, vacations, uh, . . .
employees who worked for 1 year is entitled to take a vacation—10
days. The same rules apply.

JERRY: To us?

TERRY: Uh-huh. Is that okay?

JERRY: No.

TERRY: So where you have a problem? And, also, in case [of] employee . . .
if there is some person absent . . . you know, [you can be absent] not
more than 10 days [which would be covered by sick leave], okay?

Then salary deducted automatically. [If you are] absent more than 10 days, then how the company will be compensated for that absence?

JERRY: It's a good point.

TERRY: We can deduct the pay . . . the monthly payment, portion of it?

DARYL: Let me ask a question on concept. The concept of this agreement, which is what we discussed last time, is that, what in effect we're doing is, you [LASCO Terminals] are contracting with a company. And that company, to perform under the terms of the agreement, must tender and provide the full-time productive efforts of Tom and Jerry, which is subject to your reasonable direction. And it provides that there must be a fulltime, uh, rendering of services and all other productive effort during the terms of this agreement, unless you choose to say, "Go away and stay home."

JERRY: Okay.

DARYL: You know, I kind of would hope that the form of this agreement would provide that both of you are going to work together. If they start slacking off and taking trips around the world, then you have the ability to seek remedies under the agreement. Rather than saying, you know, "You took 11 days off this year, Jerry, and, therefore, we're going to dock you a day," or something like that. Roger, is that consistent with . . . ?

ROGER: I think what the problem is, very frankly, is not the concern that they will not devote their full-time best efforts. If there was any concern about that, there wouldn't be a deal.

JERRY: Right.

ROGER: But the whole concept of their not being employees, which is what they have requested for their own tax reasons, is difficult for LASCO. And it's aggravated to the extent that they act less like employees even though they're not employees. But to the extent that people in the company . . . say, "Well, we understand that Jerry and Tom do whatever they want. They don't want to come to work, they don't come to work."

JERRY: Well, but that is a problem. Because, one thing . . . I mean, I can give you my own personal background. I get my children one month a year. In the summer. Now that one month, if I want to take a week off, or two weeks off, or a month off, I will do it. Even though I keep working. He [Tom] does the same thing.

ROGER: Well, I don't think it's just. . . . No, I don't think we're trying to put the rules the same . . .

JERRY: And, two, uh, Tom and I still have a responsibility in Europe, which we're going to have to go over there once in a while.

ROGER: I don't think that's a problem.

JERRY: Well, sure it is! Because unless it's deemed on this side to say that it is an official act, then you're taking time off to go across and do something else that there is some responsibility [to do]. . . . So there's going to be a certain amount of time there. That's one reason to have a management agreement.

TERRY: So your business in Europe is not relating to the LASCO Terminals?

JERRY: Why? . . . Well, it isn't and it is. Because sales of the product all over the world impact sales domestically. . . . [Strictly speaking], LASCO Terminals does not have any responsibility in Europe. Nor does ROCA Consulting. But Jerry and Tom have. So there will be times to be over there. Based on that, you gonna call it vacations? Time off? . . . So immediately, we can have a problem there. . . . Yet, we're still working. We're not off playing all the time. We play very little. But to be regimented, versus, say, 10 days here . . . who is the one to say these 10 days are vacation and not work?

TERRY: So . . . you have your own business as owner of ROCA Europe. You have to go to Europe. Who pays your travel expense?

JERRY: We have to . . .

TOM: It's our intent, certainly, to, uh, observe the . . . the, uh, rules and regulations of the company. Definitely. I mean, that's just . . . seriously, there's bound to be some exceptions.

JERRY: In a large company, there is no exception. That's why we're on a management contract.

TOM: But . . . uh, certainly, the employee guidelines . . . we assume the guidelines are for ourselves. . . . We have to act as employees or, otherwise, we have no respect from our [subordinate] employees. But I think that, uh, wording to the effect that, uh, we will observe the policies of the company . . . realizing, there's going to be a few basic exceptions which are reasonable. You know, . . . one of the toughest things is . . . is . . . as Matt pointed out several months ago, is that, you know, taking us from your [video terminals] group [as sales reps], and putting us into this . . . this . . .

JERRY: Structured . . .

TOM: Structure. And, you know, it's a little tough squeezing back into that, that structure. . . . So, it's a flexibility kind of thing, I guess.

As the preceding dialogue shows, the Japanese notion of appropriate qualities and behavior for a manager conflicts with the American actors' notion of autonomous action. Authority relations with respect to Tom and Jerry and their Japanese bosses became a negotiated issue in the continuing exchange.

TERRY: So the point is, uh, you guys are reporting to, uh, under [the new] organization, Sam [the Japanese manager], right? . . . So Sam is asked, you know, by Jerry. . . . Jerry takes 1 month off for some, you know, reason. In that case Sam is asking, "How I have to deal with this, unless there is some rule?" He can't say "yes" or "no." He does when he has such a rule.

JERRY: Sam is asking?

TERRY: Uh-huh.

JERRY: So this is a question from Sam, not . . .

TERRY: No, I have the same question too. And even though you both taking off for 1 month, still we have to pay monthly [salary] charges. Is that right?

JERRY: Theoretically, yeah.

ROGER: I think what Sam is concerned about—and he's not saying he has a concern because it's gonna happen and he's sure it's gonna happen— it's just [Sam wants] the understanding that there's a spirit of cooperation in that regard. And I don't think the agreement allows Jerry . . . to say to Sam, "I'm leaving, that's it. I'll see you next month." I don't think they could do that under the agreement, and Jerry's not going to do that, nor is Tom. It's the concept, I think, that Sam is concerned about. . . . Maybe the [observing] policies and regulations statement is enough.

JERRY: Yeah, but now that you bring it up, we will not . . . uh, or I won't go under that policy if it's just, uh, if everything is so strict.

ROGER: No, I think, uh, maybe we ought to say that, uh, they'll [Tom and Jerry] make every reasonable effort to comply with the policies and regulations, including matters related to vacations, time off, and the like. And, to the extent that there's any dispute, the parties will attempt to work it out in good faith.

JERRY: We most certainly don't want someone telling us, though. And if the purpose for Sam is to say, . . . "I, Sam, can tell him, Jerry," then that's something else. We plan to work with Sam, not for Sam, right? Is that the spirit of the cooperation understanding?

ROGER: Well, I think the answer is they probably mean with, as opposed to for, in the strictest sense. [Roger, nevertheless, relates a personal anecdote to remind Jerry and Tom, that "the whole is more important than you individually."]

ROGER: And I think that's what they're saying. Sam would . . . it would be expected that you would just do what I did, sort of fight the best you can, then gracefully bow out and say, "Okay, Sam."

TERRY: My . . . my understanding, you know, the definition of "with" and "for," okay. If they are employee, employee should work with his superior and for his superior.

*[I think it's still a different understanding]*

We see possible divergence in the meaning attached to the words "working with" one's superior. Additionally, there was some indication that the Japanese do not trust the Americans to behave, in their view, properly. *Japanese view are that Americans are lazy*

## CROSS-CULTURAL INTERPRETATION SUMMARIZED

The text created as the actors negotiated agreement clearly reflects the cross-national, cross-cultural context. Separate sets of cultural rules unconsciously, and perhaps consciously, "motivated" the American and Japanese players. Preliminary analysis of the text indicates that a cultural logic indeed underlies the negotiators' verbal tactics and discourse strategy; much of their communicative behavior is consonant with descriptions of American and Japanese negotiating styles found in the literature (e.g., Graham & Sano, 1984). Jerry, for example, comes close to being the stereotypical John Wayne of American negotiating, characterized by a "Shoot first, ask questions later" mentality. Matt and, especially, Terry, as anticipated, demonstrated greater concern for social harmony.

This study illustrates the implications of culturally distinct concepts of work for the negotiation process. Concepts of work shape the text in a complex process. Players not only act according to their cultural motivation, they react as well. For example, one motivation for Matt's intentionally tough stance toward Tom and Jerry was "because of the difference of their characteristics." That is, their personal qualities differed from what the Japanese expected in a high-level manager. Matt explained to me why, under the management services agreement, Tom and Jerry would hold the titles vice president of marketing and vice president of sales but would not be named executive vice president or general manager of LASCO Terminals, titles that would make them "officers" or key decision makers in the new subsidiary. He said, "They could not pass my qualification." In Matt's mind, their lack of qualification revolved around three areas: They put

*Taking one month off, for example*

self-interest above the interests of the company, they were too concerned about money, and they did not think deeply enough before taking action. In Matt's culturally informed opinion, Tom and Jerry were salesmen, not managers.

> "He is [they are] selfish individual. Normally salesman is so. They don't like to be bound by the manager or the organization. . . . He is so much concerned about money for his pocket. This is also salesman type. For a young salesman, yes, understandable [but not for an older one]. . . . For business planning or product planning, 3 years relation with them. I could not satisfy [i.e., be satisfied with] their way of approach. No evidence. I just felt no deep studies."

Tom's and Jerry's negotiation performance merely reinforced already-existing perceptions among the Japanese. Yet to most American business persons, their concern with the financial terms of the buyout and manageable risk undoubtedly seemed appropriate to the situation, as did the money-related joking of the Americans, including the lawyers. Similarly, Tom's and Jerry's desire to maintain autonomy of action also was a familiar American cultural theme (see Kleinberg, 1989). They did not realize that each time they expressed these themes through their utterances, they strengthened the Japanese resolve, however unconscious, to negotiate controls over their actions.

The American players' contribution to the text, in addition, must be understood in the context of their entrepreneurial history. Tom and Jerry were "giving up" a successful business; they felt buyout terms should reflect ROCA's value. As Tom explained to me some months after LASCO Terminals has been operating,

> "Because we were really the first and most successful worldwide sales agent in the country, we had a lot of opportunities in the final stages. That's why the negotiation was so centered on money—because we had to balance that money against what we could get on the outside."

But, just as importantly, the subtext was about giving up the entrepreneurial freedom, perhaps even their reputation in the industry, that Tom and Jerry had enjoyed. Contending that the business was being mismanaged under LASCO Terminals, Tom remarked,

> "My name is involved. . . . I started the thing [ROCA]. It was my deal. I brought Jerry and Hank [another original ROCA shareholder] in. I feel responsible for where it's gone and how it's gone. I don't like being in the position of being in a secondary position."

*Company first!*

Tom's and Jerry's self-involvement and independent thinking caused discomfort for the Japanese, who were inclined to emphasize cultural themes that focused on the organization, the center of their entire work life (Kleinberg, 1989). Thus, Matt gave Tom and Jerry lessons in interunit relations among members of the trading company's computer peripherals group. Decisions about important matters like logos or the video terminals business in Europe could not be made without the involvement of these subunits; autonomous action, personal and organizational, was exercised within narrow constraints. The future of the computer peripherals *for Matt* group took precedence over the interests of any one organizational subunit despite competition for influence within the group.

Even the Japanese notion of trust assumed an important position in the negotiation text. Matt and Terry felt that Tom and Jerry should have believed that LASCO or the trading company would not cheat them and that any problems that arose could be worked out in good faith. The long-standing relationship between LASCO and ROCA rested on such trust. The text indicates that, to some degree, the Americans did believe in Matt's good intentions; dialogue concerning ROCA's European subsidiary shows this. Nonetheless, within their business culture, trust required contractual safeguards.

*The American way NOT the Japanese*

## A FINAL WORD

As explained at the beginning, this case study views negotiation as embedded in wider organizational processes. It is not a discrete activity. The unfolding of the LASCO–ROCA negotiation illustrates this point. The drama resonates with the politics of the larger computer peripherals group, with headquarters–subsidiary relations, and with internal LASCO policy making, all of which are intertwined. Not only does the text constructed by the LASCO and ROCA players reflect their past relationships, but in constructing this text they have begun to negotiate their future work roles and relationships. They have set the stage for the next act of the drama.

## NOTE

1. The names of participants have been changed to protect their identity.

## KEY TERMS

CONTEXT: the circumstances around which events occur, or situational factors that give meaning to communication and behavior.

CROSS-CULTURAL NEGOTIATION: the process of reaching agreement between persons or representatives from at least two distinct cultural groups.

CULTURE: the acquired knowledge that people use to interpret experience and generate social behavior.

CONCEPTS OF WORK: tacit understandings widely shared in the societal culture about such things as authority, trust and decision making in the workplace

DISCOURSE STYLE OR DISCOURSE STRATEGY: the logic underlying the way a cultural group puts thoughts and words together in order to persuade.

ETHNOGRAPHY: cultural description of a social setting—that is, an ethnographer seeks to comprehend the "native's" world from the native's point of view.

INTERPERSONAL ATTRACTION: the degree to which individuals desire to establish and maintain relationships.

NEGOTIATION AS CULTURAL PERFORMANCE: the concept that, through their interaction, negotiators construct the understandings by which they make sense of their social setting; they reinforce existing cultural knowledge and create new cultural knowledge.

SELECTIVE PERCEPTION: the process by which people attend to the most important messages out of the total pool of potentially perceivable messages and use those chosen messages to make sense out of their current situation.

SUBTEXT: the underlying (not always discernable) meaning attributed to an event or action that is influenced by the constraints of the situation, the history of the participants, and the organization.


## DISCUSSION QUESTIONS

1. Based on your image of Americans and Japanese, in what ways do you feel negotiation tactics and discourse strategy reflect the respective cultures?
2. A careful reading of the dialogue shows that the Japanese negotiators, Matt and Terry, speak a kind of "Japanese English." (The written text cannot demonstrate their accents.) To what extent do you feel the "language gap" affects this particular negotiation?
3. What does the author mean by the term "concepts of work," and how does this term relate to the concept of culture?
4. Many cross-national negotiations fail because of cultural differences. How do you explain the fact that the negotiators in this case study successfully reached agreement?
5. The case indicates that Tom and Jerry were not completely satisfied with the way the Japanese were managing the new company, LASCO Terminals. What might be some specific complaints on the part of Tom and Jerry? What are some potential sources of dissatisfaction with their own role in the company?

# REFERENCES

Adler, N. J. (1996). *International dimensions of organizational behavi* Florence, KY: Wadsworth.

Friday, R. A. (1991). Contrasts in discussion behaviors of German ana American managers. In L. A. Samovar & R. E. Porter (Eds.), *Intercultural communication: A reader* (6th ed., pp. 174–185). Belmont, CA: Wadsworth.

Graham, J. L. (1985, Spring). The influence of culture on the process of business negotiations: An exploratory study. *Journal of International Business Studies,* 79–94.

Graham, J. L., & Sano, Y. (1984). *Smart bargaining: Doing business with the Japanese.* Cambridge, MA: Ballinger.

Gregory, K. (1983). Native-view paradigms: Multiple cultures and culture conflicts in organizations. *Administrative Science Quarterly, 28,* 359–376.

Kleinberg, J. (1989). Cultural clash between managers: America's Japanese firms. In B. S. Prasad (Ed.), *Advances in international comparative management* (Vol. 4, pp. 221–243). Greenwich, CT: JAI Press.

Mangham, I. L., & Overington, M. A. (1983). Dramatism and the theatrical metaphor. In G. Morgan (Ed.), *Beyond method* (pp. 219–233). Beverly Hills, CA: Sage.

Mangham, I. L., & Overington, M. A. (1987). *Organizations as theatre: A social psychology of dramatic appearances.* Chichester, England: Wiley.

Pacanowsky, M. E., & O'Donnell-Trujillo, N. (1983). Organizational communication as cultural performance. *Communication Monographs, 50,* 126–147.

Shenkar, O., & Ronen, S. (1987). The cultural context of negotiations: The implications of Chinese interpersonal norms. *Journal of Applied Behavioral Science, 23*(2), 263–275.

Spradley, J. P. (1979). *The ethnographic interview.* New York: Holt, Rinehart & Winston.

Young, L. W. L. (1982). Inscrutability revisited. In J. J. Gumperz (Ed.), *Language and social identity* (pp. 72–84). Cambridge, England: Cambridge University Press.

# CHAPTER 10

# Submerging the Emergent Culture

## A Conflict in Mission in a Human Service Organization

EILEEN BERLIN RAY

This case study recounts events that took place at a rape crisis center in a large, metropolitan city in the Midwest. It takes the perspective of the staff who were employed there at the time of the events presented. Data were drawn from interviews conducted by the author with that staff and from written documents.

## ORGANIZATION BACKGROUND

The Rape Crisis Center (RCC), founded in 1974, is a nonprofit social change agency that provides counseling for victims and community advocacy and education for issues of sexual assault. It serves a large metropolitan county of approximately 1 million residents and provides the only comprehensive service for rape survivors in the county. The agency provides free counseling for child and adult victims of sexual assault and adult survivors of childhood sexual assault for up to 4 months (approximately 200 clients are seen per month), after which they refer clients to counselors or therapists in the community. Other services, which are heavily dependent on the more than 150 volunteers, include a 24-hour hotline; community outreach programs to elementary, middle, and high schools, to a nearby urban university, and to the general community; and a hospital advocacy program. The agency is dependent on federal funding and donations for staff salaries and operations.

## THE STAFF

The RCC is headed by a director, who reports directly to the Board of Trustees. The office manager and direct service staff report directly to the Director (see Figure 10.1).

### Board of Trustees

The RCC is overseen by a volunteer Board of Trustees made up of 25 local professionals from a variety of occupations. Board members can be nominated or can self-nominate, and they serve a 3-year term, which can be renewed once.

### Directors

#### Outgoing Director

Anne Parker was the director of RCC from 1987 to 1992. She was a vocal feminist, and a strong advocate for equal rights, and she believed that all people are victimized by sexual assault. Anne saw one of her important roles as a public spokesperson about sexual and physical abuse. She was well liked by most of the staff and was viewed as a team manager. Anne spent much time informally interacting with staff and letting them vent emotions before the stress of their jobs became overwhelming. Decisions were not made until after discussion with all staff members. Weekly staff meetings were run democratically, with an open agenda. Each staff member spoke about her or his program, any concerns she or he had, and provided support for other staff.

#### Incoming Director

Linda Hall was named director of RCC in June 1992. The Search Committee was comprised of eight board members, the previous director (Anne),

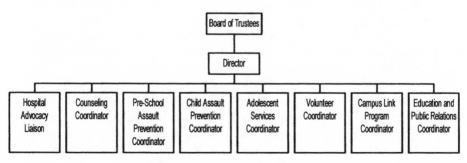

**FIGURE 10.1.** RCC organizational chart.

and two staff members. Given the decline in federal and local funding, the board was particularly interested in appointing someone who could secure grants from the community and build and clarify the board's role in the RCC.

Linda was not the top choice for most members of the search committee. Concerns were raised by staff representatives that her knowledge of sexual and physical abuse and commitment to social change appeared to be lacking. For example, in her interview Linda stated that she was not a feminist and knew little about the issues of sexual assault but was "willing to learn." However, the board liked her because her previous work experience suggested she was a competent fund-raiser. When all scores were averaged across all candidates, Linda was viewed as the most acceptable. She was offered, and accepted, the position.

## Office Manager

The office manager is responsible for maintaining the day-to-day operations of the office and for correspondence and assists the director. At the time Linda became director, the office manager was Diane Stephens. Marsha Long became the next office manager. Jane Furman followed; she was followed by Louise Darnell. Louise was succeeded by Becky Anderson, who is currently in the position.

## Direct Service Staff

The direct service staff positions, at the time the changes described here began, consisted of the hospital advocacy liaison, counseling coordinator, preschool assault prevention coordinator, adolescent services coordinator, volunteer coordinator, campus link program coordinator, and supervisor of education and public relations.

Much of the direct service staff's time is taken up with educating and counseling children, adolescents, and adults who have been sexually abused. Sexual abuse ranges from incest to acquaintance rape to date rape to stranger rape. The large majority of clientele are women and girls. Staff routinely hear horrific stories of abuse beyond most people's imagination. While they recognize the high stress of their work, they count on each other for support in the workplace and take personal days to recharge.

The staff of the RCC are a highly committed, dynamic, diverse group, predominately women, ranging in ideology from liberal to radical feminist. They see themselves as providing social service and promoting social action. Direct service staff receive little financial compensation, with the average salary about $20,000. Three have M.A. degrees, most have B.A.'s, and all have previous experience. All but one (supervisor of education and public relations) are female. The average tenure at the agency is about 5 years.

## THE CHANGES BEGIN

On Linda's first day as director, she held an introductory staff meeting. She asked the staff members to tell their names and positions. She did not ask what duties their jobs included, how long they had been at the center, or for any other information. Once the staff had finished, she said, "I look forward to meeting with each of you individually to talk about your jobs. Any questions?" The staff were caught off-guard, having anticipated the more informal style they were used to under Anne. It was very awkward. They couldn't think of any questions, so the meeting ended.

Several weeks later, at another staff meeting, Linda informed the staff that she felt they were not using their time wisely. They spent "too much time chatting in each other's offices and by the water cooler." So she decided they were to start filling out time sheets in 10-minute increments and that the sheets would be in their mailboxes soon. It was the last item on the agenda, and there was no time for discussion or questions. The stated purpose of these sheets was to help staff with their time management skills. However, the real purpose, Linda admitted to one staff member privately, was to "catch" a couple of staff members. She also told the staff there would be a planned agenda for each staff meeting. If they wanted an item discussed, it had to be submitted to her at least two days prior to the meeting for her approval. Unapproved items could not be brought up during the meeting.

By this point, several staff members were very concerned about the direction the agency appeared to be moving and about Linda's leadership. Other staff members were cautiously observing Linda but were still willing to give her the benefit of the doubt. Still others reported not experiencing the behaviors that other staff members had reported.

## STAFF CONCERNS

There was much informal talk among staff as they tried to understand how their agency was changing with Linda at the helm. This resulted in a series of staff-only meetings.

### Meeting 1

The first "meeting" occurred when Alan Michels walked into the office and found several staff members sitting around the lobby talking about Linda.

While they recognized they were doing exactly what they disliked about Linda—meeting behind her back to talk about her—they also recognized that the "meeting" had not been "called" by anyone; it was a spontaneous gathering. The concerns being discussed involved several issues. As they talked, it became clear that in private meetings with staff members, Linda had tried to fish out information about other staff members and had said negative things about their coworkers. It was also clear that she was not beyond lying if she got "caught" misrepresenting information and that she could not be trusted and felt threatened very easily. It was not uncommon for her to burst into tears at a staff meeting if questioned on a decision she had made.

Two staff members volunteered to talk to Linda about these issues and to request a chance to talk about them as a group at the upcoming staff meeting. Linda denied the request. These two staff agreed to pass on to the staff the message that if they had concerns about Linda, they should approach her individually.

The following day, at the staff meeting, Linda pulled out a magic marker and a flip-chart and tried to facilitate an exploration of what staff thought their purpose and role was as an agency. The underlying tension was obvious to most, but Linda acted as if nothing was wrong.

## Meeting 2

The second meeting of most of the staff was several weeks later. It was to be a planning and strategy session, to talk about what they could do. Instead, they discovered that many of them just needed to talk and to get validation and support from each other.

A central issue that emerged in this meeting was the staff retreat. They had requested, and even tentatively planned, one in the fall, but it never seemed to be one of Linda's priorities. It was decided that they would push hard for the retreat, with the purposes being for the staff and Linda to get to know each other better, to air out the concerns causing the underlying tension, and to begin working as a team again. As one staff member said later, "Under Anne's leadership, the staff had become a highly functioning, well-developed team. Where there was conflict, we had dealt with it openly, honestly, and fairly. But Linda was molding us into a collection of individuals, some who were for and some who were against her, some who supported her and some who attacked her."

Linda seemed reluctant to plan the retreat but agreed to research the possibilities of a site and facilitator. Several staff members supplied her with the names and phone numbers of potential facilitators. Linda never volunteered any updates on how her research was coming. At the next staff meeting she told the staff to put in writing a list of issues to be discussed at the retreat and to deliver them to her 5 days before the next scheduled staff meeting.

## Meeting 3

The third "meeting" of most of the staff took place off-site in early January. Many of the staff seemed to have a different view of the situation at the center. Where before there had not been much more than despair, now there seemed to be a glimmer of hope, and they looked forward to having a retreat. Over the next several months, since Linda was not offering updates about the retreat, many staff members, on their own initiative, asked how plans for it were coming along, but again, it did not seem to be a priority for Linda.

However, there was also increased concern as Linda, in discussions with some staff members, made it clear she would do whatever she needed to to get "rid of the troublemakers." She defined "troublemaker" as someone who questioned her decisions or authority. This was reinforced when she fired Marsha, the office manager, with no warning. Marsha was a well-loved member of the agency, and staff members were stunned and upset. Linda had never given Marsha any reasons to think her job was in jeopardy. She took Marsha's keys and that afternoon had the locks to the agency changed. When staff members tried to question her, Linda replied, "I'd watch what I say if I were you. Or you'll be out the door, too."

## Meeting 4

When the fourth "meeting" of most of the staff occurred, Alan decided to tell Linda about it. He "was sick of the secrecy and underlying tension." Linda said she knew about the other meetings. The fourth meeting was specifically about how Linda was handling the fact that some of the grants that funded staff positions were about to expire. She had asked the board for direction on priorities and was advised to let go of staff whose grants were ending. It was clear to staff members that little or no effort had been put into securing new funding for these positions. And Linda had made it clear in discussions with other staff members that she saw several of those with expiring grants as "problems who need to be gotten rid of." Linda met with each of these staff members privately, told them they could not take notes of the meeting, and informed them that their funding had ended and that they needed to find new jobs. When other staff members heard about this, they were irate. Between Marsha's firing, Linda talking behind people's backs, and this, all of the staff now agreed that the problems were very serious and that strong action had to be taken. They agreed to write detailed letters to the board asking for help. Since most had been keeping logs of all incidents regarding Linda, details were in great supply.

## THE BOARD OF TRUSTEES RESPONDS

Board meetings were held monthly. The meetings had always been open to staff, although they had no vote. As tension increased in the center, staff members attended board meetings in an effort to show solidarity and to hear firsthand what Linda was saying.

The board established an Ad Hoc Committee on Communication/ Conflict Resolution, consisting of two board members, Linda, and two staff members to discuss concerns voiced by the staff. The committee was to meet twice and then report back to the board. The board also voted that all future board meetings would be closed to staff.

Based on the Ad Hoc Committee's meetings, several issues of concern were identified, including the following:

> Poor communication: People feeling they have not been heard; lack of communication; statements misinterpreted; assumptions made without finding out facts
> Perceived authoritarian style of administration
> Lack of trust and respect
> Staff comparison of Linda to Anne
> Linda's lack of knowledge about sexual and physical abuse and concerns about her willingness to learn
> The ability to have opinions and views (particularly about abuse) that are different from those of others
> Separation between director and staff
> Linda's difficulty accepting feedback
> Linda's talking about staff members' performance to other staff members, and staff members' talking about Linda to each other rather than to her

The report presented to the Board was prepared by the two board members, Kathy O'Donnell and Mike Berger. The report recommended that the agency retreat be postponed, that a professional facilitator be hired to conduct group conflict-resolution sessions, and that the director attend an organizational communication training seminar.

The board accepted these recommendations and gave a unanimous vote of confidence in Linda and a unanimous vote of appreciation to the staff for the services they provide.

## Conflict-Resolution Sessions

A consultant, Joanne Stewart, was hired, and the staff and Linda were to meet locally for two 1-day meetings, 1 week apart. Prior to these sessions, the staff was never permitted to meet with Joanne without Linda present. Linda, on the other hand, had at least one lengthy private meeting with Joanne and had numerous opportunities to talk to board members about the staff without staff members present. The staff felt that Joanne spent the bulk of the time during the sessions protecting Linda, telling them to slow down, and silencing most attempts made by staff to air any serious grievances. By the end of the last session, any feelings of hope for change were gone.

## THE VOLUNTEERS AND STAFF RESPOND

After the sessions with Joanne morale became even lower, and many staff were actively seeking new jobs or making life changes. It was against this background that a letter from one of the volunteers was received.

### The Letter

Suzanne Briscoe's letter was the first formal acknowledgment of internal strife within the agency, as the letter was sent not only to the staff and to the board but also to all volunteers. Excerpts from this letter follow:

> *I have been an active volunteer at the Rape Crisis Center for many years and have seen the directorship change hands three times. In the past, the Rape Crisis Center has been a supportive and nurturing environment for all survivors. The director, staff and volunteers all worked together to provide a safe place for survivors to share in the healing process, while also educating the community. It was one of the few organizations in the [city] in which all members were encouraged to voice their opinions and foster change. This is no longer the case and I feel an overwhelming sense of sadness that this wonderful organization is disintegrating before my eyes.*
>
> *[Linda], 1 person has been fired, 8 people have resigned, 2 programs have been eliminated [preschool child assault prevention coordinator and campus link coordinator] and 1 program has been drastically cut, all in the nineteen months during which you have served as Executive Director.*
>
> *As you will recall, I applied for and was offered the position as Adolescent Service Coordinator after the resignation of [Becky O'Donnell]*

*and therefore feel I can speak as a respected and qualified member of
this organization. For personal reasons I did not accept the position,
however the interviewing process was enlightening. During the course of
our conversation together you "warned" me that your relationship with
the staff was a tenuous one and that you feel obligated to inform potential employees of the tension in the workplace. You further indicated that
you should have "fired the whole staff" when you came in and started
with "your own people" It scares me to think that someone coming in to
direct an existing, healthy, and supportive agency would even consider
eliminating all that has made this agency great.*

*The staff members at the Rape Crisis Center continually exhibited
their dedication to this agency by working for a common cause for very
little financial compensation. I am proud to be associated with this dynamic, diverse group. I feel I can no longer sit back silently and ignore
the tension that has plagued the agency and emotionally exhausted the
staff, forcing many to resign. Their attention should be solely focused on
our mission of helping survivors.*

## A Staff Member's Response

A Board member, Richard Whitehall, wrote a response to the letter from
Suzanne. A response to his response was written by Amy Lawrence, the
counseling coordinator, and was also sent to everyone on Suzanne's mail-
ing list. Amy's letter provides generous quotes from the text of Richard's
letter. Excerpts from her letter follow:

*I am writing as a six-year member of the Rape Crisis Center, and
as a proud member of the staff.*

*Regarding Mr. Whitehall's questioning of "the ability of those
charged with the task of 'reaching out' to survivors," I do not believe that
Mr. Whitehall is in a position to judge the staff's competency in working
with survivors. Furthermore, I and my co-workers, both past and present, have attempted to reach out to our supervisor, but the costs have
been too high in the long run. Since the beginning of her tenure as Director, Ms. Hall has made continued attempts to pit staff against staff and
to undermine individual staff members' authority to do their jobs as
they see fit. I need a cooperative and supportive working relationship
with my fellow staff members. I stopped reaching out to Ms. Hall when I
discovered that I was expected to listen to her make disparaging comments about my co-workers, and that if I disagreed with her on any
point, she was likely to either misrepresent my words and actions or ac-
cuse me of being "mean" or "unsupportive." I must stress that this is not
old history. This behavior continues to occur.*

Mr. Whitehall states that staff has been "notably absent" from fund-raising projects. I must first remind you that it is not our responsibility to raise funds. We earn our salaries by working hard at the jobs we were hired to do. We should not be expected to raise money to pay our own salaries. Nevertheless, many staff (including myself) did participate in the ticket raffles of the past, and several participated in last year's aerobithon. Several staff have also participated, or offered to participate, in grant-writing efforts.

I had originally planned to help with last year's aerobithon. Then it was decided that the name of the event should not include any reference to the mission of the Rape Crisis Center. This was justified with the assertion that people might be offended by a title that includes our name or reference to our mission. I decided, at this point, not to invest my energy in a project which would effectively whitewash and apologize for the very difficult and far-reaching issues which the Rape Crisis Center is meant to address. I felt that it would be contrary to our mission to participate in such an effort. We, of all people, should refuse to apologize for our mission, and we need to set the example of speaking out rather than camouflaging our efforts.

The claim that staff members expect staff meetings to be run as "group therapy" indicates a clear misunderstanding of what constitutes group therapy or any other kind of therapy, as well as a lack of awareness of what occurs in staff meetings. Staff meetings have never resembled group therapy, and I wouldn't expect them to. I do expect them to allow for open, honest communication, including discussion of difficult and controversial issues which an agency charged with the rape crisis mission should be prepared to face. Such communication has been thwarted in the past nineteen months.

Mr. Whitehall states that concerns raised in the past nineteen months have been "unrelated to the mission" of the Rape Crisis Center. I must challenge this assumption. All of my disagreements with the current leadership have had everything to do with the mission. It is only because I care so deeply about the mission that I have remained in this struggle for such a long time. My co-workers are also deeply committed. It alarms me that a board member, by virtue of holding a position of power, would presume to possess an exclusive understanding of the mission without consulting the experts: those who actually do the primary work, the staff and the direct service volunteers.

I am disappointed, but unfortunately not surprised, by Richard Whitehall's suggestion that those who disagree with the leadership "may well be in their best interests to move on." This is a sentiment that I and other staff members have heard numerous times from our director. Perhaps, at this point, it would be in our own best interests to leave, since we

*all pay a cost when we do such difficult work in such a tense environ-*
*ment. Nevertheless, I don't believe that it serves the interests of the Cen-*
*ter to treat skilled and dedicated members of the organization as though*
*they are expendable.*

*The message I have gotten from Mr. Whitehall's letter, as well as*
*from conversations and memos from other members of the agency's cur-*
*rent leadership is this: "Might makes right." When we asked the board*
*last spring to explain what protection is provided to the staff by our per-*
*sonnel policies, we were instead told what the laws in the State of [___]*
*would allow an employer to do (e.g., firing at will). I had hoped that the*
*Rape Crisis Center still held values and standards somewhat higher*
*than those held by the State of [___]. Might and power may give you the*
*ability to overpower us and sometimes even to silence us, but might most*
*certainly does not make right. This is everything we are supposed to be*
*fighting against.*

*I hope that at least some of you choose to listen to members of the*
*organization other than those who hold the positions of power.*

## THE AFTERMATH

Within 6 months after the final facilitation session, six of the original staff
members had left. As one put it, "It's ironic that our job is to help victims
who have been abused, and we're working in an abusive environment." For
most, the abuse took a heavy toll on their self-confidence and emotional
health. They have been replaced, but apparently the tension remains as the
new staff faces the same problems. Several of these new staff have already
left. Staff continued to try to get support from the board, but to no avail.

The conflict continued until the staff started hearing rumors that
Linda was planning to resign, along with the Executive Committee of the
board. In fact, at the board meeting, the board majority, including the Executive Committee, resigned. Linda, not wanting to quit, had asked to be
fired. Staff members and the remaining board members, anticipating these
events, had replacements in place. Because the center's bylaws state that a
minimum of 15 board members are necessary for the center to operate,
immediately after the firing and resignations, the remaining board, staff
members, and volunteer members elected 14 new board members. Two
staff members were named acting codirectors and were later replaced by a
former staff member.

It was at this point that the internal conflict at the RCC became public. The local newspaper carried a story of the turmoil and ran an editorial.
In the newspaper article, some board members suggested that the problems centered on operational control and how much input staff and vol-

unteers should have. As one board member stated, "the staff was accustomed to 'loose policies on how the office was run,' which the board directed Linda to tighten after she became executive director. . . . They were used to wearing whatever they wanted, long lunch times, and late check-in times. There was a flex-time schedule, but it was taken advantage of."

According to Linda, "I guess you could call it a coup. There's been a lot of dissension over the last two years. We [she and the board] were trying to professionalize the agency—increasing our fund-raising efforts and requiring licensing for anyone who did counseling at the agency—but it seemed that no matter what we tried, we were met with opposition from the staff and a lot of the volunteers. We finally threw up our hands and gave up."

Staff members said there was no coup, and charged that Linda and the resigning board members left in an attempt to shut down the center. There was also significant concern about the reactions of major funders. Most funders expressed concern that the agency be reevaluated in light of the new board and the mission of the center. Animosity was evident in statements from board members. As one said, echoing several others, "They wanted to be in charge; now they are. Some of them didn't have a realization of how much work is involved for pure volunteerism. Now they're going to find out." However, one staff member noted, "I'm so concerned with this being depicted as catastrophic when it's not. I've worked at a lot of other places, and I've never seen a staff so committed. Our concern with all of this is to continue providing services to survivors, children and adolescents."

Finally, about this same time, the new president of the board sent out a fund-raising letter. This letter is noteworthy because it defined the agency differently from the way it had been defined by the exiting director and board. It stated, "It is our intention to continue to rebuild our Board with community members dedicated to the historical mission of the [___] Rape Crisis Center. . . . Together we can keep the [___] Rape Crisis Center a viable and valuable social change organization in our community for years to come." At the present time, there is much healing to be done, but there is also a lot of optimism among the staff, volunteers, and the new Board of Trustees dedicated to rebuilding the center.

## KEY TERMS

BURNOUT: a reaction to chronic job-related stress characterized by physical, attitudinal, and emotional exhaustion.

CONFLICT:

  COVERT CONFLICT: conflict that is hidden, not acknowledged openly.

  OVERT CONFLICT: conflict that is out in the open.

ORGANIZATIONAL CULTURE: the values, beliefs, and practices of an organization that are created through interaction among organizational members.

SOCIAL SUPPORT:

EMOTIONAL SUPPORT: communication that tells another person they are loved and cared for.

INFORMATIONAL SUPPORT: the provision of facts or advice that helps a person cope with stress.

INSTRUMENTAL SUPPORT: physical or material aid that helps a person cope with stress.

## DISCUSSION QUESTIONS

1. Compare and contrast the organizational culture under Anne's and Linda's leaderships. How was each communicatively enacted?
2. Linda was criticized for not being a feminist and for not having knowledge of issues related to sexual assault. Are these criticisms legitimate? Why or why not?
3. What were the overt conflict issues? What were the covert issues? How are they interdependent?
4. What were the stressors faced by the staff? By Linda? How could staff burnout have been avoided?
5. What types of support, and from whom, made a difference for Linda? For the staff? How?
6. How were problems mishandled by the board? By Linda? By the staff? How could they have been handled differently?
7. What were key turning points for the staff? For Linda? For the Board?
8. Why were the sessions with the consultant not successful?
9. What potential impact could the newspaper publicity about the conflict have on funders? On staff? On clients? In the community?

## SUGGESTED READING

Buzzanell, P. M. (1994). Gaining a voice: Feminist organizational communication theorizing. *Management Communication Quarterly, 7,* 339–383.

Ferguson, K. E. (1984). *The feminist case against bureaucracy*. Philadelphia: Temple University Press.

Maslach, C. (1982). *Burnout: The cost of caring*. Englewood Cliffs, NJ: Prentice-Hall.

Mumby, D. K., & Putnam, L. L. (1992). The politics of emotion: A feminist reading of bounded rationality. *Academy of Management Review, 17,* 465–486.

Pacanowsky, M. E., & O'Donnell-Trujillo, N. (1983). Organizational communication as cultural performance. *Communication Monographs, 50,* 126–147.

Ray, E. B. (1987). Supportive relationships and occupational stress in the workplace. In T. L. Albrecht & M. B. Adelman (Eds.), *Communicating social support* (pp. 172– 191). Beverly Hills, CA: Sage.

# CHAPTER 11

## The Business Concept and Managerial Control in Knowledge-Intensive Work
### A Case Study of Discursive Power

STANLEY DEETZ

So called knowledge-intensive industries have become a major part of modern economies. An increasingly important segment of these industries provide professional services through the work of a growing and significant portion of the workforce described as "symbolic analysts" by U.S. Labor Secretary Richard Reich. These include consultancy groups; law, advertising, and accounting firms; R&D groups; some banks; software development groups; and similar organizations. They share a reliance on "intellectual capital" and a labor force that is highly professionalized. As knowledge-intensive professional service industries have become increasingly central to modern economies, so too have the studies of their management and work processes. Owing to the complex, ephemeral, and "professionalized" nature of their services, communication processes in these companies are especially rich and important. Conceptions of mission, often present as a business concept, are used to integrate and control internal processes and to relate to the market and other external groups. Studying the operation of the "business concept" can help us explore the relations among corporate cultural features, communication processes, and methods of coordination and control.

Knowledge-intensive companies provide an important context for the exploration of employee participation and limitations on the consideration of employee goals and values in decision making. New forms of workplace control are of great concern—concern by many managerial groups with how to acquire and exercise them and concern by employees and observers of organizations with new forms of domination, representational failure, and less satisfactory company performance. Older forms of self-interested managerial domination and limits on appropriate-level employee decision making clearly still exist. Research concern with oppressive work conditions, authority relations, processes of coercion, dominant ideologies, work rules, and various other forms of manipulation and oppression is still important. But new and more subtle forms of domination are emerging with new "high-end" industries, participation and empowerment plans, and shifting workforces. While it may be more difficult to have great concern with these "middle-class" problems, the limitations they put on organizational learning and on the positive use of resources, as well as the way they reduce employee loyalty and quality of life, make them of great importance.

The case study here hopes to contribute to the understanding of management and work processes in knowledge-intensive professional service organizations, to aid in understanding the relation of organizational discourse to integration and control, and to lend insight into power relations in knowledge-intensive workplaces. Analytic insights can be useful in examining other knowledge-intensive companies with attention to the relations among the business concept, power, decision processes, the relative advantages to different groups within such companies, and quality decision making. To provide a context for the case, I will initially consider the growing importance of knowledge-intensive professional services and the unique features of work processes in such companies, consider the functions of discourse constructing and reproducing a business concept or mission, and then trace these issues through an analysis of interviews with employees of a professional service division of a large multinational corporation.

## KNOWLEDGE-INTENSIVE PROFESSIONAL SERVICES

Concern with knowledge industries is certainly not new. Research on administration and work in universities, consulting and law firms, and R&D have existed for some time. But not until recently has there been so much widespread concern with knowledge work. Much of this heightened interest originated with (or better, at the same time as) Bell's (1973) work on postindustrial society. Bell's contribution in many ways has come to stand for a rather general rethinking of modern economies. While there have been many debates regarding the extent and significance of the changes he documents and forecasts, few doubt that a new type of industry has become important. Many Western societies are banking heavily that a kind of knowledge industry will replace factory and manual service industries as central to their economic health (see Drucker, 1993; Quinn, 1992; Reich, 1991).

In general the work in knowledge-intensive groups displays four dimensions not typically true of manufacturing and manual service companies: First, work groups in most knowledge-intensive organizations are characterized by high levels of autonomy and self-management. A number of personnel and work characteristics reduce the viability of direct control processes. These include employee conceptions of autonomy entitlement, the specialized nature of the expertise, the lack of clear normative standards for the product, the presence of powerful professional codes, the presence of work activity outside the employment site, and the presence of alternative employment opportunities. In light of this, a strong culture and shared internalized values often provide control and coordination in the place of authority relations and direct supervision. Most of the control processes are unobtrusive and can be best characterized as "clan" control. But employees are often subject to competing cultural influences arising from internal constituent groupings and external relations with professional groups and customer organizations that leave all control processes fragmented and tenuous and often in need of legitimation.

Second, most knowledge-intensive companies are dependent on complex communication processes. Often tasks are uncertain and ambiguous, and agreement on problem definitions and solutions requires active communication and negotiation. In these environments messages serve a number of fairly explicit social purposes in addition to providing information. For example, since the nature of an individual's work and the quality of products produced often remain uncertain and open to social determination, both work-related roles and identities and professional competency are actively established in interaction in environments that are competitive and yet depend on cooperation. While organizational positions, certifications, and seniority exert constraints, employees frequently engage in role creation and negotiation to determine what needs to be done, how to do it, and their personal responsibilities. The opportunity for high degrees of strategic interaction and productive negotiation are both present.

Third, organizations such as these are also often described as chaotic or postmodern both because of internal dynamics and because of the nature of external market environments. The activities that warrant this description have implications for the work process, evaluation systems, marketing, and decision making generally. In turbulent internal and external environments, organizations have the capacity to mobilize incredible resources toward largely unpredictable ends in which their own mobilization serves as both a determinant and effect. The market environment is fragmented and unstable, and so the organization struggles to produce the environment to which it must adjust. Adjustment, creativity, and adaptation are of great value. Role definitions are quite fluid, and many traditional managerial responsibilities, such as interfacing with the customer or determining work methods, is shifted to the employee. The result is usually a very loose work arrangement with managerial control concentrated on the outcome rather than on the work process. Such conditions provide employees with a sense of liberation and capacity for negotiated self-identity and reality, as well as potential for different operations of power and forms of domination.

Fourth, the client–service provider relationship takes on special significance. Most often the customer participates in many ways in task activities by defining needs, soliciting attention, and being the primary evaluator of service quality. The personal relationship between the employee and customer takes on special importance for several structural reasons: "(1) the problems facing the professional are not highly structured, (2) crucial information needed for task completion can be secured only by the individuals, (3) solutions must be accepted by the client to ensure implementation" (Manz & Sims, 1980). To the extent that each of these conditions is present in a high degree, power shifts from the providing firm's management to employees.

Management processes given these characteristics differ greatly from the management of manual labor or management in relatively stable bureaucracies. Generally personnel management in such organizations has focused on the symbolic realm. This has often included developing vision statements, shared value principles, company images, and active socialization programs as well as managing cultural characteristic of the work environment. Many of these symbolic elements rest on developing and acquiring commitment to a business concept.

## THE BUSINESS CONCEPT AND ITS FUNCTIONS

The idea of a business concept, often reflected in a mission statement, has been common to corporate management for some time. While the preferred term for this notion changes with the linguistic fashions of the moment, the core issue is a reoccurring feature of doing business. The business concept designates one way to think about the answer to the question "What business are you in?" While there are many ways to answer parts of this question, the business concept conception offers enough specification to consider broad issues relevant to the general character of knowledge-intensive work. As the environment becomes more turbulent, the market becomes more fragmented, or the work processes more chaotic, the presence of a strong business concept in the organizational discourse offers internal and external advantages as well as potential costs that can be seen if the conception is developed further.

Normann (1991) was one of the first to develop clearly the special function of the business concept in service industries. For Normann, the business concept pulled together three critical features of corporate functioning: First, it provides an identity to the company (and employees), giving to outsiders a clear indication of who they are, what they do, what business niche they fulfill. Second, this identity provides marketing advantages by informing potential customers of what the company does and distinguishing the company from other potentially competing services. And third, it provides guidance to internal decision making in the formulation of internal choices of business activities, reward systems, budgeting, and integration and control of work activities. The business concept, when fully implemented, permeates nearly all cultural and structural properties of work.

Given the nature of knowledge-intensive services, it is easy to see the hope that a strong business concept offers. The lack of an easily defined product or manual service leaves both personal and company identity fluid and open to strategic specification. Since many of the services offered by knowledge-intensive industries are new, customers rely on the vendor to define the need or potential advantages in a market environment where the customer has to compare neither known nor understood apples and oranges. Some authors go so far as to argue that the image and the expression of what one does is often of greater significance than the product, especially when the product is highly technical or when appropriate or shared evaluation criteria are absent (e.g., much of university faculties' work). Further, the absence of processes for easy direct control of work creates the need for clear principles to aid self-management and passive systems of integration as well as to give legitimacy to evaluation and rewards systems that have few direct measurement devices available to them.

Normann developed the business concept conception in terms of needs in strategic management. And while this has been its principal use, Alvesson (1994) has shown how the conception can be used for descriptive purposes freed from the specific interests of the management group. In his study of a computer consultancy company, Alvesson demonstrated six functions of the business concept: (1) Analytic/intellectual: The business concept clarified the business and justified the existence of a unique group to carry the business out. (2) Integrative: The business concept suggests preferred relations among subgroups and directs choices in budgeting, long-term planning, and reward systems. (3) Controlling: The business concept organizes a cluster of "recipes" or decision rules for making decisions in unclear situations, decision contexts lacking important information, or complex situations in which decision consequences are hard to predict. (4) Ideological: The business concept provides a basis for action legitimation and connects local circumstances and accounts to larger shared values. (5) Marketing: The business concept helps explain otherwise hard-to-explain products and services and provides a basis for comparison and contrast with similar services in the eyes of the customer. (6) Image: The business concept provides a "standing" for managers and other employees, both unifying them as something that they are and providing "symbolic" capital in interactions with outside groups.

Here I wish to extend this analysis by showing that the business concept is usefully reformed if thought of in a discursive sense. The business concept can be seen as an interaction move that produces and positions particular identities for employees and the company and structures the environment in specifiable ways. It partially organizes a set of discourses that, enact certain realities and reproduce particular "circuits of power" in Clegg's (1989) sense. Alvesson's (1994) functions can be seen as products or accomplishments of discursive moves, which themselves serve as resources for actors in making further moves.

The business concept is not so much a mental conception put into practice as a discursive move that partly structures mental activity and other practices. The business concept, like other signs in discursive systems, is thus largely self-referential and self-reproducing. Such discursive signs (as both signifiers and signified) in the discourse reference each other rather than an outside and produce an imaginary object that serves as the apparent referent. The power of the concept is not primarily rhetorical (though it may persuade and direct) but constitutive. The discourse enacting the business concept produces a set of objects and relations that only appear to be independent and simply referenced by it.

To fully appreciate the significance of a discourse organized around a business concept and to understand the analysis that follows, allow me to briefly detour into language theory. The expression of the business concept, like that of other words/constructs, derives meaning from the system of distinctions that it puts into play rather than from a psychological or empirical referent. The very presence of a mental or physical "object" is an outcome of the copresence of a system of distinction and ambiguous mental and empirical stuff. When an expression puts into play a system of distinction it produces a line of contrast, thus collecting a group of things that are seen as alike and another group of things that are seen as different along the line of contrast, and it holds this way of contrasting or organizing the world up against alternatives. For example, when one calls a piece of research "quantitative," the work is attached to the field of associations with "quantitative," and an oppositional class, of works that are "qualitative," is produced. With the distinction and the accompanying oppositions, tensions, and conflicts, other possible lines of contrast that would produce different sets of divisions tend to be marginalized. Even attempts to redifferentiate the world may be interpreted as a strategic move in the established conflictual realm already established rather than as the denial of that conflicting field itself. Such a system can work self-referentially since the world itself is not discontinuous nor does it itself prefer one set of dimensions on which to base contrast to others. Discourses, not the external world, produce discontinuity and preferences. The move of treating these produced objects and the discontinuities and preferences as if they were a property of the world seals the system off from discussion since it is treated as natural rather than as produced. Analysis can reclaim the unnatural, constructed quality of these productions, can demonstrate how they work to preference and advantage certain groups, and can open discussion to different differential systems.

Discursively, thus, the business concept simultaneously introduces a dimension or dimensions of interest along which distinctions are made and produces its referent as a positive object (now seen as natural rather than produced) and its produced opposite as negative. The business concept discourse simultaneously holds its distinctions as preferred (or the only thinkable ones) over competing distinctions, and its positive value over its opposite. For example in the case to follow, "integrated services" (planning, implementation, and assessment) is contrasted with "smokestack services" (piecemeal services requested by the customer). As this contrast is enacted and elaborated, definitions of activities tend to polarize. "Integrated" is ascribed with positive values and associated with positive values of new and important, and alternative ways of contrasting services based on "complexity," "empowerment," or "social good" become progressively more difficult to think and enact.

As it is elaborated, the business concept becomes narrativized, providing and being enhanced by rationalization, exemplars, justifications, and legitimation provided in descriptions and accounts. The business concept is thus core to local narratives or community stories needing to be constantly reconstructed to sustain the reality of which it is presumably about. For example, if one of the business concepts (the narrative description or story) of a university is research productivity, a faculty member who is able to write his or her identity within that is given more release time and money and is then rewarded for research productivity exceeding that of his or her peers. This confirms both the rightfulness of the authority giving the resource and the exceptional talent of the faculty member receiving the resources. The self-referentiality continues as this faculty member is now in a position to define what quality work is and thus to establish the story motifs in which others must write their lives. Alternative ways of working or alternative people who could have been successful if given the opportunity become increasingly invisible (see Martin's [1994] treatment of the marginalization of women in the university for examples of the process). The self-reproducing nature of the system becomes hidden, and alternative discourses appear self-serving, political, or simply obscure. A similar relation holds in all knowledge-intensive businesses. Advantaged people enact business concepts that give differential interpretive advantages and resource allocations; the presence of the differential resource allocation and interpretive advantages allows certain groups to sustain the business concept discourse leading to greater advantages and so forth. Such interpretive advantages can even lead to company failures with the difficulties being described as the lack of commitment to the business concept rather than as a fundamental difficulty of the business concept.

The self-justifying and self-reproducing nature of the business concept is clear in the consequences of business concepts for the relative standing of organizational members. Following Bourdieu (1977, 1991), group members have different amounts of economic and symbolic capital. As Bourdieu has demonstrated in much detail, economic and symbolic capital are mutually reproductive and together dominate discourse and interpretive practices in a variety of institutional settings. Such an analysis can be extended to knowledge-intensive work. In most knowledge-intensive workplaces, economic capital is largely held by management through their relation to financial investors and through their capacity to differentially financially reward and punish. The presence of this "capital" advantage provides advantages in enacting a favored business concept and in its use and interpretation. And further, management's power is increased to the extent that the economic interest is salient for the group. Thus a business concept that highlights a business's economic interest increases its capital and so forth in a positive spiral. This centralization of power is held in check in knowledge-intensive work by the presence of significant "symbolic" capital held by employees. Symbolic capital here can be specified as "intellectual" capital (relatively rare skills and knowledge unique to specific employees), "relational" capital (customer networks and trust relations with customers), and "artifactual" capital (databases and files containing technical and customer data). Symbolic capital can be quite valuable and tends to be somewhat more mobile (employees can take much of it with them) and difficult to acquire than economic capital. Thus management's fear of employee "exit" leaves holders of symbolic capital in a relatively strong position to define the business and to define it in ways that increase the value of their symbolic capital in contrast to the prerogatives of economic capital. The dynamics of interaction around the business concept is a struggle to use capital for group advantages and simultaneously to increase the value of a group's capital.

## THE CASE STUDY

The group studied,[1] Applied Integrated Management Systems (AIMS), is a professional service component of a large, multinational telecommunication corporation (LTC). AIMS is technically a "district" within a "division" of the Information Management Systems (IMS) company of LTC. AIMS normally employs around 90 people; about 35 of these are considered temporary since they are hired on fixed-term contracts for specific projects and receive no standard employee benefits. About two-thirds of all AIMS permanent employees (39 at the time of this study) work from the district's principal site in the eastern United States. At the end of their most recent reorganization, AIMS was composed of six work groups ranging in size from 6 to 15. Two of these are branch offices, one in a neighboring state and the other on the West Coast. The four groups at the principal site were roughly divided by function and each was headed by a manager who reported to the district manager. Most large projects had a project director who headed a team drawn from these four groups. As shown in many other organizations like this one, responsibility for individuals, accountability, and reporting functions are not always clear. Employees self-describe the organization as having a lattice structure, though in practice the structure may be somewhat more fixed than this. Several interviewees noted how loose the structure was until major decisions were considered. Economic hard times have lead to much more direct managerial control in work practices and assignments.

AIMS was founded within LTC in 1991 with a very strong mission/vision to form a consultancy-style group providing integrated solutions to various business problems mostly involving computer and network systems. "Integrated business solutions performed through a consultancy arrangement" is treated here as the most basic statement of the business concept. Prior to the formation of AIMS, most of the service functions were diffused throughout LTC in service centers or were performed on an as-needed basis by outside consultants. These services ranged from developing software for new billing and product control systems for other service and product units of LTC to various types of personnel training. Many of these groups prior to AIMS were "fully funded" through a budgeting system that treated them as a company-wide overhead cost with "funny" money keeping track of operations. They responded to the needs of other units as requested on a loose priority system.

The reorganization that formed AIMS brought together a variety of different groups from LTC to form a division within IMS. AIMS was one of the five districts within this new division. The reorganization was championed by the person who would become the divisional director as well as by others already in consulting-style services within LTC, including the present district manager of AIMS. The conceptions of "consultancy group" and "integrated solutions" clearly fit the time. The conception of internal profit centers and the ideology of consultancy were considered able to break down the bureaucracy of fully funded centers, to increase employee motivation, and to improve accountability. This was especially important as LTC was becoming more marketing centered itself and was working hard to contain costs. From a company standpoint, internal prof- it centers changed political battles for resources among service units to economic competition. Rather than managers cutting services that were less needed, the market would make the determination. As described by one manager:

"I was always in a funded, ya know, some kind of funded organization where you were on retainer to a business you knew or a project, and beginning of the year you would figure out how many people you needed for a project, it'd be eight, and you made damn sure you spent eight people because otherwise if you only spent seven, next year your budget was cut. So there was a lot of resources, ah, the other thing that happens if the project gets cut, and that is out of your con- trol, now you have to lose people. Whereas consultancy whatever you can sell, whatever services you have, your group goal'll shrink, your business goal'll shrink by what you can sell not by someone else's budget problem. That's why I like consultancy."

The concept of "integrated solutions" fit the ideology that organiza- tions worked holistically and that technological and other changes carried complex implications across the business unit. The services predicted to be the most valuable in the future were the "high end" of consultancy in- volving analysis, planning, and follow-up rather than simple service provi- sion. Again in the words of a manager:

"My vision for the organization is really to get away from the onesy, twosy little projects. We want to be the systems integrator for [LTC]. We want to be when you need to, high-tech solutions and you need to span multiple technologies. That is this organization. You come to do it when we have the expertise and the excellence to do it. You don't need to go to the outside for it. And when companies look for that when they're buying [LTC] equipment they should be coming right behind us to do the integration work."

Both of these conceptions have clear values and highlight important aspects of modern corporate life, and they have considerable rhetorical power and coordinate well with extended discourses throughout the organization. But they are partial, both in what they cover up in organizational life, what they misrecognize, and in the way their presumed neutrality favors particular interests and people. For example, although in with a consultancy model some of the time and political maneuvering is taken out of the budgeting process, the company as a whole absorbs considerable cost in internal marketing, vendor-driven "need" creation, and other attempts to show unit profitability. Themes such as these will be pursued in the analysis of the case.

During the study period AIMS was experiencing an economic crisis owing to bidding and billing mistakes and the loss of a significant contract. Even during this crisis, however, morale was high. Most employees had been through several reorganizations at LTC and were reasonably confident that even if AIMS were to be disbanded, they would be employed in a similar capacity somewhere in LTC. As will be shown, management members, however, appeared to have more to lose if AIMS was reabsorbed into LTC. They tried to increase employee loyalty to AIMS and tried to evoke some fear of AIMS's demise.

The employees of AIMS are highly educated (most with masters degrees in technical fields), well paid (upper 7% nationwide), and have high degrees of job security and potential for career mobility. Their specialities range from computer software and information system design and implementation to human resources and job design. Nearly all AIMS members interviewed have worked for LTC for their entire professional career (averaging 12 years) and for AIMS since it was pulled together out of different parts of LTC 18 months prior to my interviews. AIMS members invest a high degree of their personal identity in their work and employment situation. Many seem more connected to their work than to their families or to any outside group. Most hope to continue doing what they are doing and would be willing to take pay cuts to work on the projects they liked. Still, many of the employees and project managers work at client locations for extended periods of time and often feel cut off from AIMS. Mixed loyalties are common since client evaluations of services is a significant portion of the employees' annual review. And, predictably, it is not uncommon for employees to take jobs with client organizations (nearly all are other parts of LTC).

## THE BUSINESS CONCEPT AT AIMS

As indicated, the core business at AIMS was to provide "integrated business solutions performed through a consultancy arrangement." Before unpacking key terms here, I should emphasize how important a business concept is to an organization like AIMS. The business concept is a significant part of keeping the organization together; in fact, the definition of a unique market in relation to the goals of LTC is the primary reason AIMS exists at all. Not surprisingly, much of the discussion in this organization can be seen as articulating interests and conflicts in terms of the business concept. From a management standpoint (at least those interested in perpetuating AIMS), the defense of the business concept has become equal to the defense of AIMS. One is quickly confused with the other. As will be seen, this makes it very difficult to discuss many important business decisions. By the time the discussion is coded in terms of the business concept, many things are difficult to expresses or even to think about and to feel. The identity of different employees, as has been argued, is also shaped in relation to their subjectification in terms of the business concept. As suggested above, the business concept provides preferred distinctions and indentities and is enacted by people in power to provide a basis for that power.

At AIMS the two principal contrasts built into the business concept are "consultancy" versus "funded" groups and "integrated" versus "smokestack" services. "Consultancy group" means here a group that competitively bids for and is paid for the jobs it does rather than being "funded" by LTC. "Integrated services" are jobs that the group is involved in from the design through implementation and that support and utilize individuals with several specialities, while "smokestack services" are usually specific customer-requested applications requiring a specific talent. The following are examples of statements exemplifying these discursively produced distinctions:

> "If you're doing good work and you're getting paid for the work you do, then as long as you continue to you can do this kind of thing. If you're a funded organization you're at the mercy of someone up top who knows nothing about what you're doing, just to say, well, this morning I think I'm gonna cut by 50% so okay everyone down there, you know. With no rhyme nor reason, you know, the organization, you might be doing well and . . ."

> "I tend to think that people in funded organizations, in that type of work, tend to get lazy, ah, that may be a broad statement, but it is easier to . . . not to have something to get done in that type of organization."

> "Although that's [AIMS] goal, to be on it from end to end. That's not always, we still have our smokestack businesses."

> " . . . Have the ability to do applications development, technical architecture implementation database support, user training, development of on-line help, the whole thing, everything from cradle to

grave essentially associated with providing systems development services to a customer organization."

"But I think if we were all working together, then the smokestacks would start to go away. . . . So I think those smokestacks are existent by now but not because we're a consulting group [but] just because we haven't learned to work with each other yet."

What is of most immediate interest to the analysis here is what these contrasts produce as reifications and hide as discussion options. For example, to call AIMS a "consulting" group is very misleading in terms of the full discursive field including business features of autonomy and risks that "consulting" sets in play. AIMS is different from the consulting firms used as discursive resources. AIMS was set up within an existing company (the relation to owners and partners is different) and has a continuing ready set of customers there (the relation to marketing is different), and if they fail to make money they all have the same jobs elsewhere in the company (the risk is different). But the possibility of conceptualizing a mixed consulting–funded model or using another set of distinctions is never discussed; in fact, considerable effort is directed to minimizing of these differences from other consulting firms and in keeping the options polar.

It is thus not the rhetorical power of the term "consulting" that is of interest but its discursive effect in producing permissible contrasts, definitions of people and activities, and issues of relevancy. In a general way, the consultancy conception helped management consolidate power by making money the game. To the extent that they were able to translate "symbolic" capital in the discursive field into economic terms, management's capital was enhanced, as was their capacity to define the business. Keeping the consultancy model undiscussible aided this control. Discussion of the consultancy conception would serve to either weaken its hold by providing viable alternatives or make explicit the advantages management acquired from it. In either case, conflict could result and employees'use of their "symbolic" capital becomes greater. This becomes clearer in considering the six discursive products that become member resources that Alvesson (1994) identified.

## ANALYTIC/INTELLECTUAL

Both knowledge-intensive professional service work and the organization of it are hard to describe. This is due both to the complexity of the work and to the lack of normalization in which everyday terms would be developed to make the work and products seem simple and obvious. Both "consultancy" and "integrated" are "good" terms because of rich everyday meanings, both seeming concrete and yet containing enough ambiguity to cover many different things without obvious inaccuracy. In an industry having a difficult time saying what it does, the business concept is a quick answer. The terms here provide a "good" story appearing to have a clear conceptual basis linked to real differences out there in the world. The intellectual clarity is compelling. The terms written together make a good start to any document that denotes a unit that is different, coherent, cutting-edge, and knows what it is about. The terms' power resides in their apparent normalization and articulation with dominant themes in business today.

But equally interesting are their analytic difficulties and lack of intellectual justification. It is difficult to go beyond the terms. While "integrated services" appears to say something clearer and more distinct than "services," a careful reading suggests the opposite. To say "services" invites the question of what services; to say "integrated services" already implies an answer of all services, thus seeming to make the follow-up question unnecessary. "Integrated" adds little specification to "services," telling how they are offered but not what they are. The analytic power of the adjective is to divert attention from what is unclear, the services themselves. The term "integrated" thus distinguishes in the sense of adding value rather than adding clarity to the difference. It more stops the discussion with its implied value and clarity than adds to it. While other readings of this are possible, this one helps account for the obviously metaphorical way that "integrated" is discussed and the difficulty people had in describing what they do. For example, "integrated" was always described in the interviews with slogans, for example, "soup to nuts" and "cradle to grave." Such descriptions might pose interesting questions as to which services are "soup" or "graves," but they more divert than aid understanding. Similarly with descriptions of work activities. The feeling from the interviews is more that employees do not really have a good way of describing what they do rather than that they think that I would not understand or would not be interested:

> "We're suppose to be doing integrated solutions, you know, soup-to-nuts type of solutions. But I think a little bit more, you know, we get questions every day where people call us up and ask us to do something. And, you know, we could probably do it, but is this really what we want to do, is this our niche? I think we get, we tend to get bordered out or watered down if you do too many different things and that part of the vision is missing. Is, you know, that this is the area we wanna try to work within as opposed to just saying we're gonna do a job from soup to nuts, you know."

Certainly neither "integrated" nor "consultancy" add to the ability to explain. They make explanation seem unnecessary. Essentially the terms say, "We do whatever is needed, and you pay for our time." Both words make the specification of activities less important. Definitional power is shifted from the customer to the provider. In "smokestack" "funded" work the customer has a need to be fulfilled and seeks someone to do it. "Integrated consultancy" starts with something more abstract: "You have problems and for a price we will fix them." The presence of definitional flexibility, apparent clarity, and definitional occlusion allow the dominant coalition to control interpretive processes and to enhance their power at the same time. All opposition appears unclear, unfocused, personal, obstructionist, and frustrated.

## INTEGRATIVE

As Alvesson (1994) showed in his study at "Enator" and as appears clear in the general discussion of knowledge-intensive services, integration is accomplished mostly by symbolic means. With people working away from the site, minimal work contact with AIMS outside of one's project group, unclear and emergent tasks and products, and a relatively loose management structure, the integrative processes common to product production and manual services are not available here. The business concept is central to making choices, coordinating work efforts, and providing a point of reference for evaluation. But it also creates particular tensions.

On the surface the concept of "integrated services offered on a consultancy basis" provides a clear principle for integration. The concept directs attention to the customer. The line was often repeated, "In consulting if you don't please your customer, you're out of business." The seriousness of this construction is shown in an annual review system that puts much emphasis on customer rating forms, though oddly not on marketing or getting business, which is common in "real" consulting firms. But one does not have to follow the discourse very far to find interesting gaps and contradictions. In the conception "consulting makes money the game," but the apparent consensus does not represent well the expressed goals and values of organizational members.

Rarely is there evidence that money is the primary motivation for the individual "consultant" at AIMS. Nearly all reported satisfaction in doing a good job, in solving a problem, and in simply pleasing a customer. Even the focus on integration is advocated so that the project can be seen through to the end so that the work is more innovative and at a higher skill level, never because it is more profitable. Certainly there is no inherent contradiction between these intrinsic values and consultancy or making money, but there is no inherent affinity either. Such goals would seem just as likely in a funded agency. And most employees do not seem terribly concerned that the unit is not making money (especially since most are guaranteed alternative employment). At first glance there appears to be two independent discourses here: one about how the company works, which implies monetary motivation for the member, and another about the members' motivation, which appears to have little to do with money.

While the members may keep these separated in their talk, the discourse organizes their practice in ways that favor the economic discourse. In fact, the employees' ability to keep these discourses apart obscures for them the power of the economic logic. Little attention is paid to the way the consultancy conception instrumentalizes each of their desires for interesting work—desires, other than money, that do seem to motivate—and how it transforms social relations into economic ones. The consultancy concept remains protected from examination, provides economic benefits for the company, and strengthens management's hand in the metaphorical conception of "self-employment." Several current employee complaints—having to take jobs that they did not want and having to engage in marketing activities—certainly come with a consultancy mentality. When money is not a primary motivator, management can seek other means of increasing work effort. They could satisfy other employee desires, such as those listed above. Or, as in AIMS, they can contrive an arrangement where economic determination reenters. To the extent that a consultancy identity is accepted, the financial arrangement leads employees to control themselves rather than management having to do it even when personal financial gain is not of interest.

The instrumentalization of the consultant–client relationship created its own forms of unpaid labor and control. In placing the client as central in evaluations of work activities and in definitions of consultant identity, the employee is called upon to engage in activities that no employer could require or monitor and in activities that few employees would be willing to perform for their own employer. An example of this, though unique in being somewhat to AIMS's disadvantage, was shown in the underreporting of work time at client sites. Few employers could require that workers underreport work hours, but here it is done voluntarily, often in subtle and disguised form. More significant was the amount of "emotional labor" required. Several clients bordered on being abusive as well as making unrealistic work demands. Such clients did not appear to relate to their own employees in this way. They seemed to feel that "I have paid for this, I have a right to have it delivered no matter what you have to do." In this surrogate management situation, not only did AIMS employees lack normal worker rights since they complied voluntarily to meet the client's needs, but they were also "expected" to placate clients and maintain friendly, supportive relations. AIMS employees were generally "required" to work extraordinary hours to meet client "needs," including occasionally sleeping on cots in client worksites and working weekends to meet unrealistic deadlines that they themselves had cocreated in the bidding process. And additionally they were "expected" to be happy, engaging, and attentive. Terms like "expected" and "required" are meant here in a "consent" sense since AIMS's management could not require such behaviors. Extra work and personal relations were being sold on behalf of AIMS. If anything, AIMS's management deplored such clients (thus helping to reduce exit) and openly acknowledged such pressures and even offered support. Yet the command to please the client as a part of the consultancy "self-employment" and a reward system supporting the command enhanced consent to management control that was accomplished through clients rather than directly through AIMS managers. The customer relation thus controlled more powerfully than management could have. The consultancy concept both set up this relationship and provided financial gains to AIMS from it. The instrumentalization of the self and associated costs are certainly felt, but they do not appear to be discussable, thus to be conceptualized, clearly.

The "integrated solutions" concept has also created a number of tensions. Most centrally, "integrated solutions" is a long-term conception. Large projects may take months to get and well over a year to complete. And, as this district has already experienced, if a large contract is canceled a major financial instability is created. Even a ready supply of technically competent temporary workers does not totally solve the problem. (And it seems to make such a workforce necessary without consideration of the social or personal effects of temporary work.) Big projects have high overhead costs and require keeping many employees on the "beaches" (a commonly used military metaphor combining a sense of rest and recuperation and a pool of "surplus" or underemployed workers).

Not surprisingly with an economic downturn, customers wanted shorter, quicker solutions to technical problems. The market plus the immediacy of the economic crises at AIMS brought the consultancy model and integrated solutions into competition. While integrated solutions is presented as a business concept, as will be shown, it may well have a stronger ideological and identity connection than a rational or economic justification. In this situation AIMS needed projects fast, but all networking contacts for new work were in specific areas, and AIMS couldn't afford to have people on the beaches, so economic conditions forced a lot of smokestack work. This potentially increased the symbolic capital (through customer networks) of those traditionally doing mostly smokestack work. The management response was to develop a sales group and to reward them with $100 for each new project of any size. The effect of this was to centralize marketing and network contacts thus reducing the value of prior symbolic capital and to recapture the issue in the economic code, centralizing economic over symbolic capital. The solution itself helped point out the contradiction. Not only were there complaints about paying people extra for simply doing the job that they were supposed to do, but such a small reward system focused not on integrated solutions but, rather, on quick piecemeal jobs. As new challenges arose to the integrated concept, the dominant discourse was on deferral of integrated solutions rather than on showing the need for or desirability of mixed services or for valuing those doing smokestack work.

Despite the immediate advantages to management, one wonders why the bipolar conception was retained when mixed services seemed immediately necessary and economically advantageous even in the long run. Even in the shift to the economic discourse, the problems of the concept seemed clear. A deeper look at what the concept meant to each of the functionally divided groups provides some clues. In the small number of interviews a relation emerged that is interesting and worthy of more study. People in the more "technical" (conceptualized as based in science and mathematics and working with machines) areas, including the district manager, favored to both the consulting and integrated solution conception while people in the more "service" (conceptualized as intuitive, commonsensical, and people oriented) areas tended to argue for more a funded and smokestack conception. And, probably of little surprise given common work demographics, women were more common in this latter and less powerful group. Even with the economic losses, the dominant group can be seen as fighting for their symbolic capital.

While the amount of data is small, some tentative analysis is useful to direct exploration. First, people in the technical areas appear more focused on the project and less on the customer (most vividly characterized by the tendency for people in the service areas to underbill the customers for their time).

Second, big projects create a hierarchy favoring the knowledge and skills (the relative capital) of the technical over the service people (a hierarchy probably already gendered and captured in the descriptive labels). A big project is nearly always the implementation of a new network system or software package done by the technical people that leads to changes in work relations that requires service people to train the personnel. With a technologically deterministic mind-set, service people are always supplementary, dependent, supportive, and reactive. In smokestack work, service people are problem solvers, independent, and proactive. They are the focus of the work rather than the mop-up crew. Certainly this is not a necessary relation, but the discourse of AIMS embellishes the descriptive distinction in this way.

Third, the economics of integrated work favor the technical areas. Owing to the integrated conception, the individual groups at AIMS do not each have a financial bottom line, but the numbers were widely available and as was frequently expressed, "Everybody knows who [which group] is doing well." Part of this is historical and part, structural. When AIMS was formed, a large number of the people in the technical area were part of an intact group (including the now district manager) with several continuing contracts. As indicated above, the service area people tended to come from funded groups doing smokestack work with short-term contracts. They carried into the new unit social contacts for more contracts but not continuing contracts. Not only are their balance sheets less favorable initially, but until large integrated projects are signed, projects for which they will serve as support, their continued smokestack work is necessary for their groups to show a "profit." They must choose to fail in either the consultancy (economic) or the integrated conception. But the problem does not go away with big projects. A big project is defined as one requiring state-of-the-art technical expertise that has people consequences. I have yet to hear anyone in the company describe a big project that is initiated by a management style or diversity change that will then require some software support. The relative status of both the technical and service people is tied to integrated solutions offered on a consultancy model.

And finally, providing integrated services requires having employees in a variety of different support service areas. The combination of a division of labor, large projects requiring unit-wide commitment, and the need to select workers for each part of the project reclaims for management a relation to the customer and control of work processes that are normally shifted to the employee in knowledge-intensive consultancy work. With integrated services offered through a consultancy model, the managerial hierarchy and control is reclaimed, marketing is centralized, and deskilling is more present than in smokestack work.

## CONTROLLING

Owing to the economic crisis there appeared to be little uncertainty in decision making; thus rarely was the business concept used explicitly in choice making. But in effect the consultancy conception ruled. The economic arrangement meant that any project had to be accepted if it would improve the company's economic standing. People in the services areas had to do more low-status work to keep the unit economically sound even while being degraded for it. Integration continued to be promoted as a concept but its implementation was deferred. This is shown across a number of choices. For example, all travel and training were discontinued even though they might be competitively advantageous in the long run. As mentioned, a special reward system was established to bring in any new business.

Further, other AIMS values were disregarded. People were assigned to projects that they did not like, where before they had had considerable input on assignments. In an extreme case, a woman with two children whose husband was temporarily stationed 800 miles away was assigned to a project site a considerable distance from her home, thus requiring the children to be in day care by 6:00 in the morning and to be picked up at 6:30 in the evening. Such choices led more than one interviewee to question (off the record) whether the survival of AIMS was better than the alternatives.

The concerns were directed, however, to management choices and the "temporary" economic problem rather than to the instabilities inherent in the economically driven consultancy conception. In many ways, the combination of the consultancy concept and economic crisis strengthened management's hand. Their power resided in the co-occurrance of people wanting AIMS to survive and an economic crisis. The removal of either would weaken their control. The construction of fear of an unspecified but implied negative consequent ("What would happen if AIMS went out of business?") was a clear part of silencing alternative voices and thus reducing uncertainties and the choices offered in them. Not sharing in the dream of AIMS was heresy punishable by ostracism. This became clearer after the time period of the interviews reported here. AIMS was reorganized in January 1994 and moved to another company within LTC. "The vision saved them" were the words of one manager. But the "them" has an interesting ambiguity. Is "them" the unit or the individual employees? Both? Clearly the unit is still in existence, but what were the employees saved from, what was the price, and what were they "saved" to do?

Keeping integration as part of the dream, part of what gave AIMS and the employees a special identity, was more important than the way integration entered into choices. It is doubtful that the integrated conception would have much controlling force even at another time. When asked how they would decide which project to take if two were available, the responses referred to the intrinsic qualities of the project ("technically interesting," "I could learn from it"), clarity of the customer's need, and personal factors, but never whether it required an integrated solution. Certainly conceptually some of the intrinsic qualities were linked to integrated approaches, but none were necessarily so and both customer clarity and personal factors ("How long stationed there? Where is it?") would often tend to lean against an integrated approach. Clearly the function of the integrated conception rested elsewhere.

## IDEOLOGICAL

Both "consultancy" and "integrated solutions" have strong discursive connections to pervasive value systems in LTC and the wider society. "Consultancy" as used in this site served as an ideogram condensing and summing up a market mentality. Ideologically speaking, a market mentality holds that economic calculations are to be preferred over social or political discussions as a means of decision making, that people work harder and better if their effort is measured by money, and that a large corporation can be composed of entrepreneurial groups that, through self-interest, self-management, and economic initiative, can contribute to the greater good as if guided by an invisible hand. None of these claims were supported by much data, and none were ever tested. In interviewee descriptions most of these values appeared absolutely assumed as an intrinsic quality of a consultant mind-set:

> "I think not being funded, having to have the customer commit the dollars to the project has a lot of benefits. It validates that your organization is doing something worthwhile. Like I don't know, I guess it's like the free market economy theory of, you know, 'cause I guess having been in IMS a number of years and seeing some of the other organizations in IMS and, yeah, I think it sort of transforms the focus of the organization somewhat."

Contrary possibilities that internal marketing costs are collectively high for the parent company, that vendor-driven creation of needs is a costly inefficiency, that economic instabilities drive good people away or keep them from doing good work, or that self-interest values and their pursuit do not magically add up to company gain were not discussed, let alone assessed even in a period of crisis and relative unhappiness. Some may have questioned whether consultancy was a good way to do their work, but none questioned the dominant market economy discourse from which it drew its power. Criticisms were thus easily dismissed as backward looking ("not able to give up old ways") or simply "self-interested," "scared," and "weak willed." As one of supporters of the consultancy idea before AIMS reflected on the transitions at AIMS:

> "Uh, as we became merged into IMS and [AIMS] there was a different culture, ya know. It was the old [LTC] culture that still persists as you're regulated, you're funded, we do whatever we want. And bringing those people along kind of diluted the culture that we had and it wasn't a matter of diversity getting new ideas in, it was a matter of getting some old ideas that we got away from back in."

Proclaiming the consultancy model could thus be used to justify and legitimate any decision that could be coded in economic language.

"Integrated" also is firmly connected to dominant value discourses. Even the choice of the term "smokestack," to designate its opposite, makes it modern and progressive in distinction to an old industrial model evoking images of the rust belt and the inability to compete with economically less developed societies. It does not simply describe as a term; rather, it evaluates and legitimizes. Further, it supports big and important projects over "onesy, twosy" (in the words of the district manager), referencing (constructing) both the trivial, piecemeal, and slowly cumulative nature of the jobs and the children's game of jacks (often conceptualized as a girls' game). Integrated projects not only were considered highly technically advanced (a big value at LTC), but portrayed the customer as a part of the project, as an element needing to be integrated rather than as the buyer of a service he or she identified as needed. The term "integrated" thus legitimizes the internal ranking of personnel at AIMS. An argument for smokestack projects cannot be raised in ways that question the values and premises on which integration is based; rather, it condemns the one making the case to a secondary, but perhaps necessary, status. One who argues for smokestack projects is positioned as an "other" in the dominant game rather than being able to define the game.

## MARKETING

The business concept helps solve a very important marketing problem for knowledge-intensive services. How does one explain to a customer his or her need for a product that is very difficult to define, at least when one's professional standing requires keeping it hard to describe? Frequently the product is marketed by its proposed outcome rather than by descriptions of what is to be done ("We will improve your billing systems, reduce the need for more memory in your computer, create efficiencies . . ."). In each case since it is the outcome that is described rather than the product and activities that produce it, trust of the professional expert is essential. The customers are not given the information to assess the likelihood of the consequences for themselves. Further, since many vendors suggest they have the ability to accomplish the same ends and one cannot be easily distinguished from another by product, a vendor's distinction and uniqueness is a symbolic outcome. Both consultancy and integration serve in this capacity, but again not without costs.

Consulting helps because it carries to the customer many of the same discursive linkages found internally. The perceived risk to the customer manager, who must justify the expense and be covered if it does not pay off, is reduced ("Others have been willing to pay for this; they have to provide a good product or they would be out of business"). In an increasingly complex business environment, trust of the concept must replace trust that was interpersonally based. "Consulting" does this and at the same time reproduces the need as it puts economic over social relations. "Integrated solutions" does this and at the same time reproduces the need by displacing the employee–customer relationship. In this case, the consulting concept also helps because of some problems unique to the situation of AIMS. IMS is not terribly well respected within LTC. A funded unit within it would fight an uphill battle to get work. The ability to claim an independent and special status increases the trust. Further, since AIMS aspires to market their services internationally outside of LTC, they are able to use both the high status of LTC and consultancy as a trust factor. But consulting also carries a price. Once AIMS is in the consulting business, its comparison groups and competition change. For example, since Arthur Andersen is the contractual consulting firm for LTC, AIMS must not only show it can do as well for less cost (and be as reasonable a choice if they cannot do the job well), but they must also show that they are not overstepping their bounds into territory granted to Arthur Andersen by the LTC contract.

Offering integrated solutions on a consultancy basis also offers marketing difficulties. Big projects mean carrying high overhead costs, and there can be big mistakes that greatly increase the costs and risks to a customer. A customer understandably asks whether they are ready for this big a project. Especially in the internal market of LTC, outsider status carries credibility alone. Ten-million-dollar projects do not simply go to the lowest bidder. In fact, high cost frequently carries prestige and risk protection for the customer (if it fails, one at least has not bought a cheap product). Additionally, in a consultancy rather than fully funded arrangement the internal customer has to pay "real" rather than "funny" money and is implicitly billed for overhead that had been absorbed by LTC. Even if the financial consequences of these differences is inconsequential, the very things that gain symbolic value carry symbolic costs.

## IMAGE

Perhaps more than anything else, the business concept offers a positive image and high-status identity for AIMS and its employees. AIMS is not just another IMS (usually thought of as arrogant and inefficient) unit; it is a full-service consulting firm competing with Arthur Andersen. Even where there is some doubt as to whether employees want all that comes with a consulting business, there is little question of the goal. As a relatively new employee outside AIMS inner groups expressed it:

> "What happens is it becomes an issue of image and salesmanship which is one thing that concerns me. Although maybe I'm just naive and maybe I don't know much, everything is, it depends on that. I guess I'm just more of a technically oriented person."

The employees are not just workers offering services in a bureaucracy; they are consultants. A reoccurring theme in the interviews was the good feeling that employees got from knowing that someone was willing to pay for what they did. Interestingly, the less what they did seemed understood or appreciated by AIMS, the more pressing being defined "by being wanted" seemed to be. Certainly considerable identity is invested in being defined as good by others, a conception from which AIMS as a consulting-type company gains financially. Consulting as the discursive self-conception produces consent to having worth determined by money. A couple of quick examples:

> "As a consultant everyone you deal with you know that they want you there, because they are willing to pay."

> "I feel like they're paying me to do something I better be doing it to the best of my ability."

There seemed to be little discussion of the other side of measuring self-worth by money, the transforming of self into a commodity. Employees seemed happy to do that if it had identity payoff. They were pleased to strategize their own subordination for even uncertain payoffs. They were even thankful for the company's help in this process. The few nonmanagerial members I talked with seemed to have less identity invested in the business concept than the managers. Nonmanagerial members saw the business concept more as a marketing device and less as a definition of themselves. In many ways, the continued discursive reproduction of both "integrated" services and the "consultancy" model are better understood based on their consequences for the identity of key players than based on economic advantages.

## CONCLUSION

This study investigates the use of a business concept through a focused case study of a service division of large multinational corporation. A business conception of integrated services offered on a consultancy basis was contrasted with smokestack services offered through a funded arrangement. The discursive maintenance and elaboration of this conceptual reality both constituted and supported managerial control and a dominant coalition's centrality during a financial crisis. A careful look at the discourse of AIMS suggests an intricate set of relations between structural, economic, and personal discursive processes passing through the business concept as a central node in the circuit of power. The business concept is part of the internal politics of the organization, favoring certain groups, suppressing important conflicts and alternative thoughts and actions. The power of the concept rests in its capacity to close off certain discursive options rather than simply in its rhetorical appeal. The conception deployed allowed the discussion to seem complete and neutral thus hiding the tensions and incompletion. With such a closed set of discursive options, the employee is basically left to chose loyalty or exit but not voice. In choosing loyalty they gain membership, clarity, status, and specific identities, but they also reenact a dominant set of power relations that have winners and losers.

The dual parts of the business concept at AIMS, "integrated" and "consultancy," illustrate well how a business concept is enacted by people with different forms of capital and how the business concept organizes a way of thinking and talking about events. As a consequent it can support or rearrange the amount and relative value of different forms of capital. With the growth of processes of self-management and the continued development of different types of internal consultancy or pay-for-service groups, understanding how control and power operate in these context is important.

Certainly the particular character of knowledge-intensive professional service products and their relation to markets makes the self-referential nature of this discourse somewhat more likely and considerably more difficult for members to think through. Misrecognitions and hidden contradictions are therefore common. We have come to understand well how power and control operate in industrial firms. As knowledge-intensive work becomes of greater interest, new forms of power and control must be of interest if companies are to be efficient and effective in meeting the needs of their various stakeholders.

## NOTE

1. This study is a part of a larger multinational study of knowledge-intensive workplaces. Questions on the interviews and many of the observations concern issues different from the ones addressed in this chapter. For further descrip-

tions of the study see Deetz (1995, in press). This part of the study benefited greatly from support by the Rickart Malmsten Foundation (Sweden) and a Fulbright Senior Scholar grant for the author. This chapter was written while the author was a visiting professor at the Företagsekonomiska Institutionen, Göteborg, Sweden. I wish to thank Bobby Brody, Debra Greenberg Farber, Marsha Goddard, and Edward Troike for help at various stages of this project, including the transcription of the interviews that served as the primary data for the analysis presented here. The company and division names used in this chapter are fictitious. The company asked as a condition of access that its identity be protected. Further, the quotations from the interviews are not cleaned up. While extralinguistic notations are not given, linguistic uncertainties and self-corrections as well as moments of great fluency provide important texture to the reports.

## KEY TERMS

ANALYTIC/INTELLECTUAL FUNCTION: the clarification of the business and justification of the existence of a unique group to do it provided by the business concept.

BUSINESS CONCEPT: a conception of the primary business the company does or the market niche it hopes to fill.

CLAN AND CULTURAL CONTROL: direction of work processes based on the inculcation or utilization of values, norms, conceptual systems, beliefs, interpretive practices, or social practices shared in a work group.

CONTROLLING FUNCTION: the organization, provided by the business concept, of a cluster of "recipes" or decision rules for making decisions in unclear situations, in decision contexts lacking important information, or in complex situations in which decision consequences are unclear.

DISCURSIVE POWER: the various ways conceptions and expressions produce and privilege certain knowledge claims, particular human identities, and various social ordering principles.

DOMINANT COALITION: an informal coordination of individuals or groups who share a common interest and are sufficiently powerful to accomplish or pursue this interest over the interest of others.

EMPLOYEE DECISION MAKING: the direct and indirect involvement of lower-level work groups in decision making regarding work processes, work assignments, reward systems, and occasionally organizational goal setting.

IDEOLOGICAL FUNCTION: the provision for the bases for action legitimation and the connection of local circumstances and accounts to larger shared values provided by the business concept.

IMAGE FUNCTION: the provision by the business concept of a "standing" for managers and other employees both providing a unified identity and "symbolic" capital in interactions with outside groups.

INTEGRATIVE FUNCTION: the provision of preferred relations among subgroups and direction choices in budgeting, long-term planning, and reward systems provided by the business concept.

KNOWLEDGE-INTENSIVE WORK: work that relies on education and intellectual skills and is done by a labor force that is highly professionalized. Knowledge-intensive workplaces that provide a professional service include consultancy groups, law, advertising and accounting firms, R&D groups, some banks, software development groups, and similar organizations.

MANAGERIAL CONTROL: the capacity of managers and management groups to direct the work process and people doing it toward goals that are preferred by higher-level managers.

MARKETING FUNCTION: the explanation of otherwise hard-to-explain products and services and provision of a basis for comparison and contrast with similar services in the eyes of the customer provided by the business concept.

PERSONAL IDENTITIES: work roles and self-conceptions that a person acquires by virtue of working in an organization.

POWER: the capacity to make preferred things happen or the ability to stop or prevent less desired events either through direct control or indirectly through changing conceptions or background assumptions; also the process by which these capacities and abilities are actualized.

SELF-CONTROL: direction of work effort or processes based on observing and monitoring one's own behavior directed toward accomplishing predetermined outcomes.

SELF-(RE)PRODUCING SYSTEMS: systems that provide their own reward, environmental information, or confirmation and evaluation and are thus self-fulfilling, often becoming out of touch with external environments until they cannot sustain themselves or outside forces break into them.

SUPPRESSED CONFLICT: conflicts that are not conceptualized and rarely take place since a dominant feeling, thought, position, or group covers up alternatives and leaves them unthought, unfelt, unexpressed, or inappropriate. To the extent that such conflicts are felt or expressed, they tend to be ill-formed, vague, or systematically distorted.

SYMBOLIC CAPITAL: noneconomic resources central to work processes, including social connections with potential clients, customers, suppliers, or regulation agencies; social skills and knowledge; possession of files and other valued information sources; and status or prestige.

## DISCUSSION QUESTIONS

1. Discuss companies or divisions that perform knowledge-intensive professional services. How do these differ from places where manufacturing or manual services are the primary product? How do these differences influence processes of communication and management?

2. Why are managers more likely to use indirect, unobtrusive, or cultural control processes when directing knowledge-intensive professional service companies or units? Why are these control processes more difficult for employees to understand or see? In what ways can these control processes reduce the quality of decisions and reduce company performance?

3. In what ways can a clear business concept focus the discussion in a group, integrate activities, and lead to positive performance? And in what ways can a clear business concept exclude some members from equal participation, make important discussions more difficult, suppress meaningful conflicts, and lead to lower performance?

4. How might one tell when the discourse in a company (especially when organized around a business concept) functions more to perpetuate a dominant group's power and fulfill their self-interest in power, particular self-identities, and other benefits than to foster positive group performance and company value and profit?

5. The consultancy conception makes employment feel more like self-employment, changes managerial control into systems of "self"-control, and encourages defining the self and products in monetary terms rather than terms of intrinsic worth. Describe each of these transformations. What are the benefits and costs of each of these transformations for AIMS and potentially for other companies?

6. Identify central discursive contrasts developed in a workplace with which you are familiar (for example, production/marketing, teaching/research, curricular/cocurricular). What do these contrasts accomplish in the workplace? How do they separate and preference particular activities? Since they are inevitably arbitrary and contestable, how are they maintained and when are they contested? Who gains from supporting these distinctions rather than other ones? Try to give examples of where people have used these distinctions to acquire more power or give more value to the activities they perform.

## REFERENCES AND SUGGESTED READING

Alvesson, M. (1992). Leadership as social integrative action: A study of a computer consulting company. *Organization Studies, 13*, 185–209.

Alvesson, M. (1993a). Cultural-ideological modes of management control. In S. Deetz (Ed.), *Communication Yearbook, 16* (pp. 3–42). Newbury Park, CA: Sage.

Alvesson, M. (1993b). Organizations as rhetoric: Knowledge-intensive firms and the struggle with ambiguity. *Journal of Management Studies, 30*, 997–1016.

Alvesson, M. (1994). *Management of knowledge-intensive companies.* Berlin & New York: de Gruyter.

Barker, J. (1993). Tightening the iron cage: Concertive control in self-managed teams. *Administrative Science Quarterly, 38*, 408–437.

Bell, D. (1973). *The coming of post-industrial society.* New York: Basic Books.

Bourdieu, P. (1977). *Outline of a theory of practice.* Cambridge, England: Cambridge University Press.

Bourdieu, P. (1991). *Language and symbolic power.* Cambridge, MA: Harvard University Press.

Burawoy, M. (1985). *The politics of production: Factory regimes under capitalism and socialism.* London: Verso.

Clegg, S. (1989). *Frameworks of power.* Newbury Park, CA: Sage.

Deetz, S. (1992a). *Democracy in the age of corporate colonization: Developments in communication and the politics of everyday life.* Albany: State University of New York Press.

Deetz, S. (1992b). Disciplinary power in the modern corporation: Discursive practice and conflict suppression. In M. Alvesson & H. Willmott (Eds.), *Critical management studies* (pp. 21–52). London: Sage.

Deetz, S. (1994). The micro-politics of identity formation in the workplace: The case of a knowledge intensive firm. *Human Studies, 17,* 23–44.

Deetz, S. (1995). *Transforming communication, transforming business: Building responsive and responsible workplaces.* Cresskill, NJ: Hampton Press.

Deetz, S. (in press). Discursive formations, strategized subordination, and self-surveillance: An empirical case. In A. McKinlay & K. Starkey (Eds.), *Managing Foucault: A reader.* London: Sage.

Drucker, P. (1993). *Post-capitalist society.* New York: HarperBusiness.

Foucault, M. (1977). *Discipline and punish: The birth of the prison.* (A. Sheridan Smith, Trans.). New York: Random House.

Foucault, M. (1988). *Technologies of the self.* In L. Martin, H. Gutman, & P. Hutton (Eds.), *Technologies of the self* (pp. 16–49). Amherst: University of Massachusetts Press.

Greenwood, R., Hinings, C. R., & Brown, J. (1990). "P2-form" strategic management: Corporate practices in professional partnerships. *Academy of Management Journal, 33,* 725–755.

Hassard, J., & Parker, M. (Eds.). (1993). *Postmodernism and organizations.* London: Sage.

Heckscher, C. (1995). *White-collar blues: Management loyalties in an age of corporate restructuring.* New York: Basic Books.

Hining, C. R., Brown, J., & Greenwood, R. (1991). Change in an autonomous professional organization. *Journal of Management Studies, 28,* 375–393.

Kidder, T. (1981). *Soul of the new machine.* Boston: Little, Brown.

Knights, D., & Collinson, D. (1987). Disciplining the shop floor: A comparison of the disciplinary effects of managerial psychology and financial accounting. *Accounting, Organizations and Society, 12,* 457–477.

Knights, D., & Willmott, H. (1985). Power and identity in theory and practice. *The Sociological Review, 33,* 22–46.

Knights, D., & Willmott, H. (1989). Power and subjectivity at work: From degradation to subjugation in social relations. *Sociology, 23,* 535–558.

Kunda, G. (1992). *Engineering culture: Control and commitment in a high-tech corporation.* Philadelphia: Temple University Press.

Manz, C., & Sims, H. (1980). Self-management as a substitute for leadership: A social learning perspective. *Academy of Management Review, 5,* 361–367.

Martin, J. (1990). Deconstructing organizational taboos: The suppression of gender conflict in organizations. *Organization Science, 1,* 339–359.

Martin, J. (1994). The organization of exclusion: The institutionalization of sex inequality, gendered faculty jobs, and gendered knowledge in organizational theory and research. *Organization, 1,* 401–431.

Mills, P., Hall, J., Leidecker, J., & Margulies, N. (1983). Flexiform: A model for professional service organizations. *Academy of Management Review, 8,* 118–131.

Normann, R. (1991). *Service management: Strategic leadership in service business* (2nd ed.). New York: Wiley.

Ouchi, W., & Maguire, M. (1975). Organization control: Two functions. *Administrative Science Quarterly, 20,* 559–569.

Quinn, J. (1992). *Intelligent enterprise: A knowledge and service based paradigm for industry.* New York: Free Press.

Reich, R. (1991). *The work of nations: Preparing ourselves for 21st century capitalism.* New York: Simon & Schuster.

Shotter, J. (1993). *Conversational realities: The construction of life through language.* Newbury Park, CA: Sage.

Shotter, J., & Gergen, K. (1994). Social construction: Knowledge, self, others, and continuing the conversation. In S. Deetz (Ed.), *Communication Yearbook, 17* (pp. 3–33). Newbury Park, CA: Sage.

Slocum, J., Jr., & Sims, H., Jr. (1980). A typology for integrating technology, organization and job design. *Human Relations, 33,* 193–212.

Starbuck, W. (1992). Learning by knowledge-intensive firms. *Journal of Management Studies, 29,* 713–740.

Townley, B. (1993). Foucault, power/knowledge, and its relevance for human resource management. *Academy of Management Review, 18,* 518–545.

Zachary, G. P. (1994). *Show-stopper! The breakneck race to create Windows NT and the new generation at Microsoft.* New York: Free Press.

# CHAPTER 12

# The Politics of Information Systems

Rational Designs and
Organizational Realities

NOSHIR S. CONTRACTOR
BARBARA J. O'KEEFE

Conventional wisdom has long suggested that there is no resource more critical to an organization than timely, accurate information relevant to organizational decisions. Because of this presumption, effective information management—development of appropriate systems for production and movement of information within organizations—is seen as critical to organizational goals.

Information management has two interrelated aspects: information production and information flow. By "information production" we mean the processes through which organizations gather and organize data. The production of information is itself a complex process that involves both methodology (procedures used in rendering reality in ways useful to the organization) and judgment (decisions about what information to obtain and how to use it). By "information flow" we mean the movement of information from one system component to another. System components could be individuals, computers, departments, or libraries. As information flows, it passes through a chain of agents who have the ability to alter, suppress, or elaborate it as it is passed on.

By their very nature, information production and flow are political processes. They are political in two senses: First, they are imbued with political implications. Since decisions are made on the basis of the relevant information, or at least are held accountable to relevant information, the amount and type of information available to decision makers is consequential. The ability to control information is thus a key aspect of organizational power.

Second, information production and flow are political because they reflect the political structure of an organization. They require the participation of organizational members, whose collective decisions contribute to the overall information system of the organization. Organizational policy makers may wish to have a certain type or amount of information, but ultimately all knowledge workers in the organization control whether or not that information will be provided in the way the policy maker wishes. Changing the information environment requires active, political management to mobilize collective action toward organizational goals.

In this chapter we discuss the politics of information management in a public works department. Our case study examines the reasons for the lack of adoption of an integrated information system that has been introduced in the department. Our analysis reveals that individuals' political considerations explain their lack of interest in contributing—comprehensively and accurately—to an integrated information system that was rationally designed to serve their collective good. In the two major sections of the chapter we first describe the organization and its context and then discuss the integrated information system and its appropriation by the organization. Our description of the organization and its information systems and needs is based on detailed field notes made by Noshir S. Contractor, Barbara J. O'Keefe, Patricia Jones, and Greta Chin during repeated visits to the organization and on surveys of employee perceptions of their organizational information systems.

## THE ORGANIZATION AND ITS INFORMATION SYSTEMS

We are part of a research team conducting an information technology demonstration and assessment in the Directorate of Public Works (DPW) at a large military installation in the southern United States (which we will refer to as "the Fort"). The information technology demonstration will create a computer-based "workbench" of tools that will help in scheduling, tracking, and planning the maintenance activities of the DPW. As part of this project, we have been involved in detailed quantitative and qualitative assessments of the organization and its information needs.

### The DPW and Its Structure

The Fort is a large installation with a complex mission involving both training and specialized missions in the areas of intelligence and communications. Over 12,000 military personnel have been assigned to the Fort, and approximately 4,000 civilian employees and contractors work at the Fort. The great majority of these workers and their families live in nearby communities. The Fort also supports a large community of military retirees (10,500) and their families (17,000).

The Fort is situated on a 56,000-acre preserve near a small city, with which it shares an increasing number of services and resources. The Fort itself is highly analogous to a city of about 40,000 people: It has diverse types of housing; services such as fire and police protection, hospitals, schools, and libraries; and retail and commercial businesses. The Fort's infrastructure includes nearly 10 million square feet of space in buildings, 170 miles of roads, 6 miles of railroad track, and the complete complement of utilities (water, power, sewage, gas, and electricity).

The DPW is responsible for maintaining the entire infrastructure of the Fort. The activities of the DPW include both development and maintenance of the Fort's real property, civil services, and utilities. Much of the work done by the DPW involves routine and critical maintenance of existing facilities, although the DPW is also involved in design and construction of new facilities.

Many of the responsibilities of the DPW are carried out in partnership with the Army Corps of Engineers ("the Corps") and the civilian base contractor. For large construction projects, the Corps is involved in both the design of the project and in supervision of the contracting and construction process. For many routine maintenance activities, work is passed on to the civilian base contractor. For example, if the heating system in a building malfunctions, the problem is reported to the relevant civilian contractor, who dispatches workers to repair it.

The DPW has been undergoing a period of downsizing and reorganization. At the time we entered the organization, it had two major groups of departments, each of which was headed by a chief who reported to the division chief of the DPW ("the director"). The director reports to a lieutenant colonel, who in turn reports to the base commander.

## Engineering Plans and Services

The first group of departments, "Engineering Plans and Services (EPS)," is responsible for master planning, design, and construction of the Fort infrastructure. EPS works collaboratively with the Army Corps of Engineers. For large projects (over $300,000 for new construction or over $2 million for repairs), EPS does the initial planning, but the Corps is responsible for design and construction. Very small projects (under $25,000) are assigned to the base contractor. A different contractor is assigned construction projects of $25,000–$125,000. Any project budgeted for more than $125,000 that is not assigned to the Corps is managed by EPS. EPS develops the design and solicits bids from contractors for the project. Consistent with these activities, the personnel of EPS consists primarily of planners and engineers. It is headed by a division chief, includes a master planner, civil and mechanical engineers, and design technicians.

## Facilities Management

The second group of departments, the Facilities Management branch (FM), is responsible for management of real property (buildings), including management of utilities services. FM is responsible for evaluating, assigning, and decommissioning space across the Fort. Until recently, FM served as the recipient of all work requests (many of which are now routed directly to the base contractor). It still retains responsibility for evaluating work requests, routing them, and monitoring compliance with requirements and contracts. Consistent with these responsibilities, FM is supervised by a division chief and includes managers, sales agents, military space consultants, energy systems managers, and work reception clerks as well as engineers and technicians.

## Reorganization and Downsizing

An additional group of departments concerned with Environmental Services and Public Safety has been moved into and out of the DPW several times over the past 6 months. This reorganization, combined with personnel losses associated with downsizing, has produced a good deal of instability in the DPW staff. The number of employees of the DPW has fluctuated from over 70 to fewer than 60 during the time we have been observing the DPW.

## Information Production and Flow in the DPW

Discussions with DPW about their information and technology needs began in November 1994 at a workshop held at the Fort. In a series of meetings with DPW managers and planners, we learned about their perspectives on their goals and problems. In a subsequent workshop held in Champaign, Illinois, in December 1994, a group of employees from the DPW further discussed their perceived needs with our research team and with representatives from the Corps' Construction Engineering Research Laboratory (CERL) software design teams.

One perceived need that emerged early in our discussions with the DPW was for accurate, credible information about the status of installation facilities. In fact, virtually every supervisor and employee criticized the current system for generating and sharing information about the status of Fort facilities. Members of the DPW were critical both of the production of information about installation status and of its transformation as it flowed through the organization.

## Production of Installation Status Reports

The DPW is involved in a continuous process of assessing the state of the facilities and judging whether the facilities are "mission ready." Mission readiness refers to the ability of the Fort to perform its assigned military functions. So, for example, if the Fort is unable to house all the soldiers and their families who are assigned to the base for training, the Fort is clearly not mission ready. If the road or railroad track systems are in such disrepair that they hamper troop movement, the Fort cannot satisfactorily perform its mission.

The Installation Status Report (ISR) is used to evaluate the state of each element of the infrastructure at the Fort. It is modeled on the Unit Status Report, a system used to evaluate the mission readiness of military units throughout the Army. As with the Unit Status Report, the ISR involves a decision about whether any part of the installation is mission ready using a "red amber green" scale: A facility judged red is not able to support its mission, a facility judged amber has limitations or defects that could impair its mission, and a facility judged green is fully capable of supporting its mission.

The evaluation of a facility is guided by an extremely detailed set of procedures provided by the Army. For example, in evaluating the site and grounds around a building, they are rated red if lighting is damaged or inadequate, if sidewalks are in disrepair or not installed or if walkways from parking lot to building are missing, if no provision is made for the handicapped, or if it is impacted by surrounding incompatible activities; amber if utility services are damaged, if site lighting is provided in only some areas, if sidewalks are cracked, if only gravel surfaces the walkways, if only some provision is made for the handicapped, or if surrounding activities have a minor impact on the facility; or green if utility services and equipment are adequate, if site lighting is adequate, if sidewalks and walkways are paved and in good repair, if the site is handicapped accessible, and if it is surrounded by mission-compatible activities. These criteria (as well as those used for each element of the infrastructure) are explained and illustrated in detailed brochures published by the Army.

The ISR for a facility is completed not by members of the EPS but by other personnel designated to inspect a given facility. These individuals may be in command of units assigned to use a given facility (e.g., the sergeant whose command is housed in a particular barracks). They are generally perceived by the EPS staff as lacking the technical qualifications required to make an accurate judgment about the status of a facility.

Moreover, because ISRs are used to guide decisions about maintenance, EPS staff often question their honesty. To be a realistic candidate for repair or renovation, a facility must be rated red or amber. Those who complete ISRs know that the way to establish the need for a project is to indicate that a needed facility is red—not mission ready. EPS staff express the view that many of those who complete ISRs offer ratings that express their own sense of the importance of a repair or renovation rather than an accurate judgment about the state of the facility. In particular, they suspect that raters underestimate mission readiness to justify projects they have proposed.

However, too many red facilities make a fort look like a good candidate for closure. Particularly in the current political and economic climate, a base commander cannot tolerate too many red ratings. A fort needs to be basically mission ready. This leads staff from the EPS to worry that ratings are also distorted from the top as the base commander juggles the ISR ratings to ensure that the overall impression given by the Fort is appropriate. This concern about the quality of ISR information is aggravated by the fact that the base commander has the ability and authority to change any ISR rating at any time. One story told in one of our meetings by the EPS staff seemed to encapsulate all their suspicions about ISRs: A training course had been given to Army managers on the ISR system, and one topic discussed explicitly at the training course was the implications of ISRs for Department of Defense decisions about appropriations. EPS staff reported their interpretation of this discussion: The Fort's management personnel were being told by the Army trainers to manipulate ISRs strategically.

At the same time, the director and staff involved in long-term planning repeatedly emphasized that evaluations of installation status are critical for long-term planning and decision making. This creates a very deep ambivalence about ISRs: On the one hand, the DPW staff members believe that accurate ISRs are critical for their own infrastructure maintenance activities, but on the other hand, they have little confidence in the quality of ISR ratings.

## Flow of Information about Installation Status

To aid in assessing the mission readiness of its facilities, the U.S. Army has developed a computer-based system, Integrated Facilities System Micro (IFS-M), in which all its real property is recorded and evaluated. IFS-M, developed in the early 1990s, was an extension of an earlier system, IFS, that was developed in the late 1960s. IFS-M is a technology developed for the U.S. Army; IFS-M databases are maintained by individual installations but are used not only by that installation but also by the Department of Defense to study and evaluate facilities.

IFS-M is a computer program that automates record keeping associated with infrastructure maintenance. It stores and tracks information in 11 key areas: real property, customer coordination, projects, job costs, work estimating, contract administration, tracking requirements, supplies, scheduling, employee data, and equipment. Theoretically, IFS-M has the capability of providing an integrated picture of the Fort infrastructure, the DPW, and DPW projects (past, current, and projected).

Such an integrated representation of the Fort would be a tremendous boon to planners and decision makers, both inside the DPW and in command. In our conversations with the director of the DPW, the division chiefs, and staff responsible for planning, inventory, and tracking, it was repeatedly emphasized that IFS-M has the potential to transform the way work is done in the DPW.

However, the IFS-M program is the subject of a number of contradictory beliefs and practices within the DPW. As we show in the next section, IFS-M is a system that works better than employees of the DPW think (particularly those in management), and the perception of its weaknesses may be better understood as the product of political needs than of intrinsic defects in the technology.

## ANALYSIS OF INFORMATION PRODUCTION AND FLOW AT THE FORT

The IFS-M system is intended to meet the needs of the DPW for an integrated representation of infrastructure and maintenance activities at the Fort. In terms of the organization's goals, it is clearly desirable for each individual to collaborate in maintaining the IFS-M database and ensuring that it is as accurate as possible. In this section we discuss the reasons why the employees of the DPW have made what appears to be an irrational collective decision to ignore the IFS-M system.

A rational model would imply that an information system must be designed on the basis of matching information-processing requirements with information processing capabilities. While earlier models (Galbraith, 1973; Tushman & Nadler, 1978) assessed information-processing requirements on the basis of reducing uncertainty, more recent models (Daft & Lengel, 1986) have suggested that information-processing requirements be examined in terms of reducing both equivocality and uncertainty. Equivocality is reduced when information is processed to help identify the relevant questions that must be examined by the organization. Uncertainty is reduced when information is processed to answer these questions. According to this extended model, the design of an information system requires matching information processing capabilities that take into account the different needs of uncertainty and equivocality reduction.

Daft and Lengel (1986) describe information-processing capabilities in general, and equivocality reduction in particular, in terms of a medium's richness. The richness of a medium is judged on its capability to change understanding rather than simply convey information. Changing understanding often implies overcoming different frames of reference, clarifying ambiguous issues, and constructing (or enacting) a common frame of reference. Daft and Lengel suggest that rich media (1) have the capacity for immediate feedback, (2) convey multiple cues, (3) employ a larger number of channels, (4) offer personalization, and (5) offer language variety. In general, richer media (such as face-to-face communication, which allows a greater number of cues and feedback than, e.g., e-mail) are more appropriate to reduce equivocality, while leaner media (such as text-based computer-mediated communication) are better suited for the reduction of uncertainty.

According to the information-processing theory outlined above, the design of the IFS-M's information-processing capabilities should be evaluated in terms of its ability to match the information-processing requirements of those involved in the maintenance of the Fort. The system, and its supporting documentation, are explicitly designed on the assumption that the maintenance of the Fort is a routine, structured, scientifically driven set of tasks and decisions that do not entail the reduction of equivocality. As described in the previous section, decisions to carry out construction or maintenance tasks are made on the basis of information collected in response to a well-defined set of questions and criteria. Likewise, decisions to evaluate the "readiness" of specific fixtures or of the Fort in general are also made on the basis of preordained questions and criteria. Further, the criteria used to make these decisions do not change over time. Hence IFS-M, an information-processing system using lean computer-based media, offers capabilities that are commensurate with the uncertainty-reducing information-processing requirements of the Fort.

However, our interviews at the Fort indicate that IFS-M is only used by seven out of the 65 employees in DPW. According to IFS-M documentation and the IFS-M system manager, it is designed to be used by at least 40 of the 65 employees in the DPW. Clearly IFS-M has not been successfully adopted at the Fort.

In our preliminary interviews, the managers at DPW were very outspoken in their criticisms of IFS-M. Their criticisms fell into three categories: incomplete and inaccurate information, lack of adequate computer hardware, and poorly designed software. First, managers mentioned that the system was not being used because employees were too busy with on-going tasks to enter existing data into the system. Further, they observed, the information that was in IFS-M was not accurate. If IFS-M was current and accurate, they implied, they would have an incentive to use the system. Second, managers noted that their offices did not have the requisite computers and computer connections to be able to access and use IFS-M. If the employees were provided with better computers and dedicated computer connections to IFS-M, they would use the system. Third, managers expressed frustration with IFS-M's lack of user-friendliness. The system, they pointed out, required employees to navigate through a myriad of menus before they could access, enter, or retrieve relevant information.

Following our preliminary interviews with the DPW management, we conducted additional in-person surveys and interviews to identify the determinants of employees' attitudes toward and their use of IFS-M. Interviews with the seven users of IFS-M and the IFS-M's system manager revealed that the IFS-M data were not as incomplete and inaccurate as suggested by other employees. In fact, the production controller, who manages the routing of work-request forms, spent as much as 30 hours each week dutifully entering and updating all the work-request forms into IFS-M. Ideally, this information should be entered by the various employees as part of their workflow. Instead, the employees enter the information on a hard copy version of the forms, and this information is then sent back to the production controller for entry into the system. When DPW employees need information on the status of a work request, they contact the production controller, who then prints out a report or requests the system manager to prepare the report. As a result, the storage and retrieval of information in IFS-M is not, as intended, articulated as part of the workflow at the DPW. Instead it is conducted as a separate chore, distinct from the DPW's workflow. To validate their claim that the information is current and accurate, the production controller and the system manager pointed out that all of the information used by the outside contractors, who execute the engineering and maintenance tasks, comes directly from the IFS-M database. When asked to explain employees' claims that the IFS-M database was not current and accurate, the system manager replied, "Well, if they were to log on to IFS-M, they would see that is not the case." Clearly the lack of IFS-M adoption at the Fort was not simply a matter of incomplete or inaccurate information on the system.

The employees had also noted that a lack of computing and communication hardware prevented them from using IFS-M. This claim, too, was disputed upon closer examination. The IFS-M software resides on a mini-computer and employees use their computers as terminals to connect to the software. Hence in order to run IFS-M, employees' desktop computers do not need to be state-of-the-art machines. In fact, frequent users of IFS-

M often had older desktop computers. Most employees at the DPW had access to a computer that was capable of connecting to IFS-M. There were several instances in which computers in employees' offices had been hooked up to IFS-M and the software had been tested. These employees, including some who were in management, did not use IFS-M even after they had received training. One member of the management, who ideally should use the system every day, complained that he did not use it because each time he tried, the system notified him that his password had expired. For security reasons, the system sends this notification if the user has not logged on for 8 weeks! It takes one phone call, and a couple of minutes, for the system manager to reopen the account. Some employees had physically disconnected the communication cable from their computer. These observations indicate that the lack of computing and communication hardware was not as serious an obstacle as we were initially led to believe.

Employees at the DPW had also expressed negative attitudes about the user-friendliness of the IFS-M software. Statistical analyses revealed that employees' attitudes and use of IFS-M were not associated with their computer experience, their use of other computer software, or their training with computers. Further, employees did not rate the attributes of IFS-M software significantly lower than those for commercial word processing software packages (WordPerfect and Enable), which were used by 38 DPW employees, or e-mail software (IBM's PROFS), which was used by 26 DPW employees. In fact, the employees who reported using IFS-M reported a mean satisfaction level (3.65 on a scale of 1 to 7) that was similar to those reported for the commercial software packages. These results were surprising on two counts. First, employees' perceptions of IFS-M did not reflect the few excessively negative comments we heard from DPW management in the preliminary interviews. Second, a colleague on our research team who specializes in studying and designing user interfaces notes that the user interface of IFS-M leaves much room for improvement. Unfortunately, the system manager is not very sympathetic to such criticisms. "There is no such thing as user-friendliness," she exclaims; "you have got to learn the system, and once you learn a system it becomes user-friendly. After all IFS-M is menu-based."

To summarize, our follow-up interviews and surveys failed to uphold the reasons for IFS-M's lack of adoption offered by the management during preliminary interviews. First, the IFS-M database was more current and accurate than had been suggested. Second, while the computing hardware at DPW was not state-of-the-art, most computers were capable of connecting to IFS-M. Many had been connected; however, most were rarely used, and some had been disconnected by employees. Third, frustration with the software and user interfaces, though warranted to some extent, was neither as widespread nor particularly negative as compared to frustration with other more widely used computer software at the DPW.

The results of the statistical analysis revealed an important, and heretofore unacknowledged, determinant of employees' use of IFS-M. Employees' use of IFS-M were significantly correlated ($r = .63$) with their supervisor's assessment of its utility. This finding was echoed in several unstructured interviews with IFS-M users, nonusers, and the IFS-M system manager. The DPW management at the Fort had made few gestures to signal their support for the use of IFS-M by employees. In fact, some interpreted their actions as dissuading its use. This finding is also consistent with the social information-processing perspective on new media. This research underscores the importance of social influence on organizational members' attitudes toward and use of media (Contractor, Seibold, & Heller, 1996; Fulk, 1993; Rice & Aydin, 1991).

First, the management at DPW had staffed the IFS-M system support with just one employee, the system manager. At other bases using IFS-M, in CONUS (Continental U.S.), USAREUR (U.S. Army Europe), TRADOC (Training and Doctrination), and FORSCOM (U. S. Army Forces Command), there are between five and 10 employees charged with the support of IFS-M.

Second, none of the management at DPW log in to IFS-M regularly, thereby failing to serve as a model for other employees. They generally request hard copies of all work-request documents, thus discouraging employees who may want to provide them with this information electronically via IFS-M.

Third, as was evident from the preliminary interviews, they were among the most vocal critics of IFS-M.

Fourth, they helped shape and sustain an information culture that was counter to the norms implied in the design of IFS-M. In the ideal situation, employees who enter information into IFS-M can then access information from the system to help them make decisions; access provides an incentive for employees to contribute to a system that would in turn help them with their own decision making. These include decisions about work classification, prioritization, project scheduling, and contract surveillance as well as budgetary and technical issues related to the execution of the maintenance projects. However, at the Fort, the management wanted to be closely involved at all steps of the decision-making process and hence held several face-to-face meetings with their staff. As a result, employees, bereft of many of their decision-making opportunities, were not in a position where they could benefit from accessing information stored in IFS-M. The lack of this incentive further reduced their motivation to enter information into IFS-M.

The suspect validity of the management's criticisms of IFS-M suggest that either they were not aware of the current status and capabilities of IFS-M, or their criticisms were in pursuance of a second agenda. There was some evidence of this second agenda in management's response to the problems with IFS-M. First, weaknesses in IFS-M were used as justification for increased staffing. Management argued that to make the IFS-M database current and accurate, additional employees would be needed— an issue that was particularly sensitive given the downsizing already discussed. Second, weaknesses in IFS-M were used as a justification for equipment requests. Management argued that to improve the information system in the DPW, funds were required to upgrade the aging, but not yet completely obsolete, computers. Hence the criticisms of IFS-M made by the management, while not necessarily accurate, were consistent with the political instincts of most management teams: arguing for increases in human and material, specifically computing, resources.

While it is evident that management at DPW did not actively encourage widespread use of IFS-M, our analysis raises two further questions. First, why did the management require the production controller and IFS-M system manager to keep the IFS-M system updated? Second, and perhaps more important, why were they less than enthusiastic in their support for the IFS-M? Our analysis suggests that these two questions are more interrelated than they might appear. In both cases, the management at DPW was responding to demands in the Fort's environment, more specifically the Department of Army's (DA's) TRADOC Command. Officials at the Fort reported directly to DA-TRADOC. DA-TRADOC was directly responsible for making budget allocations and offering high-level evaluations and recommendations on the base's mission readiness. As mentioned in a previous section, DA-TRADOC had made all budget allocations to the Fort's DPW contingent on the availability of real-property records on the IFS-M. A computer at TRADOC would dial into the IFS-M computer at the Fort once every quarter for approximately 30 minutes to access this information and update their records. In addition, the system manager at the Fort was required to send this data via computer tape to TRADOC. Hence in response to the first question we raised above, not withstanding IFS-M's lack of adoption at the Fort, the management at DPW felt compelled to have the production controller and the system manager enter the requisite information into IFS-M.

Ironically, it is TRADOC's control over budgetary decisions that appears to have dissuaded management from encouraging widespread use of the IFS-M by DPW employees. As mentioned in an earlier section, the Fort is required to provide TRADOC with an ISR which is then used to assess the base's mission readiness. The ISR includes assessment of the infrastructure provided by "customers," the personnel who are using the various facilities on the base. The management at DPW has reservations about the accuracy and quality of the assessment provided by customers. In particular, they feel the need to strategically manipulate the assignment of red–amber–green ratings to various elements of the Fort's infrastructure. At present, the management at DPW is able to override the customers' assessment of the facilities by arguing that they have additional information that leads them to assign a different red–amber–green rating than the one suggested by the customer.

DPW management's desire and ability to strategically manipulate the findings of the ISR is key to understanding their lack of enthusiasm for widespread use of IFS-M. As long as the information entered in IFS-M is entered and accessed by only a handful of employees, the management has two arguments that can sustain their ability to strategically manipulate the ISR. First, by citing the lack of IFS-M use by employees, management can publicly undermine the completeness and accuracy of IFS-M, thereby reducing the credibility of any information in IFS-M that may contradict their strategic interests. Second, reducing the credibility of IFS-M data and limiting the number of employees with access to IFS-M makes it easier for management to "modify" or "correct" some of the information stored in IFS-M, thereby aligning it with their strategic interests in compiling the ISR.

## CONCLUSION: EQUIVOCALITY AND UNCERTAINTY REDUCTION IN THE DPW

Of the two key functions of an information system, reducing equivocality and uncertainty, uncertainty reduction appears to be the greatest concern for the DPW. Employees of the DPW, particularly those in management, criticize the IFS-M program and ISR data primarily in terms of their ability to reduce uncertainty. The data produced through ISRs are criticized for being biased, unsystematic, incomplete, and lacking in authority. The IFS-M database is criticized for being inaccessible, inaccurate, incomplete, and difficult to use. There is a general perception, particularly among those in management positions, that the information system is not capable of providing good answers to the questions they wish to pose.

But lurking under the surface of these complaints is considerable anxiety about the equivocality of the DPW information system. Most employees feel they have little input into what questions are asked in the process of decision making. Management personnel perceive a lack of control over how information in IFS-M might be queried and used by those above them in the organizational hierarchy, and other employees are effectively barred from using the database for decision making. These anxieties about equivocality promote a willingness, particularly among managers in the DPW, to undermine the credibility of answers provided by their information systems. As was shown earlier, ISRs and IFS-M are better than they are perceived to be, especially in terms of uncertainty reduction.

The perceived weaknesses in the information systems have in turn become exploitable resources in the never-ending process of budget negotiation. The DPW has developed a political interest in showing that current resources are inadequate since this is the preferred argument for more resources. But in the end, undermining the information systems technologies of the DPW has not been a good strategy. Employees and software developers alike have come to have pessimistic, and often cynical, attitudes toward the possibilities for effective change. Employees point to stacks of unopened software on their desks and argue that none of these tools are really designed to meet their needs. They are unwilling to invest time in learning new ways to do their work.

At the same time, without successes to point to, the case for upgrading the systems and technologies of the DPW with new resources for information technology is weak. In fact, the most persuasive evidence for putting resources into information technology upgrades in the DPW has come from the successful experiences of other installations, where other systems worked—probably in part because of the organization's commitment to change in ways that will make the new technologies most useful.

The final question then is, How can the DPW improve its performance by the strategic use of information technologies? First, the DPW should address the issue of equivocality reduction more squarely and should consider how it can use appropriate technology to address organizational needs for setting priorities and distributing participation in decision making. The second and most critical change the organization must embrace is a commitment to use and support the technology. It is particularly important for those in management positions to become advocates for the technology and provide good models to socially influence those working under them. Finally, this commitment should be carried through by allocating resources to provide proper support for the technology. This may be more feasible as more flexible and user-friendly database technologies are developed and introduced.

## ACKNOWLEDGMENTS

Preparation of this chapter was supported, in part, by a grant from the National Science Foundation (NSF-ECS-9422730). Information about this project, including technical reports based on data obtained to date, can be found at our "Project CITY" WWW site. The URL for this site is: http://www.spcomm.uiuc.edu/projects/COLLAB/projcity.html.

## KEY TERMS

COMPUTER-BASED WORKBENCH: a software program that provides a common interface and communication among a set of specialized computer programs.

EQUIVOCALITY REDUCTION: determining what questions must be answered to make organizational choices, enabling debate, clarification, and enactment more than simply seeking larger amounts of data.

INFORMATION FLOW: movement of information from one system component to another.

INFORMATION MANAGEMENT: development of appropriate systems for production and movement of information within organizations.

INFORMATION PRODUCTION: processes through which organizations gather and organize data.

KNOWLEDGE WORKERS: individuals whose primary organizational functions involve information management.

RICH VERSUS LEAN MEDIA: rich media offer greater capacity for immediate feedback, larger numbers of cues and channels, and higher levels of personalization and language variety than lean media.

SOCIAL INFORMATION PROCESSING: a perspective that suggests that individuals' attitudes and use of media are shaped, in part, by the information they process from their social interaction with others, including coworkers and supervisors.

SYSTEM COMPONENT: nodes within an organization—can be individuals, computers, departments, or databases.

UNCERTAINTY REDUCTION: the ability to collect and collate large amounts of information to answer questions that are important to organizational choices.

## DISCUSSION QUESTIONS

1. Select a group in which you are involved and describe it as an information system. What are the nodes in the system (people or other units that create or transmit information)? What are the information-production activities in this group? How does the information produced flow through the system?
2. Think of a situation you are facing in which you will have to make a decision. What questions will you need to answer to make that decision? What information will you need to answer these questions? How do the concepts of equivocality reduction and uncertainty reduction apply to your situation?
3. Why have employees of the DPW complained about the quality of information provided through IFS-M? Use the concepts of equivocality and uncertainty reduction to explain why they might exaggerate the defects of IFS-M.
4. How might the DPW implement the recommendations made in the conclusion of this chapter?
5. Improvements in information systems seldom are of direct benefit to the indi-

viduals who do the work of managing information within an organization. This results in a conflict between what benefits individuals and what benefits the collective organization. How does the case of IFS-M illustrate this dilemma?

6. More generally, there is often a conflict between what it seems rational for an organization to do and what can actually be accomplished within the organization. How does the case of IFS-M illustrate this conflict between rational and political models of the organization?

## REFERENCES

Contractor, N. S., Seibold, D. R., & Heller, M. A. (1996). Interactional influence in the structuring of media use in groups: Influence in members' perceptions of GDSS use. *Human Communication Research, 22,* 451–481.

Daft, R. L., & Lengel, R. (1986). Organizational information requirements, media richness, and structural design. *Management Science, 32*(5), 554–571.

Fulk, J. (1993). Social construction of communication technology. *Academy of Management Journal, 36,* 921–950.

Galbraith, J. (1973). Information processing model. In *Designing complex organizations* (pp. 8–21). Reading, MA: Addison-Wesley.

Rice, R. E., & Aydin, C. (1991). Attitudes toward new organizational technology: Network proximity as a mechanism for social information processing. *Administrative Science Quarterly, 36,* 219–244.

Tushman, M. L., & Nadler, D. A. (1978). Information processing as an integrating concept in organizational design. *Academy of Management Review, 3,* 613–624.

# CHAPTER 13

# Information and Organizational Development
## Enhancing Reflexivity at Alexander Center

### GARY L. KREPS

## INFORMATION AND ORGANIZATIONAL ADAPTATION

Leaders need information about the effectiveness of organizational messages, products, and programs to evaluate organizational performance and direct organizational adaptation. By encouraging representatives of relevant audiences to share their experiences and beliefs concerning these messages, products, and programs, leaders can identify any relevant problems and opportunities that are confronting the organization. Feedback from individuals who have unique insights into the organization, such as the people the organization serves and the people who work for the organization, is particularly useful. Relevant populations such as these have the unique ability to critically assess the quality of programs from firsthand knowledge. They also often have insights into how to improve these programs by suggesting strategies for organizational intervention and refinement. Feedback from such populations can thus enhance organizational reflexivity, enabling leaders to see the strengths and weaknesses in their organizations from the perspective of key internal and external audiences (Kreps, 1989, 1990, 1994).

## THE ORGANIZATIONAL DEVELOPMENT PROGRAM

An applied field study was conducted to gather information about public perceptions and attitudes toward an urban residential adolescent substance abuse rehabilitation center (the pseudonym "Alexander Center" will be used here in place of the real name of this rehabilitation center to preserve confidentiality). Alexander Center is a long-term healthcare treatment organization dedicated to helping troubled youths break their addictions to drugs and alcohol. Youths who are identified as substance abusers are referred to rehabilitation centers, such as Alexander Center, for treatment, often by the juvenile court system. Admittance to Alexander Center means that the youths actually move in to the center and live there as residents, where they participate in individual and group counseling sessions and are taught life skills to help them resist substance abuse. Alexander Center also provides follow-up and aftercare counseling and support services for youths who have completed the residential treatment program. Alexander Center has an excellent record for helping troubled youths break their addictions and resist substance abuse.

This organizational development study was designed to help Alexander Center meet community members' needs for substance abuse rehabilitation services at a time when reports of adolescent substance abuse within the surrounding geographic area indicated that this problem was at an extremely high level. A primary goal of Alexander Center is to provide needed treatment to as many of the adolescent substance abusers who were not being served as adequately as they possibly could. The data gathered in this study were needed to help Alexander Center examine the reasons why these adolescents were not receiving treatment, as well as to identify strategies for increasing public acceptance, support, and utilization of their health promotion programs.

## PARENTS AS A RELEVANT SOURCE OF INFORMATION

It was determined through analysis of archival records that the parents of adolescent substance abusers were the primary decision makers for enrolling clients for treatment in residential care facilities like Alexander Center. Parents served as boundary spanners, connecting adolescent substance abusers to the Alexander Center. Therefore parents of adolescents were identified as the population to be studied in this organizational development effort. Three different relevant groups of parents were selected for participation in this organizational development program: (1) parents with children who had already completed treatment at Alexander Center, (2) parents with children who were currently in treatment at Alexander

Center, and (3) representative parents with children who were within the potential age range and geographic region served by Alexander Center.

Focus group discussions were selected as the best method for gathering relevant information from these parents. In focus group discussions a group leader (the group facilitator) poses questions about topics of research interest to group members (respondents) and encourages them to discuss the questions and elaborate on their answers (Kreps, 1994). Effectively conducted focus group discussions stimulate disclosure of relevant information by encouraging a chaining-out of shared perceptions among group members. In focus groups outspoken respondents often encourage the more timid respondents to share information. Furthermore, by observing group members' verbal and nonverbal behaviors, the group facilitator can encourage maximum participation, information sharing, and creativity, obtaining more relevant information in less time from one focus group discussion than would be possible by conducting personal interviews with each member of the group.

The focus group technique is a popular applied research method because it reveals important information about respondents' personal experiences and interpretations of reality. It also enables researchers to learn quickly and inexpensively about the needs, values, beliefs, expectations, and behaviors of specific populations (Herndon, 1993). In this study focus group participants were selected randomly from three lists of parents (sampling frames) to ensure that the groups were representative of the larger populations of parents within the community served by Alexander Center. Names from each of the three sampling frame lists were randomized systematically to create three potential sample lists, and participants were recruited over the telephone. From these lists, nine parents were recruited for each focus group.

Letters were sent out from Alexander Center to all of the parents on the original three sampling frame lists prior to recruitment to explain the organizational development project, to identify the researcher, to inform them that they might receive a recruitment call from the researcher, and to encourage their participation in this organizational development program. After the recruitment calls were made, follow-up letters were sent to all parents who had agreed to attend to confirm the day, time, and place of their focus group, as well as to encourage their actual attendance at the focus group. Additionally, the researcher called each of the parents recruited for the focus groups 2 days prior to their group meeting to remind them of the session.

Focus group discussions were held with each of the three groups of parents to identify their key experiences, ideas, and concerns about the specific programs and services at Alexander Center, as well as to explore the more general problem of adolescent substance abuse and their sources of relevant health information about substance abuse treatment and support. The focus groups were scheduled and conducted on the same day in the same place with 90 minutes set aside for each group discussion. Each of the three focus group discussions lasted approximately one hour. To increase participation, the sessions for Group A (whose sons or daughters had completed their residential stay at Alexander Center) and Group B (whose sons or daughters were currently in residence at the center) were scheduled at times when these parents were likely to already be coming to Alexander Center. The focus group meetings were held in the conference room in the Alexander Center's main administration building. The actual size of the focus groups ranged from four to seven members, with four members (two men, two women) in Group A, six members (four men, two women) in Group B, and seven members (three men, four women) in Group C (whose sons or daughters had not been treated at the center), including the facilitator.

A general discussion guide (interview schedule) was developed to direct the focus group discussions, and minor alterations were made to adapt the topic guide to the different experiential sets of the members of the three different groups. For example, Group A was asked about their experiences with aftercare, Group B was asked about their expectations for aftercare, and Group C was asked about their knowledge about the goals of aftercare.

## RESULTS OF THE STUDY

Each group discussion was audiotaped to preserve group members' comments for later analysis. The audiotapes were then transcribed and their content was analyzed by the researcher into the following 13 primary content themes, which provided the basis for the recommendations:

1. *Motivation to seek treatment.* The most intriguing finding in this content category was that almost all of the responses to this query by members of all three groups involved confrontation themes (family crises and conflicts). It is also interesting to note how resistant the majority of parents in Group C were to seeking treatment for their children, especially in contrast to the other two groups. The theme expressed most commonly by parents in Group C was that they would not seek treatment for their children at Alexander Center, or at any other treatment facility, unless it was their very last alternative. This response suggests avoidance and denial, which is not really surprising. Since this group is the least familiar with Alexander Center and its services and is least invested in treatment (their children have probably not been diagnosed as substance abusers),

they do not want to imagine their offspring needing treatment lest those thoughts become self-fulfilling prophesies.

2. *General referral sources.* The courts were the source of general referral mentioned most frequently, which indicates that court officials must be made aware of Alexander Center and the benefits of its services. The referral source mentioned next most frequently was television advertising, which reinforces the importance of Alexander Center's using television advertising to reach potential clients.

3. *Alexander Center referral sources.* Radio and television advertising, as well as personal recommendations from parents who have used Alexander Center's services, were the referral sources mentioned most frequently. Media advertising was most important for the potential audience, which indicates that it is a good channel for reaching new customers (as mentioned in the discussion of the previous content category). Word-of-mouth referral from other parents was most important for the parents who had already been through the program and is a relatively inexpensive and highly trusted advertising channel. The majority of other referral sources are from area professionals (such as lawyers, judges, psychologists, and police), who should be kept up-to-date about Alexander Center and given current promotional materials.

4. *Positive impressions of and experiences with Alexander Center.* This was by far the largest and most impassioned of the 13 content categories. The data clearly indicate that Alexander Center is thought of highly and appreciated by all three groups of parents. Several of the comments can be used as testimonials or advertising copy for future promotional media. To be cautious, however, it should be noted that a selection bias may explain this finding. That is, the parents who were most supportive of Alexander Center were likely to be the ones who agreed to participate in this organizational development program, while the parents who were disenchanted with Alexander Center were likely to be unwilling to participate. (During the recruitment of participants, however, parents who mentioned being upset or unhappy with Alexander Center were strongly encouraged to attend the meeting to express their feelings and to help improve the system.) Regardless of this potential selection bias, the data generated in the focus group interview appear to be sincere and moving.

5. *Negative impressions of and experiences with Alexander Center.* There is a clear and troubling consistent pattern of negative first impressions and public images of Alexander Center that are held by all three groups of parents. These negative stereotypes identify Alexander Center as a place for delinquent children, orphans, runaway boys, bad boys, and rough kids. Furthermore, there is a penal-system, punishment image of the services provided at Alexander Center that discourages parents from sending their children there for treatment.

6. *Barriers that prevent parents from seeking treatment for their children.* The most significant barrier to seeking treatment voiced by members of all three groups, and mentioned twice as often as any other response, was denial. The second barrier mentioned most frequently was by Group C, who stated that they need to know the warning signals to determine whether their child is engaging in normal adolescent behavior or whether there really is a substance abuse problem. Providing parents with promotional materials that identify warning signs can be very powerful. In fact, immediately after the focus group meeting with Group C, the parents asked for handouts identifying the warning signs and even took some home for their friends and neighbors. Parents who want to handle the situation themselves have to recognize the severity and complexity of the problems their children may face. Guilt and parental problems with drugs and alcohol are additional barriers mentioned frequently that should be addressed in marketing themes and advertising messages. Cost issues are also of concern to parents, and information about insurance coverage might encourage parents to seek treatment when needed.

7. *Information sources to recognize the need for treatment.* School programs and parent networks are the information sources parents most want to use to help them identify their children's need for treatment. Parents want the schools and their peers to provide them with timely and honest feedback about their children's deviant behavioral patterns to help identify instances of substance abuse. Perhaps in promotional materials Alexander Center can present a community orientation to this problem, encouraging parents and neighbors to work together and help fight substance abuse by sharing relevant information. Parents should also be encouraged to initiate communication with representatives from the schools on a regular basis to find out if their children are behaving peculiarly or if teachers, administrators, or counselors suspect substance abuse.

8. *Suggestions for Alexander Center to help parents recognize the need for treatment.* Parents responded to this question with many suggestions for Alexander Center to engage in increased information-dissemination efforts. The suggestion mentioned most frequently for getting relevant information to parents was increased use of television and radio ads. (This finding is consistent with the data in content category 3, in which parents stated that television and radio advertisements were important sources of information in referring them to Alexander Center.) The respondents suggested using advertising scenarios that depict family breakdowns to attract the attention of parents. Furthermore, group members encouraged using public affairs, news, and other television and radio programs to present information about Alexander Center and its services. The suggestion mentioned next most often was for Alexander Center to work closely with educational institutions in offering lectures, courses, and other programs for

parents and children to inform and motivate them to recognize and deal with the prc ьiem of substance abuse. Another interesting suggestion was to widely disseminate promotional and informational literature (leaflets) about substance abuse and Alexander Center for parents to pick up at schools, department stores, grocery stores, businesses, medical facilities, police departments, and shopping centers.

9. *Experiences with other social services and treatment services.* Many respondents had experience with several other treatment services in the area. The organization mentioned most frequently was Family Anonymous, which was seen as a very good family resource. Affiliating with and working closely with Family Anonymous may be mutually beneficial to both organizations. In contrast, local hospitals were mentioned often but were generally disliked for their high levels of bureaucracy and their medical orientation, although parents did like one hospital's radio advertisements and half-day school program for children. Parents in Group B were very interested in proposed aftercare support groups (core groups) at the local high schools. Perhaps Alexander Center can help schools in the area get these groups started.

10. *Suggestions for family support services.* Interestingly, this category received the fewest responses, including no responses from Group C, even after probing. Perhaps parents in the potential group were so removed from facing substance abuse problems that they did not envision a need for any family support services. There was, however, interest expressed by parents in the Groups A and B to reinstate the sibling program (in which counseling was provided to brothers and sisters of the children receiving treatment) at Alexander Center. There was also strong agreement among the parents in Group A about the need for aftercare services for parents and families.

11. *Experiences with and expectations for aftercare services.* Parents generally supported the need for and the importance of aftercare services, especially parents in Group A, who are probably participating, and want to be more involved, in aftercare. Parents in Group A want Alexander Center to inform them about the attendance of their children at aftercare meetings, educate them about aftercare services, offer special aftercare sessions for parents and children, and start a parents' alumni group for peer support and future projects. Another suggestion for aftercare services was to provide children with healthy social and occupational opportunities, such as identifying safe (drug- and alcohol-free) places to go, establishing a youth center or halfway house, and helping children find jobs.

12. *Realistic expectations for treatment and outcome of treatment.* There is a dramatic difference between parents experienced with Alexander Center (Groups A and B) and the potential group of parents (C) with respect to expectations for treatment. Parents in Groups A and B were re-

alistic about not expecting miracle cures, recognizing that it is the children's responsibility to stay straight and to learn coping skills at Alexander Center. These parents even expected some relapse from their children. In contrast, several parents in the potential group were unrealistic in their expectation that treatment would cure their children so they would never desire drugs or alcohol again. These results indicate a strong need for educating parents about the nature of addiction and the realistic outcomes of treatment. On the other hand, several parents recognized the psychosocial elements of effective treatment, mentioning the role of support systems, ego-strength, withstanding pressure, and self-esteem in recovery.

13. *Suggestions for Alexander Center to improve its services.* This content category provides a good summary of the implications drawn from earlier questions, as many of the suggestions offered have been previously discussed. There is a wealth of ideas offered here that, with some refinement, can be of great benefit to Alexander Center. For example, information and social support programs are high on parents' list of suggestions. Several parents in Groups A and B suggested that Alexander Center do a better job at the Wednesday night meetings of educating parents about the potential for relapse, the signs of relapse, and how to handle it. Parents from all three groups suggested improving the alumni group so that children can keep in contact with each other to provide an ongoing support system after treatment. Several parents encouraged efforts to enhance community awareness of Alexander Center services through radio and television coverage and advertising, as well as offering a drug or alcohol abuse hotline. Information dissemination can also be enhanced by a videotape that describes Alexander Center, its treatment philosophies, and its programs (i.e., showing the facilities and the kinds of activities kids go through) for parents to view while waiting during the initial evaluation and during the first Wednesday night meeting. (Such a program may be able to get some free television airtime on public affairs programs.) They also suggested that when parents first bring their children in for treatment they should be given books and other reading material about substance abuse, treatment strategies, and family strategies to help children.

Parents in Group A desired follow-up telephone calls from Alexander Center after treatment is over to identify any problems and provide needed information or support. They suggested setting up a system whereby successful alumni of the program can work as peer counselors for current children going through the program. Parents are interested in Alexander Center helping to get their children back into school and making sure that they stay there. They want to be informed about whether their children are attending aftercare meetings. Parents also suggested that Alexander Center can provide parents with information about Family Anonymous, provide more privacy in the basement for families meeting with their children, and take a more preventive approach with advertising, educational services, and pamphlets. Parents also would like Alexander Center to help keep costs down by encouraging insurance companies to offer more coverage for aftercare services and providing low-cost options for aftercare services.

## CASE SUMMARY

This case illustrates how the use of focus group research can provide a wealth of information about public perceptions and attitudes toward an organization such as Alexander Center, identifying parents' concerns about adolescent substance abuse treatment and generating specific suggestions for increasing public acceptance and support for Alexander Center. The focus group interviews indicated that the public's support for Alexander Center appears to be high, although the public's image of Alexander Center is sometimes tainted by false stereotypes. Parents generally are concerned about adolescent substance abuse and indicated a clear need for more information about risks, symptoms, and services.

The data from the focus group discussions indicated that Alexander Center can attract business and community support by developing and implementing information dissemination promotional programs to meet the information needs identified by parents in this study. Many of the recommendations from this study were implemented at Alexander Center, which has helped the organization to provide the public with relevant health information, enhanced the public image of the rehabilitation center, and attracted greater public support for its programs and services. Alexander Center was also able to increase client enrollment significantly over the 6 months following the completion of this study, enabling the rehabilitation center to provide healthcare services for a larger segment of the adolescent population that was in dire need of such care.

## KEY TERMS

BOUNDARY SPANNERS: individuals who connect organizations to relevant external audiences. In this case parents were boundary spanners who connected Alexander Center with adolescent substance abusers.

CHAINING OUT: a process in which interaction among group members is stimulated when group members express ideas and experiences that other members identify with and build upon through successive messages and replies that lead to greater levels of member identification and greater sharing of information.

FACILITATOR: a focus group leader who poses questions to group members, encourages participation of all members in group discussions, and keeps the discussions on target.

FOCUS GROUP DISCUSSIONS: a research method in which a group facilitator poses questions about topics of research interest to group members and encourages them to discuss the questions and elaborate on their answers.

INTERVIEW SCHEDULE: a list of questions that the focus group facilitator uses to guide group discussions.

ORGANIZATIONAL ADAPTATION: the ability of organizations to adjust to changing situations and constraints to enable survival.

ORGANIZATIONAL REFLEXIVITY: the ability of organizational leaders to see the internal and external state of the organization.

RANDOM SAMPLE: a group of research respondents selected so that each member of the population represented has an equal chance to be selected.

SAMPLING FRAME: a list of all potential research respondents from a specific population that is as complete as possible.

## DISCUSSION QUESTIONS

1. Why is the use of focus group discussions a particularly good method to identify organizational problems, promote organizational reflexivity, and direct organizational adaptation?
2. What do you think were the most compelling findings about parents' responses to Alexander Center? How could these findings be used to improve the center's ability to achieve its health promotion goals?
3. In future advertising and promotional efforts how can Alexander Center use the theme of family confrontation that emerged in the focus group discussions as a motivating factor in urging parents to seek treatment for troubled youths at Alexander Center?
4. How can many of the comments made by respondents concerning the parents' "motivation to seek treatment" serve as potential story lines for future advertisements, pamphlets, and public relations media?
5. Do you think it would be a good idea in future advertising to confront parents with the tendency expressed in the focus group discussions to avoid and deny their children's problems? Why or why not?
6. Do you think it would be a good idea to send lawyers and court officials up-to-date promotional materials about Alexander Center? Why or why not?
7. Is it advisable for the Alexander Center staff to keep in contact with parents who have been through the program, provide them with materials, and keep them involved with Alexander Center in advisory capacities? Why or why not?
8. How can the negative public image of Alexander Center as a prison be changed? For example, do you think promotional materials that explain the historical developments and transformations at Alexander Center, that emphasize the long history of the institution and its name recognition, and that

couple this information with knowledge of the new services and philosophy of Alexander Center would be enough to change this negative image?

9. How can Alexander Center help parents recognize warning signals that their children may be having problems with substance abuse?

10. Should follow-up studies be conducted to evaluate whether Alexander Center has overcome the problems identified by the focus group discussions? If so, what kinds of studies do you suggest?

## REFERENCES AND SUGGESTED READING

Greenbaum, T. L. (1988). *The practical handbook and guide to focus group research.* Lexington, MA: Lexington Books.

Herndon, S. L. (1993). Using focus group interviews for preliminary investigation. In S. L. Herndon & G. L. Kreps (Eds.), *Qualitative research: Applications in organizational communication* (pp. 39–46). Cresskill, NJ: Hampton Press.

Kreps, G. L. (1989). Reflexivity and internal public relations: The role of information in directing organizational development. In C. Botan & V. Hazleton (Eds.), *Public relations theory* (pp. 265–279). Hillsdale, NJ: Erlbaum.

Kreps, G. L. (1990). *Organizational communication: Theory and practice* (2nd ed.). White Plains, NY: Longman.

Kreps, G.L. (1994). Using focused group discussions to promote organizational reflexivity: Two applied communication field studies. In L. R. Frey (Ed.), *Innovations in group facilitation techniques: Applied research in naturalistic settings* (pp. 177–199). Cresskill, NJ: Hampton Press.

Krueger, R. A. (1988). *Focus groups: A practical guide for applied research.* Newbury Park, CA: Sage.

Lydecker, T. L. (1986). Focus group dynamics. *Association Management, 38*(3), 73–78.

Staley, C. C. (1990). Focus group research: The communication practitioner as marketing specialist. In D. O'Hair & G. L. Kreps (Eds.), *Applied communication theory and research* (pp. 185–201). Hillsdale, NJ: Erlbaum.

# CHAPTER 14

## I Heard It through the Grapevine

Dealing with Office Rumors,
Politics, and Total Quality Management

ANGELA J. WILHELM

GAIL T. FAIRHURST

Ellen Shold was hesitant as she walked toward Joanne Moore's office. Ellen wanted to discuss a rumor with Joanne, her supervisor, but she was not sure how Joanne would react. Both women were managers at a manufacturing plant of Stanghor and Wollack (S&W), a multinational consumer goods corporation based in the Northeast. While neither of them was new to office politics, this rumor was more complicated and troubling than most. It involved S&W's total quality management (TQM) program and how their Minneapolis-based plant would stack up against the company's other plants.

As Ellen managed to weave her way through the maze of corridors that led to Joanne's office, she was reminded of the organization's rich history as she passed several posters of S&W's original product line back at the turn of the century. S&W had started as a small, family-run business and had since developed into one of the leading manufacturers of household goods. Although S&W employed millions of employees worldwide, management still referred to S&W as a "family." Ellen had never worked for a company before that put so much emphasis on being a family. True, she had wonderful memories of S&W's company picnics, holiday parties, the surprise party thrown for her promotion, and the comfort she had received from coworkers after the recent death of her mother. She could always count on her S&W coworkers to celebrate her successes and mourn her losses with her. But somehow that "family feeling" wasn't coming to mind as she thought about this rumor.

As the plant's TQM facilitator, Ellen was responsible for setting in motion the new management program that would implement W. Edward Deming's total quality management at her Minneapolis site. TQM was developed by W. Edward Deming and J. M. Juran after World War II and was the basis for the Japanese management philosophy that changed the image of Japanese industries from that of producers of inferior-quality merchandise to that of producers of high-quality merchandise. It is an approach to management that seeks to improve product quality and increase customer satisfaction largely through strong quality-oriented leadership, participation in work teams, a more efficient use of resources, and statistical monitoring of work processes.

The TQM movement swept U.S. businesses in the mid-1980s in an attempt to catch up with the Japanese. *If Japan Can, Why Can't We* was the title of one NBC documentary during that time. By implementing TQM philosophy, U.S. businesses hoped to increase worker–management interaction through the creation of teams, which appeared to be the strength of Japanese industries. S&W had a reputation for being a tightly run organization that was committed to both employee and consumer satisfaction, so TQM appeared to be a natural addition to S&W's management philosophy.

Because the adoption of TQM at S&W's Minneapolis plant was Ellen's job, she felt compelled to treat the rumor seriously. Apparently, Larry Michaels, a powerful old-guard upper-division manager, was dissatisfied with the Minneapolis plant. Larry told Ellen's source and one other manager that because the Minneapolis plant was not sending any of their group managers to a 3-week statistics course held at a Texas university, he believed the plant was lagging behind, "dropping the ball" as he put it, when it came to TQM. Michaels wielded quite a bit of power at corporate headquarters, and Ellen feared that displeasing Michaels could put Minneapolis's TQM program and plant management in jeopardy. Her dilemma was exacerbated by the fact that although statistical knowledge and training is part of the Deming program, she did not feel that a 3-week statistical course was in the best interest of the plant's TQM adoption at this time. The group managers in the plant who would be attending the course did not have a strong enough background in TQM principles yet. Since they did not yet understand TQM fully, Ellen feared that a dry, 3-week statistical course would turn them off to TQM.

Ellen hoped that Joanne would understand that the long-term goal of the organization, to implement TQM, might be harmed by this statistics class at this time, although it certainly would be necessary at a later date. Ellen was filled with anxiety about the rumor and how Joanne would respond. "Will she tell me to send the managers to the course? Will she listen to my arguments against it? Will she propose an action that would reveal

my source for the rumor? Can I keep my source confidential somehow?"
she asked herself. Ellen had always considered Joanne to be a good and fair
supervisor, the type who was willing to sit down and discuss a problem,
and to make her staff feel important. Joanne had a way of empowering
those she supervised by constantly offering support and autonomy bal-
anced by honest criticism. Because of Joanne's reputation as a collaborative leader, Ellen felt comfortable that Joanne would listen to her feelings
about the problem and that together they could figure a way out of this
mess.

Joanne pushed her work aside as Ellen walked into her office. "Come
on in, Ellen, have a seat. I'm just trying to clear off my desk for once. How
are things going?"

"Well Joanne, not so good. I heard a rumor yesterday about Larry
Michaels, and it concerns our plant." Ellen immediately retold the rumor
that she had heard yesterday to Joanne, that Michaels believed the Minneapolis plant was dragging its feet by not sending any group managers to
the statistical training course in Texas.

For her part, Joanne could see that office politics was at work again.
Although she knew that Ellen was a capable and experienced manager,
Joanne's background with Larry told her that dealing with this rumor had
to take top priority. Larry was not above using intimidation to get his way.
Joanne had seen him in action many times. While Michaels was advocat-
ing TQM and telling managers that they had to be more participative, he
was anything but that. To begin with, he himself was one of those people
who had an opinion on everything. Moreover, based on the old culture of
S&W, he rose to the position of division manager by being autocratic, aggressive, and very political. Much of how he responded to issues was based
upon how he thought his bosses would respond. For example, the corporation was under pressure to hire more women, so Larry was constantly
praising the qualities of women managers because he thought his bosses
would like that, not because he really believed they deserved the praise. After all, the onslaught of new women managers were hardly a threat to him.
He would retire by the time they were promoted up the ranks. Such behavior and thinking is hardly an endorsement for the contribution of women
at S&W.

In her early career, Joanne had by and large been able to avoid
Michaels. She suspected the motives behind his ringing endorsements of
women managers, and she recoiled at his autocratic ways. But this was
Ellen's first real experience with Michaels. As a result, Joanne felt a dual responsibility to help Ellen but also deal with Larry. She concluded that
dealing with the rumor directly was the only way to approach Michaels.

"Ellen, someone needs to work out this issue with Michaels immediately, before things get blown out of proportion. We can't sit out there and ignore that this was said. It will affect all the good work that you're doing."

Ellen knew that Joanne was just as concerned with the rumor as she was, but Ellen believed that the situation could not be dealt with in such a cut-and-dry manner. Ellen continued to explain that initially there was a misunderstanding as to how many Minneapolis managers were to go to this statistical training and what the timing would be in relation to all of their other TQM training.

She went on, however, "As the TQM manager for this plant, I'm reluctant to send our group managers to these training courses before they're ready. It's just too early. Joanne, they need more grounding in Deming's TQM philosophy before they can understand why statistical monitoring of their work processes is so essential. I can hear some of them talking about that 3-week course now, 'Why are we being asked to do all of this extra work? How does Deming justify all of this? How is the company justifying all this lost time? I can't be gone for three weeks!' If we send people away for three weeks and they have a negative experience, I'm afraid it's going to do damage to our overall Total Quality effort."

Joanne felt that Ellen's concerns were legitimate, yet the political ramifications of not sending Minneapolis managers to the statistics course had to be confronted. Joanne knew there was no need to remind Ellen that Larry was a tough guy who was not afraid to use his power. Joanne was having a hard time understanding why Ellen wasn't paying attention to the politics of the situation. "After all," thought Joanne, "Ellen was here last spring when one of the volunteer work teams was disbanded because Michaels feared that they were trying to work outside S&W's established managerial hierarchy."

"Ellen, as I see it, we have two choices. Either we follow up with Michaels directly and tell him why we object to this course at this time, or send our managers to the 3 weeks of statistical training. If we confront Michaels directly, we can address the substance of the rumor without referring to it directly. We will be operating in an information-sharing kind of way, versus 'We heard that you said this' kind of way. Politics will always be part of the system, Ellen, so we have to respond. We either get to Michaels or send the managers to the training. If we don't, everything we've done will be written off, and Minneapolis can't afford to be written off right now. We'll never be known for the strides we have made here."

Ellen, however, found confronting Michaels as unappealing as caving in and sending their managers to the training. His gruff demeanor and quick temper were not always easy to deal with. She was also very concerned about protecting the identity of her source. If Michaels heard about the rumor, he would know immediately where it came from, and this could jeopardize her source's position within the organization. Because of this, Ellen suggested another option to Joanne.

"Joanne, I have to protect my source. What about this? Why don't we go to Randy Carson and explain the problem to him? I am sure he can help us. He doesn't care for Larry's style any more than we do."

But Joanne felt bringing in the plant manager, Randy, would only delay the inevitable. Her patience was wearing thin as she lowered her voice to reinforce to Ellen one more time the importance of dealing with Larry directly. "But Ellen, what about Michaels? We need to deal with Michaels. As far as I'm concerned that's the bottom line."

"Just hear me out, Joanne," Ellen quickly responded. "As our plant manager, Carson could work out the issue with his contacts in the hierarchy. In effect, if we work around Michaels, the problem is dealt with, and I can cover my source's identity."

Joanne was silent for a moment before responding slowly and carefully. "Ellen, I understand your frustration and promise of confidentiality to your source, but as I see it we need to deal directly with Michaels or we send our people to training."

The tension between Joanne and Ellen was thick. Each was unable to convince the other to take her side because both women believed in the strength of her own argument. Both women knew that arguing would not get them anywhere, but neither was sure how long they could keep up an open discussion. "We've always had a strong working relationship before," thought Joanne, "so what's going on? The last thing I want to do is pull rank with Ellen, but she doesn't seem to understand the political fallout that will occur because of the wrong decision."

Ellen was just as discouraged as Joanne. Why couldn't Joanne see her side? Ellen knew that office politics could destroy not only her TQM goals at the Minneapolis plant but also an important working relationship with Joanne. More than anything, she wanted Joanne to understand that she believed Michaels was the source of the entire conflict and shouldn't be dealt with directly.

"Do you know that I think, Joanne? I think Michaels already signed the contract for the training without getting input from any of S&W's TQM facilitators on implementing stages. It's a lot of money. I think that no one wants to go back and either try to modify it to better meet our needs or question whether or not the need is there. To me, what's going on here is really against TQM. Michaels is trying to instill fear into folks to force them to do this training."

"I do agree with you that the statistical training course was probably not well thought out, but Ellen, you have to understand that if we don't deal with this situation appropriately, it will always affect Minneapolis. I guess that you've got to look at which is going to be better in the long run. It's going to be hard to get that negative perception off of us. The first impression from the other plants will always be 'No one from Minneapolis went to the statistics training, so how can they be any good?' Since we don't have the training information, we missed out along the way. The Minneapolis plant will always be under question. We'll never be up in the headlines of how well we're doing with TQM, no matter how well we do, no matter how right you are, unless this issue gets worked through with Michaels."

"But, Joanne, do you approve of Michaels' fear tactics? Either we send our group managers to the training course, or Michaels will consider total quality here a flop."

"No, of course not. But you have to understand, Michaels is very much the old style of management. He operates by the good-old-boy style of the division manager. He's traditional, he'll play the game. He'll play the politics. He'll put the pressure on. He'll plug the fear in. He'll make the comments. He's very much with the comments and the jabs. I've heard him praise women managers and, in the same breath, chastise them to his other good-old-boy manager friends. If we don't directly relate our concerns to Michaels, it will forever be out in the system, and we don't need that. As I said, we're dealing with one of the most political individuals in the organization. Either we go and solve the problem by dealing directly with him, or we send someone to the statistics training. We're going to end up the losers unless we can get the right information to Michaels. We have to deal with this rumor openly, otherwise Minneapolis will always have a bad TQM reputation."

Ellen could see that Joanne was trying to restrain her anger and frustration while still forcefully making her point. But Ellen was still not going to back down. This would be her last appeal to Joanne to let her handle the situation her way.

"I do appreciate that Joanne, but I just feel so strongly that this 3-week statistics course is not in the best interest of total quality management at this time, and I also feel an obligation to protect my source's identity. Surely you can understand that? As plant manager, Randy Carson can work around Michaels through his own contacts. He can let others know that we are not dropping the ball when it comes to TQM, only that we feel the need to delay our statistical training right now."

As Ellen and Joanne drew their meeting to a close, there was no clear resolution to their problem. Ellen was still against sending her managers to the 3-week statistical training course and directly confronting Michaels, but she was also concerned about protecting her source's identity. Joanne, on the other hand, felt that they must either deal directly with Michaels and the rumor or send their people to training. After considering the long debate on the issue, Joanne reluctantly agreed to go with Ellen to discuss the conflict with Carson.

This case reflects the conflicts that arise when a new company program becomes clouded by office politics. As the plant's TQM facilitator, Ellen's main concern was twofold: First, she was concerned about the possible negative implications of sending her group managers to an ill-timed 3-week statistical training course, and second, she also felt the need to protect the source of the rumor about the division manager's reaction. On the other hand, Joanne, Ellen's supervisor, knew that if the situation was handled in the indirect manner that Ellen suggested, the political fallout for the Minneapolis plant could be immense. Michaels was a powerful division manager whose manipulation of office politics was the root of the conflict.

An individual's leadership style frequently influences how office politics are managed. Given that this is a conversation between two women managers, it is interesting to consider the ways in which Ellen and Joanne may or may not reflect a feminine leadership style. A feminine leadership style is characterized by self-direction and empowerment of others. Feminine leadership lacks a sense of strict hierarchy and subordination while stressing a collective sense of group responsibility (Helgesen, 1990). However, this does not mean that a feminine leadership style avoids conflict in any way.

In contrast, a masculine style of leadership is characterized by one individual having power over and giving orders to others. A masculine style reinforces hierarchical notions of power, in which one individual is allowed to make decisions for the many. The power of one individual over many may often result in office politics, in which organizational members fight for control over others (Hackman & Johnson, 1991). This case presents an interesting mix of leadership styles, as the participants become entwined in office politics, multiple interests, and the desire to do the right thing.

## KEY TERMS

FEMININE LEADERSHIP STYLE: a leadership style that concentrates on power over self and empowerment of others. Styles of leadership that are commonly linked with a feminine style are transformational, interactive, interpersonal, or collaborative. These styles usually concentrate on creating an open, honest, inclusive atmosphere, or a feeling of being on a "team," and thus a strict sense of hierarchy and subordination is avoided (Helgesen, 1990).

MASCULINE LEADERSHIP STYLE: a style of leadership usually referred to as transactional, task, command and control, or authoritarian, styles that depend on one individual having power over and giving orders to others. This style is indicative of hierarchies, where one individual is allowed to make the decisions for many, and is considered to be the traditional manner of leading (Hackman & Johnson, 1991).

OFFICE POLITICS: the communicative manifestation of power, in which individuals seek to achieve their goals and fulfill their own self-interests by influencing others. Before asking others to support a decision or plan of action, those engaging in office politics attempt to manage the meaning of the events under scrutiny by imposing their interpretations and discounting others. Thus organizational politics can be found in the strategies and tactics individuals use to get their way in the day-to-day functioning of the organization (Frost, 1987).

RUMORS: information usually passed through the office grapevine "without secure standards of evidence being present" (Davis, 1972).

TOTAL QUALITY MANAGEMENT (TQM): a management style developed by W. E. Deming and J. M. Duran after World War II. It was the basis for the Japanese management philosophy that changed the image of Japanese industries from that of producers of inferior-quality products to that of producer of to high-quality merchandise. It is an approach to management that seeks to improve product quality and increase customer satisfaction largely through strong, quality-oriented leadership, participation in work teams, a more efficient use of resources, and statistical monitoring of work teams.

## DISCUSSION QUESTIONS

1. If you were the plant manager, what would you advise Ellen and Joanne to do? What is Joanne's responsibility to Ellen? How should Ellen respond?
2. What role should office rumors and politics be allowed to play in organizational decisions?
3. Are organizations inherently political? Why or why not?
4. What leadership styles do Joanne and Ellen use during their discussion of the office rumor? What leadership style characterizes Larry? In what ways are they masculine or feminine?
5. What does a feminine leadership style imply about conflict management? What does a masculine leadership style imply about conflict management?
6. What are some situations in which a masculine leadership style would be more appropriate? What are some situations in which a feminine leadership style would be more appropriate?

## REFERENCES AND SUGGESTED READING

Davis, K. (1972). *Human behavior at work*. New York: McGraw Hill.

Frost, P. J. (1987). Power, politics, and influence. In F. M. Jablin, L. L. Putnam, K. H. Roberts, & L. W. Porter (Eds.), *Handbook of organizational communication* (pp. 503–548). Newbury Park, CA: Sage.

Hackman, M. Z., & Johnson, C. E. (1991). *Leadership: A communication perspective*. Prospect Heights, IL: Waveland.

Haslett, B., Geis, F. L., & Carter, M. R. (1992). *The organizational woman: Power and paradox*. Norwood, NJ: Ablex.

Helgesen, S. (1990). *The female advantage*. New York: Doubleday.

Manz, C. C., & Sims, H. P. (1989). *Super leadership*. New York: Berkeley.

Wheatley, M. (1992). *Leadership and the new science: Learning about organization from an orderly universe*. San Francisco: Berrett-Koehler.

# CHAPTER 15

# The Public Electronic Network

Interactive Communication
and Interpersonal Distance

EVERETT M. ROGERS
MARCEL M. ALLBRITTON

Some 25 years ago, Smith (1972) stated his vision for something like the form of teledemocracy represented by the Public Electronic Network (PEN) system in Santa Monica, California, which has been implemented in recent years. Smith coined the terms "Wired Nation" and the "electronic highway" for American communities that were interconnected by cable television systems in France, England, Germany, Japan, and the United States. These wired cities experiences were characterized by rather modest impacts (Dutton, Blumer, & Kramer, 1987). Have the electronic telecommunities introduced in certain U.S. cities, such as Santa Monica; Taos, New Mexico; Blacksburg, Virginia; and elsewhere in recent years accomplished the Wired Nation of Smith's 1972 vision?

The purpose of this chapter is to explore a new type of organizational communication represented by computer-mediated communication among individuals. We define "computer-mediated communication" (CMC) as human communication between two or more individuals through the use of central computers that store and process message content and are connected to users in a communication network. Computer-mediated communication is one type of *interactive communication,* defined as communication in which participants have a degree of control over the communication process and can exchange roles in their mutual discourse. *Mutual discourse* is the degree to which a given communication act is based on a prior series of communication acts (Williams, Rice, & Rogers, 1988, p. 10).

Interactive communication has become much more widely diffused in recent years. For example, the Internet, a worldwide e-mail system, had an estimated 40 million users by late 1996 and a rate of adoption that had doubled over the previous year. It is estimated that 60% of all users are in the United States.

## IMPACTS OF INTERACTIVE COMMUNICATION

Computer-mediated communication has several unique qualities: The cost is minimal, compared to that of other present alternatives, the nature of the medium is digital and the messages can be manipulated fully (e.g., a message received via e-mail can be printed out, added to a database, edited and then returned to the sender, cut-and-pasted into another document, or used to create an entirely new document), and the communication structure of an organization is altered by the addition of a decentralized computer-mediated communication system. The organization usually becomes a more open system through network connections within other organizations. The introduction of an e-mail system also changes the communication structure within a work organization, such as by removing some of the effects of hierarchy and physical distance as restrictions on who communicates with whom through interpersonal network links. For example, a low-level office worker can send an e-mail message to the company president, and individuals working in different buildings or at widely separated locations can easily exchange information by e-mail, independent of their spatial distance.

For certain purposes, removing the cost of communicating interpersonally at a physical distance can be of great benefit. For instance, a work group of five company employees, located at scattered locations across the United States, can now collaborate by e-mail in writing a 5-year plan. Previously, they would have had to travel to a common site for a face-to-face meeting, at a considerable cost in time and travel funds.

Also, interactive communication systems are usually characterized by *asynchroniety*, the ability to send or receive a message at a time convenient for an individual (Rogers, 1986, p. 5). For example, say that someone sends an e-mail message on the Internet; the addressee receives it the next time that he or she logs on to the computer. Thus communication does not have to be simultaneous. Similarly, a telephone answering machine allows one to receive a message when convenient, eliminating the problem of "telephone tag." Interactive communication systems thus have the ability to overcome time as a variable affecting the communication process.

This transcendence of the barriers of time and space by interactive communication systems like the Internet leads to a very low cost per message exchanged via these communication media. Communication costs can represent a loss of time, money, coordination, and administrative cost (for example, the effort needed to plan and hold a conference), and the monetary costs of correspondence (for example, the costs of telephone calls or postage). In the case of the PEN system and the homeless in Santa Monica (described later in this chapter), CMC was a lower-cost medium of communication than face-to-face channels in that it removed the social distance barriers between the homed and homeless in Santa Monica. This lower cost of interactive communication enables people from very different affiliations, backgrounds, and interests to communicate effectively with one another about a topic and to work together to accomplish goals that are valued by the total system of which they are a part.

There are costs of communication across social distance. For example, a homeless and a homed person in Santa Monica may each have information that the other needs in order to solve the problem of homelessness in Santa Monica. But their socioeconomic differences represent a social distance that prevents them from talking about the topic of homelessness. However, interactive communication can bridge this social distance, as we illustrate in the following section.

Removing the cost of communicating interpersonally at a distance leads to such benefits as an increase in communication across long distances, which occurs because the costs are decreased (this benefit is one reason for the sharp increase in the rate of adoption of Internet-based communication in recent years), a lengthening of the physical distance of the average interpersonal network link, and a decrease in time differences as a factor in communication.

## THE PUBLIC ELECTRONIC NETWORK IN SANTA MONICA

The PEN system was established in Santa Monica, California, in early 1989 by the city government in order to provide a free electronic network to all city residents. PEN was the first municipal electronic network of its kind in the United States. The first author of this chapter, then a faculty member at the University of Southern California (USC), and with funding provided by USC's Annenberg School for Communication, directed research on this new application of an interactive communication technology. Prior to 1989, e-mail systems were widely used in large organizations, but they had not been provided for free public use in a community. The investigation of PEN represented collaboration with several colleagues at USC, the PEN system's designer, Ken Phillips, and an important user of the PEN system, a homeless man named Donald Paschal (Rogers, Collins-Jarvis, & Schmitz, 1994; Schmitz, Rogers, Phillips, & Paschal, 1995). Our research consisted of participant observation, in-depth interviews with city leaders and PEN users, and a survey of several hundred PEN users.

Santa Monica is a seaside California community with a population of about 90,000 homed residents plus several thousand homeless people (numbering from 2,000 to 8,000 in 1989, according to various estimates). Homelessness was the most important social problem facing the city in 1989, and this issue was taken up immediately by the first e-mail discussion group that was organized on PEN. By 1993, 4 years later, over 12,000 entries had been penned on the PEN Homeless Conference. From the beginning, homeless people participated in these electronic discussions along with homed people. This information exchange among socially unalike people occurred because access to PEN was possible by the homed from their home or office computers and modems and by the homeless via 20 public terminals that were located in city libraries, recreation centers, and other public buildings. Some 1,500 of the 5,000 PEN registrants (30%) make 20% of all PEN accesses via the public terminals (Schmitz et al., 1995).

Many homeless people in Santa Monica spent considerable time in its public libraries, and it was there that they first began making entries in the PEN Homeless Conference. They originally spoke up to correct misimpressions and stereotypes about the homeless that had been entered by homed individuals. For example, several PEN entries by homed individuals accused the homeless of being lazy and of not actively seeking jobs. In response, homeless individuals pointed out that they often were in a Catch-22 situation: When they applied for an advertised position, they seldom got past a receptionist because of their unkempt appearance and lack of clean clothes. And because they were unemployed, they could not afford to purchase presentable clothing, clean themselves, and prepare themselves in other ways for employment interviews.

For the first 7 months of the PEN Homeless Conference, homed and homeless people, who had not previously talked about the plight of the homeless in Santa Monica, discussed this issue on PEN. In August 1989, the PEN Action Group was formed in order to seek solutions to the Catch-22 situation of homeless people and employment. Soon a dozen individuals, including both homed and homeless, began to meet in person around a conference table. The group's first project, SHWASHLOCK (for SHowers, WASHers, and LOCKers), was launched. The Santa Monica City Council was persuaded to allocate $150,000 to renovate a storefront under the Santa Monica Pier, a central location for the homeless, in order to provide them with shower facilities. The PEN Action Group raised $5,000 for vouchers to enable the homeless to wash their clothes at a convenient laundromat. These funds were raised at a benefit event by well-known musicians and Hollywood entertainers who resided in Santa Monica. Santa Monica residents donated used clothes to SHWASHLOCK for use by the homeless.

A homeless person started a job-information bank on the PEN system in order to better inform the homeless about available positions to which they could apply. Later, in 1993, the PEN Action Group collaborated with the city government and the Salvation Army to create a new facility with showers, washers, and lockers for the homeless. This facility included a classroom equipped with computers to provide job-skills training to the homeless. As a result of these SHWASHLOCK activities, several hundred homeless people in Santa Monica secured employment, and some of them could then afford to obtain housing.

Donald Paschal, a homeless man who was one of the leaders in the SHWASHLOCK Project and who launched the job-information bank on PEN, stated, "Throughout my battles, I was considered human [on the PEN system]. . . . On the streets, one is looked on with varying measures of pity, disgust, hatred, and compassion, but almost always as something alien, from another world" (Schmitz et al., 1995). Nonverbal signals, including appearance, smell, and socioeconomic status, are absent in electronic communication via PEN, which can allow very unalike people to communicate freely. As Paschal stated, "On PEN, I have been helped, rebuffed, scorned, criticized, considered, and, in most cases, respected—as a human. PEN is a great equalizer. . . . There are no homeless or homed unless we say we are" (Schmitz et al., 1995).

## INTERACTIVE COMMUNICATION AND SOCIAL DISTANCE

The homed–homeless differences in Santa Monica made face-to-face interpersonal communication between them almost impossible until the PEN system was established. As Donald Paschal stated, "Not only might we be dirty, or perhaps smell bad, we are different. In the minds of many, people who are different must be avoided. That is why Santa Monica's PEN system is so special to me. No one on PEN knew that I was homeless until I told them. PEN is also special because after I told them, I was still treated like a human being. To me, the most remarkable thing about the PEN community is that a City Council member and a pauper can coexist, albeit not always in perfect harmony, but on an equal basis" (Schmitz et al., 1995). Thus the lack of nonverbal communication clues in interactive exchanges allows individuals to overcome social distance as a barrier to communication.

"Social distance" is defined as the perceived lack of intimacy between two or more individuals (Rogers, 1994, p. 183). This concept derived from the notion by Georg Simmel, an influential early German sociologist, of the "stranger," a cosmopolite who is oriented outside of the system in which he or she is a member. This broad orientation means that the stranger has few strong interpersonal network links with other individuals in the immediate system and is thus freer to be creative and innovative (Rogers, 1995). Early American sociologists at the University of Chicago, like Robert E. Park and his student Emery Bogardus (1929, 1933), adapted Simmel's "stranger" into their concept of social distance, which they investigated empirically in their studies of the interpersonal relationships between socially, ethnically, and racially unalike network partners (Rogers, 1994, p. 183). For instance, Park (cited in Rogers) utilized the concept of social distance in his analysis of race relations in Chicago. He found that the greater the social distance between two individuals, the less likely they were to communicate and the less effective such communication was if it did occur.

Park's generalization is supported by the lack of communication and understanding between the socially distant categories of the homed and the homeless in Santa Monica, as the following comment (entered on the PEN system) by a City Council member illustrates:

> "Last Saturday evening my wife and I walked down the Promenade. . . . On the opposite sidewalk, walking in the same direction, was a transient. He was shouting some of the filthiest profanity. . . . Several of the pedestrians commented that he was nuts, violent, on drugs, etc. . . . We found a nice place to eat at one of the outside cafes. A transient women walked in and went from table to table. She was asking for change for food. When she got to me, I asked her to leave us alone. A man at the next table . . . brought her a dinner. Thirty minutes later, I was standing in the movie line around the corner when she worked that line, asking for change for food. . . . And that is ok with most of you who read and comment on the 'homeless. . . .'" (Rogers et al., 1994)

A homeless individual responded to this message on PEN with the following comment: "Re: Mr. ———'s experiences on the Promenade: One question—how did you know that either person was truly a transient. Did you ask them?" (Rogers et al., 1994).


## THE ROLE OF FACE-TO-FACE COMMUNICATION

The solutions to the homelessness problems of Santa Monica that occurred due to the PEN system, such as SHWASHLOCK, the computer job-information bank, and the computer training program, would not have occurred without effective communication between homed and homeless people. Each party possessed certain information and other resources that the other needed in order to develop solutions to their social problems. The PEN system provided a means for these two socially different categories of people to begin talking. Note, however, that once the PEN Action Group began planning the details of SHWASHLOCK, they felt a need to complement their interactive communication on the PEN Homeless Conference with face-to-face interpersonal communication around a conference table.

A similar process occurred among female users of the PEN system. Individuals must identify their message entries on PEN with their actual names, rather than pseudonyms or computer "handles." Thus the gender of a message source is disclosed. During the first year after PEN was established, a few male users repeatedly engaged in communication activities that offended female users. For example, they incorporated the names of female users of PEN in interactive sexual fantasies with a male domination theme. Other male sexual aggression occurred on the PEN system when males made offensive remarks to female users who supported a pro-choice position in a PEN conference on the abortion issue; the female PEN users were called "Femi-Nazis," "baby-killers," and "ugly, old, and stupid" (Rogers et al., 1994). Hostility toward female users became so intense that some women dropped out of the PEN system. Others, however, responded by forming PENFEMME, a female users' support group on the PEN system. Members of PENFEMME agreed not to respond to further male aggression and formed a special PEN conference, the Abortion Issues Conference. Within a few months, members of PENFEMME began to meet in person on a regular basis, in addition to exchanging information on their PEN conference (Rogers et al., 1994).

Note that in both the case of the PEN Homeless Conference and PENFEMME, the members initially organized on PEN but then decided to meet in person to plan and implement their ideas. An interactive system like PEN can empower the information-disadvantaged (1) by facilitating their access to useful information and (2) by providing a means to organize activist groups like the PEN Action Group and PENFEMME.

## THE DESIGN OF THE PEN SYSTEM

The provision of public terminals as part of the PEN system turned out to be very important in allowing this interactive communication system to bridge social distances and in empowering the previously disadvantaged. In retrospect, this crucial decision to provide the public terminals in Santa Monica was almost coincidental. The PEN system was originally proposed by a Santa Monica City Council member who suggested that the e-mail system in use by city employees, including City Council members, be made available to all residents of the city. The director of the city's Information Systems Department, Ken Phillips, was asked to design a new interactive communication system that eventually became PEN. The Hewlett-Packard Company donated computer equipment valued at $350,000, including the 20 public terminals. The City Council thought these public terminals were a necessary component of the new e-mail system so that the city government would not be criticized for providing an elite system that the disadvantaged individuals in the city could not access.

A related policy decision, also critical, was to provide PEN services free of charge. The director of the city's Information Systems Department persuaded the City Council to allow him to donate the time of four staff persons in his department to monitor the PEN system, manage user registration, answer users' questions, and enter information into the system. These two related decisions, to provide public computer terminals and free services, ensured that any Santa Monica resident could gain access to the PEN system.

Thus our analysis of the PEN system in Santa Monica shows how an interactive communication technology like PEN recaptures certain elements of the participatory democracy once found in the small rural community, which was the model for Robert Park and his colleagues of the Chicago school, 70 years ago, for what urban life in the United States should be like.

## THE LaPLAZA TELECOMMUNITY IN TAOS, NEW MEXICO

Another example of transcending time, space, and social distance through the use of interactive communication is the LaPlaza Telecommunity, an electronic communication system established in Taos, New Mexico, in 1994. While the PEN system was initially designed mainly for the purpose of information dissemination rather than interactive communication, the main purpose of LaPlaza was to provide information to the community and to create an environment that facilitated interactive communication among members and organizations within the community. One directive of LaPlaza was to remove the economic and social barriers to information, thus making information more democratically accessible to the public (Finn & Cross, 1994).

The planning for the LaPlaza Telecommunity began in May 1993 when several citizens of Taos, a town in northern New Mexico, sought a solution to the high cost of Internet connectivity. The LaPlaza Telecommunity opened for public use in December 1994. On its opening day, 4% of the town physically came to LaPlaza's office in Taos and signed on to the system. In July 1995, 7 months later, there were 1,600 users of the LaPlaza

Telecommunity, of whom two-thirds were active users. Some 300 local people each day use the services of the LaPlaza Telecommunity. By late 1996, the LaPlaza Telecommunity World Wide Web (WWW) homepage was registering 1,400 "hits" a day (a "hit" occurs when an Internet user connects with LaPlaza's computer network through the Internet). The LaPlaza Telecommunity serves about 16% of the local population of Taos, about 10,000 people (5,000 in the town and 5,000 in surrounding areas). LaPlaza Telecommunity users are 40% women, approximately double the usual percentage of female users of an interactive communication system.

LaPlaza Telecommunity was designed from the beginning to provide as broad a range as possible of community services to the residents of Taos. LaPlaza was selected in mid-1995 as one of 36 finalists chosen from over 550 applicants nationwide to receive a National Information Infrastructure (NII) Award.

The PEN system bridged the social distance between community members, allowing them to exchange information with one another in order to solve community problems and to have a better understanding of the Santa Monica community. Even though the PEN system was not originally designed as a telecommunity, interactive communication, rather than one-way information exchange from sources such as City Hall, quickly became the most popular aspect of the PEN system. LaPlaza Telecommunity is an example of a public electronic network designed to facilitate interactive communication.

The LaPlaza Telecommunity was based on much research of previous types of public electronic networks. The LaPlaza Telecommunity provides the public with a free Internet account, a free 2-hour training course, called Quickstart, that covers the basics of using the LaPlaza Telecommunity system and the Internet, 15 hours of free use a month, and technical assistance in the form of free phone-line help services and personal assistance at the LaPlaza Telecommunity center (LaPlaza Telecommunity provides 86 hours of staffed assistance weekly at the public access terminals), located in the building complex of the University of New Mexico–North Branch Campus in Taos.

The LaPlaza Telecommunity provides public access terminals for users who do not have the equipment resources, or the desire, to use LaPlaza Telecommunity's services from their home or office. About 50 people a day visit the Telecommunity Center. One advantage of the central location of these public terminals is the interpersonal communication that occurs between the LaPlaza Telecommunity, staff and users. All of the public terminals provided by the LaPlaza Telecommunity are located at the main office of the LaPlaza Telecommunity which facilitates face-to-face interpersonal interaction between community members and LaPlaza employees. Location of the public access terminals at the LaPlaza Telecommunity main office gives the organization a physical identity as well as a virtual on-line identity.

LaPlaza Telecommunity provides the community with an electronically networked communication system that augments face-to-face interpersonal communication in the Taos community. The role of the LaPlaza Telecommunity is not to replace face-to-face communication but to augment these previously existing communication networks: "The emphasis is on supporting relationships and conversations, not on the technological tools that make this possible" (Finn & Cross, 1994).

LaPlaza Telecommunity connects individuals and organizations within the community and also connects the Taos community to national and worldwide networks through the Internet. For example, LaPlaza users can discuss specific community problems with members of other telecommunities. Taos community members, through the use of the Internet, can collaborate with members of other telecommunities and communities that are experiencing similar problems. The LaPlaza Telecommunity encourages utilization of the Internet by community members in order to create an interface between the goals and interests of the community, with opportunities to achieve these goals and develop interests. For example, community members and organizations can utilize the LaPlaza Telecommunity in order to research collaboratively and to write proposals for federal and private funding of community projects.

The neutrality of a telecommunity provides an incentive for organizations to participate in interorganizational communication. For example, community organizations can collaboratively create a proposal for funding. This lengthening of the physical communication network link may also produce access to more, and more accurate, information.

Interactive communication does not always facilitate the transcendence of social distance barriers. For example, the LaPlaza Telecommunity has had little success in integrating the Taos Pueblo, a Native American community, in the LaPlaza Telecommunity. Perhaps one reason for the disinterest of members of the Taos Pueblo rests with the technological characteristics of public electronic networks and interactive communication. In Native American cultures, such as the Taos Pueblo, communication is primarily oral and face-to-face. The social distance between the Taos community and the Pueblo may be too great for this social distance to be transcended by interactive communication.

## CONCLUSIONS

New interactive technologies allow human communication to transcend time, space, and social distance barriers. This transcendence of social distance barriers occurs in organizations as well as in communities. For instance, interactive communication allows for information exchange between a manger and a lower-level employee that otherwise might not take place. This sort of information exchange has great bearing on problem-solving efforts in organizations. Such an exchange also leads to a lengthening of the physical distance of the average interpersonal network link. For example, a major U.S. computer company utilizes an interactive computer system that connects all service technicians throughout the world. Oftentimes, an employee will answer another's questions without ever knowing the identity of the person who asked the question. A question that may take days to answer under the normal organizational structure of the company can be answered in hours by a fellow company service technician, perhaps located in another part of the world, who has come across the same technical or customer service problem.

Interactive communication can lessen the cost of communication across social distances. Public electronic networks allow community members to interactively communicate with one another and to share information with one another that would not be exchanged in other forms of communication. Interactive communication systems such as public electronic networks promote more interaction and effective communication among community members. The exchange of information between socially distanced communicators, which otherwise would probably not take place, leads to greater understanding, which in turn leads to more effective community action. Additionally, interactive communication can lead to more effective communication among communities. The mixing of organizational goals among separate organizations to create a common set of goals is possible due to the unique attributes of distributed, networked, computer-mediated communication. Other organizations can, to a certain degree, become integrated within the existing information infrastructure of a single organization. Essentially, public electronic networks allow for the creation of a community of organizations. In this case, not only is the physical distance of the average network link increased, but an entirely new network may be created.

Successful community networks aim to augment and increase the possibility of face-to-face interaction among community residents. The SWASHLOCK and PENFEMME groups on the PEN system were formed through a multistage process. Interactive communication is unique in its ability to facilitate the formation and maintenance of several different types of network structures: dyadic (two individuals), small groups, organizations, and communities. Given the Internet connection to 30 million other people at various geographic locations around the world, the types of network structures in local telecommunities can then interface with similar network structures around the world. For example, interactive communication can be utilized to connect several local telecommunities together in order to work collaboratively on accomplishing goals for the entire region in which the telecommunities are located.

The growth in telecommunities is partially due to the decreasing cost of hardware, the use of simplified software and the graphical user interface in computer networking and communication software such as the WWW, and increasing public interest in the Internet and other systems of interactive communication systems. Due to the growth of the Internet and the development of its underlying technologies, it is more feasible to create local area networks (LAN). Rather than being connected with cables to one another, several computers within an organization, office, or community can more economically be connected to one another through the Internet.

The importance of studying public electronic networks such as PEN and the LaPlaza Telecommunity is that the knowledge gained can allow for better implementation of public electronic networks elsewhere; the phenomenon of networked communities is still in its infancy, producing a need for more scholarly studies, and there is a need to learn more about perceived incentives and disincentives for participation in such electronic networks.

Perhaps the interactive technologies described in this chapter represent an entirely new form of human communication, distinct from interpersonal (face-to-face) communication and from mass communication. Perhaps.

## KEY TERMS

ASYNCHRONIETY: the ability to send or receive a message at a time convenient for an individual.

COMPUTER-MEDIATED COMMUNICATION (CMC): human communication between two or more individuals through the use of central computers that store and process message content and are connected to users in a communication network.

INTERACTIVE COMMUNICATION: communication in which participants have a degree of control over the communication process and can exchange roles in their mutual discourse.

MUTUAL DISCOURSE: the degree to which a given communication act is based on a prior series of communication acts.

SOCIAL DISTANCE: the perceived lack of intimacy between two or more individuals.

## DISCUSSION QUESTIONS

1. How did the computer-mediated communication system in Santa Monica change the nature of previously existing communication patterns?
2. How does interactive communication differ from either face-to-face interpersonal communication or mass media communication?
3. Based on this chapter, in what ways do you expect the new interactive communication technologies to change U.S. society?

## REFERENCES

Bogardus, E. S. (1929). Measuring social distance. *Journal of Applied Sociology, 13,* 110–117.

Bogardus, E. S. (1933). A social distance scale. *Sociology and Social Research, 17,* 265–271.

Dutton, W. H., Blumer, J. G., Kramer, K. L. (1987). *Wired cities: Shaping the future of communications.* Boston: G. K. Hall.

Finn, P., & Cross, P. (1994, May 4–6). *LaPlaza telecommunity.* Paper presented at the Ties That Bind Conference, Apple Conference Center, Cupertino, CA.

Rogers, E. M. (1986). *Communication technology: The new media in society.* New York: Free Press.

Rogers, E. M. (1994). *A history of communication study: A biographical approach.* New York: Free Press.

Rogers, E. M. (1995). *Diffusion of innovations* (4th ed.). New York: Free Press.

Rogers, E. M., Collins-Jarvis, L., & Schmitz, J. (1994). The PEN project in Santa Monica: Interactive communication, equality, and political action. *Journal of the American Society for Information Science, 45*(6), 401–410.

Schmitz, J., Rogers, E. M., Phillips, K., Paschal, D. (1995). The Public Electronic Network (PEN) and the homeless in Santa Monica. *Journal of Applied Communication Research, 23,* 26–43.

Smith, R. (1972). *The wired nation: Cable TV. The electronic communications highway.* New York: Harper & Row.

Williams, F., Rice, R. E., & Rogers, E. M. (1988), *Research methods and new media.* New York: Free Press.

# CHAPTER 16

# Interorganizational Diffusion

## Integrated Demonstrations and the U.S. Department of Energy

JAMES W. DEARING

Studying diffusion means studying how and why people decide to use new ideas, techniques, and technologies. Diffusing innovations across organizations is an important activity. For example, for fiscal 1995 the U.S. Congress allocated nearly $1.3 billion dollars through the Department of Commerce, the Department of Defense, the National Science Foundation, the National Aeronautics and Space Administration, and the Department of Energy to stimulate "technology transfer," a specialized type of diffusion, among federal laboratories, universities, and commercial businesses. Presented here is a case of how the U.S. Department of Energy went about developing a new way of stimulating interorganizational diffusion, the "integrated demonstration," as a means for then diffusing sets of new engineering and biology innovations from federal laboratories and universities to private businesses.

"Faster, better, cheaper, cleaner." To Dennis Miller, scientific adviser to the Office of Technology Development at the U.S. Department of Energy (DOE), this phrase captures what the department is trying to do about cleaning up toxic waste. The problem is huge and complex. Thousands of sites across the United States are badly contaminated with hazardous chemicals. The extent of environmental damage varies by site and is complicated by differing soil and groundwater conditions and different combinations of contaminants. To clean up this many problem sites the DOE needs the widespread participation of private businesses. Moreover, DOE planners hope that by adopting innovative ways of cleaning up toxic waste, U.S. businesses will have an advantage in bidding to clean up toxic waste sites in other countries, where the hazardous waste problems dwarf those in the United States (Anderson, 1993).

How did this problem occur? As much as people try to control hazardous materials, they are often unsuccessful. For example, thousands of underground gasoline tanks have over the years rusted through and leaked gasoline. And countless times people dump or pour out toxic chemicals rather than attempt to contain them. For example, tens of thousands of gallons of dirty solvents had been dumped for decades at old Army and Navy bases. Worse yet, at nuclear weapons production facilities, nuclear byproducts have for years leaked through gravel, sand, and soil, sometimes reaching underground aquifers.

Dennis Miller and other hazardous waste specialists with the DOE saw the need for new technologies that could clean up these contaminated sites *faster* than conventional technologies, produce *better* solutions to contamination problems, be *cheaper* than the use of existing techniques, and return local ecosystems to a chemically *cleaner* state than was possible using existing cleanup technologies. Hazardous waste cleanup planners at the DOE recognized that the enormous scale of this problem in the United States demanded that the DOE work with and rely on many other organizations to accomplish its cleanup goals. For example, they were having numerous successes in funding university engineering and biology researchers to create novel ways of cleaning up contaminated soil and water. New strains of microorganisms ("super bugs") that fed on contamination had been developed. High-pressure thermal pumps and piping systems for transporting the microorganisms underground to the toxic substances had also been developed. Other innovative ways for dealing with the cleanup of hazardous waste were also created, such as high-temperature incinerators and lasers, to be used at the site of cleanup activities.

So the problem is not so much in developing innovative technologies for cleaning up hazardous waste. They have been developed. The problem is in spreading (or "diffusing") the innovative practices among potential users. The DOE funds the development of new cleanup technologies, university researchers develop the technologies, but then nothing happens. The people in other organizations who actually clean up contaminated sites, such as private consultants, industrial engineers, and including state and local government regulators who mandate which technologies an engineering firm should use to clean up a site, were not adopting the new solutions to hazardous waste problems that are faster, better, cheaper, and cleaner than the old ways of cleaning up contaminated sites. Obviously, innovation is not the same thing as diffusion. In the words of one DOE official, "We've been throwing a party, but no one shows up."

## WHAT IS THE DIFFUSION OF INNOVATIONS?

"Diffusion" is the process by which an innovation is communicated through certain channels over time among the members of a social system (Rogers, 1995). An "innovation" is an idea, process, technique, or technology that is perceived by potential users as new. A central concept in diffusion is newness and the relationship of newness to uncertainty. Some innovations are high in uncertainty; that is, we perceive the decision that we are faced with—to adopt the new thing or not—as a very risky decision. We are uncertain about the consequences of the decision. Beginning to use the innovation might be a good idea, and then again, it might not! Uncertainty is reduced by gathering more information about the innovation. Having learned of an innovation, organizational members who perceive that the innovation has value for them will be inclined to seek out information about it, thus reducing their personal uncertainty about the innovation's usefulness, performance, or implications. Getting more information makes one feel more confident in making an adoption decision. Either choice, rejection or adoption, will reestablish a mental state of "cognitive consistency" by reducing uncertainty.

In addition to the need to reduce uncertainty, another key concept that drives the diffusion process is "social pressure," an increasingly strong perception by a potential adopter that nonadoption will meet with peer disapproval. Oftentimes, people adopt innovations partly to fit in with what their friends are doing or to please people who are personally important to them. The cumulative (or systemic) result of social pressure is termed the "diffusion effect," a change in the norms of the social system toward the innovation. Organizational leaders, opinion leaders, and "change agents" (those persons who are trained to know about the innovation and advocate for its adoption, like peer educators) typically seek to bring social pressure to bear on organizational members. Because people are often susceptible to peer pressure, diffusion strategies that include the use of social pressure are more effective than diffusion strategies that do not use social pressure to get people to adopt innovations.

Since the diffusion of innovations is a social process and organizations are social systems made up of relationships among people, it is not necessary to personally convince everyone in an organization to adopt an innovation for complete diffusion to occur. If influential people adopt an innovation as their own, other organizational members will "automatically" adopt the vision as part of a diffusion effect.

A goal of diffusion researchers has been to understand why innovations are adopted when they are. This goal has led diffusion scholars to study how recent adopters perceived the things that they adopted. These perceptions of adopters have been categorized as "attributes" of innovations. Understanding how people feel about innovation attributes leads to an understanding of why certain innovations spread more rapidly or slowly when compared to other innovations that may fulfill the same tasks (Dearing & Meyer, 1994).

For example, the attribute with the strongest positive relationship to adoption is "relative advantage." If a product is very expensive compared to other models, it has very low "economic advantage" in the eyes of potential buyers. Low prices are a strong incentive for most buyers. Cost is a major dimension of relative advantage, but there are other dimensions. Users perceive advantages in dependability, style, design, and status relative to other comparable innovations. For a small percentage of people, of course, the more expensive the better, since other aspects of relative advantage, such as status, are often positively correlated with cost. That is, the higher the cost, the higher the status benefit derived from owning the innovation.

"Compatibility" with existing values and beliefs and previous ways of accomplishing the same goal is a second very important attribute. Innovations that don't require a great deal of change from past ways of doing things diffuse more rapidly than innovations that have no similarity with previous practices. For example, I studied one innovation that promised great economic advantage, but using it required engineering companies to reorganize themselves into new divisions and teams. This innovation is diffusing very slowly, partly because it is incompatible with the existing structure of work in engineering firms.

A third important attribute of innovations is "complexity." New things that are very complex and difficult to understand take longer to diffuse among people. Computer software that is confusing does not sell well. Software engineers and programmers spend a great deal of time "reengineering" software after it has been created, to simplify it. Reducing the perceived complexity of innovations is a frequent reason for holding focus groups with potential customers to consider new products or services.

Two other attributes, "trialability" and "observability," are also good predictors of whether an innovation will diffuse or not. "Trialability" refers to the extent to which an innovation can be tried out on a temporary or test basis. People are more comfortable buying something if they can try it first (money-back guarantees are a type of trialability). Also, when the results of using an innovation are easily visible, people are more likely to adopt the new thing. Seeing is believing. This is termed "observability."

These five attributes of innovations are interrelated. For example, I'm nuts about kitchen gadgets. I became convinced to try out a juicemaker based on a high-status friend's recommendation (that's high relative advantage, which is good), the juicemaker's promise of dependability (again, high relative advantage), and the sales clerk's promise that I could return the juicemaker within 30 days without penalty (high trialability, also good). Yet when I got the juicemaker home and used it for the first time, I was faced with a few problems: assembly was difficult, many operational steps are necessary each time I want to use it, and cleaning up after each use is not easy (all high complexity, definitely not good). Because it is difficult to use and requires a lengthy cleaning after each use, I only used the juicemaker a couple of times in that first month (low observability of results, not good). My wife didn't like its color, and she didn't want to effectively lose what little free kitchen countertop space we have (low compatibility with the way we had organized our kitchen in terms of color and space). The juicemaker wound up in the closet. Is that successful diffusion? Probably not. I did buy it, but I won't be recommending that model to any of my friends.

So diffusion scholars have concluded that for an innovation to diffuse more rapidly, it should be inexpensive, compatible with previous ways of accomplishing the same goal and with the context into which it must fit, easy to understand, available on a trial basis, and visibly productive.

## THE DOE'S CONCEPT OF AN INTEGRATED DEMONSTRATION

An "integrated demonstration" is a collaborative display of an interrelated set of technologies, staged by an advocate, for the purpose of demonstrating utility to potential adopters, investors, and regulators. To the extent that they lead to commercial exploitation by private industry, government-sponsored demonstrations are successful at technology diffusion. Integrated demonstrations represent a special type of government-sponsored technology demonstrations.

The United States has been supporting demonstrations of new technologies for 150 years. In 1843, the U.S. Congress appropriated $30,000 for Samuel Morse to demonstrate his American Telegraph System. This successful demonstration led directly to the diffusion of telegraph service in the United States. Demonstrations can provide compelling evidence to observers that a technology should be adopted. The observability of innovations, the degree to which the results of their use can be perceived, is positively correlated with innovation adoption. Since the technologies being demonstrated are likely to be perceived as high-risk technologies by potential adopters, demonstrations must serve (1) to reduce perceived *uncertainty* about the technologies in question, and (2) to reduce perceived *differences* between technology sources and users through collaboration.

The U.S. Department of Agriculture (USDA), through its Extension

Service, state experimental stations, and state land grant colleges, made the demonstration of agricultural innovations a central part of its highly successful diffusion system. This tradition of demonstrations continues today. For example, the USDA sponsors demonstrations of environmental innovations that improve water quality. Demonstrations have been used during the past 40 years to diffuse energy and environmental innovations. The U.S. Atomic Energy Commission Power Reactor Demonstration Program of the 1950s is credited with having speeded commercial adoption of power reactor technology. The U.S. Energy Research and Development Administration demonstrated synthetic fuels. In the 1960s and 1970s, the Environmental Protection Agency demonstrated mechanized refuse collection (garbage trucks with mechanical arms), refuse burning, recycling and resource recovery, and poultry-waste-processing technologies. Another governmental organization, the Urban Mass Transportation Administration, sponsors demonstrations of intelligent highways, van pooling, dial-a-ride, and pedestrian malls.

In the DOE's integrated demonstrations, competing as well as complementary technologies are assembled and demonstrated individually and as comprehensive solutions for a specific problem that represents a generic environmental issue for hundreds of contaminated sites in the United States. For example, in Albuquerque, New Mexico, a chemical waste landfill received hazardous waste from 1962 to 1985, and a mixed-waste landfill received hazardous and radioactive wastes from 1959 to 1988. Both landfills became greatly contaminated. These landfills have been the sites of an integrated demonstration of field-tested technologies in partnerships with private companies and universities.

Some 32 integrated demonstrations were expected to be conducted by 1996. By late-1993, nine integrated demonstrations were completed or operating. Twenty integrated demonstrations were in some stage of development, and the DOE may eventually oversee 400 integrated demonstrations throughout the United States.

Integrated demonstrations are used to research, develop, demonstrate, test, evaluate, and disseminate technologies related to groundwater and soil cleanup, waste retrieval and processing, and pollution prevention. Potentially, integrated demonstrations are more than opportunities for interested persons to compare cost and performance data and the physical performance of technologies. They are collaborative learning and refining experiences for diverse engineers and scientists. Collaboration may occur at many stages of an integrated demonstration. Each integrated demonstration is divided into a series of "technical task plans." Each technical task plan is itself a set of coordinated activities organized to accomplish a goal related to waste cleanup. The mixed-waste landfill integrated demonstration in Albuquerque has occurred through the accomplishment of 32 technical task plans. A more complicated buried-waste integrated demonstration in Idaho had 66 technical task plans.

Integrated demonstrations represent first-time applications of new systems of technologies on a working scale under field conditions. The high degree of uncertainty in making these systems work in the best ways possible has necessitated collaborative partnerships between chemists, geohydrologists, geophysicists, microbial ecologists, drilling engineers, environmental engineers, computer simulation and modeling experts, and materials scientists. Collaborators in integrated demonstrations come from DOE laboratories, other federal agencies, universities and private industry.

Collaboration is required because integrated demonstrations are complex. Both the problems they address and the ways in which the demonstrations address cleaning up contamination of these problems are complicated. Hundreds of individuals may be involved in orchestrating a single integrated demonstration. The collaboration required is both among individuals as well as among their organizations. Because the demonstration sites are selected to reflect generic contamination problems that have yet to be remedied, each demonstration integrates a number of new technologies and processes in a novel way. Thus, a great deal of learning occurs during the creation of any one demonstration.

Integrated demonstrations occur over a period of years. They are not "one-shot" displays of technologies and processes. These demonstrations are complicated partly because of their involvement over time with potential adopters. Private technology vendors may be invited to bring their technologies to the site for comparative testing purposes. Since integrated demonstrations are novel, they represent a unique opportunity for technology vendors to collect data about the performance of their own technologies and other technologies in a full-scale comparative field test, over time.

Integrated demonstrations are also collaborative in their initiation. Integrated demonstration technologies can come from private industry, universities, and federal laboratories. Since the sources of technology are varied, the teams of people who work on the integrated demonstrations must also be varied, and they typically represent the sources of the technologies in the demonstration as well as other organizations.

The demonstration of new technologies matters little if the adoption, implementation, and use of these technologies does not occur. The DOE expected that integrated demonstrations would "jumpstart" widespread adoption and diffusion of demonstrated technologies. How well has this ambitious and innovative idea—the integrated demonstration—worked in leading to diffusion of new technologies? To answer this question, we conducted a case study of one integrated demonstration.

## THE FIRST INTEGRATED DEMONSTRATION

The Savannah River Site, near Aiken, South Carolina, adjacent to the Georgia border, was chosen as the test bed for the first integrated demonstration. The site measures 300 square miles and has been important to the United States in the production of nuclear materials. However, metals fabrication and degreasing activities left large amounts of volatile organic compounds (trichloroethylene and tetrachloroethylene) in the soil and groundwater. Using conventional pump-and-treat technology since 1984, over 270,000 pounds of volatile organic compounds were removed from the subsurface. Still, thousands of pounds of contaminant that the old pump-and-treat process could not remove remained in soil and groundwater. The first integrated demonstration was created to address this problem at Savannah River.

Innovative horizontal well-drilling technology for substance extraction and delivery was combined with the novel processes of in situ air stripping, in situ bioremediation, thermally enhanced vapor extraction, innovative monitoring, and characterization technologies. The demonstration integrated these technologies in complementary and competitive systems for observers. Groundwater and soils were actively treated for 384 days with only 44 days of downtime. Monitoring now shows a marked reduction in contaminant at the site.

Over 2 years, the Savannah River integrated demonstration had involved participants and consultants from 26 private companies and institutes, 13 governmental organizations, and 7 universities as well as policy makers. Rather than evolving into just another funding source for private industry and researchers employed by the DOE and local site contractors, the Savannah River integrated demonstration forced participants to work together to solve very complex first-time problems.

DOE policy makers contributed directly to the concept of the integrated demonstration, much through the vision and championing efforts of Clyde Frank. More than any other person, Frank is credited with the concept of the integrated demonstration. Savannah River was important in putting Frank's ideas to work, so that subsequent demonstrations at other sites could be improved.

Operators of more recently initiated integrated demonstrations toured Savannah River to understand the process of conducting an integrated demonstration. Hundreds of DOE and corporate personnel, as well as outside potential adopters such as technology vendors, consulting engineers, industrial scientists and managers, and government regulators, toured Savannah River to observe how the integrated demonstration was structured and how it worked. For more than 2 years, an average of 15 people per month toured the site.

The Savannah River integrated demonstration provided potential technology adopters with comparative and market studies of the technology on display as well as data about technology cost effectiveness, extent of bioremediation, extent of biostimulation, ease of use, and reliability.

In addition to touring the field sites where horizontal wells and monitoring equipment were operating, visitors to the integrated demonstration attended small group presentations by scientists and engineers and watched a computer modeling video that showed the extent of soil and groundwater contamination and the extent to which contaminant had been removed by horizontal wells. In a very real sense, the first integrated demonstration was "science and engineering in the making" in which collaborative on-site participants worked through both anticipated and unanticipated problems in the field.

## RESULTS

To what degree has the integrated demonstration at Savannah River served to diffuse new alternative technologies for cleaning up toxic waste?

The Savannah River integrated demonstration is considered a technical success by DOE personnel in the sense that it was a working example of a first-time application under real field conditions of how an integrated set of technologies could dramatically lessen contamination. But as emphasized by Clyde Frank, technical success is only a first and necessary hurdle. What really counts is not the initial innovation (in this case, the conceptualization and working model of an integrated demonstration) but its diffusion to potential adopters.

By mid-September 1993, 69 technical papers, journal articles, and reports had resulted from the first integrated demonstration about site analysis and evaluation, monitoring and characterization, bioremediation, or directional drilling. The Technology Transfer Office at Savannah River sent out close to 1,000 mailings about the integrated demonstration to potential adopters, bought an advertisement in a national industry trade journal, and sponsored public meetings on- and off-site at which researchers introduced the demonstration technologies. The integrated demonstration now serves as a test bed for technology vendors who come to compare off-gas treatment technologies developed by industry. Requests to use the facility have been 30% above that anticipated. About 100 invention disclosures were filed at Savannah River between 1989 and 1995 concerning the integrated demonstration. Ten licenses had been taken out concerning technologies and processes at the integrated demonstration by October 1993 (a license enables a company to use a process or technology from the integrated demonstration on their own cleanup problem).

Unfortunately for the Savannah River integrated demonstration, feedback from industrial representatives coupled with the data about invention disclosures and licenses demonstrates that widespread diffusion has not occurred. On the basis of personal interviews that I conducted with DOE personnel at the department's headquarters in Washington, D.C., and with the scientists in charge of the integrated demonstration in Georgia, and a review of both DOE publications and Savannah River's archival records, I conclude that only a few of the many company and government representatives who toured the demonstration then licensed the technologies on display to clean up their own contamination problems. Furthermore, many more potential adopters in cities with severe toxic waste problems, such as Los Angeles, Seattle, Chicago, Cleveland, Houston, and Philadelphia, never even knew of the Savannah River integrated demonstration. In fact, they did not even know of the DOE program that oversees all of the integrated demonstrations! Why did this case of diffusion fail?

## LESSONS LEARNED ABOUT INTERORGANIZATIONAL DIFFUSION

Many attempts at diffusion fail because innovations are prematurely pressed on their target audiences. The innovations are introduced too soon. Negative word-of-mouth then develops about the innovation if there are glitches, delays, or surprises. Unfortunately, the concept of an integrated demonstration requires a certain degree of premature release of information about the technologies on display since industrial partners are involved from early stages of creating the demonstration. From working through problems together—a commendable goal and difficult process—I conclude that negative perceptions about the complexity of the integrated set of technologies, combined with industrial partners having to work with federal bureaucrats in a slower, more cautious decision-making environment than the industrial partners are accustomed to, led to a spiraling of negative perceptions about both the technologies on display and the sponsor of the technologies, the DOE.

Demonstrations that are persuasive events calculated to influence adoption decisions increase the likelihood of technology diffusion (Baer, Johnson, & Merrow, 1977). Demonstrations are not staged for the purpose of merely disseminating information about certain technologies; rather, they are conducted to showcase technologies in a convincing manner. Their purpose is to achieve adoption, not merely to inform. Demonstrations that are exemplary rather than experimental increase the likelihood of technology diffusion. Demonstrations of technologies for which outcomes are predictably known by advocates will lead to more widespread and more rapid technology diffusion than demonstrations of technologies for which the outcomes are uncertain. Demonstrations that successfully lead to technology commercialization are rarely first-time in situ field tests. Advocates should distinguish between experimental demonstrations, whose purpose is to evaluate a technology under field conditions, versus exemplary demonstrations, whose purpose is to gain more rapid adoption of a technology.

From this case, we clearly see that demonstrations of technologies that have not been rushed through development and testing increase the likelihood of technology diffusion. There is often considerable pressure from various sources to rush technologies into demonstrations. Initial negative perceptions of innovations are very difficult to reverse. Technical problems should be fully resolved prior to demonstration of a technology.

Premature introduction of innovations is another way of saying that too much observability and trialability can be the death of an innovation that still has problems associated with its use and the results of its use. In the case of the cleanup technologies on display at the first integrated demonstration, potential adopters saw the problems and the obstacles to successful bioremediation, and those issues outweighed the Savannah River solutions to those problems and obstacles. So while more observability and trialability are usually positively associated to diffusion, they backfire when applied to innovations that are not yet perfected. The DOE staff did not conduct any formative evaluation from the perspectives of their potential adopters to systematically understand how their target audiences would perceive the technologies on display in terms of the diffusion attributes of economic advantage, compatibility, complexity, trialability, and observability. It is the responsibility of a diffusion source like the DOE to understand potential adopter perspectives prior to attempts at diffusion.

In the same way that influence among potential adopters can speed adoption, it can also block active consideration of adoption. The DOE staff and those persons in charge of the Savannah River integrated demonstration did not systematically seek to use existing social influence among their target audience members to speed diffusion. Diffusion works by taking advantage of naturally occurring influence among people and organizations. But the same opinion leaders who can create a diffusion effect among a target audience can also serve to defeat diffusion of other innovations about which they have not been persuaded. The DOE staff did advertise the integration in trade journals, make speeches, and involve certain industry representatives in technology development, but they did not systematically seek to identify which individuals and organizations were most influential with their target audiences, information that would have suggested who should have been invited to the integrated demonstration and persuaded and who should not have been invited. In the same way that there are opinion leaders who are important to sway, there are others from whom a positive endorsement will be negatively related to adoption decisions by others. They should not be sought out to attend a demonstration.

Staff within the DOE also had a very difficult time getting their own coworkers, staff in other DOE divisions, to adopt the innovations on display. Diffusion in an organization is political. Innovations are not introduced into a vacuum. Innovations are met with a variety of reactions by potential adopters, from skepticism and derision to excitement and hope (Dearing, Meyer, & Kazmierczak, 1994). Everyone assesses innovations on the basis of what he or she already knows, already owns, currently uses, and currently has invested. Comparison with the familiar—leading to the possibility of replacement—is how potential adopters make decisions about new things. This displacement function of innovations is what makes the process of diffusion so political. Diffusion creates losers as well as winners. An early backer or champion of an innovation gains stature as being farsighted when diffusion subsequently takes place. If the innovation does not diffuse, that person's early commitment is perceived as premature, ill-advised, maybe foolish. So organizational members judge proposed innovations very carefully and only willingly adopt innovations that they perceive to be in their best interests. With the DOE's cleanup technologies on display in the integrated demonstration, the vast majority of onlookers were never convinced of the benefit that they and their organizations would receive by adopting and using the technologies.

Similarly, the first integrated demonstration also affected political and economic relations among organizations. The private contractors who operate the demonstrations have a natural self-interest in retaining information, rather than sharing information and so persuading other businesspeople, about the efficacy of demonstrated technologies. Although not having the federal government directly operating the integrated demonstrations is perceived positively by industry representatives, serious conflicts of interest may exist due to the role of the private contractors. What is the incentive for them to actively diffuse the new technologies? DOE staff members were unhappy with the attitudes of some contractor employees. Is it reasonable to expect private businesses to aggressively give away valuable information to competitors? I think not.

The preferences and recommendations of contractors and local and state officials play a large role in determining the degree to which innovative technologies are portrayed positively or negatively in the integrated demonstrations. Since contractors already have invested the costs associated with older technologies and since local and state governments stand to benefit from lengthy, time-intensive, federally funded cleanup efforts, both contractors and local government present barriers to the diffusion of innovative cleanup technologies. These conflicts of interest must be resolved for technology diffusion to occur.

What made the DOE's integrated demonstrations distinct from the more typical government-sponsored demonstration model? First of all, integrated demonstrations are collaborative activities. Encouraging the communication among diverse specialists that is required for collaboration to occur is not easy (Dearing, 1995). Numerous partners are involved in each integrated demonstration, from multiple perspectives and complementary sources of expertise, in applied and theoretical, engineering and scientific, and abstract and hands-on work. Collaboration is often formalized through licenses, subcontracts, agreements, and personnel exchanges. Collaboration is difficult to initialize but can have huge benefits during implementation (Gibson & Rogers, 1994).

Second, problems are actively solved during integrated demonstrations. There is a strong sense of adapting and testing technologies to work together in first-time applications. The systems of technologies that are brought to bear in an integrated demonstration are necessarily somewhat of a custom design for a particular situation.

Third, integrated demonstrations also served as a means of testing functionally similar technologies against one another. So that customers can judge relative efficacy side by side, technology systems and system components are pitted against one another in applications to the same site problem.

Fourth, in integrated demonstrations, direct oversight and management of the innovations on display is vested with a private contractor, who in turn coordinates the roles of other private companies in the integrated demonstration. Just as the DOE contracts out many functions at its field offices, it also contracts out the management of its integrated demonstrations at those sites. Contractors identify potential industry partners and are typically partly responsible for disseminating a demonstrated technology, in accord with their particular DOE contract.

"Integration" refers to both people and technology. People from government laboratories, private industry, and academia are integrated in time and space. Since each demonstration occurs over a period of years, collaborators may work together from conceptualization through initiation, testing, and verification. Since each demonstration occurs on-site, collaborators may work side by side. Technologies, too, are expected to be "infused" into the demonstration from a variety of sources and to be integrated as a systematic solution to a complex problem through the three phases of operationalization, technical evaluation, and integration into regulatory and social contexts.

Lastly, integrated demonstrations address more than technical systems and their efficacy. Since integrated demonstrations are actual working full-scale field tests, they must be conducted within the contexts of state and federal environmental law and public acceptance. Participants in integrated demonstrations thus get a sense not only of technical feasibility but also of regulatory responses and public responses to new technologies and their effects.

In providing too much observability, these special features of integrated demonstrations probably act against the successful diffusion of cleanup technologies. For example, potential adopters probably leave an integrated demonstration with a much clearer understanding of the innovations themselves but with just as many questions, if not more, than when they arrived. Integrated demonstrations are really not operated as persuasive displays of proven technologies but as objective tests. While a promising approach for learning about cleaning up certain sites, this strategy will not stimulate adoption decisions by observers.

In summary, the DOE's innovation of integrated demonstrations is not serving to rapidly diffuse technologies for cleaning up hazardous waste in part because key diffusion concepts, such as the use of opinion leaders and change agents, and the attributes of innovations that we know are positively associated with adoption decisions have been ignored. The demonstrations are novel, they have promise, and they are a clear case of exciting technologies that address a very important national need. Nevertheless, the ways in which they are communicated to potential adopters in the United States have defeated their diffusion.

## KEY TERMS

ADOPTER: a person or decision unit that decides to implement and use an innovation.

DIFFUSION: the process by which an innovation is communicated through certain channels over time among the members of a social system.

DIFFUSION EFFECT: a change in the norms of the social system toward an innovation.

INNOVATION: an idea, process, technique, or technology that is perceived by potential users as new.

INNOVATION ATTRIBUTE: characteristics of an innovation as perceived by a potential or actual adopter.

INTEGRATED DEMONSTRATION: a collaborative display of an interrelated set of technologies, staged by an advocate, for the purpose of demonstrating utility to potential adopters, investors, and regulators.

SOCIAL PRESSURE: an increasingly strong perception by a potential adopter that nonadoption will meet with peer disapproval.

TECHNOLOGY TRANSFER: a specialized type of diffusion in which innovations are communicated to only one or a few potential adopters.


## DISCUSSION QUESTIONS

1. What is Dennis Miller's problem? Is the nature of his (and the DOE's) problem primarily technological or social?
2. What is the nature of each type of innovation attribute, and how is a potential adopter's perception of each attribute related to adoption decisions?
3. Relate the concepts of social pressure and the diffusion effect to your own life in terms of either popular music or clothing fashion. How real is social pressure? Is it possible to see the results of a diffusion effect?
4. Explain why, if you worked for the DOE you would consider the challenge of integrated demonstrations to be (1) persuading potential adopters or (2) gathering information from potential adopters to revise how integrated demonstrations are conducted.
5. What is the purpose of an innovation demonstration? What is the role of objectivity and impartiality in a demonstration?


## REFERENCES

Anderson, C. (1993). Weapons labs in a new world. *Science, 262,* 168–171.

Baer, W. S., Johnson, B., & Merrow, S. (1977). Government-sponsored demonstrations of new technologies. *Science, 196,* 950–957.

Dearing, J. W. (1995). *Growing a Japanese science city: Communication in scientific research.* London: Routledge.

Dearing, J. W., & Meyer, G. (1994). An exploratory tool for predicting adoption decisions. *Science Communication, 16*(1), 43–57.

Dearing, J. W., Meyer, G., & Kazmierczak, J. (1994). Portraying the new: Communication between university innovators and potential users. *Science communication, 16*(1), 11–42.

Gibson, D. V., & Rogers, E. M. (1994). *R&D collaboration on trial: The microelectronics and computer technology corporation.* Boston: Harvard Business School Press.

Rogers, E. M. (1995). *Diffusion of innovations* (4th ed.). New York: Free Press.

# CHAPTER 17

# Integrating Electronic Communication at Texaco

GERARDINE DeSANCTIS
BRAD M. JACKSON
MARSHALL SCOTT POOLE
GARY W. DICKSON

## TEXACO INC.[1]

Texaco is among the 10 largest publicly held corporations in the world and is the third largest oil company in the United States. Founded in 1902, Texaco today consists of four major divisions based on regional operations—Texaco USA, Texaco Middle East/Far East, Texaco Latin America/West Africa, and Texaco Europe—which altogether employ 25,000 people (see Figure 17.1). Each division is concerned to varying degrees with exploration, production, refining, and marketing Texaco products, and each is composed of numerous departments. For many years, Texaco has been an aggressive and active user of information technology, from sophisticated software and hardware for running oil refineries to multinational telecommunications lines for transporting credit card information to leading-edge workstations for analyzing marketing and scientific data. Each major business unit within Texaco has its own information technology function, which provides computing and related support to that unit. In addition, there is a corporate-level Information Technology Department that provides service and support to the business units and to service units within worldwide Texaco. The corporate Information Technology Department employed approximately 500 people during the time this case refers to.[2]

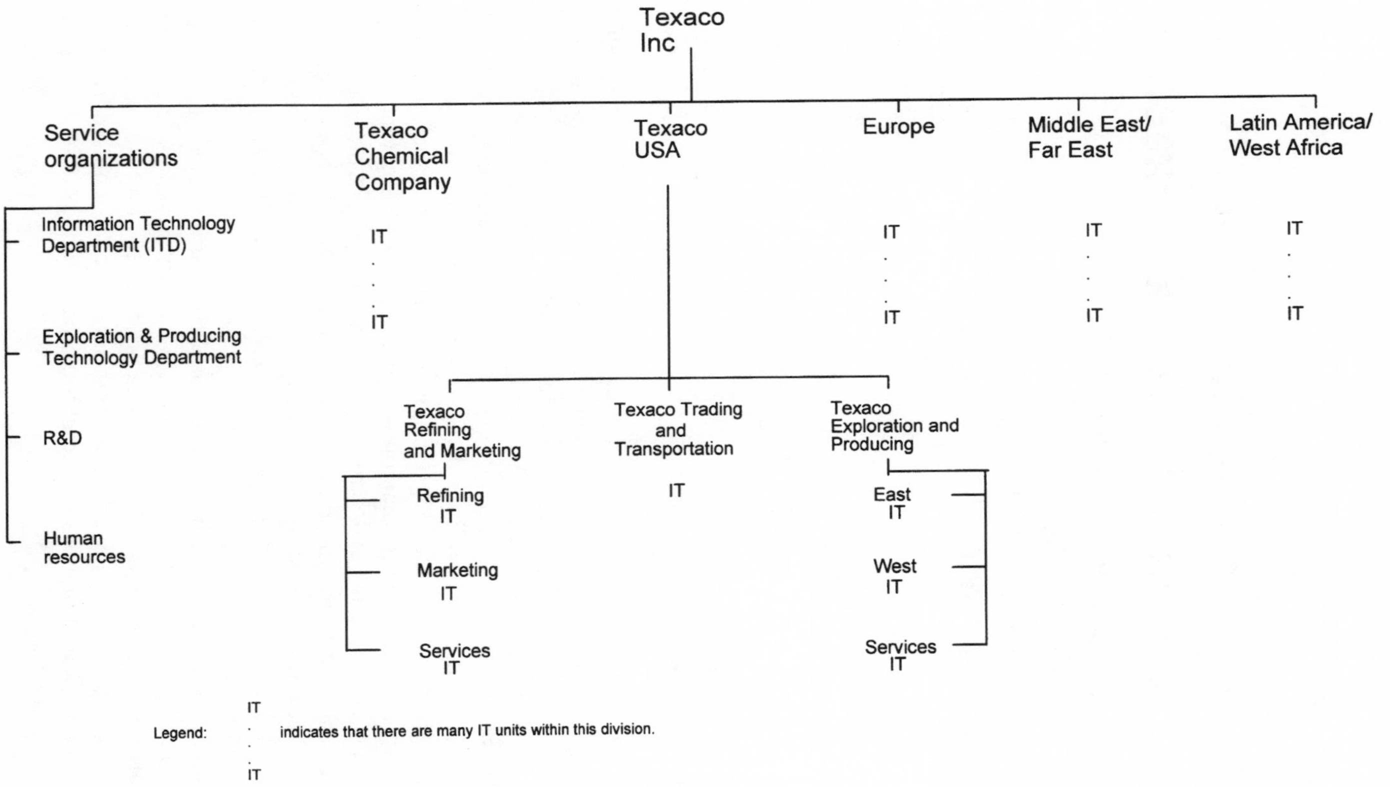

**FIGURE 17.1.** An overview of Texaco's management structure in the early 1990s.

## ELECTRONIC COMMUNICATION AT TEXACO

Texaco was an early user of computer-based communication systems, introducing e-mail, bulletin boards, and conferencing systems on a number of mainframes and minicomputers. For example, Texaco's exploration and producing units used Helium Corporation's AlphaMail product on minicomputers starting in the early 1980s. During that same time Barium Incorporated's e-mail software, BetaMail, was added to many of the Barium minicomputers located in refineries. And in 1985 the corporate Information Technology Department pilot-tested the mail package. Acquisition of electronic communication software was facilitated by developments in the latter 1970s, which had brought the minicomputer and on-line computing to end users at Texaco. Dispersed "end user computing" by the various business and service units in Texaco was gradually supplementing computer mainframe and batch processing of business transactions by the Information Technology Department. By the early 1980s engineers and other knowledge workers were rapidly discovering the use of distributed computers for support of office communication.

The early 1980s also brought the emergence of the desktop personal computer (PC), and it was not long before PCs were evident in every major business unit of the company. By 1985, PCs were not pervasive, but they were a clear and growing force within the corporation's computing environment. Early on, PCs operated in stand-alone mode, without linkage to other computing resources, but pressure quickly arose to connect PCs to the existing information infrastructure. As in other companies, the linking of PCs to mainframe and minicomputers—through other than "dumb" terminal mode, which disconnected many of the flexible features of the PCs—proved troublesome early on, and it would be many years before smooth connectivity would be possible among PCs, mainframes, and minicomputers located across the enterprise.

Due to internal demand electronic communication strategies could not wait until the computer infrastructure matured, and so e-mail grew topsy-turvy, first on local minicomputers, then on the mainframe, and later on PC-based networks. Starting in 1985 the corporate Information Technology Department began to test local area networks (LANs) for linking PCs together. Within a year, the department was deploying LANs throughout Texaco to support file sharing and printing among PCs and to link PCs to mainframes.

The vision in the Information Technology Department was to move from mainframe-centered applications housed in the department to distributed computing that linked mainframes and LANs. PCs networked into LANs could handle many tasks in local units and allow those units to develop their own applications suited to their particular problems and contexts. These LANs would then be linked into a global network that included the corporate mainframes, which were used for tasks that they could best perform, such as large database management and computing-intensive applications. The goal was a more flexible, intelligent use of computing resources that would integrate Texaco's communication system. This vision, however, could not be realized instantly; Texaco was an immense organization with varied levels of skill and computer equipment, so LANs and wide area networks had to be implemented gradually and experimentally.

Over time, two levels of networking emerged within Texaco: the global level and the local level. Globally, the company was linking mainframe computers within the United States and between the United States and Europe. Locally, the exploration, producing, refineries, and other departments were developing their own networks of minicomputers and PCs, and these local networks were not interlinked with other local networks or with mainframe networks. LAN technology was still in its infancy and could support only local architectures for PCs, not global ones. The result was two strata of electronic communication, with each level having somewhat similar functions (see Appendix).

## Corporate-Wide Electronic Communication

At the global level, the Information Technology Department saw both the customer need and the technical opportunity to make electronic communication available corporate-wide. E-mail software could operate on a mainframe system, and users could access it via dumb terminals or with their PCs running in terminal emulation mode. Since mainframe access was available to nearly all Texaco employees via the global network, the required infrastructure was in place. The software component, however, had yet to be fully developed.

The mainframe e-mail system was added after the general manager of the Information Technology Department attended the 1986 annual American Petroleum Institute (API) meeting of information technology executives from large U.S. oil companies. There he discovered that the majority of the other firms had acquired the GAMMA electronic communication system, a Flourine International mainframe product that supported e-mail, bulletin boards, phone directory listings, and calendaring. GAMMA required an expensive mainframe operating system, DollarOP, in order to run. At the time most Texaco mainframes were running a different Flourine International operating system, OPSYS. Nevertheless, the general manager became convinced that GAMMA was the right approach for Texaco. Just prior to the API meeting, Texaco had acquired Major Oil, which used the DollarOP operating system, so there was some in-house expertise on the new operating system.

So in 1987 Texaco acquired the DollarOP operating system and made GAMMA available for corporate-wide use using a mainframe for the central processor. To encourage the system's acceptance, computer access was made available for the low fee of $25 per person per month. Signups were rapid and abundant, and GAMMA quickly became—and remains today—the major corporate-wide e-mail system available in Texaco. The value of the GAMMA system is well recognized:

> "GAMMA is the most reliable source of communication available to me when working with foreign offices (Angola, Nigeria, etc.), because of the unreliability of phone and fax lines (in those countries)."[3]

> "International electronic mail has proven to be our only reliable and fast means of communication with our office in Moscow, Russia. We use it every day."

With the installation of GAMMA, it became possible for a Texaco employee to exchange messages with any other Texaco employee, located anywhere in the world. The only hitch was that the user had to acquire the computer hardware at his or her end (either a terminal or a PC and network connections) and pay for the service. In most business units, those with budget authority allocated the resources required for GAMMA use, but in some units the decision was to use only LAN communication or to forgo electronic communication altogether. Most information technology acquisition decisions were decentralized. Unit managers had their choice of what hardware and software to acquire and what services to pay for in their units.

As the application of GAMMA matured in the latter 1980s, it was judged to be robust, fairly simple and easy to use, and widely available. GAMMA provided e-mail, a "phone book" to look up user addresses, a feature that notified the sender if the receiver was away for a protracted period, and calendar services that enabled users to check on others' availability and to schedule meetings. Units with employees spread across multiple facilities and units with a strong need to communicate with people in other units benefited from the communication support of GAMMA. Employees could call in from the field and from home to access the system. GAMMA also appealed to units that did not want to set up their own (local) e-mail systems, preferring the centralized service provided by the corporate information technology department.

GAMMA had disadvantages as well. The user screen was simple but somewhat cumbersome. It required users to learn nonintuitive function key and other cryptic syntax commands, and it was unforgiving of errors. In addition, it required all users to operate their PCs in terminal mode, foregoing the flexibility of the PC. Notwithstanding these shortcomings, its universal availability made GAMMA very attractive for those interested in electronic communication.

## Local Electronic Communication

Although GAMMA filled a need for corporate-wide electronic communication, proliferation of PC-based LANs stimulated the purchase of local e-mail systems as well. As in many other companies during the late 1980s, management of LANs in Texaco became the domain of the business units who increasingly used them rather than the central information technology department. Business units installed their own LANs, selected software to suit their needs, and did their own planning and support, usually with the assistance of their local information technology function.

During this period Texaco had shifted to a decentralized management structure in which business units were given wide latitude in determining business directions and operations. This structure provided flexibility and opportunity for innovation, but it also resulted in less technology standardization for day-to-day business practices across the company. For computer-based communication, this meant the emergence of "islands of automation" in which the many office environments within Texaco were running e-mail systems that met local needs nicely but that were incompatible with and isolated from other LANs running throughout the company. For example, in one major unit, the oil and gas exploration portion utilized Delta Mail, whereas GAMMA was the standard for the production portion. While the exploration subunits had access to GAMMA, they preferred Delta Mail.

By the early 1990s at least nine different e-mail products were being used in Texaco. Some of these, like GAMMA, ran on large computers or sophisticated workstations; for example, AlphaMail was running in many exploration and producing departments; BetaMail was popular in the refineries; and Sigma UNIX was used in some of the R&D units. But most new systems were strictly LAN-based, provided by PC software vendors such as Delta Corporation, Daisy International, and SoftSystems. Personal computing and its close relative, office automation, were spreading like wildfire throughout the company, and people were discovering the power of being able to electronically coordinate with their coworkers:

> "E-mail delivers the same message at the same time to many different locations . . . allows hard copy documentation . . . minimizes misunderstandings."

"Electronic mail allows you to reach more people at one time, verify that a message was received . . . and eliminate a lot of wasted time writing down verbal notes from phone/audio messages."

Besides the benefits of speed, documentation, and asynchronous communication, e-mail also served as the conduit for coordinating meetings, exchanging files, and creating a sense of shared workspace for people who worked together:

"We use e-mail to distribute meeting minutes, announce meetings, and distribute agendas for the meetings . . . and through the LAN we exchange files often to coordinate our projects."

Before long, e-mail became core to a suite of technologies supporting interpersonal communication at Texaco, including the telephone, voice mail, fax, audio- and videoconferencing, and the Internet. Indeed, by 1994, in a survey of Texaco employees, e-mail was rated as the single most important technology impacting productivity, next to the telephone. E-mail became vital to everyday work processes, as necessary as voice conversations, and—perhaps more importantly—it came to be used in combination with voice, not just as a substitute. For example, one manager described the following:

"When writing up the findings and recommendations to evaluate the strategy of operating one of our oil fields . . . two of the members worked in two different cities, and three worked in three different departments in two different buildings within the same city. It was essential to leave voice mail and e-mail messages in order to communicate the progress we were making on the particular focus of the study we were working on. Voice mail was used to pass along ideas as well as schedules. E-mail was used to transmit notes and the write-up of the specific section we were working on. Without either of them, completion of the study would have taken much longer and cost much more (plane fares, hotels, etc.)."

## THE EVOLUTION FROM E-MAIL TO GROUPWARE

E-mail was only the beginning of the possibilities for computer-based communication within Texaco. Armed with word processing, spreadsheets, and databases at their desktops, and with LANs to link their desktops together, the next step for PC users was group-based communication. Whereas e-mail was typically one-to-one (private) or one-to-many (broadcast) communication, groupware (Johansen, 1988) provided a common workspace in which multiple parties could simultaneously participate and share work created at their desktops. The software industry was progressing—*technology push*—and users were very much wanting—*demand pull*—the emerging range of group-based applications, including:

Public folders to give members access to common information
Calendaring and scheduling
Electronic bulletin boards
Electronic discussion groups
Electronic meeting systems
Project management systems
Group writing and editing
Document sharing
Joint authoring and editing
Sharing PC-based work products
Workflow management

Groupware promises to do for teams what e-mail, the spreadsheet, and other personal utilities have done for individual workers.

Beta testing for a groupware product, DaisyChain, began in the corporate information technology department in 1986. DaisyChain is a computer conferencing system that uses a graphical user interface (GUI). In computer conferences members discuss common topics by sending entries to a common repository, where others can read them. The entries are kept in a database so there is a permanent record of the discussion. Conferencing works in asynchronous mode; that is, participation is not confined only to those times when all members can get together. Members may sign on to the conference whenever convenient, read the available items, enter any responses or thoughts, and sign off. When they sign back on, others' responses are waiting for them. This is advantageous because conferees do not have to coordinate schedules as they would for a face-to-face meeting and because it eliminates travel costs. In addition, some have claimed that the ability to type out comments before sending them leads to more thoughtful and reasoned discussion (e.g., Hiltz & Turoff, 1978)

DaisyChain has a GUI, so it is familiar to most users and user-friendly. The user has a screen of icons representing various conferences that he or she has access to. Conference topics range from very general meeting spaces open to all participants, such as "Coffeebar Talk" or "Windows Tips," to narrower team conferences of interest only to the members of a particular team, such as the "Advanced Technology Group" conference. The open conference references provide a place for all employees to interact and discuss topics of general interest such as charities, movies, and tips for working with commonly used software packages. The more focused team conference sections provide a place for members of teams to store information and keep each other informed, even if they do not see each other regularly. These conferences are particularly important to cross-functional teams, whose members work in different units, and to teams that spend a lot of time in the field and therefore have problems meeting face-to-face with regularity.

Comments are stored in DaisyChain conferences in outline format, with replies to comments indented and organized under them. Hence there is some logical organization of discussion to provide continuity to the discussions. Text and spreadsheet documents can be attached to comments as well, allowing evidence and documentation to be distributed. DaisyChain also provides an e-mail facility to allow person-to-person communication in addition to conferencing.

By 1991 DaisyChain was in "roll-out" phase at Texaco, being installed on LANs throughout the company at the rate of nearly 100 new users per month, increasing to 200 per month in 1992. DaisyChain required leading-edge PC and network technology in order to run smoothly, so many units elected not to adopt it because of the cost of replacing current equipment. However, by the early 1990s nearly all units were adopting *some* form of groupware, whether primitive (as in document sharing) or sophisticated (as in workflow management).

A key factor in the demand pull for groupware was the start of Texaco's quality program in 1989, which moved toward a team-based management structure. This necessitated a major reorganization of what had previously been a highly centralized organizational structure to enable Texaco to adapt rapidly and flexibly in the face of changing global markets and competition. The shift from a hierarchical form of management to a team-based structure created a tremendous need for interpersonal communication and interteam coordination. Individuals who had previously worked on independent tasks, reporting to a single supervisor, now had to plan their progress, monitor their outputs, and coordinate their daily work with a group of coworkers. Conflicting approaches to getting the job done had to be resolved among team members, and members had to devise ways to share information and pass work inputs and outputs to one another. Though some teams resorted to face-to-face meetings, office conversations, and manual document sharing to coordinate with another, many others came to rely on electronic communication, particularly groupware:

> "DaisyChain has helped teams easily collect and use information pertinent to the team goal. It also helps to coordinate actions and provides a single point of contact for all team members to pass ideas."

"DaisyChain has greatly benefited coordination of team activities. Through the use of the public 'Team Activities' template, all team members can contribute to future meeting agendas, track action items, and keep current on team decisions, etc."

"Delta Mail has been very useful in transferring data files, programs, source code, etc. between team members. AlphaNotes [computer conferencing tool] is useful for general info about the 'pulse' of the company and computer industry."

Communication across business units and subunits also increased following the quality initiative, since team-based management required each team to actively link its work to that of other individuals or teams in Texaco's upstream or downstream product chain. External parties typically were not in close physical proximity to the primary team, nor did they have ready access to the primary team's work. Although e-mail became an obvious conduit for coordination, groupware offered a richer communication environment:

"We use DaisyChain as a problem tracking/resolution tool for support of our process automation system. Also, several of our teams use DaisyChain as an information sharing/discussion database allowing our refinery customers in seven sites across the U.S. to interact with us on a daily basis."

"DaisyChain has helped each team that I have participated with to share information with team members and external teams. For instance, in the past 8 months one team that I work with has developed a database to hold the team's history, problems, and solutions. Since this team is primarily designed to be a service to the entire ITD [Information Technology Department] department, the database helped to increase the team's visibility and accountability along with more outside (nonteam members) participation. (Previously, the team had stored this same information in a big binder that only a few people had access to and few people were aware of.)"

In sum, as e-mail was growing in popularity, so too was groupware. Organizational demands for coordination, coupled with ever-increasing numbers of PCs and LANs throughout the company, operated as joint social and technical forces for increased electronic communication at Texaco.

## ELECTRONIC COORDINATION OR ELECTRONIC CHAOS?

By 1993 Texaco had invested millions of dollars in electronic communication technology of one form or another and in associated training, services, and support. Increasing levels of desktop technology were continually being rolled out to more people, and networks were busy with ever-increasing volumes of electronic communication traffic. But the two strata of communications networking had not yet merged. GAMMA remained the major electronic highway for global, corporate-wide communication; but it was mainframe-based, and users increasingly preferred the local world of PCs and LANs for their work, due in large part to the functionality and ease of use of these technologies. As the local world flourished, users aspired to take their groupware facilities worldwide. Whereas the 1980s had been the era of decentralization and a distributed approach to management, the 1990s were bringing downsizing, process streamlining, and a growing need to integrate work across units. There was a greater need for cross-organizational communication, but, unfortunately, this was not easily done in the decentralized LAN-based world that had evolved.

In 1988 the corporate Information Technology Department had installed a software gateway, known as SwitchWitch, which served as a mechanism to interconnect and translate between disparate e-mail systems. Using SwitchWitch, for example, a Delta Mail e-mail user in Denver could send a message to a DaisyChain Mail user in New Orleans; transparent to the user, SwitchWitch would translate the message to DaisyChain Mail format and route it to the appropriate place. But the SwitchWitch translation was perceived as cumbersome and unacceptable to many users, who preferred that their coworkers use the same office software systems as they did, for easy exchange of files, data, and messages. The islands of e-mail had grown large and numerous, and there was no smooth navigational chart for integrating them.

> "My work involves communication with engineers in a variety of Texaco departments. But because IT [Information Technology] is so decentralized, we're all on different electronic mail systems. If I want to send the same memo to three people, I may have to send it as many as three times using three different hardware and software platforms because we all use different systems!"

> "There are too many electronic mail systems at Texaco; every unit uses a different one to communicate. It is difficult to keep up to date on all of them. Mail begins to stack up and important documents get lost in the mess."

> "High-level management needs to pick *one form* of electronic communication (i.e., GAMMA, Delta Mail, DaisyChain, etc.) platform and stick to it. It is to redundant to have multiple data forms of communications."

In the western U.S. exploration and production unit, a manager in the production group observed,

> "Since migrating from GAMMA to SoftSystems Mail, I can send a document to Midland [Texas] or Sacramento [California], but I can't send one across the street [to the exploration unit, which is still on GAMMA]."

Electronic communication had progressed to the point of ultimate paradox: E-mail use was pervasive, yet many employees could not satisfactorily communicate with one another. File and document exchange among various LANs was cumbersome for some and impossible for others. Everyone recognized the need for a standard electronic communication system, yet issues of cost, training, and learning made a corporate-wide transition a major management concern. Further, attention had to be paid to the political tension of individual business units having to abandon the network infrastructure they had developed to suit their internal needs, should the company move to a standard e-mail system. As one observer put it, "Everyone is basically saying, 'I think we need standards; everyone else should use mine!'" What was management to do?

## SYSTEM INTEGRATION OR MIGRATION?

### The Problem

Texaco technology managers found themselves confronted with the classic conflict between centralized and decentralized forms of organization. The global level networks were centrally managed, and the local networks were decentralized. Would it be possible to impose some orderly infrastructure on the chaos that had emerged in the business units? The issue extended beyond electronic communication systems.

Since 1989 each major business unit had been operating its own information technology function, independent of the corporate technology department and all other information technology functions within the company. Problems of inconsistent architectures, incompatible systems, and lack of alignment with global corporate concerns had arisen in many technology areas (such as software development, databases, and IT personnel management), not just electronic communication. Given the corporate structure, there had been no real incentive to view information technology as a singular, company-wide resource. In fact, accounting and tracking of computing technologies had become nearly impossible, as each information technology function had developed a "stovepipe" mentality—managing systems to suit the business unit's needs but not the needs of the larger organization. Decentralization had made happy users—until they had to communicate and share information via their incompatible networks.

*A question:* At this point in the case, what would you recommend that Texaco do? Stop for a minute and formulate a plan that addresses the problems raised up to this point. Once you are finished, proceed and find out what Texaco actually did.

## Texaco's Approach

In 1992, after a series of roundtable meetings in which the directors of information technology from the various operating units discussed common problems and issues with one another, the corporate Information Technology Department formed a cross-functional team consisting of 16 people from the various business unit information technology functions and chaired by the general manager of corporate information technology. This team, called the Information Planning Group (IPG), had the general goal of achieving synergy among the many information technology groups throughout Texaco.

The IPG team was used as a mechanism to spawn other cross-functional teams. First, the IPG created an Asset Management Task Force, which was a temporary committee charged with conducting an inventory and valuation of computer and telecommunications hardware and software throughout Texaco. The findings of this task force provided a foundation for the IPG's initial planning efforts. Major areas in need of cross-functional coordination were identified, and a series of subteams were established to address each area (see Figure 17.2).

Like the IPG, each subteam was responsible for defining its own objectives, strategies, and operating approach. Each subteam included one IPG member, with the rest of the members constituting a collection of technology professionals from across Texaco. The subteams reported to the IPG, but, as before, there were no formal reporting relationships across information technology units; participation in the IPG and subteams was voluntary. One subteam of the IPG that was particularly important in shaping organizational communication in Texaco was the e-mail subteam.

## The Battle for the Desktop: Daisy versus SoftSystems

The e-mail subteam of the IPG initially worked on identifying requirements for a corporate e-mail system. If the team could get consensus on system requirements, the next step would be to evaluate vendor products meeting those requirements and select one to serve as Texaco's standard.

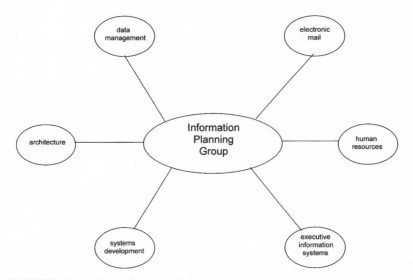

**FIGURE 17.2.** Cross-functional planning teams for information technology.

Business units that were not using the selected standard product would have to agree to migrate to that product over time.

After about a year of meetings and intense analyses of the electronic communications dilemma, two major camps were forming, both within the team and across Texaco. On one side were the DaisyChain users, who were continually growing in numbers and were fervently devoted to their product. DaisyChain was not an e-mail package per se, but it contained an adequate (some would say minimal) e-mail facility that enabled communication and file sharing among the many DaisyChain users across Texaco. Opposing the DaisyChain camp were those who advocated migration to a SoftSystem product suite, particularly SoftSystems Mail, which was reputed to be simpler, cheaper, and easier to support and use than DaisyChain and other supplemental utilities. Many users of Delta Mail, BetaMail, and AlphaMail were gradually shifting to SoftSystems Mail as they standardized on SoftSystems products for desktop and office applications. DaisyChain users argued that although their product was more expensive and complicated to manage, it was far richer in capability, offering a full range of groupware facilities that were not available in SoftSystems Mail. Daisy International and SoftSystems were competing not only in the marketplace of the software industry, it seems; they were also competing within the offices and networks of large corporations, including Texaco. A feud was brewing, and though the stakes were down to two major products, sentiments were deep on each side, and systems integration proved to be a formidable technical and political goal.

## The MAPI Standard

The e-mail subteam came to the conclusion that the goal of a single, enterprise-wide product for electronic communication was probably not going to be met in the short term. Instead, they decided that rather than focusing on *products*, they would focus on *standards* that products must meet. They identified three layers of technology for which standards had to be specified: client, server, and network backbone. The *client* layer resided in the PC and was the interface between the user and the technology, the place where users accessed the functions they needed in a display format that was familiar. The *server* layer was hidden from the user and was the hub for collecting communication and distributing it to the appropriate parties. Clients and servers resided at the local level, linked via a LAN. The *network backbone* linked servers together to form an integrated network, much like a telephone network links local systems into a worldwide network. The e-mail feud had been centered around products at the client level. But if the three layers could be logically separated, then users could choose their preferred system to run at the client level, and standardization could take place at the server and backbone levels. Following this line of reasoning, the decision to be made by the e-mail subteam was not the selection of an e-mail package but the selection of a standard messaging protocol for exchange of information through the network, a protocol that particular products must satisfy.

In 1994, the e-mail team decided on the Messaging Application Programming Interface (MAPI) protocol as Texaco's corporate messaging standard. The recommendation was made to the IPG, and eventually approved, that Texaco should migrate toward products that met the MAPI standard. SoftSystems had announced a commitment to MAPI standards in future e-mail and groupware products, but their current system, SoftSystems Mail, did not meet this standard. SoftSystems's anticipated use of MAPI was enough reason for many Texaco units to migrate to SoftSystems Mail and other SoftSystems products and to advocate that others in the corporation do the same. Commitment by Daisy International to MAPI was less certain, and in 1995 Daisy International was purchased by Flourine International, bringing additional uncertainty about their conformance to MAPI. Still, DaisyChain users within Texaco were not about to abandon their product for the less rich, non-MAPI SoftSystems mail product. Indeed, DaisyChain installations continued to grow within Texaco through 1995, and there was no apparent reverse in this trend.

As they look ahead to the future, Texaco information technology managers now ask themselves, Will software vendors provide us with MAPI-based products so that we can integrate our disparate communication technologies? Or, will we ultimately be forced to migrate everyone to one common product? Can Texaco afford to keep investing in multiple, incompatible platforms for electronic communication, or should the company try more forcefully to shift the tide in favor of one product? As management mulls over these questions, electronic communication continues to grow exponentially throughout Texaco. The local world of electronic communication is growing like a monster . . . but the only way to communicate to everyone today is still through that old centralized dinosaur GAMMA.

## APPENDIX: A CHRONOLOGY OF
## ELECTRONIC COMMUNICATION AT TEXACO

1982–1987    A variety of mainframe and minicomputer-based e-mail products are installed throughout Texaco (e.g., AlphaMail, BetaMail).

1985    Initial testing begins of token ring LANs to link personal computers.

First groupware product is used: The Facilitator.

1986    ITD begins to deploy local area networks throughout the company to support file sharing and printing among PCs and to link PCs to mainframes.

Beta testing of DaisyChain begins.

1987    GAMMA is installed and quickly becomes available corporate-wide.

Information technology function is decentralized.

1988    "Islands of e-mail" emerge as business units install various e-mail packages on their minicomputer networks and LANs.

The SwitchWitch system is installed to interconnect disparate e-mail systems.

1989    Quality process is introduced and team-based management begins.

1990    By now, business units have acquired a range of software applications for their desktop computers and LANs; demand for ability to exchange information (e-mail, files, databases) grows.

DaisyChain begins to roll out throughout the company; other groupware systems are used on a trial basis.

1992    Multiple e-mail systems are used across business units: AlphaMail, Sigma Unix, Delta Mail, DaisyChain Mail, BetaMail, SoftSystems Mail, etc.; SwitchWitch is available to interconnect e-mail systems, but support in the business units is uneven, and many users remain unaware or unable to send mail across systems. Frustration mounts.

DaisyChain use grows to 2,000 users.

Cross-functional Information Planning Group is formed. A subgroup is formed to address the e-mail problem.

| 1993 | DaisyChain use grows to 5,000 users; other groupware systems are implemented on a more limited basis. |
|------|------|
| 1994 | The Messaging Application Programming Interface (MAPI) is selected as the corporate messaging standard. The decision is made to migrate toward products that meet the MAPI standard, though few do at the time. Both SoftSystems and Daisy International promise MAPI products. |
| 1995 | Some business units migrate from Delta Mail, BetaMail, etc., to SoftSystems Mail; others add DaisyChain. Tension intensifies between those desiring standardization on SoftSystems products and those preferring DaisyChain. |
| 1995–1998 | Integration or migration? Texaco has a common direction (MAPI standard) but not a common product. Will vendor developments provide smooth integration of competing communication products, or will Texaco migrate to a common (standard) product for everyone? |

## ACKNOWLEDGMENTS

The authors thank the Information Technology Department of Texaco Inc., particularly Ed McDonald and Gary Richardson, for the opportunity to conduct this case study. The research was supported by National Science Foundation Award SES-9109167 and by a grant from Texaco Inc. The views expressed here are solely those of the authors and not of the research sponsors.

## NOTES

1. This case was developed for instructional purposes only and is not presented as an evaluation of management practice. All names of corporations other than Texaco and of hardware or software products are pseudonyms.
2. The projected size of the department in 1996 is 250 employees, as Texaco continues to outsource information systems services.
3. All quotations come from interviews and surveys of Texaco employees conducted by the authors. The information in this case is based on the comments of six primary informants and members of 80 teams, who were interviewed over a 2-year period. In addition, numerous corporate documents and records were consulted. Statements are anonymous unless otherwise indicated.

## KEY TERMS

BACKBONE: a high-capacity network that links together major computer and communications resources in an organization.

BETA TESTING: installation of an early version of software to determine how well it works in the field and to identify any flaws or bugs. The developer uses this information to improve the programs and move the software toward full commercialization.

CLIENT: a PC that communicates over a network both with other PCs and with a larger computer, called a server, which typically stores data and programs that many users need access to. The client has just one user; the server many.

CROSS-FUNCTIONAL TEAM: a team that has members from more than one functional department in an organization. Such teams are often used for special projects or to coordinate activities among functional departments.

DEMAND PULL: innovation that is driven by demand on the part of users for a new technology.

DISTRIBUTED COMPUTING: the type of computing that networks support. With combinations of PCs and servers, an organization's data may be scattered among different computers.

DOCUMENT SHARING: the ability for different users on different computers to have access to and work on the same document, where "document" refers to any meaningful computer file, such as a word processing file or a spreadsheet.

ELECTRONIC MAIL: memo-format messages sent from one person on a computer network to another. E-mail can also be copied to a whole list of receivers.

GRAPHICAL USER INTERFACE (GUI): an interface between user and computer that is based on pictures, graphics, and text. Users can input commands via either mouse or keyboard, and programs and utilities are often represented by icons.

GROUPWARE: computer programs and hardware that facilitate the work of organizational groups or teams. The technologies labeled as groupware range from very simple devices such as a shared display that all members can see to very complicated and expensive group decision support systems, which help groups analyze problems and come to decisions. Various types of groupware are designed to support groups working in a wide range of conditions. Some groupware supports only groups meeting face-to-face, while other groupware can support distributed groups whose members "meet" across the network. Some groupware supports groups whose members are all working at the same time — synchronous work—while other groupware supports groups whose members sign on and work at any time they choose —asynchronous work.

LOCAL AREA NETWORK (LAN): a group of computers connected by cable that can share data, software, storage, printing, and communication devices. They are required for client–server computing.

MAINFRAME: a large computer that typically does large-scale calculations and maintains large databases. It can be the connection point for terminals, which are "dumb" devices that depend on the mainframe to do their computing. When a PC is in "terminal mode" it is basically acting like a terminal connected to a mainframe.

MINICOMPUTER: a computer between PCs and mainframes in size and memory capacity. In recent years minicomputers have been used to do computing-intensive applications on networks, replacing more expensive mainframe computers.

OPERATING SYSTEM: a series of programs designed to handle many of the essential processes of a computer. Mainframes, minicomputers, and PCs all have operating systems of different types. Popular operating systems for PCs include DOS, Windows, and Macintosh.

QUALITY PROGRAM: a program designed to improve the quality of organizational products and processes through having workers analyze their work and come up with improvement suggestions. Also called "total quality management."

SERVER: a larger computer that contains data and programs needed by clients on a network. Servers also may be the "traffic cops" of a LAN, managing message traffic, and the gateway into and out of the LAN to other networks.

STANDARDS: a set of specifications and rules for the design of hardware and software that make it compatible with other computer and communication devices. Standards ensure that different versions of a product from different companies will operate in the same way and be compatible with other devices.

TEAM-BASED MANAGEMENT STRUCTURE: an organizational structure that vests responsibility and control for a team's activities in the team itself. This turns the organization into a hierarchy of teams with overlapping membership. Usually the object is to make the organization more flexible and responsive to its environment.

TECHNOLOGY PUSH: innovation that is driven by the development of new technologies so promising that they are adopted on their merits.

WIDE AREA NETWORK: multiple local networks tied together by telecommunication and sometimes satellite links. Wide area networks may connect users in different buildings or countries.

WORKFLOW MANAGEMENT SOFTWARE: software for scheduling and coordinating a complex series of tasks carried out by multiple workers and, sometimes, by multiple units.

WORKSTATION: a powerful personal computer, generally running at a higher rate and with much larger memory.

## DISCUSSION QUESTIONS

1. Looking back on Texaco's strategy of implementing e-mail, is there anything they could have done to avoid the problems of systems incompatibility that led to the current state of affairs?
2. The development of the global and local worlds of electronic communication can be analyzed from both social and technical perspectives. What were the key social factors that shaped the development of global and local worlds? What were the key technical factors and events?
3. What do you recommend that Texaco do at this point? Why?

4. How would you go about assuring the success of your recommendation? Be specific.
5. Throughout this case, the issue arises of local autonomy versus the view of what is best for the overall organization. How should executive management reconcile these differences?
6. How do you balance "control" and "innovation" with respect to new communication technologies?
7. How does the traditional telephone fit into this case? Do you see any relationship between voice mail, e-mail, teleconferencing, and groupware?

## SUGGESTED READING

Hiltz, S. R., & Turoff, M. (1978). *The network nation: Human communication via computer.* Reading, MA: Addison-Wesley. (An old source, but a classic on the potential of computer conferencing.)

Johansen, R. (1988). *Groupware: Computer support for business teams.* New York: Free Press.

Scott-Morton, M. S. (1991). *The corporation of the 1990s: Information technology and organizational transformation.* New York: Oxford University Press.

Sproull, L., & Kiesler, S. (1991). *Connections: New ways of working in the networked organization.* Cambridge, MA: MIT Press.

# CHAPTER 18

# Telemedicine in Kansas

Using Technology to Bring
Healthcare to Rural Areas

## PAMELA S. WHITTEN

Chances are that if you live in rural America, you do not have the same access to healthcare that is available to your fellow urban citizens. Currently more than 28 million Americans live in medically underserved rural communities (Office of Technology Assessment, 1990). This means that a cancer patient may live hundreds of miles from the nearest oncologist; a heart attack victim may have no access to a cardiologist; or an elderly person with pneumonia may simply have no doctor in town at all. The irony in this is that the U.S. population located in rural areas tends to be poorer and sicker and consequently in greater need of health care. Yawn (1994, p. 2) explains that residents of rural areas are unique in that they "tend to be more conservative, more self-directed, less well educated, older, poorer, more likely to be self-employed or unemployed, and more likely to have an acute or chronic illness." Unfortunately, it is very difficult to recruit any type of physician to a rural setting, and as a result there is a serious shortage of primary care physicians in rural areas of the United States (Vanselow, 1990).

Rural areas face a number of serious challenges that threaten the very existence of their healthcare infrastructures. The problems currently facing rural healthcare systems include professional isolation, lack of access to specialists, declining hospital use, discontinuity of care when patients are transferred to tertiary centers, financial difficulties, and trouble recruiting and training physicians (Kane, Morken, Boulger, Crouse, & Bergeron, 1995). Although levels of severity differ, virtually all rural communities share similar problems.

There is, however, hope for rural residents. Telemedicine has been offered as one possible solution to some of the problems that currently plague rural healthcare. Telemedicine has been defined in a variety of ways ranging from very specific to more general. A number of those involved in telemedicine view it solely in terms of the technology. Park (1974), for example, defined telemedicine as the utilization of interactive, or two-way, television to provide health care. Higgins, Conrath, and Dunn (1984, p. 285) broadened the definition somewhat by defining telemedicine as the "use of telecommunications technology to assist in the delivery of health care." Willemain and Mark (1971) simply describe telemedicine as a situation in which the physician diagnoses or treats a patient who is at a different location, but Bennet, Rappaport, and Skinner (1978) used the term "telehealth" to include education, administration, and patient care.

Traditionally, telemedicine occurs when a physician or other health-care provider sits in front of a device that enables him or her to talk to and see a patient at a remote site, which can literally be hundreds or thousands of miles away. The health provider diagnoses or treats the patient just as he or she would if the patient were in the same room, except that there is a monitor between them. In many ways, the provision of healthcare via telemedicine is very similar to traditional, face-to-face delivery. Physicians interview patients; they synchronously listen to heart and breath sounds; they look at the coloring and disposition of the patient. Yet there are some differences as well. The physician is dependent upon the heath provider at the rural end to quite literally be his or her hands. So for example, when using a telemedicine stethoscope, the specialist is dependent upon the nurse to place the remote stethoscope upon the patient's chest and to move it as directed. (See Figure 18.1.)

Telemedicine actually has a rich and interesting history. The technologies paralleling the current notion of telemedicine developed in the late 1950s in Omaha, Nebraska. Wittson, Affleck, and Johnson (1961) were the first to employ telemedicine when they set up telepsychiatry consultations between the Nebraska Psychiatric Institute in Omaha and the state mental hospital 112 miles away. In the 1970s, there was a flurry of telemedicine activity as several major projects developed in North America and Australia, including the Space Technology Applied to Rural Papago Advanced Health Care (STARPAHC) project of the National Aeronautics and Space Administration (NASA) in southern Arizona; a project at Logan Airport in Boston, Massachusetts, and programs in northern Canada (Dunn et al., 1980). This growth in telemedicine during the 1960s and 1970s came to a screeching halt in the 1980s as federal funding opportunities dried up. However, the 1990s have evidenced a rebirth of this healthcare technology for a variety of reasons. The technology itself is faster, better, and cheaper. The current political climate of impending healthcare reform has also led to a search for alternatives in the delivery of health services. So, not surprisingly, telemedicine programs have increased from

**FIGURE 18.1.** Dr. Gary Doolittle, an oncologist at the University of Kansas Medical Center, treats a patient located 250 miles from where he sits in Kansas City, Kansas. On the left monitor, Dr. Doolittle sees the patient and nurse located at the remote site. On the right monitor is the image of Gary Doolittle being sent to the rural site. On the table in front of Dr. Doolittle sits an electronic stethoscope, which enables a physician to synchronously listen to heart and breath sounds of a patient located many miles away.

four in 1991 to 26 in 1994. With the number of telemedicine programs doubling each year since 1993, projections are for at least 50 active programs in 1995 (Allen & Allen, 1995).

As perhaps the most innovative technology to be introduced in the healthcare arena, telemedicine has a potentially bright future. At this point, the crucial challenge facing telemedicine proponents is learning how to manage development and growth. The proliferation of programs is rather certain in the near future, yet currently we are just beginning to understand organizational issues related to new healthcare innovations. For most of the programs, questions remain unanswered regarding issues of power and authority, interpersonal stress and technostress (stress from new job-related technology), information load, conflict management, role expectations, and ethics, just to name a few. The purpose of the following case study is to illustrate some of the crucial organizational communication issues that unfolded as a telemedicine program was created, launched, and developed at the University of Kansas Medical Center (KUMC).

## TELEMEDICINE AT KUMC

The University of Kansas Medical Center is the sole medical school for the state of Kansas. With campuses in Kansas City and Wichita, the medical center's mission is to provide healthcare education and to supplement clinical services for residents throughout the state. In 1989, a rural Kansas pediatrician, weary of weather-related cancellations of specialty clinics, approached KUMC for a solution to this problem. In late 1991, a telemedicine demonstration project was launched between KUMC in Kansas City and a KUMC outreach office located in a rural town 250 miles west. By 1994, there were telemedicine systems in seven rural Kansas medical facilities. Initially, the Information Technology Department was in charge of implementing and coordinating telemedicine services. The focus was on implementing a safe and effective medical technology.

By 1994, the telemedicine program appeared to be functioning adequately. Preliminary data indicated that patients were satisfied with telemedicine consultations. Feedback from physicians indicated that they saw telemedicine as a viable tool for many medical services. However, telemedicine providers expressed frustration with low utilization of the telemedicine system for consultations and general confusion about and dissatisfaction with the way telemedicine was being run. It became clear that organizational issues were having an impact on the effectiveness of the telemedicine program. This case study chronicles the early years and focuses on present problems by showcasing key players who contributed to the program's growth and development.

This research project was launched in the spring of 1994. Three data-collection methodologies were employed to study KU's telemedicine program. During the *observation phase*, which occurred during the entire data-collection process, about 100 hours were spent observing telemedicine participants at work. Observations included a variety of telemedicine consultations, periodic shadowing of the scheduler at KUMC, at least one full day at each of the seven rural telemedicine sites, and 6 weeks at KUMC. During the *interview phase*, approximately half of the telemedicine providers in the state were interviewed. Of these, 75% of the subjects ($n = 27$) came from the six rural sites, and the other 25% ($n = 9$) came from the University of Kansas. Interview participants included administrators, nurses, therapists, technicians, physicians, and clerical staff who participated in providing telemedical care. Interview data provided input into the construction of a survey that was mailed to all telemedicine providers and that had a 74% response rate. The survey asked for information regarding structure and boundaries, goals, leadership, decision making, and membership roles and responsibilities. The following case study is based on the data generated from observations, interviews, and the survey.

## THE CASE IN KANSAS

Don Page tossed and turned and finally gave up on trying to sleep. The bright red digital numbers on his alarm clock told him that it was 3:15 A.M. How much longer could he continue the stress of being one of two pediatricians for the entire town of Lincoln? This meant he had to be on call every other night. It wasn't the emergency calls that were so stressful. These were the easy ones, because there was no choice to make—he threw on his clothes and got to the hospital. No, it was those young children with moderately high temperatures. He soothed the parents by telling them how to treat the fever and asked them to bring the child to the office in the morning. Then, for the rest of the night he prayed that it was not some terribly serious disease that could threaten the child's life. Don sighed; he wasn't going to get any more sleep on this night.

He quietly climbed out of bed to avoid waking his wife and went to look out the window. Don groaned as he saw the snow coming down in drifts. This meant that once again the pediatric cardiologist from Kansas City wouldn't be able to fly into Lincoln for his monthly clinic for the children with various heart problems. Some of these children desperately needed to see a specialist this month. This would mean that their parents would have to drive the 5 hours from Lincoln to Kansas City for access to this type of specialty care for their children. Yet the citizens in Lincoln have it easy compared to more rural Kansas towns. Bob thought about his patients who drove from Bigelow, Kansas (about 60 miles from Lincoln), just to see him. There was no pediatrician in Bigelow, and only one family practitioner for the entire town. The more Don thought about the health-care situation for the folks in western Kansas, the more frustrated he got. He decided it was time to do something about it.

The next day, Don Page called the Information Technology Division at several hospitals in the state challenging them to come up with a solution to the health woes of rural Kansans. Rich Franklin at KUMC in Kansas City called him back and invited him to come to Kansas City to meet with him. Don was a little bit nervous as he drove from Lincoln to Kansas City in 1988 to meet with Rich Franklin. As a retired Air Force general, Rich had a reputation for being pushy and opinionated. When Don Page met Rich, he thought Rich's reputation was warranted. He also found that Rich Franklin was determined to find a solution for rural Kansas.

It wasn't long before Rich Franklin and his Information Technology staff found a potential solution: telemedicine. Interactive video technology offered the ability to let physicians see and hear patients without having to leave Kansas City. However, there was a host of issues to work out before the technology could be implemented. Rich had to come up with project funding, which he found through a state grant. Rich also had to come up with a telecommunication infrastructure that would enable the telemedicine machines to talk to one another over long distances. He found the answer in the state phone company, and by 1990 the telecommunication backbone was in place throughout the state.

Suddenly KUMC was in business. Within a year, the first telemedicine connection was made between KUMC in Kansas City and the KU Area Health Education Center (an outreach office for KUMC) in Lincoln. Don Page was ecstatic; his dream had come true. Or so he thought.

## The First Years of Growth

Initially, Don and Rich were very enthusiastic about telemedicine. For the first few months, they busily tested various applications and recruited a handful of other believers to work with them on this "salvation" for medicine. Antonio Morelli, a pediatric cardiologist, was very active in performing efficacy tests on the stethoscope equipment. Ace Allen, an oncologist, implemented oncological care via telemedicine while simultaneously launching a research agenda that would garner international attention within 2 years.

For the first 12 months, Rich Franklin maintained total control of all telemedicine activity. He insisted that either he or his right-hand man run the equipment for any telemedicine event. However, as the information technology director for KUMC, Rich had many responsibilities beyond telemedicine. So he decided to hire a technical coordinator to "do whatever was needed" for telemedicine. Rich hired Kelly Kraus, who came from California with several years of technical experience in the movie industry. Kelly came on board in 1993 anxious to fulfill his job description of "doing what was needed."

By 1993, Don and Rich and Kelly were getting discouraged. There were now five telemedicine sites in Kansas, yet the actual volume of medical consultations was disappointingly low. Instead, the vast majority of activity was for meetings and some educational use. In an impromptu phone conference to discuss the current status of telemedicine, Rich said to Don and Kelly, "I don't get it. We put the technology out there. We know it works. Yet rural physicians just don't seem to want to use it for consults." Kelly Kraus chimed in, "I know. I sit here and sit here and the phone just doesn't ring." Don Page listened in frustration. By this time, he had changed his whole lifestyle to devote himself to telemedicine. He had quit practicing medicine and had been hired by the executive vice chancellor's office at KUMC to work on telemedicine. However, Don continued to live in Lincoln because he felt it was important for KU to have someone in rural Kansas. Don decided to break the news to Rich that he had decided to drop down to half time with KUMC and would be accepting a half-time appointment with the private hospital in Lincoln to "do telemedicine" for it as well. Don continued to tell Rich and Kelly that he knew that there was something wrong with telemedicine in Kansas; he just didn't know how to fix it. All three men sighed and hung up their phones in frustration.

## The Rural Perspective

It was a cold, wintry day in Belmont, Kansas, when hospital administrator Jay Fenster picked up his phone to call his friend Leigh Pine who ran the hospital in Bigelow. When Jay and Leigh got on the phone, they made their usual jokes about city life in Belmont and Bigelow (towns with less than 1,000 people), which housed the hospitals that supported farmers sprawled throughout their huge respective counties. Eventually, Jay brought up the subject that had prompted him to place his call to Leigh.

"Listen, Leigh. We've decided to purchase telemedicine equipment and get a program going. But we need some help. The problem is, I just can't find anybody to call and ask. I've called KUMC and there's no telemedicine office. I can't find anybody in charge of telemedicine in Kansas. Do you have any ideas?"

"Jay, this is just the beginning of your troubles. We've had our system in for a while now but are very unhappy with the progress we've made and the level of our utilization. But it's just so darn tough to try to use this thing. Let me give you an example. The other day our local doctor had a patient that he wanted to refer to a psychiatrist for a consultation. He thought that the telemedicine system would be a good way to get this patient fast access with a psychiatrist and prevent him from having to travel a long distance. Well, here comes the nightmare. We call KUMC's psychiatric department in search of a psychiatrist for this consult. Nobody in that department has heard of telemedicine before and they all think we are nuts—no pun intended, Jay. It took my nurse six calls to finally just find a psychiatrist. Then it took her an additional three calls with the psychiatrist to schedule his time for the consult. Then we had to schedule our own room and make sure someone would be free to present the patient from this end. Then, we had to call this Kelly Kraus guy at KUMC to schedule their room and his time. Then we had to call the state agency to reserve the line time for the consult. Then our local doctor asked us if we had asked the psychiatrist if he wanted any special tests done prior to the consult. So we called the psychiatrist, and sure enough he wanted to see some blood workups to rule out any physiological causes. It took us over 16 phone calls just to SET UP the consult. Then the actual day of the consult, we had some audio problems and had no idea who to call for help. This thing is a nightmare to use!"

"Well, Leigh, you certainly haven't made me feel any better."

"Jay, to add insult to injury, our local physician has refused to use the system on several specific occasions. When I finally confronted him about it thinking maybe he was afraid of the technology, he admitted that nobody had ever educated him about specific applications for his patients. He asked if a postsurgical patient could be seen over the system for a follow-up visit to see if the wound had healed properly or if a patient with a seizure problem could be seen by a neurologist? And, he added, that it was easier to just send his patients to specialists in Kansas City that he knew from medical school. He knew he could trust these people because they were old friends."

"Well, Leigh, I'm not sure where we'll go from here."

"Jay, hang in there. Somehow we made things happen and you will as well. Good luck."

About 9 months later, Jay related this story when I was in Belmont. He seemed impressed that someone from KU had driven out to talk to him. He thought no one at the Medical Center would ever come to him. During the interview, he was quite open when asked about a wide range of issues concerning telemedicine. He said that he had not meant to talk for more than 2 hours, but there were just so many stories about how telemedical care was delivered to patients. As I walked to my car, I couldn't help but wonder how the telemedicine program in Kansas had become world famous with all the organizational problems Jay discussed.

## Meanwhile, Back in Kansas City

By the summer of 1994, Rich Franklin, the information technology director, retired and moved to South Carolina. His replacement, Andrew Davis, was radically different from Rich. Andrew Davis was a physician who loved computers and technology and was always thinking about where KUMC should be in 5 years. He didn't worry about details; he thought other folks could handle these. However, he did recognize early on that all was not right with the telemedicine program. Among other things, he knew the telemedicine technician he had inherited, Kelly, was qualified to run the equipment, but he also knew that was not enough to make the program successful.

In September 1994, Andrew, Ace Allen, and I gave presentations about KU's telemedicine program at a national organization of healthcare management information system professionals in Washington, D.C. Our conclusion was that Kansas was not like the movie *A Field of Dreams;* you just couldn't put the technology out there and expect people to come. We agreed that the technology itself mandated a unique organizational infrastructure to facilitate this kind of healthcare.

The week after we returned to Kansas City, Andrew began to argue to the chief administrator at KUMC that it was a mistake for telemedicine to be housed in the Information Technology Department. His department was a support department that simply serviced technical needs. It would never be capable of providing the organizational structure needed for a telemedicine program, he argued. After several months, the executive vice chancellor agreed to move telemedicine to an academic department, Family Medicine, where Ellen Winters was the chair. Ellen was known throughout KUMC as a "mover and shaker who got things done." Although her plate was full with efforts to move primary care to the forefront of medical education, she was excited at the prospect of revamping telemedicine at KUMC. With Andrew and Ace's encouragement, Ellen created the position of director of telemedicine services. The job required a revamping of the way telemedicine services were delivered to residents in Kansas. In the summer of 1995, I was appointed director of telemedicine services and formally became part of the next phase of Kansas's telemedicine program.

## Telemedicine's Second Life at KUMC

Ellen Winters created a new division within her Family Medicine Department at KUMC to house the telemedicine program, which she named Information Technology Services and Research. Even though Andrew Davis argued that this name would create confusion with the Information Technology Department, which he ran, Ellen decided to give the division this name to reflect its ultimate goal of disseminating all kinds of technologies to rural Kansas. My job was to run the services side of the program, and Ace Allen was to run the research side. Ellen recognized that in some ways our jobs would overlap, but she knew that we had developed a good working relationship and assumed we would negotiate our roles as we went.

Even though I had been involved in the telemedicine research for over a year, I was not prepared for the outstanding organizational issues within the KUMC as a whole. While there was a lot to do to determine the state of telemedicine in Kansas, there was a lot of uncertainty about the role of telemedicine in KU's Medical Center.

Our initial challenge was to design a service we called "one stop telemedicine." In an effort to save rural sites the dozens of calls necessary to set up a consult, we implemented a hot line whereby one KUMC contact would schedule the room and line time for the rural requester. A number of people were involved in organizing "one stop telemedicine," and not surprisingly, some did not like the changes. Paving the way for change is never easy; failing to solicit the advice of those involved in having to change will undoubtedly create tensions. The director of the department that coordinated planning of the rooms at KUMC was one such person who had not been involved in the "one stop" concept, and she was not happy with the changes we were trying to implement. The change meant rural sites would no longer have to call her department.

She said that her department had taken over scheduling the room and line time at KUMC because the Information Technology Department had done such a dismal job. "We're finally doing it right and you want to change? So that the rural requester calls you and then you call us?" she asked.

She spent weeks fighting this change, but finally the change was made. Telemedicine could finally be scheduled with one phone call to the Medical Center, even though the rural participants reported that the new process was much improved and the departments who lost first contact with the rural sites vented their anger at all of us who were pushing the next plan.

Another goal of the plan to revamp the telemedicine program at KUMC was to develop readily accessible clinical and educational services. For example, input from administrators and physicians at the rural telemedicine sites indicated that they were looking for the opportunity to obtain more continuing education in their own hospitals so that they would not have to leave town. KUMC had sporadically been using the telemedicine system to provide physicians with continuing medical education (CME), education legally required for physicians to maintain their licensure. We decided that a more systematic approach to CME through telemedicine could provide physicians with more classes to meet their needs. To do this, it was necessary to pull together all the KUMC personnel located centrally in Kansas City and at outreach offices throughout the state who were responsible for coordinating CME. At first some of these continuing education coordinators argued that it could not be done. Those who had been running continuing education in northeast Kansas for some time felt that physicians could not come to CME offered via telemedicine. Others warned that we could not "just throw a program together in two months." However, other continuing education coordinators were more visionary. Rita White from northwest Kansas argued that "this could be just the tool that offered KUMC a marketing advantage over other hospitals trying to take educational business away from us."

The project took weeks of hard work and coordination among the people who organize and provide CME for physicians throughout the state; after just 3 months, however, the program was considered a success. But some staff in the continuing education department at KUMC were questioning why those of us from the telemedicine program were "doing continuing education. After all, it should all come from our department." Just like the reorganization of scheduling, developing a more systematic approach to continuing education heightened the visibility and viability of telemedicine at KUMC, but neither change came without considerable negotiation with those involved.

After just 6 months, we had hired a full-time scheduler, and two physicians had been recruited to act as liaisons with the physicians at the KUMC in Kansas City and in Wichita. As a result, KUMC had a deep repertoire of specialty physicians providing services over the telemedicine system. There was a broad range of telemedicine services now readily available to rural Kansas and accessing those services was now fairly easy. Yet there still was no rural liaison dedicated to traveling the state to train and educate folks about telemedicine. There was also a need for continued funding for the project. It was pretty clear that the program needed more financial support than the Medical Center had allocated. However, more was needed than financial support. We struggled with a bigger question concerning the long-term direction the telemedicine program should take. Even though those of us close to the program knew of its problems, top administration continued to view telemedicine at KUMC as one of the positive things being offered by the university.

In an early winter meeting in 1995, Ace Allen, Ellen Winters, and I presented our plan to the Medical Center's top administrators. Among them was the new chief executive officer, who really knew nothing of the program's turbulent history. He only knew that Ace Allen was famous because of his telemedicine work. We explained that KUMC's telemedicine program was at a crossroads. Telemedicine could go in two directions, but it could not effectively proceed in both. The first path would require that KUMC's telemedicine program operate as a head-on competitor with other telemedicine programs that were springing up at private hospitals throughout the state. In this case, telemedicine would compete with the growing number of programs seeking to garner telemedicine market share. The advantage of this road seemed obvious: the generation of revenue for KUMC. However, the main disadvantage was the amount of resources KUMC would have to provide in order to allow telemedicine to compete on an equal footing with other private telemedicine programs. There was the example of the internationally known psychiatric hospital that was offering to pay for all hardware and telecommunication expenses for any rural hospital who would refer only to them.

On the other path, KUMC telemedicine would become the state facilitator. KUMC would continue to provide telemedicine services, but it would also act as a centralized state resource. For example, when an out-of-state telemedicine program asked KUMC to coordinate a means for it to link up with all the sites in Kansas, KUMC would serve to facilitate that connection. The advantage of this path lay in providing a funding niche for KUMC in a telemedicine market that is growing increasingly competitive.

Perhaps the choice of paths was symbolic of the ambiguous mission of the entire medical center. Was a state medical center that ran a hospital supposed to compete just like any private health facility or was it instead to serve solely as the educational resource for the entire state? The Medical Center's administration continues to debate this choice for the organization as a whole as well as for the telemedicine program.

## The Present

Later that same November, I flew to Owensville, Kansas, located about 350 miles west of Kansas City. The local hospital in Owensville was one of the recipients of a federal telemedicine grant to fund equipment for its hospital. The grant provided almost $50,000, which meant that the hospital would have to come up with another $30,000 to cover additional hardware and telecommunication expenses. The rural physicians were very excited about the grant. They were very familiar with telemedicine and knew many of the KUMC doctors who provided consultations via telemedicine. Yet the hospital administrator, Sam Long, was rather guarded in his enthusiasm. Sam worried about whether telemedicine would meet his hospital's needs. As the head of this hospital, Sam was showing hesitancy in accepting the grant funds. He was concerned about the potential changes the technology might mean for healthcare in Owensville. He worried about how it might impact the need for rural healthcare providers if people could just sit in front of the telemedicine equipment and access physicians from all over the world.

Sam was also unsure of how to handle what he called the "inevitable role conflict and overload" that this technology would cause. He didn't have adequate funds to hire a full-time telemedicine coordinator, so he had decided that the hospital's education director, Sheila Filmore, would also be the interactive video coordinator. At dinner that evening, Sheila had asked me how she would balance these two jobs. Which should have priority? How should she decide who should run equipment during interactive video (ITV) events or which hospital a nurse should get pulled from to present a patient over the telemedicine system during a telemedical consult?

As I flew home, I thought about Sam's concerns; they were quite legitimate. Just a short year ago, a rural site contemplating whether to implement a telemedicine system had no formal office to call to ask for help. There was no formal telemedicine leadership or accountability at KUMC. In the new system, someone from KUMC would go to Owensville to assess their physical facility and would help them select an optimal room to house equipment and make recommendations for room modifications. Again, a year ago this would have been next to impossible because the staff was chained to KUMC because there was nobody else to schedule events or run equipment. Even 9 months ago, Owensville would have had great difficulty scheduling a medical consult. It would have been virtually impossible for Sheila to be the education and ITV coordinator because it would have taken her all day just to schedule events. There certainly wouldn't have been the availability of such a wide array of subspecialists willing to do consultations via telemedicine without the vital communication link played by the physician liaisons.

Yet we still had a long way to go. We needed to strengthen the communication linkage with rural Kansas by having a full-time liaison who traveled the state on a regular basis to address concerns, answer questions, and provide training.

Internal working relationships with other KUMC departments had vastly improved, though there were still several departments that feared this technology might make them unnecessary. A secretary at a KUMC outreach office in Lincoln voiced concern about the need to fund expensive outreach offices in the state if people could hold meetings, educational sessions, and clinical consults via this technology. How would this ultimately affect her job? I wondered if we would discover the appropriate balance of seeing people face-to-face in person and over an interactive video system? I was also still waiting for an answer to the unclear mission of our telemedicine program. Were we to be a centralized resource for the entire state or a program that aggressively sought to obtain "more business" via telemedicine?

## KEY TERMS

CHANGE: occurs when organizational members are expected to perform their job functions in a new or different way.

DATA COLLECTION METHODOLOGIES: the strategies and tools employed to gather information in a research project.

DELIVERY OF TELEMEDICAL CARE: provision of medical services via telecommunication technologies.

INFORMATION LOAD: the amount of information an individual processes.

INTERACTIVE VIDEO TECHNOLOGY: means by which two or more parties participate in a mediated event where simultaneous audio and video communication occurs among all participants.

LEADERSHIP: an individual's attempt to influence others to accomplish group goals.

MISSION: broadly defined purpose of an organization.

ROLE CONFLICT: contradictory or inconsistent expectations of a person in a particular position.

ROLE EXPECTATIONS: the jobs and functions an individual anticipates he or she is responsible to fulfill.

ROLE OVERLOAD: when a focal person has multiple roles that he or she is unable to fill because of competing demands on his or her time and energy.

STRUCTURE: social system created through communication.

TECHNOSTRESS: anxiety or tension experienced by an individual when new job-related technology is introduced.

TELEMEDICINE: the use of telecommunication technologies to provide medical information and services. Physician and patient are at two different sites and consults are made through video technology.

## DISCUSSION QUESTIONS

1. What factors have prompted the need for new communication technologies in healthcare?
2. Are there universal communication issues that must be addressed in any organization, regardless of whether it is based on a technology or not? If so, what are these issues?
3. How important is a clear mission to the success and effectiveness of the telemedicine program?
4. Compare and contrast telemedicine with the traditional delivery of healthcare in terms of such attributes as potential speed of communication, sensory channels employed, development of interpersonal relations between and among healthcare providers and patients, and how healthcare providers organize themselves.
5. Discuss potential ethical issues related to telemedicine.
6. What should the formal structure of a telemedicine program look like?
7. What impact did the creation of formal leadership have on this telemedicine program?
8. What are the outstanding organizational issues from KUMC's point of view? From a rural site's point of view?
9. How should KUMC address the potential technostress felt by telemedical providers?
10. Is it possible that the real concern people felt about telemedicine was because telemedicine represented "change"? If so, how should KUMC go about introducing this "change" to new telemedicine sites?

## REFERENCES

Allen, A., & Allen, D. (1995). Telemedicine programs: Second annual review reveals doubling of programs in a year. *Telemedicine Today, 3*(1), 10–14.

Bennet, A. M., Rappaport, W. H., & Skinner, E. L. (1978). *Telehealth handbook*

(Publication No. [PHS] 79-3210). Washington, DC: U.S. Department of Health, Education, and Welfare.

Dunn, E., Conrath, D., Acton, H., Higgins, C., Math, M., & Bain, H. (1980). Telemedicine links patients in Sioux Lookout with doctors in Toronto. *Canadian Medical Association Journal, 22,* 484–487.

Higgins, C. A., Conrath, D. W., & Dunn, E. V. (1984). Provider acceptance of telemedicine systems in remote areas of Ontario. *Journal of Family Practice, 18*(2), 285–289.

Kane, J., Morken, J., Boulger, J., Crouse, B., & Bergeron, D. (1995). Rural Minnesota family physicians' attitudes towards telemedicine. *Minnesota Medicine, 78,* 19–23.

Office of Technology Assessment. (1990). *Health care in rural America* (OTA-H-434). Washington, DC: U.S. Government Printing Office, 052-003-0125-7.

Park, B. (1974). *An introduction to telemedicine: Interactive television for delivery of health services.* New York: Alternate Media Center, New York University.

Vanselow, N. A. (1990). Medical education and the rural health crisis: A personal perspective from experiences in five states. *Academic Medicine, 65,* 527–531.

Willemain, T. R., & Mark, R. G. (1971). Models of health care systems. *Biomedical Science Instrument, 8,* 9–17.

Wittson, C. L., Affleck, D. C., & Johnson, V. (1961). Two-way television group therapy. *Mental Hospitals, 12,* 2–23.

Yawn, B. P. (1994). Rural medical practice: Present and future. In B. P. Yawn, A. Bushy, & R. A. Yawn (Eds.), *Exploring rural medicine: Current issues and concepts* (pp. 1–16). Thousand Oaks, CA: Sage.

# CHAPTER 19

# The Uncooperative Cooperative

## Attempting to Improve Employee Morale at Weaver Street Market

### THEODORE E. ZORN

Weaver Street Market (WSM) is a 10,000-square-foot cooperatively owned natural foods store, located in Carrboro, North Carolina. It was opened in June 1988 by two men who had been co-managers of another co-op natural foods store in a nearby community. The store looks like a medium-sized grocery store with a café, yet its shelves and bins are filled with organic and health-oriented products. The market was begun with a blend of democratic idealism and capitalist entrepreneurial spirit. Its mission, redefined in 1992, is

- To provide the community with healthful, high-quality, affordable foods in an environment that emphasizes exceptional service and consumer education;
- To provide financially and personally satisfying jobs in a working environment that promotes cooperation and welcomes diversity;
- To operate a profitable, socially and environmentally responsible cooperative business as a successful model of community and worker ownership;
- To engage in projects that make a positive contribution to the local and global communities.

Members of the co-op are called "shareholders." The store has over 50 employees, about half of whom are "worker–owners," meaning, among other things, that they have invested $400 in the store and have the opportunity to share in the profits. Weaver Street Market is dedicated to the community and has supported such endeavors as the relief effort for Hurricane Hugo, the San Francisco earthquake, saving the Central American rain forest, and the local high school's fund-raisers. In their first year, sales tripled initial projections. Today, the store has $5 million in sales annually.

The management structure of the market consists of a Board of Directors, a general manager (GM), department managers, and nonmanagement employees. The board consists of seven members: the GM, two worker–owner representatives, two consumer-owner representatives, and two appointed members. Ron Simmons,[1] one of the two founders, has been GM since the store opened. He holds primary responsibility for the day-to-day operations of the store, including personnel scheduling, meeting the payroll budget, profits, and sales goals.

The focus of this case is the organization's efforts to address chronic employee dissatisfaction and low morale, which took two major forms. The first was a series of changes in structures and processes, including implementing a system of committees and teams and implementing policies and practices suggested by total quality management (TQM) (Jablonski, 1991; Walton, 1986). The second way the organization attempted to address employee dissatisfaction was a series of attempts to "fix" the GM, who some perceived as the source of continuing morale problems. The interrelatedness of these two efforts is most apparent in the establishment of the Organizational Development Committee (ODC) by the Board of Directors in 1991. The board established the ODC as a response to negative evaluations of the GM's "people skills." The ODC then became the primary instigator of process and structural changes intended to increase employee participation and improve communication and morale.

I will focus primarily on the period from mid-1991 through the end of 1993, when I served on the Board of Directors of WSM and during which time the primary efforts to improve employee morale took place. Prior to that, in early 1990, I had been employed to conduct an assessment of employee attitudes and communication for the store and to conduct management training sessions as a follow-up to the assessment. As a director, I became an integral part of the efforts to restructure management and improve morale. So I was deeply immersed in this organization for a period of about 4 years.

In constructing this case, I relied on three sources of data: First, I drew on my personal experiences as a participant-observer, using both field notes and recollections. Second, I relied heavily on various written artifacts, including minutes of meetings, memos, and reports. Finally, I asked two longtime members of the organization (the GM and the personnel manager) to read my first draft of this case and to provide feedback on facts and interpretations.

In order to fully understand the efforts to improve employee morale,

I first need to trace the events that led up to them. The next section provides background on events leading up to the change efforts.

## THE EARLY HISTORY OF WEAVER STREET MARKET

Ron was in his early 30s at the time WSM opened. He is well educated, low-key, and soft-spoken and rarely displays emotions. He is highly intelligent and has an exceptional ability to grasp complex problems and offer solutions to them. In meetings, after a group had struggled with problems for what seemed like hours of disagreement, Ron would often explain a way out that made perfect sense. He is a "big picture" person; he constantly has new ideas for improving things. Yet because of the stream of new opportunities and concepts, the big picture is continuously changing, and he sometimes does not communicate the changes he envisions. This problem is compounded by the fact that Ron tends to take on every job that appears to need doing, from serving on committees to sweeping floors; while he works long hours, he often leaves little time for delegating and communicating. While I found Ron to be friendly, courteous, and appreciative, some employees complained that his only interactions with them were to correct and criticize. For example, a department manager, in an exit memo, wrote that she "received many more criticisms of what I purchased ... than *constructive* criticism or even compliments." Other employees complained that people were afraid to speak up for fear of Ron's retaliation.

Ron described the period of June to December 1988, the first 6 months of the store's existence, as the period "from euphoria to exhaustion." Sales tripled projections, bringing euphoria about the initial success but exhaustion at attempting to cope with limited staffing. Shortly after this period, management was expanded. A store manager, reporting to the GM and supervising the department managers, was hired, as was a personnel manager, a marketing manager, and a finance manager.

In the summer of 1989, the worker–owner group took a retreat to the beach to, among other things, develop and agree on a mission statement. Also in 1989, management experimented with a collectively managed department, which failed, according to Ron, "because the employees would not fire a nonperformer. I had to step in and fire the problem employee." A similar experiment in another department was ended because of the same problem. A traditional bureaucratic hierarchy evolved, with the GM meeting with the department managers weekly to disseminate information and the department managers supervising employees in their departments.

A worker–owner organization existed separately from the management structure. This organization included all employees who had bought shares, and thus it included the GM and some department managers. Its role wasn't completely clear to members. Some seemed to want it to operate as an advocate for workers' interests, much like a union, which was clearly impossible with the sizable management representation in the group.

WSM had been open about 18 months when I was contracted to conduct an assessment of employee attitudes and communication. The assessment included three focus groups and a questionnaire survey of the employees. The assessment revealed both strengths and weaknesses. The mean for the scale measuring various components of job satisfaction was 3.39 on a scale of 5, and questionnaire and focus group data showed a wide range of attitudes regarding the many facets of the store. The means for most items were between 3.0 and 4.0, indicating general but not overwhelming satisfaction with the store. However, there were some employees who were very unhappy. Two of the focus groups, one consisting of department managers and one of nonmanagers, expressed general satisfaction, even though they had areas of concern. The third, all nonmanagers, was overwhelmingly negative and very critical of management. After I presented the report of the findings to the employees, one employee followed me to the parking lot to express how upset she was that I hadn't portrayed a more negative picture. Some specific findings of the assessment with particular relevance to this case were these:

- Employees expressed a generally positive attitude toward Ron (scale mean = 3.96). His highest ratings were for being trustworthy, caring about people, and being competent. His least positive score was "communicates well with employees" ($\bar{x} = 3.25$).
- Some areas of particular dissatisfaction expressed were with the lack of participation by employees in decision making, lack of clarity in upper management's job responsibilities (upper management was defined as the GM, store manager, finance manager, and personnel manager), and keeping employees informed.

The personnel manager at the time, Mary Bains, was my primary contact for the assessment. She met with me after the assessment report to discuss potential follow-up actions. Among other things, she was interested in providing guidance to Ron, whom she perceived needed some assistance in fulfilling his role as GM. We decided to design several training sessions for all the managers, which focused primarily on leadership skills. The training focused on strategies for developing employee performance and empowerment, which seemed consistent with the store's worker–ownership philosophy. The managers, especially Ron, expressed very favorable reactions to these sessions. A tangible result was that they redesigned their manager-appraisal process to emphasize the dimensions of leadership presented in the training sessions.

Management also followed up on the assessment by developing and circulating a memo entitled "Management Response to Areas of Concern Highlighted by Employee Survey." In this memo they identified eight problem areas, a suggested response for each, and an implementation timetable. Many of the areas of concern focused on personnel issues, such as lack of evaluations and training. This document was then discussed at a store meeting, in which (as was typical) all employees were invited. These meetings were usually held about every 6 weeks, on Sunday nights immediately after the store closed.

However, when I joined the Board of Directors in May 1991, over a year after the assessment was completed, the suggested responses had either not been implemented or had been implemented initially but not sustained. All of the problems that were targeted to be addressed after the assessment were still problems a year later. For example, a former department manager said in an exit memo that she had "yet to receive a formal oral or written review since January 1989, even after several requests" and that she had received "little or no training." As a further example of the focus away from personnel issues, the personnel manager (Mary) had relinquished her personnel duties and had begun managing the "front end"—customer service and checkout. The personnel manager position had not been filled.

One reason for the lack of follow-through on these planned responses was that, shortly after the assessment, WSM learned that Wellspring Grocery was opening a store nearby. Wellspring is a very successful, privately owned natural and gourmet foods store. This news posed a threat to WSM's survival, and management's emphasis shifted to improving its financial picture in preparation for the competition. Personnel issues and organizational development efforts were put on hold. While this may have been a reasonable response, it foreshadowed a continuing trend and led to a frustration expressed by many WSM employees: management's failure to follow through on its plans, especially those focused on personnel issues.

In the spring of 1991, Mary and Ron asked me to be on the Board of Directors, which I agreed to do. I filled one of the two appointed positions on the board, positions they tried to fill with people who had expertise in areas that would benefit the store. The other appointed position, for example, was filled by an attorney. They hoped I would be able to help in improving management and organizational communication processes in the store.

Two things stand out from my first few meetings with the Board of Directors. First was the meeting process. Board members received a packet from Ron a day or two before the meeting. The packet included an agenda for the meeting, a "General Manager's Report" summarizing key developments that had taken place in the past month, and detailed financial information documenting the store's financial performance for the period, with comparisons to goals and performance in previous periods. The meetings consisted largely of the GM reviewing these documents and responding to questions from the Board members. Items on the agenda were identified as "for approval," "presentation," "discussion," or a similar description denoting the suggested means of handling them. Even for items labeled "discussion," Ron usually had well-thought-out suggestions, which he often made to initiate the discussion. Thus the communication process at board meetings in mid-1991 was largely one-way and controlled by Ron.

The second issue that stands out was my first major assignment: to participate on a subcommittee that would conduct an annual evaluation of the GM. This was important for two reasons: First, evaluating Ron's performance was a major ongoing concern of disgruntled employees and the Board of Directors. Second, the results of the evaluation were the primary impetus for many organizational change efforts.

The evaluation of the GM consisted of several parts. First, we designed surveys to be completed by board members, department managers, employees, and the GM himself. We also interviewed former board members and considered the financial performance of the store since the last evaluation. Finally, while it was not part of the group's plan, one member of the subcommittee (a nonmanager worker–owner) solicited letters from former WSM managers who no longer worked at the store. These were uniformly critical of Ron. While we read them and were influenced by them, they did not play an explicit role in the evaluation report. The primary reason for not including them more explicitly was that they were given to us after the evaluation committee's report was complete. In addition, the common themes in these letters echoed the concerns that had emerged from the other parts of the evaluation.

Following is an excerpt from the evaluation subcommittee's report:

> Ron's skills in the areas of marketing, operations, and accounting are exceptionally strong. He has propelled WSM to a superior sales level, developed an innovative and effective marketing program, and has a strong working knowledge of the natural foods industry.
>
> Ron's abilities in the area of personnel management need improvement. . . . Principally, one could view the substantial management turnover at WSM as indicative of this problem. Turnover is high in the industry, but primarily among hourly employees. The number of department managers who have left WSM since its inception indicates that the managers were either poorly selected and not suited to their jobs (one type of problem) or poorly managed after they were hired. Many former managers would cite the latter reason for their departure.

In discussing the evaluation, the board considered implementing a training program for the GM; hiring an assistant manager or comanager (especially someone with strong "people" skills); becoming a board-led, rather than manager-led, organization; creating a committee to address restructuring the organization to free the GM of some responsibilities; and more frequent GM evaluations. While all of these were adopted in principle, the immediate concrete actions taken by the board were to hire Kara Schwartz to act as a temporary assistant store manager and to create the ODC.

## CHANGES IN PROCESSES AND STRUCTURES: THE ODC INITIATES TQM

In September 1991, immediately after creating this action plan, the Board of Directors distributed a letter to employees that reintroduced the board and their objectives and new priorities. The letter informed employees that the board hoped to improve personnel development, motivation, and communication by reevaluating the current management structure. The board announced that they had created the ODC to explore and recommend solutions and that it would hire Kara to free Ron and Mary to focus on organizational development issues. Members of the ODC initially included Ron, myself, one other board member, Mary (as a representative of the management team), and two employee representatives.

The ODC met twice weekly at first, since we were asked to make recommendations quickly. We began by discussing our charge, discussing how WSM arrived at this state of low morale, identifying goals, and deciding upon initial steps. The minutes from the second meeting indicate "lack of empowerment and [employee] accountability were identified as major contributing factors to this dissatisfaction." We distributed an open-ended questionnaire to employees, asking for their input on changes needed or desired to improve WSM's functioning. Based on our charge and responses to the survey, we created a mission statement for the ODC: "To examine the organizational structure and management processes, with the goal of recommending specific steps that would maximize morale, communication, satisfaction, and teamwork." I had this mission statement enlarged, framed, and placed visibly in the conference room for our meetings. The ODC began researching and discussing articles on alternative management structures, such as self-managed teams, employee involvement, and TQM.

After several meetings, Ron presented a four-page plan to the ODC, complete with four major recommendations. Following are excerpts:

1. Hire an assistant manager for six months. . . .
2. Institute a TQM program in each department. . . .

3. Institute . . . functional committees and teams. . . .
4. Consolidate the functional committees with the existing worker–
   owner committees. . . .

Ron's plan incorporated ideas that others had proposed and the group had discussed. Each recommendation was accompanied by implementation steps, a timetable, and cost estimates. After discussion, the committee modified these into three recommendations that were presented to the Board:

1. Institute a system of "functional committees" to address organizational concerns that are being missed now . . . including training
   and orientation, benefits, communication. . . .
2. Institute changes in the way we work in every department. . . .
3. Hire an assistant manager to assume responsibility for important
   areas of the store that are not adequately covered.

Notice that recommendation 2 emerged from discussion of Ron's second recommendation ("Institute a TQM program . . ."). As is apparent by the more ambiguous phrasing, the entire committee was not ready to commit to TQM yet. However, TQM was presented orally to management and employee audiences as the framework we were considering for this recommendation.

These recommendations were written and distributed to all store employees. Two open meetings were scheduled in which employees were invited to attend, ask questions, and give feedback. The meetings had high attendance. While employees had lots of questions, their responses were generally positive. One of the consumer-owner board members who attended the store meetings said with hopeful enthusiasm that "something is different this time." The ODC conveyed its recommendations to the board, along with the perceived support for the recommendations given by employees in the open meetings. The board supported the recommendations. It is worth remembering that three of the seven board members were on the ODC.

In addition to the three major recommendations, some more specific changes were identified by the ODC and implemented. First, a bulletin board was cleared and set aside for board and ODC agendas and minutes; this was an attempt to keep employees informed about the issues addressed by and the progress of these two groups. Additionally, an employee suggestion process was implemented, with small rewards provided for implemented suggestions. I pushed this idea, in part because so much of the apparent payoff for our plans was long-term and I felt we needed some immediate improvements to show progress and build momentum for the change efforts. Finally, the ODC recommended that the board provide a clear sense of direction for the organization, in part by revising the store's mission statement, which we felt was too unfocused and not useful as a guide in making difficult decisions.

In the next several months, the ODC continued to learn about TQM through additional reading, ordering and watching videotapes from the Deming Library (W. Edwards Deming was considered by many to be the originator of TQM principles), and inviting a professor from the University of North Carolina Business School to discuss TQM. One important message that came from several sources was that TQM could not be viewed as a quick fix. Most recommended that the payoffs should not be expected within five years.

Tape-viewing sessions were scheduled so that employees who wished to attend could do so. It became clear to us that the question was not only whether or not to implement TQM but *which version* of TQM to implement. TQM is a set of principles, not all of which are agreed upon by its various proponents (Bowles & Hammond, 1991; Jablonski, 1991; Walton, 1986). Most TQM programs have several features in common: a commitment to continuous improvement of critical processes through employee involvement and scientific methods (especially statistical process control). However, the specific ways these are implemented vary substantially from one TQM guru to another and from one organization to another. Thus much of our discussion was focused on figuring out which version or which aspects of TQM were best suited for WSM.

We also agreed to bring in a local consultant to assist by facilitating meetings and teaching meeting facilitation skills to employees and to help us develop a means of building consensus within the store on the various organizational changes. The professor from the Business School had suggested that developing group process skills was more important in the early stages of TQM than was learning statistical process control methods, another major component of most TQM programs.

Several suggestions were submitted by employees through the new suggestion process. Initially, the ODC planned to solicit recommendations from relevant department managers on whether and how to implement suggestions, then to make the final decisions. However, we were overwhelmed with the other aspects of the change effort, so a subcommittee was formed to manage this process. A number of questions arose (e.g., concerning staffing for and costs of implementing suggestions) that the subcommittee failed to resolve, and the suggestion process seemed to stall. Responsibility for managing the process was eventually turned over to the "management team." This is what we began to call the group that included Ron and the department managers, who, like the board, began using group facilitation methods to make their meetings more interactive rather than one-way communication controlled by the GM.

In early January, after 4 months of intensive work, the ODC members felt overwhelmed by the various initiatives (e.g., implementing TQM, managing the suggestion process, revising the mission statement, reviving the worker–owner program, and reevaluating the need for an assistant manager). We decided to organize ourselves by establishing cochairs of the ODC. The group agreed that Donna Parks, a worker–owner, and I would serve as cochairs. TQM was identified as the most important priority. We worked extensively on an implementation plan, which included action steps such as building internal support for the changes, training, and pilot-testing TQM methods.

To build support from management, a joint meeting of the ODC and management team was held in which the ODC explained TQM and the implementation plan, then asked for feedback. One department manager's comments reflected the general reactions of the group: "I feel positive about the plan. My concerns are getting enthusiasm [from employees] and that it will require a lot of training, but it can be done. It'll take a lot of work." The group wanted more specifics, such as how a TQM team would actually work and whether we would adopt Deming's "14 Points" (Walton, 1986) or an alternative TQM framework. These issues were addressed in a follow-up meeting, and the management team agreed to support the implementation of TQM.

In the spring of 1992, with the management team's approval, the ODC began steering WSM through the first 6-month implementation phase of TQM. Two pilot projects with volunteer team members were selected to begin using TQM methods to solve problems, thereby addressing issues of importance to the organization and experimenting and learning about TQM methods. Subcommittees of the ODC developed a TQM training plan and a process for developing employee consensus around a store culture (specifically, a set of core values) that would support TQM. The training included "just-in-time" training by community experts for the pilot teams, monthly leadership training at management team meetings, and group facilitation training for selected employees. Additionally, employee excellence awards were given renewed emphasis and visibility at store meetings, and the board facilitated a process to rewrite the store's mission statement to make it more focused and memorable, thus more usable. The mission statement presented at the beginning of this case is what was created from this process.

## "FIXING" THE GM: EVALUATION AND COACHING

Meanwhile, scrutiny of Ron's performance continued. An April 9 memo from a new evaluation subcommittee of the board to all employees stated, "[We are] meeting at the request of the Board of Directors to develop a follow-up evaluation process for WSM's General Manager. The follow-up is focused on communication and morale issues that were identified during the Board's yearly GM evaluation." Note that the yearly evaluation (to which this was a follow-up) had taken place 9 months earlier. The evaluation subcommittee consisted of four board members—including Ron and me—and a worker–owner. We explained in the memo a 2-month process that included an employee survey focused on communication and morale issues and lunch discussions between evaluation subcommittee members (except for Ron) and small groups of employees. Additionally, the memo explained that the GM would be creating a personal action plan (to work on his perceived weaknesses) and would be coached by other members of the evaluation subcommittee.

The follow-up evaluation of Ron showed ongoing employee dissatisfaction with his performance in the areas of communication and personnel management. While some employees had positive evaluations, others expressed anger and frustration, especially at what they described as the impersonal manner in which he dealt with them, his lack of organization and follow-through, and his not keeping them informed. One manager explained his view that Ron's disorganization and focus on minutiae resulted in his waiting until the last minute on decisions, allowing no time for communication with and input from others. This manager thought Ron ended up making decisions himself, decisions that often undermined things managers had done.

The evaluation committee's report recognized that several factors made the evaluation difficult: "With the commitment to implementing . . . TQM . . . and the changing role and restructuring of the Board, WSM is obviously in a state of transition, temporarily leaving blurred lines of authority and accountability, especially with regard to Ron's role and priorities as General Manager and confusing a fair evaluation process. Also . . . focused coaching sessions with clearly defined goals have not occurred." The evaluation report noted areas of improvement, plus areas continuing to need improvement:

> TQM . . . has given Ron the opportunity to allow others to involve themselves in store structure and decisions. It has encouraged him to be open to ideas and to be supportive of ideas being expressed. Some survey responses and lunch reactions reflected Ron trying to take advantage of this opportunity—they were positive with regard to . . . his efforts to improve. Actively relating to people, holding people accountable and following-up, however, continue to provide opportunities for consistent improvement.

The report made several recommendations, including clarifying guidelines for accountability, clearly prioritizing the GM's annual goals, and 3 months of biweekly coaching sessions.

In response to the evaluation, Ron wrote to the Board of Directors to make some requests. His response demonstrated frustration in a number of areas. In general, he felt the store's focus on its "internal dynamics" was too limited. For example, he suggested the significant attention given to TQM as a means of improving "internal dynamics" was "unusual," since TQM usually placed customers as the primary focus. Second, he suggested the board had sent conflicting messages: 2 years earlier it had placed "pressure on [Ron] to be more aggressive in meeting financial goals" (when the Wellspring opening was the most pressing concern) and then, after he began emphasizing financial goals, "almost immediately de-emphasized these goals in favor of a focus on internal dynamics instead of profit." He expressed confusion at what roles he was expected to play: "I am getting the message that you would like me to exert more leadership and I am happy to do this." But, he said, many obstacles had been placed in his path to doing this: "It is hard to play a leadership role in an area that has been publicly identified as one's weakness. If the reason to begin this process was my weak evaluation (which is still mentioned frequently), it has . . . led me, particularly in the beginning, to play a more passive role." He asked that the board clearly define a comprehensive and consistent direction for the organization and to define what role they wanted him to play in this plan. Ron requested more public support from the board, along with the promised coaching sessions, and the creation of a steering committee to help guide "the transformation that we all want." Ron wanted this steering committee in part because of what he perceived was a political agenda on the part of the ODC: "In an effort not to side with management's (mostly Mary's and my) ideas, the group tends to adopt the ideas advanced by the non-management workers."

The coaching sessions took place, as planned. Ron seemed to appreciate the suggestions, and he set personal goals and reported progress on them each time. For example, he set a goal of interacting more frequently with nonmanagement employees and began keeping a log of his interactions. In addition to focusing on developing Ron's management and leadership skills, the coaching sessions became a sounding board for decisions Ron had to make or ideas he was considering. After about 2 months of coaching sessions, it seemed to me that Ron competently managed many specific issues but often failed to exert leadership in some ways that were crucial for managing the change effort and addressing the ongoing criticisms of his efforts. In a memo to Ron, with a copy to the other members of the board who were involved in coaching him, I summarized my perceptions. Following are excerpts:

> It seems to me that *your* highest priorities in providing leadership to the store's change efforts and addressing the interpersonal issues that have been the thrust of our evaluation [should be]:
>
> a) *Communicate the big picture/vision for the change effort.* People . . . need to know where we're going and why, and that what we're doing makes sense given our mission and vision. You can do this in several ways. For example,
>
> - make the store's mission statement and TQM the guiding rationale for *every* new initiative (such as the expansion, the suggestion process, more frequent store meetings, etc.). If you cannot justify an initiative with either the mission or TQM, that may suggest the initiative isn't appropriate.
> - Put yourself on the agenda at *every* store meeting for a discussion of "The Big Picture." Remind people where we've come from, what we're striving toward (mission statement and TQM vision), and what concrete steps have been and are being taken to move us toward that end. The *Market Messenger* [the store's employee newsletter] is another vehicle for accomplishing this. Hammer home these themes through multiple channels. . . .
>
> b) *Empower others to accomplish important tasks, then hold them accountable for doing so.* There are almost an overwhelming number of things to do as part of our change effort, but your time needs to be free to provide leadership *and* we need to make sure so many things don't fall through the cracks, such as training, communicating to the store, and promoting the mission statement. I believe this priority will address the criticisms regarding the lack of trust, follow-through, and accountability. [I then made some specific suggestions for accomplishing this]

We discussed these suggestions very briefly at a coaching meeting, and Ron said he agreed with them "in principle." I saw little concrete evidence that he acted on them, however.

## CHANGES IN PROCESSES AND STRUCTURES: FROM INITIATING TO IMPLEMENTING AND MONITORING

The ODC had originally been created to recommend changes to store operations that would address the problems in morale and communication identified in the fall of 1991 GM evaluation. Since our recommendations had been accepted and implementation begun, we found ourselves in the summer of 1992 asking what our role should be. As a result, we revised our mission statement to be "to monitor management processes, personnel programs, and employee attitudes, with the goal of supporting ongoing programs and recommending specific steps that will maximize organizational effectiveness, morale, communication, and teamwork." Thus the focus shifted from creating programs to monitoring them. We also reorganized, identifying the information we would need to fulfill this monitoring function and how we would get it. Finally, we agreed we needed to meet less often, given our change in emphasis.

Two other major developments occurred at this time. First, on Ron's recommendation, the board approved hiring an assistant manager for the store. The position was to have two primary responsibilities. The person hired was to act as the personnel manager, and he or she was to provide supervision to the bakery, café, and deli departments. The person hired, Mark Powell, was chosen largely because of his experience in the restaurant business, since the store had had ongoing difficulties with the café and bakery operations. He was also known to be a very effective "people person," which was important to many in agreeing to hire him. He had never functioned as a personnel manager, however.

The second major development was that the board began seriously considering a major expansion and renovation of the store. A take-out and delivery pizza restaurant adjacent to the store had failed to renew their lease, and the mall management gave WSM the option to take over the space. Initially, we considered this as an opportunity to expand the café, in part because it was physically adjacent to the available space and in part because it was the department that seemed to have the greatest potential for increasing profits. Eventually, this expansion evolved into a major reorganization and renovation of the entire physical layout of the store. This development was important because the enormity of the task was to sap much of the time and energy that would have been devoted to implementing TQM and improving the internal dynamics of the store. As an example of its effects, the newly hired assistant manager found that the planned 50% of his job that was supposed to be devoted to personnel issues was impossible. Instead, almost all of his energy was channeled into managing the expansion and the troubled café and bakery departments.

In September, a year after the ODC had been created as the primary initiator of organizational change efforts, there were three different committees focused on managing various organization development and personnel issues: the ODC, the GM coaching committee, and the TQM steering committee. It soon became apparent that the functions of these overlapped substantially. Furthermore, Ron and I were a part of each of these groups. As the coaching committee neared the end of its 3-month commitment, we merged its functions into the TQM steering committee. Additionally, the ODC membership was reduced to four members: me, two worker–owners, and Mark.

August 15, 1992, marked the 6-month anniversary of the TQM implementation plan. The steering committee formally evaluated progress and created an implementation plan for the next year. Following are excerpts from the progress report on TQM implementation:

- The management team set up only one TQM team, the "bottle project," although it was projected that a new pair of projects would be set up every six weeks.
- The management team continues to use group process and decision-making methods associated with TQM. There has not been as much emphasis on using a methodological decision-making process.
- There has been no progress toward improving the staff training program.
- At a store meeting, employees collectively identified elements of an ideal store culture. In department meetings that followed, specific improvements to be focused on were identified. . . . However, it does not seem as if, at this point, management is relaying the connection between organizational culture and TQM to the employees.
- Twelve employees have been trained in facilitation skills, and the department managers have been practicing facilitation at the management team meetings. The "bottle project" participants have received on-the-job training as part of the project.
- An attempt has been made to re-energize [the worker–owner program] through a series of three meetings of the worker–owners.

The report then laid out next steps. The steering committee met regularly over the next 6 months to monitor, revise, and communicate progress on these next steps. This committee was comprised of Ron, Carl Weeks (the marketing and communication manager), Mark (the assistant manager–personnel manager), Katrina Hopkins, and myself. Katrina was a graduate student with interest and training in TQM, who had begun observing processes at WSM on a research assistantship with me. Her contributions were so substantial that she eventually was put on the payroll as a "quality advisor" and then (over a year later) as personnel manager.

One of the "next steps" was a plan for training managers in TQM. Over the next several months, managers and others continued to receive group process training. Additionally, Katrina and I presented four sessions on leadership skills to the management team. One tangible result of this was the creation of a vision statement for the store by the management team (formally accepted in spring of 1993). Additionally, managers planned to set aside 30 minutes to discuss TQM ideas in those weeks in which we did not have training sessions scheduled. They did this on several occasions in these months, but not every week.

The steering committee also created a communication plan, intended to heighten employees' understanding of TQM and keep them informed of the progress the store was making toward its TQM goals. The plan also was intended to "generate enthusiasm for TQM" and "create an environment in which TQM principles gain top-of-mind awareness among staff" (quoted from the Steering Committee Report). This was a multifaceted plan, primarily to be implemented by Carl, the marketing and communication manager. Some actions taken over the next several months were (1) a communications audit to identify perceptions and opportunities for improving employee communication, (2) regular articles in the *Market Messenger and Quality Informer* (note the change in title of the employee newsletter) on TQM principles and updates on the progress of specific TQM projects, and (3) changing the "employee excellence awards" to "Quality Performance Awards" and modifying the guidelines to be consistent with TQM goals (formally implemented March 1993).

A "next generation" of TQM teams was created: one to reorganize the produce department, one to make improvements in the grocery department, and one to address the expansion of the deli and bakery. An evaluation after 4 months showed that each of the groups had learned a great deal about using TQM methods but had difficulty pointing to concrete improvements they had made. Only the grocery team seemed to be a clear success, which was largely attributed to the enthusiastic support of the new grocery manager, Jerry Baldwin. The bottle project team, created in March 1992, formally ended its work in March 1993. It created a list of recommendations but failed to show a tangible payoff from these.

## CHANGES IN PROCESSES AND STRUCTURES: ONE STEP FORWARD, TWO STEPS BACK

The year 1993 was another mix of progress and frustrations. The store expansion dominated the WSM scene, since it required an enormous amount of attention from the board, who struggled to negotiate alternative and changing floor plans, to address cost overruns, and to cope with the disruption to work. Similarly, the everyday operation of the store was disrupted by the expansion, which was finally complete in August. A "Grand Re-Opening" was held in September.

Personnel changes created still more difficulties. In early 1993, a department manager who had been one of the most enthusiastic supporters of the change effort died of a long-term illness. He had played a crucial role in the early days of the ODC and was a worker–owner representative on the board at the time of his death. Thus a major source of knowledge, insight, and commitment was lost. Around the same time, a new consumer-representative joined the board. Dave Chapman came to the board as a well-known local activist, the spokesperson for the local chapter of the Green Party. He came to have a great deal of influence on the board as a spokesperson for a group of employees dedicated to opposing Ron's leadership.

Another critical personnel change took place in early 1993. Carl, the marketing and communication manager, left and was replaced by Jane Billings. Carl was affectionately referred to in one newsletter as an "all round skeptic," and that certainly describes his initial attitude toward TQM. However, he eventually became a very positive force for change. As mentioned earlier, he designed the communications part of the steering committee's TQM implementation plan. He was replaced by Jane, who turned out to be a close friend of Dave's (the new board member), and another adversary for Ron. Jane showed little interest in TQM, as was evident by her changing the name of the newsletter from *Market Messenger and Quality Informer* to *Market Messenger: Musings to Munch On.* Instead of weekly articles about and updates on TQM, the *Messenger* included weekly "Affirmations by John" (the accountant) and chatty stories about employees' personal lives. Once the adversarial role between Jane and Ron developed, Ron said he felt he could do little to influence her performance, for fear he would be seen as persecuting an employee, in this case one closely connected to an adversarial board member.

That summer, Mark, the assistant manager–personnel manager, resigned to return to his old job as kitchen manager at a local restaurant. He stated that his reason was that he missed his old work, but the exit interview revealed some frustration. He mentioned being overwhelmed by the committee work and said he felt employees thought TQM was a

"smokescreen, something that is talked about for them, but it's not *seen* as something for them. . . . People come in with great expectations that they're going to be a part of it, and they're not. They're set up with great expectations. Their input *is* considered, but if the decision doesn't look like they envisioned it, they think they weren't listened to."

While he had contributed minimally to progress on personnel issues (since most of his attention was devoted to the expansion), he had been a stabilizing force, a person that employees generally liked and trusted.

The one major, positive personnel change was the more visible role taken by Jerry, the grocery manager. His leadership was given credit for the success of TQM methods in the grocery department. Jerry replaced Mark on the steering committee and became meeting facilitator for board meetings. He was considered by nearly everyone as likable, energetic, and competent, and he had 15 years of experience in grocery store management.

A major emphasis of the steering committee's implementation of TQM in 1993 was to integrate it more into the daily operations of the store. The centerpiece of this effort was an "alignment" process, in which the mission and vision statements, along with a set of standards defining "quality" individual performance, were used to communicate expectations to employees and then to align performance through a top-down process, starting with the GM, through the department managers, and down to the nonmanagement staff. The plan had four major parts: (1) "Communicate clear direction," which included communicating the vision, mission, and quality performance standards and regular clarification of direction and progress through such means as store meetings and the *Market Messenger*; (2) "Develop alignment with the direction," which addressed selecting and orienting new employees in light of the direction and individualizing expectations for employee performance; (3) "Ensure everyone's working in the same direction," which included a 360-degree assessment of performance relative to expectations, plus feedback (or "alignment conferences"); and (4) "Provide support and systems to change employee and management practices," which included means to support quality performance, such as training, recognition, and corrective action.

The performance standards were derived from the ideal store culture discussions held in 1992, plus TQM literature. They included three major areas: teamwork, customer courtesy and responsiveness, and professionalism, each of which included from five to nine more specifically defined standards. Additionally, four "quality management ideals" were identified as performance standards for managers: make employees successful, make customers successful, make suppliers successful, and make the business successful. Again, each of these included more specific standards. We intended for "alignment cycles" to last 6 months, and one full cycle was completed in 1993. Additionally, managers went through training in conducting alignment conferences, and the management team implemented the quality management ideals incrementally, through addressing one per month in training, discussion, and on-the-job emphasis.

Other positive developments in 1993 included the promotion and financial sponsoring of off-site training available in the community, the opening of board meetings to employees and inviting them to come, and, at long last, a clear, workable structure for the worker–owner program.

The revised worker–owner program clarified the role of worker–owners in decision making and clarified the mechanisms of participation. Finally, an employee grievance procedure was formally put in place late in 1993, allowing workers to address grievances with management to a council that included managers and worker–owners.

After the development of mission and vision statements over the previous year, a logical next step was a long-term strategic plan to translate the vision and mission into more tangible, operational goals. A task force including members of the board and the management team worked to develop a strategic plan, to get input from others, and to revise the plan. It was approved by the board in June.

## "FIXING" THE GM: HOPE AND HOSTILITY

Thus the summer of 1993 was a tumultuous time at WSM. The fiscal year was ending, the expansion was nearing completion, the assistant manager–personnel manager resigned, the strategic plan was completed and was ready to be translated into annual goals for the new fiscal year, and the alignment process was ready to begin its initial cycle. Not surprisingly, it was a time of excitement, anticipation, fatigue, and tension. The process of replacing the personnel manager brought the tension to a head.

Dave and Ron met in August to finalize an announcement of the personnel manager opening. Apparently, Ron had reservations about the announcement, which he suggested were shared by two other board members. Dave, however, felt he had been authorized by the board to go ahead with the announcement and insisted that they do so. Ron suggested that they call a worker–owner board member for input, but Dave said this was unnecessary. Ron's account of the conversation, detailed in a memo to the board, was as follows: He said Dave stood up and asked:

> "Are you refusing to work on the task assigned by the Board?" I told him I wanted to work on a document with him, but I wanted him to consider the viewpoint of the other Board members. . . . He said he would take the lack of a direct answer as a "no." . . .
>
> He then said, "The hell with you Ron. I've put in a lot of time on this because the Board asked me to. All of this because you can't do your job. You know you can't do your job. Your evaluation said so. . . ."
>
> I then followed him into the store and caught up with him as he was handing his draft to Jane. He said that she could put this in the *Market Messenger,* although her boss doesn't want her to. . . .
>
> At this time, seeing no alternative except a struggle between he and I in front of several employees, I relented.

Ron wrote an eight-page memo to the board relating his concerns from this incident and more generally concerns about how the board was working together, the way the board was gathering feedback from employees ("haphazard, confusing, divisive, and undermines the feedback processes that we are implementing"), and the way the board was treating him.

In the August and September board meetings, when the board had planned to identify and agree on the goals for the next fiscal year (which were already behind schedule), we spent the entire meetings focusing on our internal dynamics and considering (once again) whether we should reevaluate the management structure of the store.

At the September meeting, a message signed "Members of the Staff at WSM" was delivered to board members. Excerpts follow:

> We request that you consider the Board's historical role in attempting to improve working conditions and that you recognize that these well-intended efforts have been wholly ineffective. . . . We believe that these attempts fall short for two basic reasons: 1) attention to specific issues has lead [*sic*] to "band-aid" solutions that fail to address the severity of the ongoing pattern of mismanagement; 2) and procedures concentrate authority in the hands of a few individuals. . . . Another element of the pattern of leadership we endure is harassment whenever we outwardly express desires to improve employee representation. Most recently, this occurred following the last worker–owner meeting. And so it is with disappointment that we recognize that it is not prudent to sign this letter.

The board members read the letter in silence, with heavy sighs the only sounds. When we finally discussed it, several of us suggested that we were dismayed but that the lack of specifics about the "harassment" left us little to go on in terms of addressing the concerns. Furthermore, we had no idea whether this memo represented the view of three or 30 employees, and we were putting processes in place to address such concerns (e.g., a grievance procedure).

The end of 1993 marked the end of my tenure on the board. My last major project was the same as my first: to evaluate Ron's performance. I did so with little pleasure, since I felt that although we (including Ron) had worked extremely hard over the previous two-and-a-half years to implement changes to address communication, morale, and teamwork, employee satisfaction was little better, if at all, than it had been when I arrived. Developing an evaluation process was a monumental task in itself, since we wanted it to coincide with the alignment process, while some were adamant that Ron be evaluated under the "old system"—that is, in a way comparable to previous evaluations to see if he had improved. We ended up doing both.

The evaluations were mixed once again. There were many positive evaluations, especially by the management team and by new workers. This was an improvement, since some managers had expressed negative opinions about Ron in the previous evaluations. For example, one manager in this evaluation commented, "Ron has a belief that we can solve problems, so he always looks for answers in a positive way. Recently, also, he told me how much he appreciated my extra work. Also, he has nominated several people for quality awards."

On the other hand, long-term nonmanagement worker–owners still had more negative than positive evaluations. The criticisms focused on lack of trust and poor communication. For example, one nonmanagement worker–owner commented, "I have been in meetings here and he is so optimistic that the truth is left out. I have heard other managers report similar experiences. As for praising others for a job well done, he has not commented on any aspect of my performance in over a year—neither positively or negatively. I have no idea what he thinks and have long since stopped caring."

## CONCLUSION

After 4 years of intense, often frustrating work, I walked away from my last board meeting wondering if things were any better than when I started my work at WSM. The question is not an easy one to answer. On the one hand, communication was different in some obvious ways. More people were included in decision making and in problem-solving meetings. And the meetings were more carefully organized and were led using group facilitation methods. Roles had changed, too. The GM no longer ran the board meetings, and he played less dominating roles in other key meetings, such as those of the management team. The board had functioning officers and a clear structure, with standing committees. And I had reason to hope when I left that the store would, for the first time, hire a personnel manager who was a dedicated professional in that position. Finally, a number of programs and processes were put in place that had the potential for making the quality of work life better at WSM: the suggestion process; TQM; the steering committee; the grievance process; the alignment process; updated, more consistent personnel policies; and a better functioning worker–owner organization, to name a few.

On the other hand, TQM and our various attempts to improve satisfaction and morale were not clear successes. Quality and service had not improved in a measurable way. And, as the GM evaluation and September 1993 letter from the staff showed, there were still some people who were very unhappy with Ron, with the board, and with life at WSM generally. I take some hope in the warnings of those who have implemented TQM and attempted to change organizational cultures in other ways that such changes take time. Don't expect a payoff from TQM for five years, we were told. That seems like forever to someone in the middle of it.

## EPILOGUE

The fiscal year 1995–1996 was WSM's most profitable yet, and 1996–1997 looks to be more profitable still. Worker–owner membership and bonuses are also at an all-time high. An organizational audit by a consulting firm specializing in auditing and advising co-ops reported in 1995 that WSM had "achieved significant progress and success" given its relative youth and suggested that the organization had perhaps attempted to tackle too much too soon. The audit report suggested that perhaps members of the organization had had unrealistic expectations for how quickly WSM could achieve its "ambitious mission." It concluded that since "the organization . . . holds an ambitious vision and ideal . . . when that vision is not fully realized after six long years, frustrations, criticism, and contention arise." "Employee morale and job satisfaction" they concluded, "is mixed . . . with a good number of the staff liking their jobs overall," but "there is a definite level of frustration in some workers, and a fair amount of employee turnover."

The organization hired Katrina as personnel manager, and she left in late 1996. The personnel manager position was filled immediately, and the current personnel manager describes the morale of the store as "upbeat" with little of the rancor that seemed to characterize earlier years. She added, "Exit interviews are very positive about storewide climate. They still point to a need for more communication from top down."

The term "TQM" is not used at the store any more, although many of the processes implemented in the name of TQM remain.

## ACKNOWLEDGMENTS

The author wishes to thank Kim Weller for her help in organizing and summarizing data for this case, Krista Hicks for her help in data collection, and the employees of Weaver Street Market for their help in sharing information and insights.

## NOTE

1. All names of WSM employees and board members have been changed.

## KEY TERMS

COACHING: a process of one person or group helping another person or group learn to perform more effectively, by observing the other's performance, making suggestions for improvement, and helping the other to solve problems and make improvements by acting as a sounding board for the others ideas.

COOPERATIVE, OR CO-OP: a form of organization, typically characterized by the users or purchasers of its services having ownership in the organization. Weaver Street Market is a "hybrid" co-op, with consumers and workers sharing ownership.

EMPLOYEE SUGGESTION PROCESS: at many organizations, a process through which employees may identify problems or opportunities and recommend ways of addressing them; accepted suggestions are often rewarded with money or prizes.

FOCUS GROUP: a means of collecting data on or gaining understanding of a set of issues that typically involves a facilitator asking questions to, and recording answers from, a group of people who have something in common, such as type of job, level in the organization, or years of experience; the advantage over separate interviews is that group members can enforce, supplement, or disagree with others' answers.

JUST-IN-TIME DELIVERY: a means of managing processes, such as inventory control and training, such that they are delivered just at the point at which they are needed; often associated with TQM, the value of just-in-time delivery is that products are used immediately (and often, as a result, more completely) and the company avoids additional costs, such as the space needed to store inventory delivered too early or refresher courses for training that was delivered too early and thus not retained.

MEETING OR GROUP FACILITATION: a process for planning and conducting meetings in which one person, often not the person in charge, serves to facilitate the meeting process by staying out of discussions of substantive issues and by monitoring, suggesting, and getting group commitment to processes that will help the group accomplish its goals.

ORGANIZATIONAL ASSESSMENT: the process of systematically collecting, analyzing, interpreting, and feeding back data about organizational effectiveness, often as a first step in an organizational development process.

ORGANIZATIONAL DEVELOPMENT: any systematic intervention that focuses on changing organizational processes or structures or enhancing organizational learning to improve organizational effectiveness (i.e., organizational productivity, communication, or quality of work life).

PERFORMANCE ALIGNMENT: a cascading process by which each level of the organizational hierarchy, or each major organizational unit, sets goals deemed to contribute to those of the overall mission, vision, and goals of the organization, and individuals within those levels or units set their individual goals and evaluate their performance based on these larger unit goals.

PERFORMANCE EVALUATION: in most formal organizations, a process that involves evaluating the performance of individual employees on a variety of criteria deemed necessary to effectiveness; these evaluations are often used as a basis for personnel decisions (e.g., retention and salary increases) as well as a basis for suggesting areas for improving performance.

360-DEGREE FEEDBACK: a process of providing performance feedback to individuals based on input from coworkers, subordinates, and supervisors.

TOTAL QUALITY MANAGEMENT (TQM): a philosophy of management and a set of management practices that emphasize identifying critical work processes and problems and making continuous improvements to them through the use of employee involvement and statistical measures; sometimes referred to as "continuous quality improvement," or CQI.

VISION STATEMENT: a description of what a leader or a group of people want an organization to work toward becoming; in contemporary leadership literature, what leaders should convey and get commitment to as a means of directing people's energies and decisions; sometimes considered the same as a mission statement, although the mission is usually a more general description of purpose, whereas visions typically describe more specifically the ideal outcomes toward which the organization should work.

## DISCUSSION QUESTIONS

1. How might worker–ownership influence employees' expectations of communication, job satisfaction, and participation in decision making? What role might these expectations play in the morale problems of WSM?
2. This case raises questions about the ability of leaders to change their basic style of leading. How would you deal with Ron's apparent inability or unwillingness to change his "task-oriented" style of leadership?
3. The board's continuing concern with evaluating Ron's performance suggests they were concerned with whether he was the right person for the job. Was he? Should they have replaced him or made more sweeping structural changes?
4. One premise of TQM is that performance problems are usually caused by weak systems, not by weak people. Deming even suggests that organizations should "drive out fear" and get rid of performance evaluation systems. Was the board's focus on evaluating Ron's performance undermining their TQM implementation?
5. What is the role of communication in supporting organizational change, such as the structures and processes changed at WSM?
6. What is the role of communication in supporting a change in leadership style, such as what Ron was attempting (or what the board wanted him to attempt)?

## REFERENCES

Bowles, J., & Hammond, J. (1991). *Beyond quality: New standards of total performance that can change the future of corporate America.* New York: Berkley Books.

Jablonski, J. R. (1991). *Total quality management: An overview.* San Diego: Pfeiffer.

Walton, M. (1986). *The Deming management method.* New York: Perigee Books.

# CHAPTER 20

# Men Will Be "Boys" and Women Will Be "Whores"

## The Case of the U.S. Navy's Tailhook Scandal

### MICHELLE T. VIOLANTI

The United States Navy's purpose is to protect and serve its country as a fighting force of great efficiency and responsibility. Serving in the military is a privilege, not a right, and those who serve must be willing and able to follow orders, be obedient, and focus on fidelity. Like many other organizations, the Navy has traditions and customs associated with being a member. One of these traditions is the annual Tailhook convention.

Tailhook conventions began in 1956 as a reunion of Naval officers in Tijuana, Mexico. Tailhook is the name used to describe a hook that snags a restraining cable on a carrier deck so that aircraft may land safely. In 1958, the conventions moved to San Diego, California, and were designed for past and present Navy aviators to meet and share stories. In 1963, the conventions moved to Las Vegas, Nevada, and were held there until 1991. The late 1960s brought a symposium format to the convention as a means of briefing attendees about the weapons and developments in the Vietnam War. Over time, these symposiums became a central part of the convention and brought a more professional atmosphere to the proceedings. However, the social dimension of the convention also remained extremely important. At the end of each day, there were "no-host" cocktail parties that eventually developed into all-evening parties hosted by various squadrons in what they called "hospitality suites."

Prior to the 1991 Tailhook convention, there had been reports of inappropriate behavior at these social events. For example, at a special Tailhook Board of Directors meeting following the 1985 convention, one squadron commander commented, "Dancing girls performing lurid sexual acts on naval aviators in public make prime conversation for the media." Similarly, during the 1990 convention a civilian woman had her breasts, crotch, and buttocks grabbed as well as her blouse unbuttoned and ripped. When she described this to the male Navy officer who brought her, his response was, "Boys will be boys." Over time, these hospitality suites became very competitive, and the squadrons took great pride in outdoing each other. Navy officers believe this competition led to overconsumption of alcohol and increased lewd behaviors.

About 6 months after the 1990 convention, the U.S. Navy instituted a "zero-tolerance" policy on sexual misconduct and sexual harassment in the military. The policy was introduced by distributing materials informing personnel of what constituted inappropriate sexual behavior. Also, leaders were charged with educating individuals under their responsibility. However, the ways in which and the extent to which this education was to take place were unclear. At the same time, the Navy created a Women's Study Group to examine measures that could be implemented to improve the situation of women in the military. Regarding the zero-tolerance policy, Secretary of the Navy H. Lawrence Garrett said, "Our goal in the Department of the Navy must be to cultivate . . . an environment where actions demeaning to women are as a matter of course considered unacceptable—and even more, where behaviors and attitudes reflect respect for women and the valuable contribution they make as an integral part of the Navy team" (Department of Defense, 1992, Enclosure 7, p. 1).

Approximately 5,000 people attended the 1991 Tailhook convention in Las Vegas from September 5th through 8th. Of these 5,000, only about 2,000 were registered for the official events; the remaining 3,000 were present for the social activities that took place at the end of the convention days. Approximately 1,600 of the 5,000 people were transported to Las Vegas using the Navy's C-9 passenger aircrafts. The Tailhook Association planned an association-wide meeting; briefings on aviation safety, advance aircraft, aviation personnel issues, and aviation budget; a symposium on Desert Storm operations; a Flag Panel forum by Navy and Marine officers; and no-host cocktail parties. Except for the cocktail parties, the Flag Panel was the best-attended event.

Flag Panel is a time when high-ranking Navy and Marine officers assemble to answer "tough questions" from the audience. Audience members do not wear uniforms, so their ranks and identities are basically unknown. The forum is designed to be open and free of stifling military protocol so that officers cannot "avoid the questions." In 1991, one woman asked when females would be able to take part in combat activities. Vice Admiral Richard Dunleavy's answer was, "If Congress directs SecNav [the Secretary of the Navy] to allow qualified women to fly combat aircraft, we will comply" (*Tailhook Report*, 1993, p. 110). Generally, a new policy would be open for discussion at such a forum. However, none of the questions asked was about the zero-tolerance policy on sexual harassment, and it was not mentioned as part of the Flag Panel.

The other major event at the Tailhook '91 convention was the hospitality suites on the third floor of the Hilton Hotel. Different military squadrons sponsored these in the evening hours. Each participating squadron collected money from its members to rent the suite, purchase alcohol, pay bartenders (usually female), and provide entertainment. In most suites, entertainment included strippers, skimpily clad women, and pornographic movies. What occurred over the course of the three nights (September 5, 6, and 7) took entertainment to a new level despite a two-page letter, which included the following excerpts, from Captain Frederic Ludwig, Jr., president of the Tailhook Association:

> This year we want to make sure everyone is aware of certain problems we've had in past year's [sic]. . . . In past years we have had a problem with under age participants. If you see someone who does not look like they belong in our group, or look [sic] under age please ask for a [sic] ID. If they are under age, or do not have ID, please ask them to leave or contact Security. . . . Also, in the past we have had a problem with late night "gang mentality." If you see this type of behavior going on, please make every effort to curtail it either by saying something, calling security or contacting someone from the Association. We will have people on the floor in blue committee shirts should you need them for any reason. . . . Remember, when bringing in your suite supplies do so with discretion. We are not allowed to bring certain articles into the Hilton. Please cover your supplies by putting them in parachute bags or boxes. DO NOT BORROW LAUNDRY BASKETS FROM THE HILTON. THEIR SENSE OF HUMOR DOES NOT GO THAT FAR!!! Supplies may be purchased in town from "WOW". They have a number of items that may be purchased or rented for your suite. The lanai suites do not have wet bars. You will need to set up your own wet bar. . . . Please make sure your duty officers are SOBER and prepared to handle any problems that may arise in your suite. . . . REMEMBER . . . THERE ARE TO BE NO "QUICK HIT" DRINKS served. LEWD AND LAS-CIVIOUS behavior is unacceptable. The behavior in your suite reflects on both your squadron and your commanding officer. (Department of Defense, 1992, Enclosure 2, pp. 2–3)

While the letter acknowledges that inappropriate behavior has occurred in the past and provides indications of precautions that should be taken, it does not indicate what the "punishment" or "retribution" would be if these behaviors were to occur in 1991.

At the 1991 Tailhook convention, at least 90 men and women experienced sexual harassment and/or sexual assault. Some of the terms that were used in conjunction with these events were "shark," "ballwalking," "zapped," "a pressed ham," and the "rhino room." "Shark" was used to refer to a man who repeatedly bit women on the buttocks. Men exposing themselves (their penis and testicles) were commonly referred to as "ballwalkers." Many women, particularly those who were working as bartenders or hired entertainment, were "zapped" (had squadron stickers slapped on the breasts and buttocks) on a frequent basis. A "pressed ham," naked buttocks pushed up against a window, actually cracked one of the windows on an upper floor at the Holiday Inn; luckily, no one below was injured. Finally, the "rhino room" was the term used for Room 308, one of the squadron hospitality suites on the third floor. This room contained a hand-painted $5' \times 8'$ mural of a rhinoceros, the squadron mascot. At the point where the tusk of the rhinoceros would be placed hung a dildo that was used as a drink dispensing mechanism. Women were cheered and jeered until they went up to stroke, kiss, or suck the dildo for a "Rhino spunk" alcoholic beverage.

On the night of September 5, 1991, Lisa, a civilian woman, was standing in the patio area near the hotel pool. A man came up behind her and bit her on the buttocks. Lisa responded by saying, "Don't ever do that again." About a half-hour later, the man returned to bite her again on the buttocks and she again admonished him verbally. Later that same evening, Lisa was still standing in the pool area talking to Navy officers when a third man came up from behind her and began fondling her breasts. One of the men she was talking to said, "There are some people you don't do that to." The third man apologized but held up a "flight tag" and said, "See this ID, this gives me the right." To this man, being part of the military system and present at the Tailhook convention gave him the right to fondle Lisa's breasts.

That same night, about an hour after the incidents Lisa experienced, Sherry, a lieutenant in the U.S. Navy, was on the third floor of the Hilton in Suite 307. She and two other military officers were having a conversation when an unknown male approached her from behind. This unknown male attempted to place his hand up her dress. Sherry turned around, grabbed the man by the collar, and smashed him up against a wall. She said, "I'm a Navy officer and an aviator. Do not touch me." When the man returned a few minutes later and bit her on the buttocks, Sherry slammed her elbow into his body. The man fell to the floor and proceeded to crawl out of the suite into the hallway.

Friday night brought similar events in the third floor hospitality suites. Suzanne, an employee of the Tailhook Association, was standing in front of Room 356, an administrative suite, when a man came up behind her, grabbed her around the waist, bent down, and bit her on the buttocks. Beyond the shock of being bit, she was not hurt. She turned around. When the man saw her name tag, he got down on his knees and said, "I'm sorry. I'm sorry, I didn't know who you were." Her reply was, "You are going to hurt someone or get in trouble. You could be ejected from the convention for such behavior." The men to whom she was talking asked if she wanted them to take action or report the incident and Suzanne replied, "I'm just going to let this one go."

The worst of the behaviors occurred on Saturday night. Around 10:00, Nadine, a U.S. Navy lieutenant junior grade from California, entered the third floor hallway. Nadine attempted to find someone she knew to escort her to the hospitality suites. She found no one and when the hallway looked safe for passage, she attempted to walk through. "My arms were either held down at my sides or behind my back. I remember one guy was behind me and had both hands grabbing my breasts. I think maybe they were trying to pick me up off the ground so I was struggling downwards. I don't recall specifically how or when it stopped" (Tailhook Report, 1993, pp. 222–223). Nadine bit one of the attackers on the arm and those around began to "boo" her. During the attack, she spotted a Navy captain she knew and could not believe that he saw what was happening and did nothing about it. When he was interviewed about the incident, he denied seeing anything other than a woman punching a man in the face; he did not see what had prompted the punch. About two months after the Tailhook '91 convention, Nadine again saw the Navy captain and he told her, "men have been treating women like that since 'caveman days.' . . . It was your fault for being there in the first place. Since you're not a Naval aviator, you had no business being there in the first place" (*Tailhook Report*, 1993, p. 223). Finally, he implied that Nadine should have known what would or could happen to her if she attempted to walk through the hallway.

Lieutenant Paula Coughlin, who made the incidents at the Tailhook '91 convention public, entered the hospitality suite area about an hour and a half after Nadine. The hallway was loud and rowdy with men lining each side. As she began walking down the hallway, one of the men intentionally touched her and another yelled, "Admiral's aide!" While she was attempting to figure out who had done this, another man pinched her buttocks with such force it knocked her forward a step. She turned and yelled at the man, "What the f___ do you think you're doing?" Following that statement, a group assault known as the "gauntlet" began:

> "The man with the dark complexion moved in immediately behind me with his body pressed against mine. He was bumping me, pushing me forward down the passageway where the group on either side was pinching and then pulling at my clothing. The man then got both his hands down the front of my tanktop and inside my bra where he

grabbed my breasts. I dropped to a forward crouch position and placed my hands on the wrists of my attacker in an attempt to remove his hands. . . . I sank my teeth into the fleshy part of the man's left forearm, biting hard. I thought I drew blood." . . . The man removed his hands and another individual "reached up under my skirt and grabbed the crotch of my panties. I kicked one of my attackers. . . . I felt as though the group was trying to rape me. I was terrified and had no idea what was going to happen next." (*Tailhook Report,* 1993, p. 214)

After having her route into a few of the hospitality suites blocked by men, she finally escaped into one of the suites that was dark. She sat there crying, trying to figure out why this had happened to a fellow officer and admiral's aide.

As part of the investigation, other people who were reported to be present during Lieutenant Coughlin's attack were interviewed. In each case, the response was similar to that of a federal government civilian, "I remember Coughlin entered the hallway. . . . As she advanced through the area, the gauntlet collapsed on her blocking her from my view. I recall Coughlin wrenching around as she disappeared from sight. I never saw her exit the gauntlet" (*Tailhook Report,* 1993, pp. 214–215). Even though this man said there were approximately 100 people present in the hallway taking part in the festivities, he could not identify any of them. During the course of the investigative interviews, several witnesses attempted to discredit Lieutenant Coughlin for making the assaults public by claiming that she had also engaged in inappropriate sexual behavior. All of these allegations were second- or third-hand stories, and none of them could be substantiated.

While most of the people who reported inappropriate sexual behavior at the 1991 Tailhook convention were women, six of the reports came from men. John, a Navy lieutenant commander, was in an administrative suite when a "tall woman in a knit dress" grabbed his genitals, yelled "package check," and offered to perform a sex act for money. Also, Jim, a Marine captain at the time, had two women pull down his shorts while he was in Room 308, another administrative suite.

Over the course of the three evenings, Candy served as a bartender for one of the squadron hospitality suites. During this time, she had drunken and sober men pulling on the front of her T-shirt so that they could get a better look at her chest. Others asked her, "Are those your tits, are they real?" and told her, "I want to get down your pants." Finally, some of them were even more blatant and stated, "I want to f___ you." Even though all of these repeated comments were made on the first night, Candy returned to work on Friday and Saturday because she needed the money as a single parent to support her children. Candy did not report her experiences until she was questioned as part of the Department of Defense investigation.

Many other women were also reluctant to report their experiences. One civilian woman who attended the social events with her husband was wearing a formal black cocktail dress when a couple of men lifted her above their head. Her dress was lifted above her waist and because she was not wearing nylons or pantyhose, the men attempted to get their hands inside her panties. All of the men around were laughing and appeared drunk. Since the woman did not want to appear to be a prostitute, she went to her room and changed into shorts after the incident. When she told her husband what had happened, they jointly decided to keep her experiences silent because they did not want to jeopardize her husband's military career.

Heather attended the social events as the guest of her boyfriend, who was a Navy lieutenant. Men ripped off Heather's tube top and grabbed her breasts and buttocks while she attempted to cover herself. After the attackers finally let her go, Heather was crying and a Marine aviator came up to her. He said, "It is an annual tradition at Tailhook conventions to harass women physically and verbally in the hallway. Don't worry about it." Heather told her boyfriend what had happened and he advised her not to tell anyone because they would think she was a "slut." In a similar vein, a civilian woman's brother witnessed another military man exposing his penis and wrapping it in her long hair. When asked about the incident, the brother replied, "Even if I could, I don't think I would identify the guy. What happened to my sister was not wrong in the context of the Tailhook party. Nobody was hurt."

Just as Candy knew what to expect when she returned to work, there were women who had heard rumors about previous Tailhook conventions or experienced them firsthand and chose to attend. On Saturday night, a civilian named Pam entered the third floor and asked a male she called "Smiley" if he would escort her to one of the hospitality suites. Prior to attending the convention, Pam had heard rumors that men grabbed and pawed at women as they walked down the hallway. Despite the fact that she had an escort, males in the hallway still pinched and groped at Pam. Others knew that it was not a good idea to go to the third floor after 11:00 P.M. because the hallway could get "crazy." While most of the stories center around men inappropriately touching women, there were some men present who did their best to help the women in attendance. For example, one women's purse was dumped on her way through the "gauntlet," and an unknown military person ordered those lining the hallway to find her missing items. All of the items were retrieved and returned to her. Other men apologized for the behaviors of their fellow military personnel but felt 'ss to do anything about the inappropriate behavior because "one person can't control this crowd."

The investigative process into the Tailhook '91 convention began on Sunday, September 8, 1991, when Lieutenant Coughlin telephoned her superior, Rear Admiral John Snyder, to report the incident. He did not follow up on her complaint and several weeks later she wrote to Vice Admiral Richard Dunleavy. Recognizing the severity of the allegations, Vice Admiral Dunleavy notified his superior and instructed the Naval Investigative Service to undertake an investigation. Acting as the Naval criminal investigative and counterintelligence agency, the Naval Investigative Service has approximately 1,100 civilian investigators.

On October 11, 1991, Captain F. G. Ludwig, Jr. (president of the Tailhook Association) wrote a debriefing memorandum to all of the Tailhook Association members. In the letter, he talked about how this was the "Mother of all Hooks"—close to 5,000 people attended the convention, important information was exchanged at the symposium, and frank, animated questions were asked and answered at the Flag Panel. Additionally, the senior Naval leadership were impressed with and enjoyed their time at the convention. Tailhook '91, however, was also the "Mother of all Hooks" because of the unprofessionalism that occurred there. In his letter, Captain Ludwig included the ways in which the line of responsible behavior was crossed:

> This year our total damage bill was to the tune of $23,000.00. . . . We narrowly avoided a disaster when a "pressed ham" pushed out an eighth-floor window which subsequently fell on the crowd below. Finally, and definitely the most serious, was "the Gauntlet" on the third floor. I have five separate reports of young ladies, several of whom had nothing to do with Tailhook, who were verbally abused, had drinks thrown on them, were physically abused and were sexually molested. . . . Our ability to conduct future Tailhooks has been put at great risk due to the rampant unprofessionalism of a few. *Tailhook cannot and will not condone the blatant and total disregard of individual rights and public/private property!* . . . I need you to get these "goods" and "others" briefed to all of those under your purview. Further, I need you, as the leaders of our hardcharging JOs [junior officers], to make them realize that if future Tailhooks are to take place, attitudes and behavior *must change.* We in Naval Aviation and the Tailhook Association are bigger and better than this (Department of Defense, 1992, Enclosure 3, pp. 1–2)

On this same date, the Naval Investigative Service officially opened their criminal investigation of the Tailhook '91 convention.

October 29, 1991, brought a response to Captain Ludwig's letter from Secretary of the Navy H. Lawrence Garrett. In his letter, the secretary expressed his outrage at the events and his personal disappointment at the unprofessional behavior that had taken place at the Tailhook convention. His letter continues:

> There are certain categories of behavior and attitudes that I unequivocally will not tolerate. You know the phrase: "Not in my Navy, not on my watch." Tailhook '91 is a gross example of exactly what cannot be permitted by the civilian or uniformed leadership of the Navy, at any level. No man who holds a commission in this Navy will ever subject a woman to the kind of abuse in evidence at Tailhook '91 with impunity. . . . Last April I sent a message to every command in the Navy about the progress of our women officers and sailors. I said then that I would reinforce a position of zero tolerance of sexual harassment and I meant it. . . . Also in April, with my strong concurrence, Admiral Kelso made specifically clear in a parallel message that a Navy free from sexual harassment or intimidation is a leadership issue. Together we made certain that the whole Navy knew: "Each of you, from the most junior sailor to the most senior officer, has a responsibility to build working and living spaces free from unprofessional conduct, fear, and prejudice." The Tailhook Association most certainly did not live up to that responsibility. (Department of Defense, 1992, Enclosure 4, pp. 1–2)

Finally, the letter, based upon a discussion between Chief of Naval Operations Frank Kelso and Secretary Garrett, terminated the Navy's business relationship with the Tailhook Association. In a memorandum written the same day to the under secretary of the Navy, Secretary Garrett asked for a "thorough investigation of any non-criminal abuses or violations of law or regulation that may be associated with the Tailhook Association, or subject symposium" (Department of Defense, 1992, Enclosure 5, p. 1).

After receiving Secretary Garrett's memorandum, Dan Howard (Under Secretary of the Navy) wrote to the Naval Inspector General. He provided them with more specific directions for completing the investigation. For example, they were to look into improper use of Naval resources (especially those used for transporting people to the convention), the relationship between the Navy and Tailhook Association, the alcohol consumption and sexual abuse, and any violations of administrative policies and procedures. This investigation was to be completed within 30 days and a report of any criminal misconduct should be forwarded to the commander of the Naval Investigative Service for further action. Under Secretary Howard later modified his instructions: Only the business relationship between the U.S. Navy and the Tailhook Association should be investigated because the Navy did not have the resources necessary to do a full-fledged investigation. At this point, two parallel investigations were occurring, one by the Naval Investigative Service and one by the Naval Inspector General. From this point until April 1992, weekly briefing meetings were held by both groups with Secretary Garrett.

During the course of its investigation, the Naval Investigative Service had to hire a second agent because the number of identified victims was growing. Approximately 2,900 witnesses were interviewed over the course of the investigation. A tone of "What's the big deal?" pervaded the interviews. Many of those interviewed had no idea that what had occurred at Tailhook '91 constituted sexual harassment or even worse, criminal behavior. Regarding the gauntlet behavior and general social activities, James Ravage (a retired rear admiral) said, "The behavior was juvenile, but it certainly wasn't criminal. Obviously there was activity we weren't very proud of. But there was no one raped" (Gross, 1993, p. A-1). In Lieutenant Coughlin's statement, she used the "f" word to ask her assailants what they were doing. When he read her story, Lieutenant Coughlin's superior Rear Admiral Williams's response was that "any woman who would use the 'f' word would welcome this sort of behavior [being practically gang-banged in the gauntlet]" (Department of Defense, 1992, p. 16). Rear Admiral Williams felt that he had been misunderstood and tried to convince the Naval Investigative Service agent that he said that because he was concerned that the defense could use Lieutenant Coughlin's words to reflect negatively on her credibility during a hearing or trial.

Only assault-related information was supposed to be revealed in the Naval Investigative Service interviews. While some of the people talked about the assaults, many of the interviewees also mentioned other improprieties that occurred both at the Tailhook '91 convention and previous conventions. These behaviors included indecent exposure and conduct unbecoming to an officer. Even though these improprieties were revealed, the investigation was not expanded and the information was not forwarded to the Naval Inspector General. During the course of these investigations, none of the senior officers present at the Tailhook convention was interviewed to find out what he or she may have witnessed or in which activities he or she may have participated. Over the course of the investigation, the Naval Inspector General "determined we had a cultural problem," and "it was our contention in that group around the table, the Under and all these people, that the corporate 'we' had allowed this to take place" (Department of Defense, 1992, p. 10).

April 28, 1992, brought the first briefing and draft copies of reports to Secretary of the Navy Garrett regarding the Tailhook investigations. During the briefing, the assistant secretary of the Navy expressed her concerns at the way the investigations were conducted. Even though both the Naval Investigative Service and Naval Inspector General would have their reports ready for release within 3 weeks, they were instructed to hold on to their reports until Secretary Garrett was satisfied that the investigations were complete. Part of the incompleteness revolved around 55 pages of interviews concerning two officers suspected of improprieties (assault and obstructing justice) and placing Secretary Garrett in the hospitality suites. Prior to leaving for a 2-week vacation in Australia, Under Secretary Howard authorized release of the incomplete reports to the media because he feared a leak to the press. During the month of May, Secretary Garrett attempted to determine the options available to him for handling the incomplete investigations that indicated a potential cover-up.

The month of June was the climax of the Tailhook investigations. On June 2, 1992, Secretary Garrett wrote a memorandum to the chief of Naval Operations and the commandant of the Marine Corps about the behavior and attitudes toward women during the Tailhook '91 convention. Excerpts from his memorandum follow:

> Military officers—entrusted with life-and-death responsibilities—must embody a strict sense of what is right and wrong. Duty and honor bind them to behave in an appropriate manner, to be responsible for their behavior. The inexcusable conduct of some naval aviators in Las Vegas, compounded by their subsequent refusal to assume responsibility for their conduct, has brought shame upon them personally and upon the Navy and Marine Corps as a whole. . . . We cannot—and will not—tolerate the demeaning and insensitive behavior and attitudes of the past. Our goal in the Department of the Navy must be to cultivate through education an environment where actions demeaning to women are as a matter of course considered unacceptable—and, even more, where behavior and attitudes reflect respect for women and the valuable contribution they make as an integral part of the Navy/Marine Corps team. (Department of Defense, 1992, Enclosure 7, p. 1)

The memorandum continues by stating that all individuals involved in the Tailhook '91 scandal be held responsible. To that end, six assault suspects, 57 people identified as being part of the gauntlet, 5 individuals suspected of violating standards of conduct, and 2 individuals suspected of hindering the investigation were recommended to the chain of command for appropriate action.

Even though individuals should be held responsible for their actions, the Navy commanding officers as hosts of the hospitality suites bear an additional responsibility for enforcing the zero-tolerance policy toward sexual harassment. Thus, Secretary Garrett reopened the investigation to determine responsibility (what commanding officers knew, found out about, or did not prevent) for the activities in and around the squadron suites as well as what commanding officers did before, during, and after the Tailhook '91 convention to ensure that all individual behavior toward women was appropriate under the zero-tolerance policy. On June 24, 1992, Lieutenant Paula Coughlin went public with her story because she felt that 9 months should have been enough time for the Naval Investigative Service and Naval Inspector General to complete their investigations and bring the assailants to justice.

Because of the media attention, particularly surrounding the problems associated with the investigations, Secretary of the Navy H. Lawrence Garrett resigned on June 26, 1992. Over the course of time, the number of people accused of misconduct rose from 70 to 140; some were demoted or moved to other sections of the Navy, others resigned, and still others experienced no repercussions for their actions. Admiral Kelso was the last resignation in 1994. He will receive a total of $89,000 per year in pension because his "performance on Tailhook 'was not sufficient to offset the 38 years' of service to the Navy" (Admiral Should Not Be Demoted, April 13, 1994, p. A-4).

Since the Tailhook '91 convention and investigation, several measures have been undertaken to address the cultural problems present in the U.S. Navy and inappropriate values enacted at the 1991 Tailhook convention. Prior to the convention the Navy had distributed materials informing members of what constituted inappropriate behavior and charging officers with educating those under their purview. Following the investigation, they created an organization-wide training program on what the core values of the Navy should be: integrity, moral conduct, equal opportunity, and mutual respect. Based upon recommendations from a Navy Women's Study Group, a Standing Committee on Women in the Navy and Marine Corps was created and charged with the following:

- assessing the adequacy of present policies, procedures, education programs and other initiatives to (i) enhance opportunities for women in mainstream Navy and Marine Corps activities, (ii) eliminate demeaning behavior and attitudes toward women and (iii) ensure that all Department of the Navy personnel are sensitive to and respect the rights, concerns and contributions of women;
- developing and presenting for review and approval initiatives to accomplish these objectives;
- overseeing implementation of approved initiatives; and
- providing periodic updates regarding progress. (Department of Defense, 1992, Enclosure 7, p. 5)

While these measures have been proposed and implemented by the Navy, the way they are portrayed in the media and people's reactions to being a female in the Navy have not changed much. For example, a greater number of women are now enlisting in the Navy, but they continue by some accounts to be regarded as "aliens" and "intruders" ("How the Navy Treats Women," 1992). Similarly, bonding has been considered a "male activity" and women have been "left to attach themselves to this male system wherever they could, like velcro to a cement block" (Goodman, 1992, p. B-5). Two places in the Navy remain closed to women: submarines and combat duty. Finally, 2 years after the reports were released and the beginnings of the changes made, 4 women testified before a House of Representatives committee. In their testimony, they indicated that the women who complain of sexual harassment are the ones who end up being punished. One woman testified that she was ordered to undergo 3 days of psychiatric examination when the Navy found out she reported to her congressional representative that her superior had sexually harassed her (Schmitt, 1994).

In the past, we have seen a series of three sexual harassment cases involving different branches of U.S. government. In 1989, Anita Hill claimed Clarence Thomas sexually harassed her while she worked for him. In 1992, Lieutenant Paula Coughlin claimed sexual harassment at the Tailhook '91 convention, and that was later expanded to include the everyday happenings of the Navy. Finally in 1993, former employees of Senator Robert Packwood (R.–OR) revealed instances that they believed constituted sexual harassment. In each case, we have heard government officials claim that "We get it; we understand what sexual harassment is and are going to do everything we can to stop it." The question that still remains for the Navy is how best to convey the zero-tolerance message to its members. Until we stop separating sexual harassment as something that is a "women's issue," that happens only to women, that is seen as an "other" behavior problem, and that blames either the harasser or harassed without recognizing both people play a part in the interaction, sexual harassment will continue to pervade both organizations and U.S. society.

## NOTE

1. The events described were recreated from accounts published in newspapers, news magazines, and two publications produced by the U.S. Navy (*Tailhook '91: Part 1—Review of Navy Investigations* and *The Tailhook Report*). All of the names of Navy personnel are real; with the exception of Lieutenant Paula Coughlin, all of the "victim's" names are fictitious. All of the accounts and events are real.

## KEY TERMS

HARASSMENT-PRONE CULTURES: a setting having certain characteristics—such as an inconspicuous or no policy statement regarding sexual harassment, a male-dominated work setting, license to tell jokes that denigrate women—that indicate potential problems with sexual harassment in an organization.

PERSONAL REMARKS: comments, jokes, teasing (e.g., sexual slurs), or questions about sexuality and appearance (e.g., asking for one's body measurements) of a nonsolicitory nature directed toward a woman.

POWER: the ability to influence that thoughts or behaviors of another person; power may be emotional, physical, positional, or psychological in nature.

RELATIONAL ADVANCES: repeated, unwelcome request for a social relationship.

SEXUAL ADVANCES: an unwelcome request for sexual intimacy such as "Will you be my lover?" or "I'd like to take you to bed."

SEXUAL ASSAULT: a prolonged, intense, and aggressive form of unwanted physical contact.

SEXUAL BRIBERY: a request for sexual behavior with the promise of a reward or threat of a punishment.

SEXUAL CATEGORICAL REMARKS: sexually based comments about "women" in general or witnessing the requests or remarks of a harassing nature directed at others.

SEXUAL HARASSMENT: unwelcome sexual advances, requests for sexual favors, and other verbal or physical conduct of a sexual nature when submission to the conduct is made a condition of employment, when submission to or rejection of the conduct is the basis of an employment or educational decision, or the behavior seriously affects the person's work performance or creates a hostile working of learning environment.

SEXUAL MATERIALS: pornographic or sexually related materials or objects that are considered unwelcome in a particular context, such as the workplace.

SEXUAL POSTURING: unwelcome invasions of one's personal space and unsuccessful attempts at physical contact.

SEXUAL TOUCHING: brief, sexual, and sexualized touching such as a pinch or grab.

SUBJECTIVE OBJECTIFICATION: remarks about a woman that imply she is not present when they are said; examples include rumors about sexual promiscuity or alleged lesbianism.

SUBTLE PRESSURE: statements in which the unwelcome sexual nature is implied by the interaction's context.

## DISCUSSION QUESTIONS

1. What steps should the Navy have taken when they introduced the zero-tolerance policy on sexual behavior and sexual harassment?
2. Do you think the Navy was correct in labeling the women who reported sexual-

ly inappropriate behavior as "victims" when they did not consider them to be victims?
3. Are there more effective means that the "victims" of sexual harassment and sexual assault could have used to respond to what happened to them?
4. What type of leadership exists in a bureaucracy such as the Navy? To what extent could the leadership introduce and enforce a policy of zero tolerance for sexual harassment? What changes in leadership practices might be more appropriate for addressing the sexual harassment and sexual misconduct?
5. Is it possible for the Navy to change a culture that currently devalues women? If yes, what steps must the Navy undertake if it is truly going to change the values enacted by its members? If no, why not?

## REFERENCES AND SUGGESTED READING

Admiral should not be demoted, panel told. (1994, April 13). *Kansas City Star*, p. A-4.

Bingham, S. G. (1991). Communication strategies for managing sexual harassment in organizations: Understanding message options and their effects. *Journal of Applied Communication Research, 19,* 88–115.

Booth-Butterfield, M. (1989). Perception of harassing communication as a function of locus of control, work force participation, and gender. *Communication Quarterly, 37,* 262–275.

Cleveland, J. N., & Kerst, M. E. (1993). Sexual harassment and perceptions of power: An under-articulated relationship. *Journal of Vocational Behavior, 42,* 49–67.

Department of Defense. (1992). *Tailhook '91: Part 1—Review of Navy investigations.* Washington, DC: Department of Defense, Office of Inspector General.

Goodman, E. (1992, September 28). Navy makes right moves on Tailhook. *Kansas City Star,* p. B-5.

Gross, J. (1993, October 10). Trying to play down a scandal. *Kansas City Star,* pp. A-1, A-7.

Gutek, B. A., & Koss, M. P. (1993). Changed women and changed organizations: Consequences of and coping with sexual harassment. *Journal of Vocational Behavior, 42,* 28–48.

How the Navy treats women. (1992, September 26). *Kansas City Star,* p. C-6.

Pryor, J. B., LaVite, C. M., & Stoller, L. M. (1993). A social psychological analysis of sexual harassment: The person/situation interaction. *Journal of Vocational Behavior, 42,* 68–83.

Schmitt, E. (1994, March 10). Military women say complaints of sexual harassment go unheeded. *New York Times,* pp. A-1, A-11.

Stockdale, M. S. (1993). The role of sexual misperceptions of women's friendliness in an emerging theory of sexual harassment. *Journal of Vocational Behavior, 42,* 84–101.

Strine, M. S. (1992). Understanding "how things work": Sexual harassment and academic culture. *Journal of Applied Communication Research, 20,* 391–400.

*The Tailhook report.* (1993). New York: St. Martin's.

Terpstra, D. E., & Baker, D. D. (1989). The identification and classification of reactions to sexual harassment. *Journal of Organizational Behavior, 10,* 1–14.

Wells, D. L., & Kracher, B. J. (1993). Justice, sexual harassment, and the reasonable victim standard. *Journal of Business Ethics, 12,* 423–431.

# CHAPTER 21

## Sexual Harassment on the Menu

### SHEREEN G. BINGHAM

*— The Culture of Pasta Roma*

*Gina is faced w/ the subcultures*

Gina[1] stepped back to check her appearance in the bathroom mirror. The digital clock on the dresser flashed 3:35. She had more than enough time to get to Pasta Roma for her 4:00 interview.

Walking from the bright outdoors into Pasta Roma was like descending into a cave. As Gina's eyes began to adjust she could make out the form of someone she assumed was Mrs. Cornaggia, a tall, angular woman in her 50s, menus in hand. "You're early," Mrs. Cornaggia announced. "Come with me."

She handed Gina a stack of menus and some square slips of paper on which the word "calamari" was inscribed in black ink. Mrs. Cornaggia motioned for Gina to sit. "Calamari is the special on the menu tonight," she instructed. "Insert them in all the menus and then meet me in the kitchen. And put your coat and scarf on the coatrack behind the cash register."

Gina removed her coat and scarf and laid them over a railing. She scooted the chair up to the table and got to work. There was a flap inside the menus into which the specials slid neatly. This is an odd way to conduct an interview, she thought, as she inserted "calamari" into the last menu and laid it on top of the others. Then she scooped up her winter clothes, picked up the stack of menus, and went in search of the coatrack and kitchen.

Gina pushed open a swinging door and stuck her head into a small white room overcrowded with kitchen appliances. She stood silently, unsure whether she should make her presence known. She was startled when Mrs. Cornaggia spoke, without looking up, as though she had sensed Gina standing there all along: "Gina, this is Leonardo." Her voice was controlled and even. "Our son Tony, our number one cook, is sick tonight, so Mr. Cornaggia here—Leo—is doing his best to put us out of business."

*Leo & Bella Cornaggia*

353

Leo smiled broadly at Gina, wiped a hand on his apron, and extended it in Gina's direction. "My Bella is such a perfectionist," he said with a sigh. Gina stepped further into the kitchen with her arm outstretched. Leo took her hand in his and shook it more slowly and with a firmer grasp than she expected. He looked at Gina from head to toe. "Such a beautiful Italian girl!" he exclaimed. "You look like you could be one of the family!"

Gina extracted her hand from Mr. Cornaggia's, feeling a little uncomfortable. "What about the interview?" she asked.

"We did that on the telephone," Mrs. Cornaggia replied, as she placed the lid on the pot of sauce and turned to give Gina her full attention. "You start tonight, if you're interested."

"I'm interested all right," Gina said enthusiastically, forgetting her discomfort. "The specials are in the menus and I'm ready for my next assignment."

"Fine," Mrs. Cornaggia replied. "Please, call us Bella and Leo," she instructed. "We're all in the family here. We go by first names."

"Right," Gina responded. "All in the family. Bella and Leo. Got it."

"Leo, why don't you introduce Gina to the other girls and get her started," Bella suggested. "It's almost time for the rush."

"It will be my pleasure," Leo said suavely, squeezing his arm around Gina's waist and promenading her out of the kitchen. Gina casually escaped Leo's embrace as soon as they were through the door. She didn't like him getting so close. Leo smiled and kept walking toward the dining room.

In the dining area two muscular young men wearing dress pants and short jackets were pushing a pair of tables together. "Those are our nephews, Ronnie and Dennis," Leo informed Gina. "They're both just out of high school. My brother's kids. Twins. Ronnie's the taller one. Good boys. Hard workers."

Leo raised his voice. "Boys, come here to say hello to our pretty new waitress."

"Hello," the two men called out, laying a white cloth over the tables and rapidly assembling four place settings.

"Boys, listen to me," Leo said more firmly. "Don't be disrespectful. Come over here to meet Gina."

"We don't have time now Uncle Leo." Ronnie said in an irritated tone. "We've got more groups to set up."

"What's the matter, Uncle Leo?" Dennis asked playfully. "Are you getting too old to keep the pretty girls occupied?"

"I'll teach you a few things about occupying pretty girls," Leo called back, winking at Gina. "They have no respect for their elders," he remarked, shaking his head with feigned exasperation. "I think you'd be surprised at what a man of my age can still do with the ladies," he continued, leaning toward Gina and peering down her neckline. Gina took a step back and crossed her arms.

"Come," Leo said suddenly, glancing at his watch and adopting a more professional tone of voice. "Let's get you acquainted with the other waitresses. You'll meet the boys later." Leo headed toward the back of the dining room and Gina followed.

"My darlings," Leo called out musically as he approached three women hunched over a long counter that lined the back wall. Two of the women were preparing salads while the third placed squares of butter and ice into tiny, shallow bowls. "I've brought you a new sister."

"Good," said the woman slicing butter, eyeing Gina. "Welcome to the family. Now come here and start cutting the bread." The other two women laughed.

"Gina, meet Ellen," Leo said, gesturing toward the petite woman wiping her buttery fingers with a towel. "She's not much on formalities."

"That's just not so," Ellen said, pretending to be defensive. "I'm pleased to meet you, Gina. I'd shake your hand, but I'm afraid mine is too well greased."

"Ellen is soon to marry our son, Antonio," Leo added. "It's Tony's sore throat that has forced me to dust off my chef's apron tonight."

"And it appears that your apron has shrunk around the middle!" said a short, heavy set woman with an enormous smile. She giggled and poked a finger at Leo's protruding stomach.

"And this is our Donna," Leo announced, winking at Donna and sliding his palms over his rounded tummy. "She was a college girl like you when we hired her. But now she's an executive secretary for a big shot computer company. She only comes around when we need her on weekends. Now I think maybe she wants to be a comedian."

"I'm glad to meet you, Gina," Donna said, snatching up Gina's hand and shaking it vigorously.

"And this is my sister-in-law, Sue," Leo continued, turning to a slightly older woman who was busy garnishing salads with tomatoes and peppers. "My brother, Al, was lucky enough to make this pretty lady his bride a few years ago. Ronnie and Dennis are Sue's boys now."

"Welcome, my dear," Sue said gently.

"Thank you very much," Gina responded, feeling touched. "It's really nice to meet all of you. I'm happy to be here. Just point me in the right direction and I'm ready to work."

"That a girl!" Leo exclaimed. He hugged Gina awkwardly while he ran his hand down her back and bottom. "You're going to fit right in," he said into her ear in a breathy voice.

Gina cringed and broke away from Leo's embrace. She searched the other women's faces for validation that Leo was out of line, but they appeared to be disinterested.

Suddenly Bella's voice resounded from the kitchen. "Leo Cornaggia, where are you? We have no time for idle chitchat on a Friday night."

Leo stiffened. "I'm being paged, girls," he said, managing only half a smile. "Ellen, get Gina set up and ready for the rush, will you sweetheart?" He glanced at his watch again and loped toward the kitchen.

"Don't mind him," Ellen remarked casually, having noticed Gina's reaction to Leo. She handed Gina an order tablet and a money apron, which Gina tied around her waist. "He's just a lovable old flirt. He gets a little raunchy sometimes, but they all do. He doesn't mean any harm. It's just his way of having fun. As they say, boys will be boys!"

"I don't know about that," Gina responded.

"You just have to dish it right back to them," Donna offered. "I can get just as bawdy as they can, and I think they respect me for it."

"Well I don't know about that," Sue chimed in. "Sometimes that just eggs them on. I've always just ignored it. When they don't get a rise out of you, they leave you alone. Well, sometimes they leave you alone," she added with a chuckle.

"The main thing," Ellen advised, "and I think we'd all agree on this, is that you shouldn't let it bother you." The other women nodded. "It's no big deal, really," Ellen continued. "As long as the paychecks keep coming in, I just laugh it off."

"I guess you're right," Gina said congenially. What else could she say? This was her first day on the job and she didn't want to make an issue out of it. If the others didn't mind Leo's behavior, then maybe she would have to tolerate it, too. Was it possible that she was being oversensitive? Well, there was no time to belabor the point now.

Gina could hear Bella's voice at the front desk, greeting customers as they entered the restaurant. "Mr. and Mrs. Sorino, so nice to see you! Would you like to have a drink at the bar before dinner?" "Mrs. Elliot, hello! My, what a lovely dress. Reservation for four at six o'clock? Yes, right this way, ladies!"

As Bella led four well-dressed women to a table in the right front quarter of the dining room, Gina's stomach churned. "My first customers," she thought, as she watched the women slide into the booth and make themselves comfortable.

Gina walked promptly to the kitchen window to place her first order. When she looked into the kitchen she noticed a man she had not met yet working by Leo's side. "Mozzarella sticks please," she called out to this man, hoping he instead of Leo would respond.

"Ah ha!" Leo replied immediately. "Music to my ears! My Italian beauty needs me! But I didn't hear you clearly. Can you ask me once more?"

Gina paused. Leo was going to make this difficult. "I asked for mozzarella sticks please, for four. It's an appetizer on the menu, right?"

"Oh, yes, mozzarella sticks, one of my delicious appetizers. And you would like them for four? Such a smart girl. They are indeed the perfect foreplay to my main courses. You do know about foreplay, don't you, Gina?" The other man in the kitchen snickered.

*[handwritten margin note: everything has sexual connotation]*

"Just make the mozzarella sticks, please," Gina said dryly, rolling her eyes. She didn't have time for this. She needed to put in an order for some wine.

A tall, slender man with curly brown hair and a bushy mustache startled Gina when he popped up from behind the bar.

"Oh, I'm sorry," Gina said, "I thought you were away from the bar. I need a carafe of burgundy in a hurry. And four glasses."

"No problem." The man replied. He quickly filled a carafe with red wine and placed it on a round tray. "My name's Andy, by the way." He pulled four large wine glasses from a shelf and arranged them around the carafe. "I'm a nephew on Bella's side. And you're Gina, right?"

"Word spreads around here quickly," Gina responded with surprise.

"No doubt about it," Andy chuckled. "Like Aunt Bella always says, we're one big happy family here."

"Then just call me sis!" Gina remarked jovially, regaining her composure. She picked up the tray. "Thanks for the wine."

"Wait a minute," Andy said, stroking his mustache and looking up at the ceiling as though he were trying to remember something. "Have you come in here for drinks before?"

"No, I don't think so," Gina replied.

"Seems like I've seen you around," Andy said slowly, still stroking his mustache.

"I don't know," Gina said. "I'm a student at the university. Maybe we've run into each other on campus."

"Not a chance!" Andy replied. "School and I never got along. But my wife Teresa took some courses last year in psychology. Teresa Marino?"

"Oh, yeah, I know Teresa! I sat by her in class sometimes. She's really nice. You two are married?"

"With two kids!" he said, pulling his wallet from his back pocket and flipping out a photo of his family.

Gina glanced at the picture. "Cute kids," she offered.

"Thanks," Andy replied proudly. He closed the wallet and slipped it back into his pocket. "But I wonder when I've seen you before."

"I don't know," Gina responded, beginning to feel impatient. The tray was getting heavy and she needed to check her tables. "Listen, Andy, I've got to get back to work now."

"Oh, yeah, me too," he replied, glancing over at a man who had just seated himself at the bar. "But I know I've seen you around someplace." He squinted his eyes at Gina. "Oh well, it'll come to me."

"Whatever," Gina said casually. "See ya."

By the end of her shift Gina was psychologically exhilarated, but her feet and body were so exhausted that she practically had to crawl to her car. As she pulled out of the parking lot she reflected on the members of her newly acquired family. First there was Mom. What a tough character Bella was, though Gina thought she had glimpsed a soft spot beneath that rough exterior.

Then there were all the kinfolk. Gina hadn't been able to meet everyone yet, but almost everybody she'd talked to was somehow related to the family. Gina couldn't have asked for better coworkers than Ellen, Sue, and Donna. Each of them had rescued her at least once, answering questions or helping out with a customer, even if it meant keeping their own tables waiting. Andy was nice to have around, too. He was an excellent bartender and easy to talk to, though his small talk was distracting at times. Gina wondered if he was right about having met her before. He did seem vaguely familiar. Then there were Ronnie and Don. They were agile at bussing tables, and Gina enjoyed their energy and upbeat attitude, but she noticed that their sense of humor got offensive at times.

In fact, Gina was uneasy about the whole joking climate that was pervasive behind the scenes and especially in the kitchen. She liked the casual atmosphere; the humor and familiarity made work more interesting and fun. But on the other hand, it appeared to be routine for them to entertain each other with degrading comments and jokes about the customers. At one point Ronnie told a racist joke to mock an interracial couple who had come in for drinks. And later in the evening, when Dennis realized two men having dinner together were gay, he walked into the kitchen swinging his hips and waving his hands around on limp wrists. The others laughed along with him, but Gina felt uncomfortable. And the way the other women made excuses for Leo's sexual jokes and comments bothered Gina, too. They seemed to expect her to accept whatever Leo might dish out, as though it were just another item on the menu.

Luckily, things had gotten so busy that Leo pretty much left Gina alone after that first order of mozzarella sticks. Or maybe he finally got the message that she didn't appreciate his remarks. At any rate, Leo—Dad— was a complex character. He actually seemed to have an understanding and reasonable side. The time she got a customer's order wrong, for instance, he took back the plate and prepared a new dish without even a comment. Gina decided she would reserve judgment on the whole group and give Leo a chance.

Anyway, work was over for the night. Now it was time to relax and share the rest of the evening with someone special. Gina glanced at her watch: It was 11:30. Maybe Karen would still be up.

As Gina pulled into Karen's driveway, she could see that the light was on in the living room. She walked up the porch steps and tapped on the front door. There was no answer, so she walked in. Karen was sitting on the sofa, with her back to the door, reading a paperback and munching on popcorn. Gina tiptoed up behind her and whispered in her ear, "You really should keep your front door locked, sweetie."

Karen looked up calmly. "Where were you tonight?" she asked affectionately. "I missed you. I called to find out about your interview."

"I got the job! And they had me start tonight!" Gina said in a tone that revealed her own astonishment.

Karen stood up, wrapped her arms around Gina, and gave her a kiss on the lips. "That's wonderful!" she said softly. "Sit down and tell me all about it!"

"Gosh, I almost don't know where to start!" Gina began. "I had six tables to cover, which was plenty. They want me to work every night except Sunday plus lunches on weekends, which will leave my weekdays free for classes and studying. And the tips are supposed to be really good; mine were good tonight. All my coworkers seem okay, except I'm not so sure about the owners. It's a family business, which I like, but the wife is really hard-nosed and the husband keeps coming on to me."

"Did you come out to them?" Karen asked.

"No way," Gina replied, widening her eyes. "You should hear their jokes. Total homophobes."

"It makes me so angry that an employer can fire somebody because of their sexual orientation in this state," Karen remarked. "It's none of their business what we do."

Gina nodded. "I know. I really hate it. We shouldn't have to hide our personal lives. Straight people need to know we exist and we don't fit the media stereotypes. But if I don't hide it I could lose the job."

"Do we know anyone who works there?" Karen asked.

"No," Gina replied, then she reconsidered. "Well, maybe. The bartender, Andy, seems familiar and he thinks we've met before. I know his wife."

"Well, everything will probably be okay," Karen said reassuringly. "Anyway, I'm tired. Let's worry about this tomorrow."

The next day Gina got to the restaurant early for the lunch shift. As she walked across the parking lot toward the restaurant she was startled when she saw Leo standing off to the side, smoking a cigarette, watching her.

"You're early, my beauty!" he called out when she saw him. "I like your enthusiasm!" Leo took a long draw on his cigarette and exhaled slowly.

"It's a little cold out here, isn't it?" Gina asked from a distance. Her voice was tense, but she tried to sound cordial.

"I was keeping a close eye on you last night," Leo said, ignoring her question. "I like your style. You're a very enthusiastic worker."

"Thanks." Gina replied, crossing the lot toward him. She relaxed a little; he was going to talk about work.

"The thing I like best about your performance," Leo continued, "is that you really try to please your customer. You really try to satisfy him. That's something I'm sure your boyfriend enjoys a great deal," Leo added as Gina stopped a few feet from him.

"What's that supposed to mean?" Gina asked with irritation.

"I think you know," Leo responded in a half whisper.

"Listen, Leo," Gina began. She took a deep breath, trying to remain calm.

At that moment a car pulled into the parking lot and a dark-haired man in his 30s hopped out. "Good morning!" the man called in a hoarse voice as he approached Leo and Gina.

"Tony, you've come to rescue me from the kitchen?" Leo asked. "Are you over your laryngitis?"

"Sorry, Dad, but I don't think I'll make it until Monday," Tony croaked. "I'm here now because Ellen forgot to bring me my paycheck last night."

"It's on my desk in the office," Leo informed him. "I need to make a phone call, so I'll go downstairs to get it for you. You stay here and get acquainted with Gina, the new waitress."

"Okay," Tony replied. He looked at Gina and smiled. "It's freezing out here!" he said. "Let's go into the lobby." Gina nodded and followed the two men inside.

Tony sat down on the sofa in the lobby and gestured for Gina to sit beside him. "So, I hear from Ellen that this is just your second day," he remarked politely. "What do you think so far?"

"So far so good," Gina responded. "The others were really helpful last night, especially Ellen. I hear you and Ellen are getting married soon?"

"Yes, in June," Tony said matter-of-factly. "Time is passing quickly."

"Time!" Gina exclaimed. She looked at her watch and leaped to her feet. "It's time for the lunch shift!"

"Get going then, or Mom will have your head!" Tony responded with a chuckle. "I work the dinner shift on weekends, so maybe I'll see you next Friday."

"I hope so," Gina replied sincerely. "And I hope you feel better soon," she called out as she rushed off to the dining room.

The next few months passed quickly. As Gina got better acquainted with everyone at Pasta Roma, she realized that her first impressions were fairly accurate. Gina liked Tony and Ellen the best. Whenever she needed help or someone to talk to about a work problem, she turned to one of them. Gina also got along well with Bella, since Gina was such a diligent worker. As Gina had suspected, Bella was strict, but a kind woman deep down. Sue and Donna were friendly and easy to work with, though Gina didn't feel that she knew them very well. Andy, in contrast, often disclosed personal information about himself and seemed to want a closer relationship than Gina preferred. Gina eventually became adept at cutting off their conversations when she wanted them to end. With Ronnie and Dennis, however, Gina was less successful. She hated their jokes and comments about the customers, but they ignored her when she asked them to change their behavior in her presence. Leo's behavior also continued to make Gina uncomfortable, and she tried to fend off his sexual comments and gestures in a variety of ways. She was tempted to ask him overtly to stop his behavior, but she suspected that might inflame the situation. Besides, the whole work climate was filled with sexual innuendo; sexual humor was used to help time pass more easily. Since the family was so tight-knit, Gina was concerned that complaining might mark her as an outcast.

Between being a full-time student and working full-time at the restaurant, Gina had very little leisure time. One rare evening when she had the night off from both work and school, she and Karen dropped by Pasta Roma for a pizza to go. They decided Karen should wait in the car to avoid raising curiosity about their relationship. Ellen and two women Gina had not met were waiting tables that night.

"Can't get enough of this place, eh girl?" Ellen asked jovially when she saw Gina.

"Oh, I dream about this place," Gina responded with a laugh. "Actually, I'm here for a pizza," she added.

"Have you met Margie and Tammy yet?" Ellen asked, gesturing toward the two women who were serving in the dining room. "They've both been here a few months, part-time. Neither of them is family. That's Margie pouring coffee, and the one fending off Leo is Tammy." Gina watched as Leo put his arm around Tammy and whispered something in her ear.

"Hey, what are you doing here?" a low, familiar voice asked from behind.

"Hi, Andy," Gina responded before turning around. "I'm just here with a friend to pick up a pizza."

"Where's the friend?" Andy inquired, looking around the dining room.

"She's in the car," Gina replied. "How long will it be for a pepperoni and mushroom pie?" She wanted to change the subject.

"I'm off work now," Andy remarked, putting on his jacket. "I'll go out and keep her company."

"No, that's not necessary, Andy," Gina responded quickly. But Andy was already headed outside.

When Gina got back to the car with the pizza, Andy was leaning on the car and talking to Karen through her open window. "So how long have you known Gina?" he asked her.

"A couple of years," Karen replied shortly.

"You two must be pretty close, then," he suggested.

"I guess you could say that," Karen responded vaguely. Andy was making it difficult to avoid being rude.

Gina got into the car and handed the pizza to Karen. "We've got to get going, Andy," she said abruptly, turning the ignition and releasing the brake.

Andy stood up straight and took a step back from the car as it pulled away. "Okay, see you tomorrow," he called out.

"He was really curious. I felt like he was trying to pry," Karen remarked as they drove toward her place. "If he figures us out and tells Leo, it could be trouble for you. Maybe you should reconsider that internship you heard about at school last week."

"But it only pays minimum wage!" Gina protested. "But you're right," she conceded after a pause. "I'd better look into it."

The next evening business was slow at the restaurant, so Gina didn't mind when Andy waved her over to the bar to talk. He slid a glass of club soda toward her on the counter. "How's it going?" he asked.

"Not much happening," Gina replied, taking a sip of soda.

"I had a breakthrough," Andy announced with a sly expression on his face. "I remembered where we've met. Becky's Place. I saw you and Karen there a year ago." Andy looked at Gina closely, waiting for her to react.

Gina froze. "Oh, yeah?" she asked as nonchalantly as she could. Becky's Place was one of the few gay and lesbian bars in town, the only one where Gina and Karen liked to hang out on occasion. It was a nice place that served decent food and drinks and played good dance music.

"Yeah," Andy replied. "I used to go there a lot. It's a fun place."

"You used to go there?" Gina asked with surprise. She didn't know very many straight men who hung out at Becky's.

"It was before Teresa and I got married," Andy replied. He paused for a moment. "Things used to be different for me, and I miss it sometimes."

"You miss what?" Gina asked.

"You know," Andy replied. "Being with men."

"You're bisexual?" Gina asked bluntly.

"You're a lesbian?" Andy retorted.

"Listen," Gina said. "I'm not out with the Cornaggias, and I would appreciate it if you would keep this to yourself, Andy."

"No problem," Andy replied. "But like I said, I really miss it, and I was hoping you might be able to set me up with one of your gay friends."

"What about your wife?" Gina asked.

"She wouldn't know," Andy said quietly.

"Sorry, but I have a lot of respect for Teresa; she's a good person. If you're going to cheat on her, I don't want to know about it, and I certainly don't want to be part of it."

"Just think about it?" Andy pleaded.

"No way, Andy. And you'd better not spread the word about me here. My personal life is no one's business but my own."

"Hey, don't worry about it," Andy replied, adopting a more distant tone.

Gina tried not to worry about it, but during the next two weeks at work, she could sense that something was different. Whenever she walked into the restaurant, it seemed as though the others would stop talking and watch her walk by. Donna, Sue, and Andy didn't seem as friendly, and Gina sensed that Ronnie and Don were snickering behind her back. Leo seemed to look at her differently too, as though there was something on his mind that he wasn't expressing.

One night at the end of Gina's shift, Leo pulled her aside. "I want to ask you about something in my office. Come with me downstairs," he ordered.

"What's up?" Gina asked nervously. She always detested being alone with Leo in the office, but now she felt particularly wary.

"Just come with me," he repeated, leading the way downstairs.

When they got to the office, Leo leaned on the edge of his desk, crossed his arms, and stared at Gina expectantly.

"What is it?" Gina asked in an impatient tone. She stood near the doorway.

"Well, Gina," Leo began, "the word around here is that you have, uh, certain preferences."

"What are you asking me?" Gina asked.

"Well, um, I was just wondering. Are you gay?"

"No," Gina replied.

"You're not gay?"

"No, I'm not gay. I'm a lesbian," Gina replied. " 'Gay' refers to males."

"Well, you like women, right?" Leo asked.

"Leo, I appreciate your coming directly to me to talk about this. But who I am personally has nothing to do with my employment here or my work performance."

"Hey, don't get excited," Leo replied in an appeasing tone. "Your secret is safe with me. This is the '90s. If you have certain preferences, it's your own business."

Gina was surprised. "Well I appreciate that, Leo." She was almost speechless.

"Oh, yeah. I'm a progressive guy," Leo said. "I just want to know one thing, though," he said, lowering his voice and stepping close to Gina, putting his arm around her shoulders. "If I pay you, will you let me watch?"

"What are you talking about?" Gina asked, hoping she misunderstood his implication.

"I've always had a fantasy about seeing two women together," Leo continued. "And I'm willing to pay." He pulled his money clip from his pocket and began leafing through a thick fold of 20-dollar bills. "How much do you want? I'll pay double if you let me participate."

Gina was fuming. "You couldn't afford it," she retorted.

"Well, you just let me know when you're ready," Leo responded.

"When Hell freezes over!" Gina exclaimed, struggling to hold her temper.

"Just let me know," Leo repeated, laughing. Gina stormed out of the office. "I'm really wealthy!" Leo called after her as she bounded up the stairs.

Gina hoped Tony would be in the kitchen. She was upset, and she thought talking to Tony might help her feel better. Instead, she found another cook, Paul, one of the nephews whom she had never really met. Tony's brother, Tom, was in the back cleaning up the pizza counter.

"Do you know where Tony is?" Gina asked Paul, but he didn't reply. Instead, he began to make gross facial gestures, sticking out the tip of his tongue and moving it rapidly up and down. "Would you be willing to give me lessons?" he asked Gina. "You could probably teach me a few things. What do two women do together, anyway?"

"I don't appreciate your sense of humor," Gina said dryly.

"How about going out for drinks sometime to discuss it?" Paul asked.

Gina ignored his comment. "Tom, do you know where Tony is?"

"He already went home," Tom replied.

Gina decided it was time for her to go home too. She could talk to Tony the following night.

The next evening Gina asked Tony to speak with her outside. "It's really important," she told him.

"Does this have anything to do with your being a lesbian?" Tony asked bluntly as they walked out of the building.

"You heard?" Gina asked.

Tony nodded. "Ellen told me," he replied.

"I'm worried about my job now," Gina disclosed. "I told Leo that this shouldn't have anything to do with my employment, and he said he agreed, but I'm still worried."

"Well, don't be," Tony said, trying to reassure her. "It doesn't make any difference to me, and it shouldn't to anyone else."

"But they're all treating me differently," Gina said. "And it's upsetting. I think this might be a good time for me to take an internship that was offered to me. It only pays minimum wage, but it sounds interesting. It's at a local TV station."

"It sounds like good job," Tony remarked. "What about taking it and cutting back your hours here?" he suggested.

"Do you think they'd go for that?" Gina asked.

"Lot's of our employees are part-time," he assured her. "Go ask Bella."

"Thanks, Tony! That's a great idea," Gina said, feeling a little relieved. Putting up with Leo would be much easier on a part-time basis. "But enough about me," Gina said. "Tell me about what's happening in your life. Are you ready for the wedding?"

"Things are pretty hectic," Tony replied. "Less than a month away, you know."

"How's Ellen holding up?"

"Terrific," Tony replied. "She's great."

"Looking forward to married life?" Gina asked.

"I guess so," Tony said hesitantly. "I'll tell you, though, it's hard to face the prospect of being with just one woman for the rest of my life."

"Do I sense cold feet?" Gina asked playfully.

"They're in a cake of ice!" Tony replied, laughing.

"Hey, you're so lucky to be getting Ellen. You don't know how lucky you are!" Gina remarked.

"You sound envious!" Tony said jovially. "I thought you already had a girlfriend."

"All I'm saying is that you'd better treat her right, or else," Gina responded, laughing.

"Or else what?" Tony asked in a challenging tone.

"I just might have to swoop in and take her away from you!" Gina said lightheartedly.

"Should I take that as a threat?" Tony quipped, grinning.

"Believe me, Tony, one night with me and she'd never want to go back to you!" Gina retorted.

"Oh, you think so?" Tony replied.

"What's going on here?" a voice asked inquisitively. Gina looked up to see Ellen standing with her hands on her hips.

"I was just telling Tony that he'd better treat you right or I'll come in and steal you away and take care of you myself!" Gina said.

"Oh, how sweet. Isn't that sweet, Tony?" Ellen asked.

"What, are you thinking of taking her up on it?" Tony asked. His smile was not quite so broad.

"Tony, are you jealous?" Ellen asked.

"Don't be ridiculous," he responded.

Ellen put her arm around Gina. "Hey, Gina, maybe we should go out for a romantic dinner some time," she said.

"That's enough, Ellen," Tony said. His voice was strained.

"Tony's jealous! Tony's jealous!" Ellen chanted.

"I said that's enough!" Tony said emphatically.

"Oh, you're no fun," Ellen retorted, and walked away.

Gina looked at Tony incredulously. "She wasn't serious," she said.

"I know," Tony responded. "I was just kidding around."

"Well," Gina continued, changing the subject. "I guess I'll go talk to Bella about cutting back my hours."

"Okay," Tony said. "I think she's downstairs in the office. Let me know if you have problems."

Gina went down to the office and tapped on the open door. "Can I talk to you?" she asked.

"I'm busy," Bella snapped. "What do you want?"

"I've been offered an internship at a TV station, and I'd like to cut back my hours to about 20 a week. I'd like to work maybe three nights—Thursday through Saturday—since I know those are your busiest nights."

"No," Bella replied sternly. "Twenty hours a week is impossible. You can keep Saturday nights, but that's it."

"I don't understand," Gina contested. "What's wrong with 20 hours?"

"We can't do it," Bella replied. "We're going to have to replace your full-time position. We can use you on Saturday nights, starting tonight. Take it or leave it."

"Okay, fine," Gina replied. "I'll work Saturday nights."

"Fine," Bella stated. "Now if you don't mind, I have work to do."

When Gina got up to the dining room, Leo pulled her into the lounge. "Leo, I don't have time to talk," Gina told him. "I have to get ready for my shift."

"This will just take a moment," he insisted. "Do you see the two women sitting over there?" He pointed to the bar.

"Yes," Gina replied impatiently. "What about them?"

"I know the shorter one," he said.

"So what?" Gina asked.

"She'd sleep with you and let me watch," Leo whispered.

That was the last straw for Gina. It was time to confront Leo about his behavior once and for all. "Leo, I've got to talk to you about this kind of thing," Gina said firmly.

"You want to give it a try?" Leo asked, grinning.

"Leo, listen to me," Gina said adamantly, looking him directly in the eyes. "I only want to have to say this once. I'm not comfortable with your sexual comments anymore. I'm not okay with your jokes and innuendoes. I'm not okay with you asking to watch me and offering to pay. Do you hear me? I don't like it. I want it to stop."

"Hey, it's all in fun," Leo replied. "I don't mean anything by it."

"Well it's not fun to me," Gina continued. It felt good to finally stand up to Leo. "I don't want anything to do with your little fun and games. You all have been good to me here. I've made good wages. You've given me time off when I needed to study. I just talked to Bella and I'm cutting my hours to one night a week so I can take an internship, so I appreciate your flexibility. I like you people. I just don't want to be subjected to your sexual comments anymore."

"Hey, I said it's no big deal. I'll stop. Don't worry about it," Leo said. He flung his hands in the air and walked into the kitchen.

The next Friday night, however, Leo approached Gina again in the lounge and put his arm around her. "Bella and I were talking about you," he said.

Gina prepared for the worst. "What about?" she asked.

"She has always wanted to be with a woman," he replied.

"Leo, I don't think you've been talking to Bella about this."

"Yes I have; you can ask her."

"Well it doesn't matter whether you have or not. I'm not interested! I told you last week that I wanted this behavior to stop. Didn't you hear me? I want it to stop!" Gina was yelling.

"Okay, okay. It's all in fun," Leo muttered and walked away.

At that moment Gina made an important decision. She felt she had no choice but to quit her job. The money was excellent, and quitting put her into a financial bind, but she couldn't subject herself to the situation any longer.

If Gina thought her encounters with the Cornaggia's had come to an end, she was mistaken. A month later she got a call from Margie, one of the servers working at Pasta Roma the night that Gina and Karen picked up a pizza. "Tammy and I got fired last week," Margie told Gina somberly. "I heard what Leo did to you before you quit, and I thought you should know about this."

"Why should I know about it?" Gina asked curiously.

"Leo attacked Tammy in the basement," Margie replied. "He kissed her and grabbed her breasts. Now he's saying we were fired for being incompetent."

"You're kidding!" Gina exclaimed. "Did he do anything to you?"

"Plenty," she replied. "He never touched me, but he made a lot of sexual comments. He was always asking me to perform sexual acts on him."

Gina paused to let it all sink in. "Why are you telling me about this?" she asked.

"He has to be stopped," Margie said. "Both Tammy and I are reporting him to the state EEOC [Equal Employment Opportunity Commission]. We want you to file a report, too."

"I don't want to have anything to do with a lawsuit," Gina replied immediately. "I'll get dragged through the mud and they'll end up winning and laughing at me. None of them would turn on Leo; he's got his whole family on his side. It would be my word against theirs. Who'd believe me?"

"We need you," Margie persisted. "If we all file sexual harassment complaints against him they'll believe us."

"Sexual harassment?" Gina asked. She hadn't thought of it in those terms before. "I'll think about it," she promised.

Margie had given Gina a good deal to think about. Gina was disturbed by the knowledge that Leo would go on harassing other women if he weren't stopped. She talked to Karen about the situation, who suggested that Gina discuss the case with their friend, Deborah, an attorney who was willing to work with victims in sexual harassment cases.

After several days of reflection, Gina decided to obtain legal assistance from Deborah, and she, along with Margie and Tammy, filed a sexual harassment complaint with the state EEOC office. When the EEOC began their investigation several months later, the story told by Leo Cornaggia and his family was drastically different from Gina's experience. The Cornaggias claimed that Gina's accusations were completely fabricated and vindictive. They claimed that Gina was frequently late for work, that she repeatedly made sexual passes at the female employees, and that after being reprimanded numerous times, she was finally fired. Gina attempted to contact Tony, Ellen, and Andy to ask if they would testify on her behalf. As Gina predicted, however, they refused to speak with her.

The EEOC investigation is still under way at the time this chapter goes to print. The Cornaggia's attorney has written a number of letters to Deborah hinting that the Cornaggias would be willing to settle out of court. But Gina isn't interested in a monetary award. She would rather lose than settle. She firmly believes Leo Cornaggia should be exposed and stopped.

## NOTE

1. This chapter is based on an in-depth interview with the woman referred to as "Gina." Names and other details and events that might reveal the identity of the

parties or the business involved in this case have been altered to protect anonymity.

## KEY TERMS

EQUAL EMPLOYMENT OPPORTUNITY COMMISSION (EEOC): a commission created by Congress to insure that employers comply with the spirit and letter of the Civil Rights Acts and other laws prohibiting discriminatory practices.

HETEROSEXISM: the ideological system that assumes everyone is and should be heterosexual. Heterosexism denies, denigrates, and stigmatizes nonheterosexual forms of behavior, identity, relationship, and community (Herek, 1995).

HOMOPHOBIA: the fear and hatred of gay, lesbian, and bisexual people. It is expressed through discriminatory laws and policies and through hostile behaviors ranging from derogatory jokes and abusive language to physical violence and murder.

SEXUAL HARASSMENT: unwanted sexual communication (verbal, nonverbal, physical, visual) that is implicitly or explicitly connected to terms or conditions of employment or decisions affecting employment; that unreasonably interferes with one's work performance; or that creates an intimidating, hostile, or offensive work environment.

## DISCUSSION QUESTIONS

1. Do you think Gina was sexually harassed? Why or why not?
2. Why do you think some people repeatedly subject others to unwanted sexual conduct at work, as depicted in this case? Are the causes primarily individual, situational, organizational, or social? To what extent do you think misunderstanding comes to play in sexual harassment situations?
3. How effective and appropriate do you think Gina was in dealing with the situations she encountered? If you think she could have handled the situations more skillfully, what would you recommend?
4. Do you think Gina will win the sexual harassment case in court? Why or why not?
5. Do you think Mr. Cornaggia should be punished? If so, how? If not, why not?
6. Why do you think many people tolerate sexual harassment at work?
7. What can organizations do to prevent sexual harassment?

## SUGGESTED READING

Bingham, S. G. (1991). Communication strategies for managing sexual harassment in organizations: Understanding message options and their effects. *Journal of Applied Communication Research, 19,* 88–115.

ı, S. G. (Ed.). (1994). *Conceptualizing sexual harassment as discursive prac-* . Westport, CT: Praeger.

ı, S. G. (1996). Sexual harassment: On the job, on the campus. In J. T. ..ood (Ed.), *Gendered relationships* (pp. 233–252). Mountain View, CA: May-field.

Clair, R. P. (1993). The use of framing devices to sequester organizational narratives: Hegemony and harassment. *Communication Monographs, 60,* 1–24.

D'Augelli, A. R., & Patterson, C. J. (Eds.). (1995). *Lesbian, gay, and bisexual identities over the lifespan.* New York: Oxford University Press.

Herek, G. M. (1995). Psychological heterosexism in the United States. In A. R. D'Augelli & C. J. Patterson (Eds.), *Lesbian, gay, and bisexual identities over the lifespan* (pp. 321–346). New York: Oxford University Press.

Keyton, J. (1996). Sexual harassment: A multidisciplinary approach. In B. R. Burleson (Ed.), *Communication Yearbook 19* (pp. 93–155). Thousand Oaks, CA: Sage.

Kramarae, C. (1992). Harassment and everyday life. In L. F. Rakow (Ed.), *Women making meaning: New feminist directions in communication* (pp. 100–120). New York: Routledge & Kegan Paul.

Kreps, G. L. (Ed.). (1993). *Sexual harassment: Communication implications.* Cresskill, NJ: Hampton Press.

Stockdale, M. S. (Ed.). (1996). *Sexual harassment in the workplace.* Thousand Oaks, CA: Sage.

# CHAPTER 22

# The Dispossessed

Case Studies in Reconstructing Identities
at the End of the Organizational Age

H. L. GOODALL, JR.
ERIC M. EISENBERG

## THE CRASH

Charlie and Gwin[1] met when they went to work for Eastern Airlines in Miami in the summer of 1968. Both skilled mechanics, they met during the company's orientation program, dated for a year, then married. They were respected workers whose performance evaluations consistently ranked them in the top 5% of most categories related to their jobs. Eventually, both of them were elected officers in their union, where they worked hard to defend workers' rights and to help the company cut costs and remain competitive. Charlie bragged that he had never missed a day of work in 21 years; the only days Gwin missed were when she gave birth to each of their two children. Trained as highly skilled technicians who also loved airplanes and cared about the safety of their customers, they were "in deep" with Eastern.

Charlie and Gwin had organized their lives around the idea that they would work for Eastern until they retired. They bought a home on a fixed 30-year note, confident that it would be paid off early. They were active in their community, largely because they believed it was where they would be living and working for the rest of their lives. They were volunteers for Greyhound Rescue, a group that provides adoptive homes for ex-racing dogs who would otherwise be killed. They also volunteered weekends to help clean up their neighborhood roadways and tend vacant properties and lots. "What we wanted," Gwin says, "is to help make where we lived a better place."

Eastern Airlines filed for bankruptcy in 1989. "When the crash came, we never even heard it," Charlie says. "We got up one morning and found that we had been 'locked out.' We couldn't even go inside to get our personal stuff." After months of failed attempts to help resurrect the company, and faced with mounting bills and continued unemployment, Charlie and Gwin called it quits. Both of them had been successful employees, but Eastern's sudden demise put many workers with similar backgrounds, skills, and resumes on the street at the same time. It was hard to find comparable work: other major airlines, seeing how quickly Eastern had fallen, were cautious about taking on new employees. People they had known for 20 years suddenly became competitors for the same jobs, jobs that were usually for lower pay. Friends who had shared their local neighborhood—other Eastern employees as well as newly unemployed workers from smaller companies who had depended on contracts with Eastern—began leaving Florida for jobs in other states, some even in other countries.

What bothered Charlie and Gwin most was that they were now not able to help their children as much with college or with getting started on their own. For many years, Gwin had told her daughter that they would make sure she could finish school, no matter what, and now Gwin wondered how she would keep this promise. They also noticed that conversations with their children about the future seemed strained and strange, as if all the usual success stories no longer applied. Their son, Al, talked about going into business for himself, probably in landscaping; their daughter, Liz, talked of becoming a freelance writer. But the kids agreed on two things: that they would only work at what they loved and that they would never trust a company to take care of them the way their parents had. In fact, it never even crossed their minds that this was any longer a possibility.

Charlie eventually found a job with a small airline transport company in North Carolina, and Gwin got a position as a telemarketer selling timeshares at a beachfront resort. They sold their home in Miami, moved out of their neighborhood, and, as Charlie puts it now, "joined the ranks of the dispossessed." Two years later Charlie quit this new job because he was getting not so subtle messages to "sign off" on repairs that he felt were borderline unsafe. Charlie had dedicated his life to the high standards he had helped create at Eastern, and this was the final blow to his dignity and to what he knew, in his heart of hearts, was right. Gwin, on the other hand, discovered that she had a talent for sales and made a good living with her new firm. This helped send the kids to school, but she often felt that they were drifting and wondered what line of work they would go into once they finished.

## THE WAY THINGS WERE

Elaine and Rich grew up in a middle-class neighborhood on Long Island. They were reared in a town where most people graduated from college and went to work for an electronics manufacturing firm located there. It was "how things were," as Elaine puts it. "You didn't ask too many questions because there really was only one good answer."

Friends since high school days, Elaine and Rich went away to college together. Rich majored in business, Elaine in math, good choices for people who planned to return home after graduation and go to work "for the company." Sometime during their junior year they fell in love. When they graduated they got married but stayed on at school so that Rich could finish his M.B.A. and Elaine could take additional coursework in engineering. Chances were good that with his M.B.A. degree and her additional training, both of them could "begin in management at home," by which they meant at the local electronics manufacturing company in their hometown.

And that is exactly what happened.

Three years passed. Elaine was happy with her job in Quality Assurance and Rich was doing well in Product Development. But rumors of a leveraged buyout began to circulate. Someone, or some larger company, was interested in buying this firm. "I thought, 'no big deal,'" recalls Rich. "I had studied this kind of takeover in college and the general rule was that if your management was solid the new owners would keep it intact. I mean, why change what already works?"

Rich never got a chance to ask anyone that question. The company was bought by an Asian electronics giant more interested in reducing competition than in preserving jobs—or, for that matter, in preserving a U.S. community. Within 6 months the plant was closed, with most engineering operations having been relocated to Singapore and manufacturing operations to Mexico. The well-tended community suddenly found itself without resources for change, and business after small business—all dependent on incomes from plant employees—closed up shop. The local public park, once full of children and families, these days seemed mostly abandoned, a haunt for the homeless. Pick-up basketball games for men continued in the afternoons, but the start times were earlier and the fouls were harder. Homes in all the neighborhoods were sold, many at vastly reduced prices because there were no buyers. "How things were," as Elaine had phrased it, had changed forever.

Rich found work in Rhode Island through an old friend, and eventually, so did Elaine. They joked about how it would be nice to move "from island to island, no big deal" but in truth the idea of going from New York to New England frightened them. Still, it was another nice community to live in, another company town, another electronics manufacturing firm. Sure, it was "away from home," but to tell the truth, home had changed so much that they hardly recognized it anymore. "It was scary," Rich recalls, "in 2 years, our hometown went from prosperity to zip. We figured we had lived through it once, and that was enough." Buoyed by the new jobs and the promise of new lives in a new town, Elaine and Rich decided to have children; not long afterwards, their son, Scott, was born. Becoming parents made them miss their families even more, but they didn't see many options. Like Elaine said, "I guess you just have to make some sacrifices, to go to where the work is."

But these intimations of stability and prosperity also proved to be short-lived. Another huge company, ironically a Korean firm in competition with the Japanese giant that had bought their first employer, moved in and purchased the Rhode Island operation. "They assured us they would keep loyal, hardworking employees," Elaine remembered. "But nobody read the small print in that agreement." The new owners were required to keep the current employees for 1 year, but after that they began slowly replacing them—and in particular the managers—with Koreans. "Because we had only been with the company a relatively short time, we were let go early on," Rich said. "We learned firsthand about global economic competition, the hard way." And Elaine added, "In some strange way I feel we were lied to, not by any one person, but by—I don't know—society? Everyone talks about how much they value good employees and about the importance of balancing work with the life of the family, the community, and the individual. But it's all talk. When it comes right down to it, everything is for sale to the highest bidder. And once you've paid the price, it seems it's yours to do with what you will."

Rich and Elaine moved back to Long Island, to a less prosperous neighborhood not far from their old hometown. Rich is still looking for work and dreams about starting a market research firm with some friends from college who live nearby and who are also unemployed. Elaine works part-time out of her home for a Florida-based computer software firm. This gives her more time to spend with her son, but there is still a lot of tension in the house. For the first time, Rich and Elaine are having trouble with their marriage, and they fight often about whether Scott should be in day care, about Rich's lengthy job search, and about who should do most of the housework. "The truth is," said Elaine, "we really have no idea what to do. We just weren't prepared for this kind of life. Is anybody?"

## THE FUTURE OF HISTORY

When Tony Logan graduated from the University of Michigan in 1992, his future seemed preordained. While not tops in his class, Tony was tops in his major—history—and was often approached by his professors about the possibility of graduate school. Although there was a tiny part of him that wondered whether more school might just be a cowardly way of postponing the inevitable—getting a job and becoming an adult—most of him agreed with his teachers. He liked university life, he liked teaching and writing, and he loved history. He applied to four leading graduate programs and was accepted at all of them.

Choosing where to go to pursue graduate work was tough. On the one hand, Tony was struck by how much legal jargon there was in each of the offer letters. It seemed that although, yes, he had been admitted, his funding and future in the program were "contingent" upon a hundred other things, all of which seemed out of his control and none of which he truly understood. And although Stanford appealed to his ego, the University of Illinois was closer to home and eventually became his choice. "My parents are older and not in the best of health," he said of his decision, "so as much as I would have loved to try California, Illinois made the most sense overall."

Tony did all the right things while in graduate school. He affiliated early with a professor he very much respected, and while other members of his committee came and went, the professor stayed with him and provided much-needed support. He earned excellent grades in all of his courses and was a central figure in the department's graduate student association. He was active at conventions, giving papers in his specialty area, Australian and Polynesian history. By the time he received his Ph.D., he had delivered four convention papers, published two articles in regional journals, and won a dissertation award from a national historical association.

When Tony started graduate school, his major professor had cut short any attempt on his part to talk about employment once his degree was done. "Just focus on the work," she had said, "and the jobs will take care of themselves." Recently, however, Tony had noticed that the topic of jobs came up more frequently—and now she was initiating it. "Have you thought of where you might go," she asked, and Tony supposed maybe it *was* time to start thinking about just that.

The year Tony was working on his dissertation he also applied for every history job posted in the *Chronicle of Higher Education*. He continued to attend conferences and signed up for their placement services. He told everyone he knew that he was "on the market" and to please "keep your eyes open."

There was only one response Tony had not been ready for: nothing happened. Most of the people he sent letters of application to never even responded. "Don't these people have any manners," he wondered, "or even a sense of professional courtesy? This is my life they're playing with, you know!" His disillusionment had been growing for nearly 2 months when the phone call finally came. It was the search committee chair at Rutgers University, and they wanted to interview Tony right away. They also said that they would be bringing in two other candidates for interviews.

Tony prepared for the Rutgers interview like a man on a mission. He did a very good job, he felt, but was told he wouldn't know anything until the others had been brought in. Another 6 weeks passed, and still no news. The search committee chair was slow in returning his calls, and finally one Friday afternoon called with the bad news: The position had been pulled by the university, and they would not be hiring this year. Tony was devastated. After having been in control of his education for so many years, he was frustrated to see all these forces beyond his control have such a significant impact on his life. "What's the secret code?" he often wondered. "I just can't seem to figure out how to crack this."

Tony finally landed a 1-year position at California State University at Fullerton. "I had always dreamed of California," he says, "but not this California, not this way. They've got me teaching five courses a semester, so I have no time to read or write. And I don't even want to unpack my stuff, since I'll most likely be moving again in June. People are nice enough, they give me some hope that one day a permanent line might come along, but exactly when—no one seems to know." The Cal State position was followed by two other 1-year jobs, one in Oregon and one in Maine. In his quiet moments, Tony wondered what went wrong. "Was it my specialty area—is it too narrow, too unpopular? Should I develop new interests? Find a new career altogether? Or is there something wrong with me?" But usually, his train of thought stopped here: "I guess I was just born at the wrong time in history."

## THE END OF THE ORGANIZATIONAL AGE

We live at the end of the organizational age. The vast public and private bureaucracies spawned by an expanding economy are being rapidly downsized or dismantled. In some cases, they are being replaced by global megacorporations that do not respect the interests of nations or communities (Barnet & Cavanaugh, 1994; Deetz, 1992) and in most cases cutting out—permanently—large numbers of middle-income jobs. By some estimates, the world of 2025 will contain approximately 8 billion human beings, but jobs will exist for only about 2 billion of them, with the vast majority of the remaining work being done with far less dignity than today (Aronowitz & DiFazio, 1994; Rifkin, 1995).

Improvements in information technology, combined with the flexibility and speed required by global economic competition, have combined to produce a worldwide demand for smaller, flatter, and more customer-driven organizations and agencies that at the same time require highly flexible skill sets and new learning by employees. Companies have also discovered that many jobs that used to be routinely performed "in-house" can now be "outsourced" to temporary agencies and other providers who are not on the company payrolls and therefore do not require company benefits. And as labor costs in the United States have risen, intense global economic pressures have forced many manufacturers to move their operations overseas, often to Third World countries, where the wages are much lower and there is less government interference or regulation.

One result of these changes is a call for a "new social contract" (Chilton & Weidenbaum, 1994). Since the advent of the Industrial Revolution, most people in the West have organized their institutions, their economies, and their lives around one central concept: Who a person was was largely defined by what job he or she did, and performing a job meant exchanging loyalty, commitment, labor, and time for wages. Human beings have always worked, but it is only in the last few hundred years that they have had jobs in which they have developed such a highly dependent relationship (both economically and psychologically) with employers.

The old social contract that virtually guaranteed lifetime employment for good workers is gone. Loyalty no longer pays when companies downsize, relocate, outsource, or are bought out by megacorporations. No longer can commitment to a specific company or a specific job be equated with success. There is no guarantee that the job one prepares for today will even exist tomorrow. The numbers are bleak. In 1995 alone, for example, there were just over 1.1 million college graduates in the United States and they faced a world in which there were less than 500,000 new jobs for them (*All Things Considered,* National Public Radio, May 11, 1995).

These changes are indeed dramatic, and more clearly so when one considers their impact on the lived experience of people like those described in this case study. What is common to all of them is a profound sense of disorientation, even betrayal: "Where did the old world go?" or "Why is no one playing by the rules?" they may be asking. Charlie and Gwin learned to survive by getting out of the jobs and away from the companies that they had grown up believing would always be there for them; Elaine and Rich had to switch careers completely and relocate to another region of the country, where, to their dismay, they learned there is nowhere to hide from the sweeping hands of this revolutionary change. Tony, like many others in academia, assumed that universities would be immune to market pressures, that there would always be room for the best people in any field. But it was not to be.

The effects of these changes on local communities also has been devastating. In every major industrial city in the United States, it is possible to drive by what used to be thriving manufacturing operations that today are abandoned and disfigured and that all too often serve as temporary quarters for increasing armies of homeless persons or street gangs or simply as the local neighborhoods that nobody visits after dark. In the cities and suburbs, people everywhere who worked hard and played by the rules have discovered that hard work isn't enough and that while the old rules have changed, the new ones are not yet written. In the rural regions and agricultural centers, those who grew up working on family farms are seeing their farms disappear and their way of life along with it.

## WHAT TO DO

The stories told here do not make up what might be considered "a traditional case study." What they do, instead, is direct attention to some taken-for-granted assumptions about working and living and ask some hard questions about the role of organizations, and of organizational communication, in our brave new world. The issues here are large and complex. The lives depicted here are, unfortunately, not atypical.

Our work world does not respond well to any fixed, recognizable set of answers, because the questions we need to ask have not as yet been articulated (Eisenberg & Goodall, 1993). This, then, is a case study whose best answers are perhaps questions, questions about the nature of the "new social contract," about the future of work (and not just the future of jobs). What is it that we must know about the connections between communication and the changing nature of the workplace (see Goodall, 1996)? About communication and work under the new social contract? About communication and the future of communities? Of nation-states? Of our species and the planet?

Similarly, what can we say about who we *are* when what we *do* is no longer stable? What are the skill sets and understandings that can help us rebuild—or perhaps forge anew—a sense of self that is neither stable nor isolated but constituted in dialogue with others in highly individualized, dynamic, and mostly ambiguous situations?

Finally, are the answers to questions about working and identity really just metaphors for how we approach and solve the larger questions of life, such as Who are we? What are we here for? What kinds of things are worth doing? At our very best, we are "playing ball on running water" (Reynolds, 1984), coping with our current challenges while simultaneously inventing the future.

## NOTE

1. The people featured in this case do not exist, and the events described herein are not literally true, but are a composite of many similar people and situations unfolding today all over America.

## KEY TERMS

BANKRUPTCY: a situation in which a company declares it is no longer able to pay its debts. A company may declare bankruptcy or may be forced to do so by its suppliers or employees. At first, bankruptcy provides a period of protection during which the company may find a way to get back on its feet. If this is unsuccessful, the court appoints managers to help in the systematic demise of the company, attempting to fairly distribute monies owed to debtors in the process.

CAREER: an idea developed initially in relation to bureaucracy and referring to the natural progression of a qualified individual through a hierarchy of offices in a company. Careers no longer exist within companies, nor do they correspond to hierarchical position. Today a successful career looks more like a series of interesting and worthwhile contractual arrangements with a range of companies, all focusing on a developing set of skills for the individual concerned.

GLOBAL MEGACORPORATIONS: enormous companies whose interests and influence routinely cross national boundaries.

LEVERAGED BUYOUT: a situation in which an individual or group of individuals purchases controlling interest in another company with the help of other financiers who put up a large percentage of the money (the "leverage") needed to make the purchase.

NEW SOCIAL CONTRACT: the developing expectation on the part of most employees that companies cannot be counted on to provide long-term employment and consequently that all workers must take personal responsibility for their professional development and career.

OLD SOCIAL CONTRACT: not a formal legal document but an expectation that has developed over the years on the part of employees that if they work hard and stay out of trouble, their job is secure.

OUTSOURCING: the process by which companies contract with people or businesses outside of their operations to do work that is critical to the development of their products and services. Nearly anything can be outsourced, from computer service support to subassembly manufacturing to human resources.

PERFORMANCE EVALUATION: a written document prepared by a supervisor (often collaboratively with the employee) evaluating the employees' business performance in the recent past.

## DISCUSSION QUESTIONS

1. How has communication between management and employees changed under the "new social contract"?
2. Given the changes in the global economy described in this case, what role do communication skills now play in getting and keeping steady work?
3. Under the new social contract, how has the relationship between communication at home and at work changed? Does the greater interdependence between

family and work put different communicative demands on people who value both?
4. What is the relationship between all of these changes in communication and expected changes in worker identity?

## REFERENCES

Aronowitz, S., & DiFazio, M. (1994). *The jobless future.* Minneapolis: University of Minnesota Press.

Barnet, J., & Cavanaugh, D. (1994). *Global dreams.* New York: Simon & Shuster.

Chilton, K., & Weidenbaum, M. (1994). *A new social contract for the American workplace: From paternalism to partnering.* St. Louis, MO: Center for the Study of American Business.

Deetz, S. (1992). *Democracy in an age of corporate capitalism.* Albany: State University of New York Press.

Eisenberg, E. M., & Goodall, H. L. (1993). *Organizational communication: Balancing creativity and constraint.* New York: St. Martin's Press.

Goodall, H. L. (1996). *Divine signs: Connecting spirit to community.* Carbondale: Southern Illinois University Press.

Reynolds, D. (1984). *Playing ball on running water.* New York: Quill.

Rifkin, J. (1995). *The end of work.* New York: Basic Books.

# About the Authors

**Marcel M. Allbritton** (M.A., University of New Mexico) recently completed a thesis on Project H, an invisible college of about 100 scholars at universities scattered around the world, who communicated with each other by e-mail for a 2-year period in the early 1990s. Allbritton's scholarly interests center on new communication technologies, organizational communication, and technology transfer. He is now a doctoral student in the School of Information Studies at Syracuse University.

**Brenda J. Allen** (Ph.D., Howard University) is an Assistant Professor in the Department of Communication at the University of Colorado at Boulder. Her research centers on computer-mediated communication, feminism, and diversity in organizations. She has published articles in the *Journal of Applied Communication Research* and *Sex Roles.*

**James R. Barker** (Ph.D., University of Colorado) is an Assistant Professor in the Department of Communication and Journalism and a Research Associate with the Institute for Organizational Communication, which are both at the University of New Mexico. His research interests include the development and evolution of organizational control and the consequences of organizational change and innovation. He has studied worker participation innovations in both service and manufacturing industries and in federal research laboratories and site-based managed schools. He also consults with organizations on team problem-solving and development. He has authored and coauthored articles in *Administrative Science Quarterly, Communication Monographs, Human Communication Research,* and the *Journal of Applied Communication Research.*

**Shereen G. Bingham** (Ph.D., Purdue University) is Associate Professor of Communication at the University of Nebraska at Omaha. Her research focuses on the ways communication is used to enact, perpetuate, prevent, and resolve sexual harassment in organizational and educational contexts.

She teaches courses in gender, interpersonal, and organizational communication, and provides conflict mediation services in the Omaha community.

**George Cheney** (Ph.D., Purdue University) is an Associate Professor in the Department of Communication Studies at the University of Montana–Missoula. His teaching and research interests include issues of identity and power in organizations, the quality of work life in contemporary society, democracy at work, and ethics in business and other institutions. He has published one book, *Rhetoric in an Organizational Society* (University of South Carolina Press, 1991), and numerous journal articles, book chapters, book reviews, and editorials. He received a Golden Anniversary Monograph Award from the Speech Communication Association (SCA) in 1996 for his essay "Democracy in the Workplace" (*Journal of Applied Communication Research*, 1995). He is at work on several projects that attempt to link practical experience with theoretical knowledge in the interest of making organizations more humane and more effective, including a book on workplace democracy. He is currently chair of SCA's Organizational Communication Division.

**Noshir Contractor** (Ph.D., Annenberg School for Communication, University of Southern California) is Associate Professor of communication and psychology at the University of Illinois at Urbana–Champaign. He teaches courses and doctoral seminars on organizational communication processes, communication network analysis, computer-mediated technologies, and quantitative research methods. His research interests include applications of systems theory to communication, the role of emergent communication networks in organizations, and information technologies in the work place. His current research focuses on the role of computer-based tools to augment collaboration and group decision-making processes. His articles have appeared in *Decision Science, Organization Science, Human Communication Research,* and *Management Communication Quarterly.* He has served on the editorial board of *Human Communication Research,* and currently serves on the editorial board for *Management Communication Quarterly* and the *Electronic Journal for Computer-Mediated Communication.*

**James W. Dearing** (Ph.D., Annenberg School for Communication, University of Southern California) is an Associate Professor in the Department of Communication at Michigan State University. He teaches graduate courses in research design, program evaluation, mass communication theory, and social change. He has been principal investigator for research sponsored by the U.S. National Science Foundation, the U.S. Environmental

Protection Agency, and the U.S. Agency for Health Care Policy and Research. In 1994, he was a Visiting Assistant Professor at the University of Michigan, and was awarded the Thomas J. Kiresuk Award for Excellence in Scientific Research by the U.S. Knowledge Utilization Society. He has authored *Growing a Japanese Science City* (Routledge, 1995) and coauthored *Agenda-Setting* (Sage, 1996), with Everett M. Rogers.

**Stanley Deetz,** (Ph.D., Ohio University) is a Professor of Communication at Rutgers University, New Brunswick, New Jersey, where he teaches courses in organizational theory, organizational communication, and communication theory. He is author of *Transforming Communication, Transforming Business: Building Responsive and Responsible Work Places* (Hampton, 1995), *Democracy in an Age of Corporate Colonization: Developments in Communication and the Politics of Everyday Life* (SUNY, 1992), and has edited or authored eight other books. He has published numerous essays in scholarly journals and books regarding stakeholder representation, decision making, culture, and communication in corporate organizations and has lectured widely in the U.S. and Europe. In 1994, he was a Senior Fulbright Scholar in the Foretagsekonomiska Institutionen, Goteborgs Universitet, Sweden, lecturing and conducting research on managing knowledge-intensive work. He has served as a consultant on culture, diversity, and participatory decision making for several major corporations, and as President of the International Communication Association, 1996-1997.

**Gerardine DeSanctis** (Ph.D., Texas Tech University) is Professor of Management at the Fuqua School of Business, Duke University. Before joining the Duke faculty, she was Professor of Information and Decision Sciences at the University of Minnesota. Her research interests are in the general areas of organizational computing, computer-supported cooperative work, and management of information systems. She currently serves as a Senior Editor for *Organization Science*. She serves on the advisory board for *Information Systems Research*.

**Gary W. Dickson** (Ph.D., University of Washington) is Professor and Head of the Business Management Department of North Carolina State University. He was the founding editor of the *Management Information Systems Quarterly* and the chairman of the first *International Conference on Information Systems*. He has conducted research programs in the areas of decision support systems, management of the information systems function, managerial graphics, and group-decision support. He has published extensively on these topics. He is coauthor of *The Management of Information Systems* (McGraw-Hill. 1985).

**Eric M. Eisenberg** (Ph.D., Michigan State University) is Professor of Communication and Chair of the Department of Communication at the University of South Florida. He specializes in the role of communication in promoting organizational change. He directed the Master's Program in Applied Communication at Temple University and was on the faculty of the University of Southern California for 10 years. While in California, Dr. Eisenberg established his reputation as a successful communication consultant, assisting major corporations in strategic change efforts across a variety of industries. He has twice received the Speech Communication Association Award for Outstanding Research Article of the Year. In 1993, he was awarded the Burlington Resources Foundation Faculty Award for Excellence in Teaching.

**Gail Fairhurst** (Ph.D., University of Oregon) is Professor and Head of Communication at the University of Cincinnati. Her research centers on leadership communication and language analysis in organizational settings. She is coauthor of *The Art of Framing: Managing the Language of Leadership* (Jossey-Bass, 1996) with Robert Sarr. She also has been widely published in communication and organizational science journals, and in 1994 received the Speech Communication Association Award for Outstanding Research Article. She is a fellow of the Center for Environmental Communication Studies and the Institute for Data Sciences at the University of Cincinnati. She has also served as a consultant for a number of Fortune 500 organizations, including Proctor and Gamble, General Electric, The Kroger Company, and Cincinnati Bell.

**H. L. Goodall, Jr.** (Ph.D., Pennsylvania State University) is Professor of Communication Studies and Head of the Department of Communication at the University of North Carolina at Greensboro. He has authored and coauthored 14 books, most recently *Divine Signs: Connecting Spirit to Community* (Southern Illinois University Press, 1996), and, with Eric M. Eisenberg, *Organizational Communication: Balancing Creativity and Constraint, 2nd Edition* (St. Martin's Press, 1996). His scholarly focus is organizational and community ethnography and his consulting work deals with managing change processes.

**Patricia L. Goode** (M.B.A., University of Southern California) currently works for LAC (the company discussed in Chapter 8). She has held positions with production, engineering, product assurance, and supplier development, spanning 20 years. Projects managed include installation of coordinate measuring/laser measurement equipment, information system design and implementation, multigroup consolidation. Her focus with LAC has been on developing processes based on the knowledge of the individual performing the work, eliminating unnecessary steps, and using measures as feedback to the process. Strong interpersonal and effective cross-boundary communication have been the basis of her success in managing tough culture change.

**Brad M. Jackson** (M.S., University of Houston) is currently a partner at Cogos Consulting in Boston, Massachusetts. Prior to joining Lotus, he was Assistant to the General Manager of the Information Technology Department of Texaco Inc. While at Texaco he held positions in marketing, telecommunications, technology research, and refining. He has published articles in the *Management Information Systems Quarterly, Journal of MIS,* and *Journal of Organizational Computing.* His research interests include electronic support for teamwork and architectural planning for information technology.

**Jill Kleinberg** (Ph.D., University of Michigan) is a cultural anthropologist who has done extensive field research on Japanese business organization in Japan as well as Japanese firms operating in the United States. Her research in the United States has focused on the special problems of managing cultural differences between Japanese and American employees. An Associate Professor in The School of Business at the University of Kansas, she teaches courses on comparative and cross-cultural management, business and society in Japan, organizational behavior, and organizational ethnography.

**Gary L. Kreps** (Ph.D., University of Southern California) is Professor and Executive Director of the Greenspun School of Communication at the University of Nevada, Las Vegas. He has served as a faculty member at Northern Illinois University, Rutgers University, Indiana University at Indianapolis (IUPUI), and Purdue University–Calumet. He has expertise in organizational communication, intervention, and learning; health communication; health promotion; interpersonal/group interaction; multicultural relations; communication theory; leadership and empowerment; conflict management; and research methods. He has written many books, chapters, and scholarly articles concerning communication, management, education, and health care. He is the editor of two Hampton Press book series: Communication and Social Organization and Health Communication. He was the founding editor of the Speech Communication Association's Applied Communication Publication series, and edited special issues of *American Behavioral Scientist* and the *Journal of Health Psychology.*

**Dean H. Krikorian** (M.A., Annenberg School for Communications, University of Southern California) is a doctoral candidate in the Department of Communication at the University of California–Santa Barbara, and a visiting lecturer in the Department of Communication at Michigan State University. As an electrical engineer at LAC (the company in Chapter 8) for 6 years, he facilitated hundreds of technical decision-making meetings and helped determine causes and corrective actions of satellite failures. Other projects included implementation of database systems, electronic mail, and video-conferencing in everyday technical operations at LAC. His current research interests include group decision making, analysis of communication networks, and communication technologies in the workplace. He has also been investigating corporate "reengineering" in terms of self-organizing systems theory.

**Bruce L. Lambert** (Ph.D., University of Illinois at Urbana–Champaign) is Assistant Professor of Pharmacy Administration and Clinical Assistant Professor of Pharmacy Practice at the University of Illinois at Chicago. His research interests include provider–patient interaction, the development of communication competence, and the personal, organizational, and health consequences of individual differences in communication competence. Dr. Lambert has recently developed a computerized content-analysis system that automatically extracts thematic features from machine-readable texts. He is a member of the Consumer Interest and Health Education Advisory Panel of the U.S. Pharmacopeial Convention. His publications have appeared in *Health Communication, Communication Yearbook, Social Science and Medicine,* and *The Quarterly Journal of Speech.*

**Carol A. Lambert** (B.S., University of Florida) is President of Lambert Management Consultants, Inc., of Lake Forest, Illinois. She has more than 11 years experience in executive search and management consulting as well as over 10 years experience in R&D and manufacturing in the pharmaceutical industry. She also consults in organizational development, conflict management, team building, and communication. She has been selected for inclusion in *Who's Who of American Women, Who's Who in the Midwest,* and *Who's Who in Illinois.*

**Debra C. Mazloff** (Ph.D., University of Kansas) is an Assistant Professor in the Department of Communication at the University of St. Thomas in St. Paul, Minnesota. Primarily, her research focuses on the role of communication in the underutilization of employee assistance programs. She is also interested in how communication allows people to cope with the stressors in their lives. Specifically, her work examines coping mechanisms at work and as people age. The case study presented in her chapter is part of her doctoral dissertation completed at the University of Kansas under the direction of Beverly Davenport Sypher.

**Katherine Miller** (Ph.D., University of Southern California) is Associate Professor of Communication Studies at the University of Kansas. Her research interests center on communicative aspects of stress and burnout among human service workers and the development and maintenance of occupational identity. Her research has been published in a wide range of outlets, including *Communication Monographs, Communication Research, Human Communication Research,* and *Management Communication Quarterly.*

**Barbara J. O'Keefe** (Ph.D., University of Illinois at Urbana–Champaign) is Professor of Speech Communication at the University of Illinois at Urbana–Champaign. Her research has contributed to the development of a general theory of communication and coordination—constructivism—that has been applied to the analysis of managerial and supportive communication in a variety of settings including cooperative work. Her most recent work is concerned with two interrelated topics in a theory of interpersonal communication: (1) explicating the logics-in-use that govern the adaptation of messages to their circumstances; and (2) explicating the ways that communication technologies and group goals and norms structure the circumstances to which messages must be adapted.

**Marshall Scott Poole** (Ph.D., University of Wisconsin) is Professor of Speech–Communication at Texas A&M University. He has conducted research and published extensively on the topics of group communication, computer-mediated communication systems, conflict management, and organizational innovation. He has coauthored and edited four books, including *Communication and Group Decision-Making* (Sage, 1986), *Working through Conflict* (Longman, 1996), and *Research on the Management of Innovation* (Harper & Row, 1989). He has published in a number of journals, including *Management Science, MIS Quarterly, Human Communication Research, Academy of Management Journal,* and *Communication Monographs.* He is currently an associate editor of *Information Systems Research.*

**Eileen Berlin Ray** (Ph.D., University of Washington) is an Associate Professor in the Department of Communication at Cleveland State University. Her research interests are in organizational and health communication, primarily focusing on the functions and dysfunctions of supportive communication and its relationship to job stress and burnout in human service organizations. Her work has been published in numerous books and journals, including *Communication Monographs, Management Communication Quarterly, Communication Quarterly,* and *Health Communication.* She is currently on the editorial boards of six journals and has edited four books. In 1995, she was a Visiting Scholar at Lincoln University, Canterbury, New Zealand.

**Everett M. Rogers** (Ph.D., Iowa State University) is Professor and Chair of the Department of Communication and Journalism at the University of New Mexico. He has been teaching and conducting research on the diffusion of innovations, and other types of communication research, for the past 42 years. Rogers is particularly known for his book, *Diffusion of Innovations* (Free Press, 1995), now in its fourth edition. Rogers currently conducts research on the effects of an entertainment/education radio soap opera about HIV/AIDS prevention and family planning in Tanzania, and on the effects of Mothers against Drunk Driving's Victim Impact Panels on drunk drivers in New Mexico. Rogers also directs research on technology transfer from Federal R&D laboratories in New Mexico and on the performance of university-based research centers.

**David R. Seibold** (Ph.D., Michigan State University) is Professor of Communication, University of California–Santa Barbara. Author of nearly 100 articles on organizational change, group decision making, interpersonal influence, and health communication, he is currently Editor of the *Journal of Applied Communication Research* and serves on the editorial board of several journals. He is chair of the Interpersonal and Small Group Interaction Division of the Speech Communication Association, and Vice-Chair of the Organizational Communication Division of the International Communication Association. He also works very closely with many business, government and health organizations.

**Sherianne Shuler** (M.A., University of Illinois) is a Ph.D. candidate in Communication Studies at the University of Kansas. Her research interests broadly include organizational and interpersonal communication, especially how talk makes organizing and relationships possible. Her dissertation focuses on the discourse of emotional labor.

**Beverly Davenport Sypher** (Ph.D., University of Michigan) is Professor of Communication Studies and Divisional Dean for Social Sciences at the University of Kansas. This is the second volume of case studies that she has edited for The Guilford Press. Her work has appeared in a variety of communication, psychology, and management journals, and she continues to focus on the kind of organizations created by the communication practices of employees. Most often she studies large-scale manufacturing organizations, but she has also helped employees of small nonprofit groups; local, state, and federal agencies; and various corporations sort out the consequences of communication choices and the possibilities of person-centered messages. She has received the Speech Communication Association's Ecroyd Award for Outstanding Teaching in Higher Education and a Kemper Fellowship for Teaching Excellence at the University of Kansas.

**Phillip K. Tompkins** (Ph.D., Purdue University) is Professor of Communication and Comparative Literature at the University of Colorado at Boulder. He is a Fellow and Past President of the International Communication Association. He has published articles in such journals and magazines as the *James Joyce Quarterly, Human Communication Research, Communication Monographs, Esquire,* and *The Quarterly Journal of Speech.* Tompkins has authored and edited several books on organizational communication; he is the founder of a research program dealing with communication and control and organizational identification. He is currently the chair of the Boulder Faculty Assembly, the campuswide governance body for the faculty at CU-Boulder.

**Michelle T. Violanti** (Ph.D., University of Kansas) is an Assistant Professor at the University of Tennessee. Most of her research has centered around how people talk about and how organizations respond to instances of sexual harassment. During 1993 and 1994, she worked as a consultant for the American Association of Retired Persons to develop and disseminate their messages on health care reform in a five-state area. She has authored and coauthored articles in the *Journal of Applied Communication Research, Management Communication Quarterly, Women's Studies in Communication,* and *Communication Education.*

**Pamela S. Whitten** (Ph.D., University of Kansas) is Director of Telemedicine Services and a faculty member in the Department of Family Medicine at the University of Kansas Medical Center. Her research focuses on new technologies in health care settings, with a specific research agenda centering around telemedicine from an organizational communication perspective. She is currently researching provider and patient perceptions of this technology as well as how this technology impacts the provision of health services.

**Angela J. Wilhelm** (M.A., University of Cincinnati) intends to pursue a Ph.D. Her research interests include popular culture studies, feminist rhetorical theory, and organizational communication.

**Theodore E. Zorn** (Ph.D., University of Kentucky) is a Professor in the Department of Management Communication at the University of Waikato in Hamilton, New Zealand. His research and teaching focus on interpersonal communication in organizations, particularly managerial influence processes. He has published articles in *Human Communication Research*, the *Journal of Constructivist Psychology*, *Management Communication Quarterly*, the *Journal of Applied Communication Research*, *Communication Yearbook*, and the *Southern Communication Journal*, as well as in a number of edited books and trade journals. Prior to his career in academia, Dr. Zorn worked in the field of human resources development, and remains active as a consultant and trainer. He has served many large and small organizations, including Arthur Andersen, Andersen Consulting, Burroughs–Wellcome, Corning Glass, Frito-Lay, G. E. Capital, Gulf States Utilities, the Rank Corporation, and the State of North Carolina.

# INDEX